Pelican Books

Medicine, Patients and the Law

Margaret Brazier was born in 1950. She graduated from the University of Manchester in 1971 and was called to the Bar in 1973. She is a Senior Lecturer in Law and Legal Studies Director of the Centre for Social Ethics and Policy at Manchester University. Her publications include several articles on torts and medico-legal problems and she is the editor of the current edition of *Street on Torts* and has been an editor of *Clerk and Lindsell on Torts* since 1975.

MEDICINE,
PATIENTS
AND THE LAW

Margaret Brazier

Penguin Books

PENGUIN BOOKS

Published by the Penguin Group
27 Wrights Lane, London W8 5TZ, England
Viking Penguin Inc., 40 West 23rd Street, New York, New York 10010, USA
Penguin Books Australia Ltd, Ringwood, Victoria, Australia
Penguin Books Canada Ltd, 2801 John Street, Markham, Ontario, Canada L3R 1B4
Penguin Books (NZ) Ltd, 182–190 Wairau Road, Auckland 10, New Zealand

Penguin Books Ltd, Registered Offices: Harmondsworth, Middlesex, England

First published 1987
10 9 8 7 6 5 4 3 2

Printed and bound in Great Britain by
Cox & Wyman Ltd, Reading
Photoset in Linotron Times by
Rowland Phototypesetting Ltd, Bury St Edmunds, Suffolk

In memory of
L. T. Jacobs 1914–85
and
Harry Street 1919–84

Contents

Preface   ix
Table of Cases   xiii
Table of Statutes   xix
Table of Statutory Instruments   xxiii

Part I
Medicine, Law and Society

Introduction   3
1 The Practice of Medicine Today   5
2 Medicine, Moral Dilemmas and the Law   19
3 A Relationship of Trust and Confidence   32

Part II
Medical Malpractice

Introduction   53
4 Agreeing to Treatment   55
5 Medical Negligence   69
6 Medical Litigation   86
7 Drug-induced Injuries   105
8 Hospital Complaints Procedures   125
9 Radical Reform: An End to Fault Liability   142

Part III
Matters of Life and Death

10 Pregnancy and Childbirth   157
11 Problems of Infertility   179

Contents

12 Abortion 199

13 The Handicapped Newborn: Whose Rights? Whose
    Decision? 211

14 Doctors and Child Patients 222

15 General Practice 242

16 Family Planning 259

17 Organ Transplantation 272

18 Medical Research 285

19 Defining Death 297

20 Death, Dying and the Medical Practitioner 305

21 Reviewing and Reforming the Law 325

Some Suggestions for Further Reading 339

Notes 341

Index 365

Preface

Rarely a day passes now without the press or television focusing on some issue of disputed medical practice, medical ethics or medical litigation. The medical profession finds itself in the limelight. Its image undergoes drastic changes. One day the doctor is hailed as a saviour. The next he is condemned as authoritarian or uncaring. The rapid progress of medical science, extending life at one end and bringing new hope to the childless at the other, has thrown up intricate problems of ethics and morals. At every level of medical practice the law now plays a part. The number of actions for malpractice against doctors, once virtually unknown in England, is growing apace. Doctors fear an epidemic of American proportions. Patients find the English legal system obstructive and cripplingly expensive. Nor are patients' grievances limited to the lack of provision for compensation for medical mishap. Increasingly patients demand a greater say in their treatment. The extent to which it is their right to have such a say becomes ultimately a question for the law. Meanwhile, medical progress has created new problems for the law's definition of the beginning and end of life. Research on embryos, abortion, the damaged newborn baby and euthanasia excite lively legal and moral debate. The lack of any common moral stance in our society prompts other issues of law and morality too. For over two years the courts of the land tackled Mrs Gillick's campaign to bar girls under 16 from receiving contraceptive treatment without their parents' agreement. Despite a decision from the House of Lords, the highest court in the land, the legal wrangle continues.

The object of this book is to examine the regulation of medical practice, the rights and duties of patients and their medical advisers, the provision of compensation for medical mishaps and the framework of rules governing those delicate issues of life and death where medicine, morals and law overlap. It is intended to provide a picture of the role of the law in medical practice today and to highlight those areas where the law is woefully inadequate. So in Part I, I consider the general legal framework within which medicine is practised today. In Part II, I look at legal remedies available to the patient injured by, or unhappy with, treatment he has received. And finally in Part III I examine in detail specific issues relating to the treatment of the living and the dying which have posed awkward problems of law, morals and medicine. Throughout the book I concentrate on the provision of health care for the mentally competent patient. Some mention is made of the problems arising when a patient is temporarily or permanently mentally incompetent, but the detailed and specific legal rules governing the care of the mentally ill or handicapped patient are beyond its scope. The book is intended for a wide audience. It is designed to be read by lawyers and law students seeking an introduction to the law relating to medical practice, by members of the medical professions, and above all by the lay public, looking for a guide through the maze of current issues confronting them every day in their daily newspaper. I make no judgment on medical practice in the eighties. I am not qualified to do so. I do evaluate the state of the law and too often find it sadly wanting.

Originally this book was to have been the joint project of Professor Harry Street, Professor Gerald Dworkin and me. Professor Street died in April 1984 having worked on early drafts of parts of Chapters 4, 5 and 8. He inspired the writing of the book. His example as colleague and teacher created a debt which I can never repay. Gerald Dworkin's many commitments prevented him from completing his planned share of the work. He has kindly allowed me to use the drafts he prepared of Chapters 17, 19 and 20. His wise advice and meticulous reading of other chapters has assisted me greatly.

I should like to acknowledge the help given to me by many of my colleagues in Manchester, from the disciplines of both law and medicine. Their patience in listening to me as I chewed over awkward problems, and advising me as the work progressed, has been invaluable. In particular I thank my friend and colleague Diana Kloss, whose encouragement and shrewd insight supported me during the writing of the book. I must also thank my students, who challenged my views on several occasions and forced me to think again on many issues. I acknowledge the especial efforts of Margaret Scotland and Julie Stone in helping me track down materials. I thank all the secretarial staff at Manchester and Southampton who struggled valiantly with so many drafts, and my special thanks go to Margaret Croston and Diana Hindle.

No criticisms made in this book are the result of any personal experience of medical practice. The care which I and my family have received from our general practitioners, and from Withington Hospital where my daughter was born, has always been of the highest standard.

I submitted the typescript to the publishers in January 1986. I was able to make some amendments to update the work in September 1986.

Margaret Brazier

Table of Cases

A. v. *C.* (1978) 197, 198
A.B. v. *C.D.* (1851) 35
A.B. v. *C.D.* (1904) 35
A Baby, In re (1985) 197
Allan v. *New Mount Sinai Hospital* (1980) 55
Anns v. *Merton L.B.C.* (1978) 115
Appleby v. *Sleep* (1968) 108
Archard v. *Archard* (1972) 261
Argyll v. *Argyll* (1967) 33
Ashcroft v. *Mersey A.H.A.* (1983) 79, 95, 148
Attorney-General v. *Able* (1984) 309, 323
Attorney-General v. *Jonathan Cape Ltd* (1976) 33
Attorney-General of Canada v. *Notre Dame Hospital* (1984) 312

B., Re (1981) 213, 216
Barber v. *Superior Court* (1983) 314, 315
Barnes v. *Crabtree* (1955) 247
Barnett v. *Chelsea and Kensington H.M.C.* (1969) 69, 71
Bartling v. *Supreme Court of California* (1985) 313, 323
Baxter v. *Baxter* (1948) 260, 261
Beatty v. *Illingworth* (1896) 67
Bhandari v. *Advocates' Committee* (1956) 11
Blyth v. *Bloomsbury A.H.A.* (1985) 65, 265
Bolam v. *Friern H.M.C.* (1957) 60, 62, 71, 72, 73
Bravery v. *Bravery* (1954) 259, 261

Canterbury v. *Spence* (1972) 60
Carmarthenshire C.C. v. *Lewis* (1955) 41
Cassidy v. *Ministry of Health* (1951) 82, 87, 98, 99
Chatterton v. *Gerson* (1981) 58–9, 61, 287
Chin Keow v. *Government of Malaysia* (1967) 78, 244
Church of Scientology v. *Kaufman* (1973) 39, 40

Table of Cases

Clark v. *MacLennan* (1983) **76, 100, 163, 292**
Clarke v. *Adams* (1950) **74**
Coles v. *Reading and District H.M.C.* (1963) **244**
Collins v. *Hertfordshire C.C.* (1947) **79**
Colton v. *New York Hospital* (1979) **283**
Corder v. *Banks* (1960) **80**
Crawford v. *Board of Governors of Charing Cross Hospital* (1953) **75**
Crompton v. *G.M.C.* (No. 1) (1981) **10**
Crompton v. *G.M.C.* (No. 2) (1985) **10**
Cull v. *Butler* (1932) **56**

D. v. *N.S.P.C.C.* (1977) **43**
D., Re (1976) **238–9, 289**
Davies v. *Eli, Lilly & Co.* (1986) **123**
Department of Health and Social Security v. *Kinnear* (1984) **121, 122**
Devi v. *West Midlands A.H.A.* (1980) **56, 67, 266**
Dinnerstein (1978) **319**
Distillers Co. (Biochemicals) Ltd v. *Thompson* (1971) **115**
Donoghue v. *Stevenson* (1932) **110**
Dunning v. *United Liverpool Hospitals' Board of Governors* (1973) **92**

Edler v. *Greenwich and Deptford H.M.C.* (1953) **248**
Emeh v. *Kensington, Chelsea and Fulham A.H.A.* (1983) **167–8, 171, 187, 268–9**
Evans v. *G.M.C.* (1985) **11, 253**
Eyre v. *Measday* (1986) **83, 270**

Freeman v. *Home Office* (1984) **56, 58, 312**

Gartside v. *Outram* (1856) **34**
Gibbins v. *Proctor* (1918) **216**
Gillick v. *West Norfolk and Wisbech A.H.A.* (1985) **35, 209, 222 ff., 233, 289, 331–2**
G.M.C. v. *Browne* (1971) **232**
Gold v. *Haringey A.H.A.* (1986) **65, 264, 271, 287**

Hall v. *Avon A.H.A.* (1980) **94, 97**
Halushka v. *University of Saskatchewan* (1965) **287**
Hatcher v. *Black* (1954) **60**
Hills v. *Potter (Note)* (1984) **59**

Hotson v. *Fitzgerald* (1985) **69, 80, 101**
Hubbard v. *Vosper* (1972) **39, 40**
Hucks v. *Cole* (1968) **78, 244, 245**
Hunter v. *Hanley* (1955) **74, 77**
Hunter v. *Mann* (1974) **34, 44**

Initial Services Ltd v. *Putterill* (1968) **38**

Jones v. *Manchester Corporation* (1952) **72, 79, 104**

Kavanagh v. *Abrahamson* (1964) **248**
Kitson v. *Playfair* (1896) **38**
Kralj v. *McGrath* (1986) **125, 176**

L. v. *L.* (1949) **184**
Langley v. *Campbell* (1975) **77, 246**
Lazenvnick v. *General Hospital of Munro City* (1980) **165**
Lee v. *South West Thames R.H.A.* (1985) **92, 330**
Leigh v. *Gladstone* (1909) **311**
Lim Poh Choo v. *Camden and Islington A.H.A.* (1979) **298**
Lion Laboratories Ltd v. *Evans* (1984) **34, 35, 173**
Little v. *Little* (1979) **276**

McFall v. *Shimp* (1978) **275**
MacIvor v. *Southern Health and Social Services Board, Northern Ireland* (1978) **91**
McKay v. *Essex A.H.A.* (1982) **157, 162–8, 170, 171, 172, 184, 201**
MacLennan v. *MacLennan* (1958) **182**
Mahon v. *Osborne* (1939) **98**
Maynard v. *West Midlands R.H.A.* (1984) **71, 73–4, 78**
Megarity v. *Ryan (D.J.) & Sons* (1980) **94**

Nettleship v. *Weston* (1971) **72**
Newton v. *Newton's New Model Laundry* (1959) **77**
Nickolls v. *Ministry of Health* (1955) **244**

O'Brien v. *Cunard S.S. Co.* (1891) **57**
O'Malley-Williams v. *Board of Governors of the National Hospital for Nervous Diseases* (1975) **60**

P., Re (A Minor) (1981) **209, 230**

Table of Cases

Paton v. *British Pregnancy Advisory Service* (1979) (1980) **208**
Pfizer v. *Ministry of Health* (1965) **108**
Phillip B., Re (1979) **236**
Phillips v. *William Whiteley Ltd* (1938) **71**
Pickett v. *B.R.B.* (1980) **100**
Prince Albert v. *Strange* (1849) **34**
Pritchard v. *J. H. Cobden* (1986) **268**

Quinlan, Re (1976) **316–18, 323**

R. v. *Adams* (1957) **215, 308**
R. v. *Bateman* (1925) **85, 174**
R. v. *Bourne* (1939) **199**
R. v. *Brain* (1834) **215**
R. v. *D.* (1984) **227**
R. v. *Donovan* (1934) **9, 260**
R. v. *G.M.C. ex p. Gee* (1985) **13**
R. v. *Lennox-Wright* (1973) **277**
R. v. *Lowe* (1973) **216**
R. v. *McShane* (1977) **309**
R. v. *Malcherek* (1981) **301**
R. v. *Poulton* (1832) **215**
R. v. *Price* (1969) **202**
R. v. *Reed* (1982) **323**
R. v. *Secretary of State for Social Services, ex p. Hincks* (1979) **16**
R. v. *Senior* (1832) **174**
R. v. *Senior* (1899) **216, 234**
R. v. *Smith (John)* (1974) **20**
R. v. *Sockett* (1908) **199**
R. v. *West* (1848) **206**
R. v. *Whitchurch* (1890) **199**
Rahman v. *Kirklees A.H.A.* (1980) **94**
Reibl v. *Hughes* (1980) **59, 60**
Rodgers v. *G.M.C.* (1985) **11, 12, 13, 254**
Roe v. *Ministry of Health* (1954) **75, 79, 87, 98**
Royal College of Nursing v. *D.H.S.S.* (1981) **207**

S. v. *Distillers Co.* (1970) **157**
S. v. *S.* (1972) **290**
Satz v. *Perlmutter* (1978) **312, 313, 316**

Sidaway v. *Board of Governors of the Bethlem Royal and the Maudsley Hospital* (1984) (1985) 59, 61–5, 68, 74, 93, 148–50, 287, 332, 335
Sindell v. *Abbot Laboratories* (1980) 107
Smith v. *Brighton and Lewes H.M.C.* (1955) 83
Spring (1980) 318
Storar (1981) 318
Strunk v. *Strunk* (1969) 276
Sullivan v. *Sullivan* (1970) 261
Superintendent of Belchertown v. *Saikewicz* (1977) 318
Sutherland v. *Stopes* (1925) 259
Sutton v. *Population Services Family Planning Ltd* (1981) 82, 262

Tarasoff v. *Regents of the University of California* (1976) 41
Thake v. *Maurice* (1984) 17, 269, 270
Tucker v. *Lower* (1972) 300
Tuffil v. *East Surrey A.H.A.* (1978) 77

Udate v. *Bloomsbury A.H.A.* (1983) 269
Urry v. *Biere* (1955) 80

Watson v. *Buckley and Osborne, Garrett & Co. Ltd* (1940) 110
Waugh v. *B.R.B.* (1980) 92
Wells v. *Surrey A.H.A.* (1978) 267
Whiteford v. *Hunter* (1950) 75
Whitehouse v. *Jordan* (1980) (1981) 73, 95–7, 143–4, 147–9, 176, 326
Williams v. *Luft* (1978) 157
Wilsher v. *Essex A.H.A.* (1986) 72, 82, 87
Wilson v. *Inyang* (1951) 9
Wilson v. *Pringle* (1986) 55, 56
Wood v. *Thurston* (1951) 77
Wright v. *Dunlop Rubber Co. Ltd* (1972) 112
Wyatt v. *Wilson* (1820) 34

Younghusband v. *Luftig* (1949) 9

Table of Statutes

Abortion Act 1967 **29, 164, 167, 199 ff.,**
   212, 221, 320, 335
Administration of Justice Act 1970   – ss. 32–5 **91**
Administration of Justice Act 1982   – s. 5 **102**
                   s. 6 **101**
Adoption Act 1958   – s. 50 **196**
California Natural Death Act 1976 **323**
Children Act 1975   – s. 26 **182**
                   s. 85(2) **197**
Children and Young Persons Act 1933   – s. 1(1) **216, 234**
                   s. 1(2) **216**
Civil Jurisdiction and Judgments
   Act 1982 **115**
Civil Liability (Contribution) Act 1978   – s. 1 **103**
                   s. 2 **103**
Congenital Disabilities (Civil Liability)
   Act 1976   – s. 1(1) **177**
                   s. 1(2)(b) **165, 176**
                   s. 1(3) **177**
                   s. 1(4) **159, 176**
                   s. 1(5) **162, 163**
                   s. 1(7) **159, 162**
                   s. 2 **159**
Corneal Grafting Act 1952 and 1986 **277**
Criminal Law Act 1967   – s. 5(1) **38**
                   s. 5(5) **38**
Data Protection Act 1984   – s. 29 **47–8**
Family Law Reform Act 1969   – s. 8(1),(2),(3)
                   222–3, 225–6
Fatal Accidents Act 1976
Guardianship of Minors Act 1973   – s. 1(2) **197**

Table of Statutes

Health and Social Security Act 1984   – s. 5 **243**
                                              Sched. 3 **243**
Health Services Act 1980   – s. 1(7) **242, 243**
                                              Sched. 3 **242**
Hospital Complaints Procedures Act 1985 – s. 1 **125, 126, 131, 330**
Human Tissue Act 1961   – s. 1(1) **277**
                                              s. 1(2) **278**
                                              s. 1(4) **277**

Infant Life (Preservation) Act 1929 **204**

Law Commissions Act 1965 **180**
Law Reform (Personal Injuries) Act
    1948 **102**
Limitation Act 1980   – s. 11 **90**
                                              s. 14 **90**
                                              s. 33 **90**
Medical Act 1983   – s. 2 **10**
                                              ss. 30–34 **10**
                                              s. 35 **10**
                                              s. 36 **11**
                                              s. 37 **10**
                                              s. 40 **11**
                                              s. 41 **13**
                                              s. 46 **9**
                                              s. 47 **9**
                                              s. 49 **9**
                                              s. 50 **13**
                                              Sched. 1 **10**
Medicines Act 1968   – s. 2 **113**
                                              s. 4 **113**
                                              s. 6 **112**
                                              s. 7 **112**
                                              s. 19(1) **113**
                                              s. 19(2) **113**
                                              s. 20(3) **113**
                                              s. 21(5) **114**
                                              s. 24 **113**
                                              s. 28 **113**
                                              s. 35 **112**
                                              s. 38 **113**

Mental Health Act 1983	– s. 131(2) **223**
Misuse of Drugs Act 1971 **44**	
National Health Service Act 1977	– s. 1 **15, 16**
	s. 3 **15, 16**
	s. 17 **126**
	s. 29(1) **242**
	s. 30(1) **243**
	s. 46 **252**
	s. 89 **137**
	ss. 106–20 (Part V) **127**
	s. 109 **127**
	s. 110 **127**
	s. 111 **128**
	s. 113 **128**
	s. 114 **128**
	Sched. 5 **87**
	Sched. 9 **252**
	Sched. 13, Part I **128**
	Sched. 13, Part II **133**
Nurses, Midwives and Health Visitors Act 1979	– s. 17 **173**
Offences Against the Person Act 1861	– s. 58 **199**
Perjury Act 1911	– s. 4 **180**
Police and Criminal Evidence Act 1984	– ss. 8–14 **44**
	Sched. 1 **44**
Prevention of Terrorism (Temporary Provisions) Act 1984	– s. 11 **38, 44**
Prohibition of Female Circumcision Act 1985 **239**	
Sale of Goods Act 1979	– s. 14(2)(b) **108, 257**
	s. 14(3) **108, 257**
Sexual Offences Act 1956	– s. 28 **230**
Suicide Act 1961 **309**	
Supply of Goods and Services Act 1982	– Part I **88, 108, 257**
	s. 13 **88**
Supreme Court Act 1981	– s. 33 **46, 91**
	s. 34 **46, 91**
	s. 35 **46, 93**
Surrogacy Arrangements Act 1985 **31, 195–6**	

Table of Statutes

Theft Act 1968 – s. 15 9
Unfair Contract Terms Act 1977 – s. 2 83
Uniform Anatomical Gift Act
  (U.S.A.) 283
Uniform Brain Death Act
  (1978) (U.S.A.) 304
Vaccine Damage Payments Acts 1979 120–23
Venereal Disease Act 1917 9

Table of Statutory Instruments

National Health Service (General Medical and Pharmaceutical
Services) Regulations 1974
(S.I. 1974, No. 160) **224, 243, 244, 249**

	Regulation		
		9	**250**
		10	**255**
		16	**248**
		17	**250**
		18	**250**
		25	**248**
		26	**248**

National Health Service (General Medical and Pharmaceutical
Services) Regulations 1975
(S.I. 1975, No. 719) **224, 243**

National Health Service (Service Committees and Tribunals)
Regulations 1974
(S.I. 1974, No. 455)

	Regulation		
		4(1)	**251**
		10	**251**
		11	**252**

National Health Service (Vocational Training)
Regulations 1979–1984
(S.I. 1979, No. 1644) **242**
(S.I. 1980, No. 1900) **242**
(S.I. 1981, No. 1790) **242**
(S.I. 1984, No. 215) **242**

Prosecution of Offences Regulations 1985 **203**

Part I

Medicine, Law and Society

Introduction

In contrast to most European countries, the law of England is not to be found neatly encapsulated in any Code. The task of the non-lawyer seeking to establish his rights or ascertain his duties is therefore far from easy. The law relating to medical practice is to be discovered from a variety of sources. Parliament has enacted a number of statutes governing medical practice. The regulation of medical practice and the disciplining of the defaulting doctor are entrusted by Act of Parliament to the General Medical Council in the Medical Act 1983. The structure of the health service is provided for by several statutes on the National Health Service. Those same statutes embody most of the rules dealing with complaints procedures within the N.H.S. too. The Medicines Acts are concerned with the safety of drugs, and a number of other Acts of Parliament will be seen to be crucially relevant to issues of medicine, patients and the law. An Act of Parliament can deal only with the general framework of legal rules. Acts of Parliament therefore commonly empower government ministers to make subsidiary regulations known as statutory instruments. These regulations may determine crucial questions. For example, most of the duties of general practitioners within the N.H.S. are dealt with by regulations and not by Act of Parliament.

Nevertheless, statute and statutory regulations alone by no means give the whole picture of English law. Much of English law remains judge-made, the common law of England. Decisions, judgments handed down by the courts, form the precedents for determining later disputes and define the rights and duties of doctors and patients in areas untouched by statute. The common law governs questions of compensation for medical accident, the patient's right to determine his own treatment, parents' rights to control medical treatment of their children and, as we shall see, several other vital matters. I deal with English law. The common law is not confined to England. Decisions of courts in America, Canada and elsewhere are mentioned from time to time. Such judgments do not bind an English court. They can be useful as examples, or warnings, as to how the same basic principles of law have developed elsewhere. Finally it must be remembered that for the lawyer Scotland counts as a foreign country. Scotland maintains its own independent legal system. On many of the questions dealt with in this book English and Scottish law coincide. Occasionally the law of England and Scotland diverges. I confine myself to stating the law as it applies in England and Wales, although I try to point out some areas where the law of Scotland differs from its English counterpart. And the problems of law and medicine embodied in the book are common to Britain as a whole.

Chapter 1
The Practice of Medicine Today

Few professions stand so high in general public esteem as that of medicine. Popularity polls of professionals in the press regularly result in doctors at the top of the poll and lawyers near the bottom! Yet few individuals attract greater public odium than the doctor or nurse who falls from the pedestal. The revulsion occasioned by Nazi atrocities in the concentration camps was nowhere as marked as in the case of Dr Mengele. That he used his skills as a doctor, taught to him that he might heal and comfort the sick, to advance torture and barbarism causes horror even now, forty years and more after the end of Nazi rule and when the man himself is probably dead. The transformation of a supposed angel of mercy into the angel of death makes the blood run cold.

Public passion is rightly aroused by the likes of Mengele. But passion is never far away from ordinary everyday relationships between doctor and patient. Clients can usually remain relatively impartial about their solicitor. If he does a good job they may appreciate him. If he is incompetent they sack him. He will rarely be loved or hated. The family doctor by contrast arouses more intense feelings. For many of his or her patients the doctor is almost a member of the family. He is expected to feel for them as well as to provide professional care. When the doctor meets the patient's expectations he will be rewarded by admiration and affection. Woe betide him if he does not. One error, one moment of exasperation or insensitivity, may transform the beloved doctor into a hate figure. The hospital consultant enjoys or endures a similarly ambivalent role. The consultant, at any rate until comparatively recently, was accorded an almost godlike status. He was a figure inspiring awe in the patient, visiting the ward attended by a retinue of junior doctors and nurses. The consultant's exalted status insulated him from personal contact with the patient and protected him from the sort of complaints voiced freely to nursing staff. He paid a price. Gods are expected to work cures. They are not expected to be subject to human error. When the consultant proved to be human, when medicine could not cure, the patient found it hard to grasp and rightly or wrongly, and often wrongly, regarded the doctor as personally incompetent.

Attitudes are changing slowly. Family doctors are becoming a different breed. Some of them try hard to persuade their patients to see the doctor as a partner in promoting good health. Doctors are urged to prescribe less freely and to talk more to their patients. The good G.P. is as interested in the prevention of ill-health as its cure. A new generation of consultants is gradually taking over in the hospitals. They are in many cases less grand and more prepared to listen to patients and nursing staff. Entrenched attitudes take time to change. Doctors may be changing slowly, but the perception of many patients has not changed. They still regard the doctor as a miracle worker, and the publicity attaching to and money poured into high-technology medicine reinforce that perception. Stories rarely appear in the press applauding the good work of the geriatrician or praising the community health physician. Doctors in such unglamorous specialties, it is reported, rarely win the coveted N.H.S. merit awards which can boost the senior doctor's salary. Money, fame and publicity are usually reserved for the transplant surgeon, the gynaecologist running a 'test-tube' baby unit, and so on. The medical marvels with which the public are bombarded reinforce the image of the doctor as superman. And so when a member of the public becomes a patient and 'superman' lets him down he is unsurprisingly aggrieved. Nor can doctors entirely blame the media for their image. Doctors decide on who get merit awards. Doctors vote with their feet as to which branch of medicine they enter. Many continue to vote for the glamorous world of 'high-tech' medicine.

Quite apart from the question of medical 'image', there are certain inescapable features of the profession of medicine which will always render the doctor more vulnerable to attack than fellow professionals. The doctor deals with the individual's most precious commodity, life and health. On a mundane level he may determine whether patient X is to be sanctioned to enjoy seven days off work for nervous exhaustion brought about by overwork or classified as another malingerer.[1] At the other end of the scale he may hold in his hands the power of life and death. He is the man with the skill and experience. In his hands, as the patient sees it, rests the power to cure. Only recently have the lay public become more aware that cure is not always possible. As Ian Kennedy has said, the patient appears before the doctor '. . . naked both physically and emotionally. However unwilling we may be, however well-intentioned the doctor, it is hard to overstate the power which this vests in the doctor'.[2] The price of power is that those who exercise it can today expect constant scrutiny from those subject to it and from the public at large. The age of deference is past.

The power inevitably held by the doctor in our society is matched by the cost of any error he may make. When an overstretched, overtired accountant makes a mistake he will probably get a chance to put it right next day. When an articled clerk's inexperience lets him down the likelihood is that his principal will notice and correct the error. For the junior doctor who has been working continuously for over 36 hours there may be no second chance. Nor, of course, is there a second chance for the patient. The accountant or the solicitor may lose his client money or property. Monetary compensation paid for out of the professional's insurance cover will go some way to placate the client. For the patient for whom the doctor's mistake resulted in disability or death, money is poor compensation. Finding out why things went wrong may be more important to the patient and the family. And inability to find out 'why' may explain the bitterness which attends many claims against the medical profession.

When the price of a momentary error is so high, it follows that concern to prevent error is acute. Every profession has its black sheep. Some are merely incompetent, others are venal. The failure of the Law Society to pursue and discipline its members has been a subject of recent debate. There is no evidence that the medical profession is any better or worse than its brethren in other disciplines in maintaining and policing standards. Its failures will always attract greater attention. A solicitor who grossly overcharges, fails to keep proper records or conducts his client's business dilatorily will arouse public concern as well as private anger. But the outcry will not reach the same level of passion as that occasioned by reports of a doctor failing to visit a child when the child later dies. The medical profession may rightly claim that doctors make no more mistakes, that there are no more 'bad' doctors than in any other profession. The claim is futile. The cost of a medical error is such that doctors will always be expected to be better than others and the standards of the profession as a whole to be of the highest.

Nor are the consequences of a failure in medical skill the only reason for the medical profession's susceptibility to virulent attack. The decisions which face the doctor can so often touch on sensitive areas of moral and religious concern. This is in itself nothing new. For example, until the advent of safe Caesarian surgery doctors could be called on several times in a year to decide whether to save the life of mother or baby in a difficult confinement. Two developments have intensified the modern doctor's dilemma. Technology has given the doctors power to save and prolong life undreamed of twenty years ago. The doctors now have to decide when to use the technology. In many cases life can be prolonged; the question is whether that life is worth prolonging? Secondly, there is no longer any general consensus on the sanctity of life, when life begins, or when it ends, or should end. Abortion, once illegal and hazardous to the mother, can now be carried out safely and cheaply in the early months of pregnancy. The debate on the morality of abortion has not abated. The legality of some abortions in England is unclear. The divide between pro- and anti-abortion campaigners is greater than ever to the extent that in the U.S.A. abortion clinics have been bombed and doctors carrying out abortions have received death threats. In this country in 1981, Dr Leonard Arthur, a leading paediatrician, stood trial for murder as a result of his decision as to the management of the care of a severely handicapped baby. His lengthy ordeal ended in acquittal. At the core of the issue was a dispute between medical professionals and within society itself as to the treatment of severely damaged babies. In what other profession would an ethical and professional dispute result in a criminal prosecution of this sort?

The power in the hands of the doctor explains the concern that the public and patients have in its exercise. It places the medical profession in the limelight, a limelight some doctors appear to relish. Nor is the profession averse to publicizing its successes. Doctors cannot then be surprised when failure, incompetence or controversy attract equal notoriety. Alas, the representatives of the profession too often react in an over-defensive manner, so exacerbating the original criticism or complaint. What the profession, patients and the public have in common is a need for: (1) the medical profession to be properly regulated and controlled, (2) an adequate and rational system of compensation for patients suffering injury, (3) effective means of investigating medical accidents, and (4) provision for doctors to be given comprehensible guidance on those areas of medical practice of moral and ethical sensitivity. The extent to which the law does and can meet these needs is the theme of this book.

Regulating medical practice

The regulation of the medical profession is entrusted by statute, the Medical Act 1983, to the profession itself acting through the General

Medical Council. The G.M.C. controls medical education and maintains a register of qualified practitioners. Surprisingly, no law expressly prohibits any unregistered or unqualified person from practising most types of medicine or even surgery! A criminal offence is committed only when such a person deliberately and falsely represents himself as being a registered practitioner or having medical qualifications.[3] The rationale of the criminal law is that people should be free to opt for any form of advice or treatment, however apparently bizarre, but must be protected from rogues claiming a bogus status and from commercial exploitation of untested 'alternative' medicine. On its own the penalty for falsely claiming to be qualified is not much of a deterrent, a maximum fine of £2,000. The fraudulent 'doctor' out to make money is deterred in other ways. He will not be able to recover his fees in a court of law.[4] If money has been handed over voluntarily where the 'doctor' led the patient to believe he was qualified he may face additional charges of obtaining property by deception and conviction may result in imprisonment.[5] The herbalist and the faith-healer are left free to practise, but they must be honest with those who come to them for help and not pretend to be registered doctors.

Few would quarrel with the liberality of the law where the unqualified adviser limits himself to advice. The nightmare is that some unqualified person might resort to surgery. Any physical contact with a patient permitted by him under the impression that he is dealing with a 'real doctor' will be a criminal assault. A biology teacher who set himself up in private practice in Lancashire was imprisoned for assault causing grievous bodily harm for carrying out gynaecological operations on unsuspecting women.[6] A more difficult question is raised where the patient agrees to surgery by an unregistered practitioner knowing full well that he is not dealing with a conventionally qualified doctor. I would tentatively suggest that a prosecution for assault would still succeed in most cases even if nothing went wrong with the 'operation'. The consent of the 'victim' of an assault is not always a defence when bodily harm is done.[7] The public interest in preventing unqualified persons from engaging in surgery may be sufficient to render the 'doctor's' conduct punishable as a crime.

The General Medical Council

The General Medical Council, the governing body of the medical profession, is composed of elected members chosen by the profession at large, appointed members selected by universities and other bodies and a group of nominated members, nominated by the Queen on the advice of the Privy Council.[8] A majority of the nominated members must be lay people. As elected and appointed members are required to be registered practitioners the lay element on the Council is minimal. The Council's duties include maintaining the register of practitioners,[9] and providing '. . . advice for members of the medical profession on standards of professional conduct or on medical ethics'.[10] The Medical Act 1983, which defines and delimits the Council's powers, illustrates the importance of the Council's role in relation to medical education and in ensuring that registration is granted only to suitably qualified and experienced aspirants. Over one half of the statute deals with this issue. We shall not go further into the details of qualifications for registration. Public concern focuses rather on the Council's exercise of its powers to require registered doctors to maintain standards. Those powers are perhaps more limited than the public appreciates. The Council is required to establish a Health Committee which may suspend a doctor unfit to practise by reason of physical or mental illness or may make his registration conditional on compliance with certain conditions, for example, he may be obliged to accept medical treatment himself.[11] Elaborate procedural safeguards are erected to ensure that a doctor alleged to be unfit is treated fairly. Complementary to the Health Committee is the Professional Conduct Committee. With this Committee lies the power to discipline any doctor who has been found guilty of a criminal offence in the British Isles or who '. . . is judged by the Professional Conduct Committee to be guilty of serious professional misconduct'.[12] Such a doctor may (1) have his name erased from the register, or (2) be suspended from the register for one year, or (3) have his registration made conditional on compliance with conditions set by the Committee, for example undergoing additional training or attending a refresher course. Once again the procedure is scrupulously fair to the accused doctor and he has an automatic right of appeal to the Privy Council.[13]

What amounts to serious professional misconduct?

The efficacy of the General Medical Council's disciplinary powers as a means of maintaining standards of competence and care within the profession and in protecting the patient depends largely on what the Council treats as 'serious professional misconduct' and on the penalties imposed on guilty doctors. The G.M.C. is '. . . not ordinarily concerned with errors in diagnosis or treatment, or with the kind of matters which give rise to action in the civil courts for negligence unless the doctor's conduct in the case has involved such a disregard of his professional responsibility to his patients or such a neglect of his professional duties as to raise a question of serious professional misconduct'.[14] Isolated error or even incompetence as such is thus excluded from serious misconduct: so what does meet the bill?

Earlier legislation defined punishable misconduct as 'infamous conduct in a professional respect'. Echoes of that wording persist. Serious professional misconduct is defined in Halsbury's *Laws of England* as conduct '. . . reasonably to be regarded as dishonourable by professional brethren of good repute and competency'.[15] So adultery with a patient or a patient's spouse remains serious misconduct. Drug abuse, alcoholism and fraud join the list. Added to these are touting for custom and a number of offences to prevent unseemly competition among doctors. From the patient's viewpoint two areas of potential misconduct are of prime importance: breach of confidence, which I deal with later in Chapter 3, and failure to attend and treat the patient.

In the G.M.C. 'Bluebook' giving guidance on what constitutes misconduct, neglect of the doctor's duties to his patients is given as the first example of potential misconduct. Yet there is widespread suspicion that doctors who fail their patients are let off lightly. Are there any grounds for this suspicion? First a high degree of proof is demanded before a doctor will be 'convicted'.[16] This is no different from the standard pertaining in any other professional disciplinary committee, for the doctor may well stand to lose his livelihood and reputation. There is, however, force in the criticism that once 'convicted' the penalty does not fit the crime. In November 1984 two doctors who had faced the ultimate penalty of being struck off the register appealed against their sentence. One had failed on two occasions to attend two desperately sick little girls.[17] The other had committed adultery with a patient.[18] Her husband instituted the complaint. Neither denied misconduct but they said they should merely have been suspended, not struck off. The appeal hearings revealed that since 1970 no doctor had suffered the ultimate penalty of striking off for failure to attend a patient. By contrast, between 1975 and 1984 four doctors out of ten disciplined for sexual misconduct were struck off. Both doctors lost their appeals. But has the G.M.C. got its priorities right in punishing the adulterer with greater vigour than the uncaring doctor?

At the heart of the dilemma lies the notion that it is not negligence, nor an isolated failure in caring, that constitutes serious misconduct. The doctor's action or inaction must bring the profession into disrepute. Hence the emphasis the Council places on adultery and alcoholism. The Council should respond to public feeling. In 1987 the doctor who fails to visit a dying child, brushes off a sick patient as neurotic or neglects the elderly brings greater dishonour to medicine than the occasional adulterer.

Public unrest about the medical profession's ability to police its members led to the introduction of a Private Member's Bill[19] to amend the Medical Act 1983. Nigel Spearing M.P. proposed a modest reform. The G.M.C. was to be given power to impose its *minimum* penalty of making registration conditional on compliance with stated conditions for up to three years, for example undertaking a refresher course or working under supervision for a while, where the doctor has 'behaved in a manner which cannot be regarded as acceptable conduct'. The G.M.C. opposed this Bill. Doctors, they said, understood what was entailed in serious professional misconduct. 'Acceptable conduct' was too vague a test. The Council itself, it was claimed, had revised its guidelines on failure to attend patients and made it clear that the precedent of 1984 where the doctor in a bad case[20] was struck off should be a warning to all. Outside the G.M.C. other doctors' organizations are not so optimistic that internal reform can answer the public's concern. The British Medical Association (B.M.A.), an organization representing many doctors, has backed Mr Spearing.[21] The B.M.A. does not regard the revised guidelines on misconduct as sufficient to allay legitimate public concern. What the G.M.C. has done in its latest guidance[22] on professional conduct is to outline a good standard of medical care. The criteria for proper care are unexceptionable. Emphasis is laid on conscientious assessment of the patient, consideration for him, prompt attention and a willingness to take a second opinion. But the guidelines still beg the question as to when departure from the standards set constitutes *serious* misconduct. No solid guidance by way of illustrative example is given to answer criticism that the G.M.C. is too ready to find there has been misconduct, and admonish the doctor, rather than categorizing his conduct as serious; and unless serious misconduct is proved the G.M.C. has no power to take any positive steps to punish the doctor and/or protect other patients.

The G.M.C. has responded to public concern. It has acted on a number of malpractices, notably unsafe prescribing practices. And doctors who failed to warn the parents of a child who died of the dangers of the surgery agreed to were suspended swiftly. Have they yet done enough? Publicity may next focus on the Council's power to restore a doctor to the register after erasure.[23] Whether the G.M.C. would find this desirable is open to question. The G.M.C.'s role is far from easy. While if it is insufficiently severe with defaulting doctors the Council will become the target of public criticism, should it lapse from strict fairness to a doctor the Council may face legal proceedings by him for breach of natural justice.[24] Yet if the Council wishes to retain pre-eminence in the regulation of medical practice it cannot shirk its responsibility to the profession and the public.

The role of the Privy Council

I have mentioned in passing the right of a doctor to appeal against any decision of the Professional Conduct Committee to the Privy Council. The hearing will not be before the entire Council of politicians, ex-politicians and assorted dignitaries but before two Law Lords and usually one other Privy Councillor. There will be a complete rehearing of the evidence. The system throughout is designed to ensure total fairness to the doctor. The complainant has no right of appeal if he is dissatisfied with the G.M.C. decision. Perhaps he should have, to ensure fairness between patient and doctor. At the hearing the Privy Council examines the evidence in detail, but is unwilling to interfere with penalties or to take a lead in condemning any particular variety of misconduct.[25] In the exercise of general supervisory powers over the G.M.C. the Privy Council does act directly to protect the public. The Medical Act 1983 grants the Privy Council default powers to require the General Medical Council to exercise any powers or duties conferred on it.[26] In this context the Privy Council monitors G.M.C. action, and it is reported that in 1985 the Council in concert with the Department of Health put pressure on the G.M.C. to extend its definition of serious professional misconduct to include a greater range of omissions to treat patients.[27]

The action for malpractice

Whatever the General Medical Council should be doing, it is not ordinarily concerned with isolated medical accidents, because even the best doctor can err, nor has the Council any power to compensate an injured patient. That is the function of the courts by way of an action for malpractice, that is, an action for negligence. More and more patients are resorting to litigation. The reaction of the doctors is one of unsurprising horror. For a start, insurance against professional liability costs them more and more each year. In 1986 premiums for doctors insured by the Medical Defence Union were increased by 70 per cent. Secondly, distinguished doctors see the threat of litigation as harmful to the development of medicine. They claim it will lead to defensive medicine. Doctors will take the course of action least likely to result in a court case rather than that which they judge to be medically desirable. They cite the experience of the U.S.A., where malpractice actions are epidemic. For example, the rate of Caesarian birth in certain states has climbed steadily because if the baby is delivered by surgery and proves to be damaged the risk that the doctor will be sued is minimized. Finally, doctors see a finding of negligence against them as a blot on their career. The lawyer may perceive the negligence action as providing a means of compensation for injury, a finding that a man on one day committed an error as all men do. The doctor sees it differently. And so do many patients.

The malpractice action is not much more popular with patients either, once they are enmeshed in the process of law. The majority of doctors are insured against liability by the Medical Defence Union or the Medical Protection Society. There are one or two other small protection societies. The protection society will provide the doctor with legal and other expert help. The claim will in many cases be defended all the way. The burden is on the patient to prove negligence. He must get expert witnesses to back him. There will be no investigation of *why* things went wrong. Instead there will be a gladiatorial contest between lawyers and the experts called as witnesses. The outcome of the trial may depend on whose lawyer asks the right questions.[28] In Part II we look at the malpractice action in detail and consider what changes are necessary in the way the law works. We shall look, too, to see whether, if the malpractice action fails to provide any mechanism for impartial investigation of medical mishaps, other complaints procedures fill the gap.

The National Health Service

No investigation of the control of medicine in Britain would be complete without looking at the operation of the N.H.S. I do not attempt a survey of health services law as such; that is done elsewhere.[29] Throughout this book, though, it can be seen that the existence of the N.H.S. and the framework of statutes and regulations which make up the rules for the health service dramatically affect the legal relationship of doctors, patients and other medical staff. Attention will be drawn to these features of the N.H.S. in Part II and in Chapter 15 on General Practice.

N.H.S. statutes such as the National Health Service Act 1977, the Health Services Act 1980, and the Health and Social Security Act 1984 are largely concerned with the constitution of the service. Parliament creates by statute the authorities who administer the health service, and provides for the services available and payment to those who administer them. The last ten years have seen constant change in the details of the service's administration. Powers and duties have been transferred through different tiers of authorities. It has not made for stability or efficiency.[30] Supplementing the legislation is a mass of regulations made by ministers under powers granted them by statutes. Regulations deal with some of the patient's most crucial concerns, for example the general practitioner's obligations to the service and his patients. Finally a mass of literature emanates from the D.H.S.S. in London giving information and guidance to health authorities and to individual doctors. Guidance on matters of long-term general importance comes in health circulars. Circulars cover a number of issues affecting patients' rights. The present procedure for dealing with hospital complaints and the procedure for managing claims by patients are just two examples. Circulars up-dating doctors on medical developments may be crucial to a malpractice action. If a circular has warned of the danger of a particular drug, this may help a patient prescribed the drug prove that his doctor was at fault. Finally, health circulars themselves may provoke litigation, as did the D.H.S.S. circular advising doctors on the right of girls under 16 to confidential advice on contraception.

Ultimate responsibility for the health of the N.H.S. lies with the Secretary of State for Social Services. The National Health Service Act 1977 provides in Section 1:

It is the Secretary of State's duty to continue the promotion in England and Wales of a comprehensive health service designed to secure improvement:

(a) in the physical and mental health of the people of those countries and
(b) in the prevention, diagnosis and treatment of illness and for that purpose to provide or secure effective provision of services in accordance with the Act.

Section 3 of the Act imposes on the Minister a further duty to provide to such extent as he considers necessary to meet all reasonable requirements a whole range of services including hospital accommodation, medical, dental, nursing and ambulance services and such other services as are required for the diagnosis and treatment of illness. High-sounding sentiments and expressions of political will, but is there any legal significance in this 'duty' imposed on the Health Minister? In 1979 four patients who had spent long periods vainly awaiting hip-replacement surgery went to court alleging that the Health Minister had failed in his duties under section 1 to promote a comprehensive health service and under section 3 to provide the appropriate hospital accommodation and facilities for orthopaedic surgery. The patients alleged: (1) that their period on the waiting list was longer than was medically advisable, and (2) that their wait resulted from a shortage of facilities, caused in part by a decision not to build a new hospital block on grounds of cost. The patients asked for an order compelling the Minister to act and for compensation for their pain and suffering. The Court of Appeal[31] held that (i) the financial constraints to which the Minister was subject had to be considered in assessing what amounts to reasonable requirements for hospital and medical services; (ii) the decision as to what was required was for the Minister, and the court could intervene only where a Minister acted utterly unreasonably so as to frustrate the policy of the Act. An individual patient could not claim damages from the Minister for pain and suffering. The patients lost the immediate legal battle. They gained valuable publicity.[32] And the courts did not entirely abdicate control over the Minister. A public-spirited patient, resigned to getting no damages himself, might try again for an order against any Minister who he alleged had totally subverted the health service, for example a Minister using his position and powers exclusively to benefit private medicine at the expense of the N.H.S. Chances of success are not high, and of course the government of the day could always change the law but they can be made to do it openly and not be permitted to pay lipservice to a duty to a health service which may have been abandoned.

Public and private medicine

Ten years ago private medicine was of marginal interest in England. The trend has been reversed. Private health insurance is booming and luxury private hospitals are mushrooming throughout the country. The morality of public versus private medicine and the medical merits of the two systems are for others to assess. The differences in the operation of the law relating to doctor and patient depending on whether the patient is N.H.S. or private may surprise some.

At the basis of the legal difference between public and private patient lies the fact that the N.H.S. patient has no contract with his doctor or anyone else. The private patient has a contract with his chosen doctor. That doctor must personally carry out any agreed treatment or surgery. The N.H.S. patient may be operated on by any doctor employed by the health authority. He has no choice of surgeon. N.H.S. and private doctors are both obliged to do their skilful best. A contract may impose more stringent obligations. One patient paid £20 for a vasectomy. Nature reversed the operation. The trial judge held that the surgeon contracted to render the man sterile. When his wife conceived again, the surgeon, albeit his surgery was faultless, was in breach of contract.[33] The Court of Appeal reversed that decision, deciding 2–1 that that contract did not guarantee sterility.[34] Private practice shuddered with relief. The advantages in legal terms by no means always lie with the private patient. We shall see that when it comes to proving negligence the N.H.S. patient has the edge. Something goes wrong in the operating theatre and it is not denied that someone must have been careless. The N.H.S. patient simply sues the health authority, claiming that one of their employees is responsible, and the authority has to pay. The consultant operating privately will not be acting as the employee of the hospital or clinic. If all the medical staff put up a wall of silence and refuse to give evidence, the private patient will be unable to show who was careless and thus must lose his action.[35]

The state of the law

I set out earlier in this chapter four objectives for the law relating to the practice of medicine. The regulation of the profession by the profession has been shown to fall short of what the public demands. I have indicated that the provision for compensation for injured patients is not ideal, and in Part II I elaborate on this theme and cast doubt too on the adequacy of complaints procedures. The value of the law's role in relation to difficult ethical and moral issues of medicine is dealt with in the next chapter and in Part III. Doctors and lawyers regard themselves as practitioners of ancient and honourable professions. A fraternal respect exists between senior members of the two professions. Judges, we shall see, have been hesitant to criticize doctors but have fewer inhibitions about intervening in other professions. Attacking the medical profession is easy, and in certain circles is becoming a popular pastime. Doctors as we have seen are a vulnerable target. They may doubt whether the law at present serves them well. We shall see that astute lawyers can use the law, to keep the doctors out of court,[36] to defeat claims against them, and to prevent investigation of errors.[37] In the long term this may damage the doctors as much as it now frustrates and infuriates aggrieved patients.

The summer of 1986 saw the problems of law and medicine attract renewed concern in many quarters. Doctors' representatives in the B.M.A. initiated talks with the legal profession on replacing the action for malpractice with a comprehensive compensation scheme for medical accidents. The Labour Party were reported to be considering similar proposals. Complaints procedures within the N.H.S. came under fire after Wendy Savage, a consultant obstetrician, endured and survived, at enormous public expense, an inquisition into her competence launched not by dissatisfied patients but by her own professional colleagues. Above all, dire warnings continued to be issued as to the effect of escalating medical litigation and awards against doctors. Doctors receiving their demand for steeply increased insurance premiums also received an explanatory letter in which a leading Q.C. wrote of an 'air of unreality' developing in assessing compensation in medical negligence cases. He warned his own colleagues that any assumption that a bottomless bucket of insurance money would pay out on claims was false. Change is in the air. Let us hope the nettle of necessary reform will be grasped firmly and without delay.

Chapter 2
Medicine, Moral Dilemmas and the Law

Medical ethics make news today but are far from new. From the formulation of the Hippocratic Oath in Ancient Greece to the present day, doctors have debated among themselves the codes of conduct which should govern the art of healing. These days philosophers, theologians, lawyers and journalists insist on joining the debate. Outside interest, or interference as doctors sometimes see it, is not new either. Hippocrates himself was a philosopher. The Church through the centuries has asserted its right to pronounce on medical matters of spiritual import, such as abortion and euthanasia, and to uphold the sanctity of life.

The Hippocratic Oath makes interesting reading. Its first premise is that the doctor owes loyalty to his teachers and his brethren. Obligations to exercise skill for the benefit of patients' health come second. Abortion, direct euthanasia and abetting suicide are prohibited. Improper sexual relations with patients are banned. Confidentiality in all dealings with patients is imposed. In 2,500 years these basic precepts of good medical practice changed little. Dramatic change in the kinds of moral and ethical problems confronting the doctor came only in the last fifty years. The art of the Greek philosopher physician became a science to many of its practitioners. Science has given the doctor tools to work marvels undreamed of by earlier generations. Women whose blocked Fallopian tubes prevent natural conception can be offered the hope of a test-tube baby. Women who have never ovulated can become mothers via egg donation. Babies born with spina bifida and other disabling handicaps can be saved from early death by delicate and complex surgery. Ventilators keep alive accident victims whose heart and lungs have given up. Dialysis and transplant surgery save kidney patients from certain death. The list of technological miracles is endless. They have placed in the hands of the doctors powers which through the ages men have ascribed to God alone.

Technological progress has been matched by social change. People are less and less willing to accept without question the decisions of those who exercise power, be they judges, politicians or doctors. Paternalism is out of fashion. Feminists ask why doctors should determine which infertile women receive treatment. Lawyers and philosophers, not to mention parents, wonder why the doctor is best qualified to judge whether a damaged baby's quality of life is such as to make life-saving surgery desirable. The power of the doctor to end life, whether by switching off a ventilator or by deciding not to give a patient a place in a dialysis unit, disturbs us all. These acute moral dilemmas are just as acutely felt by the doctor. His difficulty is accentuated by the fact that the new technology cannot be made available to all those in need. There is just not enough money or resources in the National Health Service.[1] Above all, the medical profession in 1987 faces a society more deeply divided on virtually every moral question than ever before. The public demands a say in medical decision-making on sensitive ethical issues. Yet from the hot potato of whether doctors should help lesbians to have children by artificial insemination, through the debates on abortion to euthanasia, the doctor who seeks guidance from public opinion will discover division, bitterness and confusion.

Questions of medical ethics arise throughout the whole field of medical practice. The ethics of the doctor–patient relationship are discussed in Chapter 3 and throughout Part II. Of the ethical and moral questions before the doctors today the most divisive revolve around matters of life and death and the concept of the sanctity of human life. It is the application of views on the sanctity of human life that is dealt with in this chapter, and to which we return in detail in Part III of the book.

The sanctity of life: Judaeo-Christian tradition[2]

For the devout Roman Catholic the concept of the sanctity of life is relatively straightforward. Human life is a gift from God and thus is literally sacred. Any act which deliberately ends a life is wrong. Life begins at conception and therefore abortion, and research on or disposal of an artificially created embryo, a test-tube embryo, is never permissible. Indeed the truly obedient Catholic will abstain also from any form of non-natural contraception. Life ends when God ends it. No degree of suffering or handicap justifies a premature release effected by men. Yet even so there remain grey areas in the application of belief that life is sacred. The Roman Catholic Church forbids abortion even when pregnancy threatens the woman's life. But a pregnant woman with cancer of the womb may be allowed a hysterectomy albeit that the child will then die. This is called the doctrine of double-effect. Abortion is banned because the only intent of that operation is to kill the child. An operation for cancer incidentally destroys the child but that was not its primary purpose. At the other end of life, the Church while condemning euthanasia does not demand that extraordinary means be taken to prolong it. Where is the line drawn? Should a grossly handicapped baby be subjected to painful surgery with a low ultimate success rate? Must antibiotics be administered to the terminal cancer patient stricken with pneumonia? The doctrine of double-effect, the application of a distinction between ordinary and extraordinary means to preserve life, have generated substantial literature and debate. Even accepting that areas of doubt exist for him, the orthodox Roman Catholic remains fortunate in the security of his beliefs on the sanctity of life, beliefs shared by many fundamentalist Christians of the Protestant tradition.

Many other practising Christians, who subscribe in essence to the doctrine of the sanctity of life, see further problems once they seek to apply their faith. Contraception is morally acceptable to the majority, and indeed to very many Roman Catholics now. The exact point when life begins and becomes sacred then becomes of the utmost importance to determine the morality of certain contraceptive methods. Abortion to save the mother's life is accepted by many Christians, as it always has been in the Jewish faith. The child's life may deserve protection but not at the expense of his mother's. This step taken, the extent to which the child's life may be sacrificed to his mother's has to be ascertained. Is a threat to the mother's mental stability sufficient? What about the women who suffer rape and conceive as a result? Today there is the question of the status of the early embryo created in the test-tube. These and many other issues have caused dissension and distress in the councils of the Church of England and the other Christian traditions. Nevertheless the Christian, Jew, or adherent of any religious faith at least enjoys a framework of belief. The sanctity of life has meaning for him because that life was given by God.

The sanctity of life in a secular society

In Britain today the numbers of people practising any religious faith are in a minority. A fair number still describe themselves as Church of England when entering hospital or joining the army. Churches are still popular for weddings and funerals. Thriving communities of Jews and Muslims remain committed to their traditions. But Britain is overwhelmingly a secular society. The majority of the population is un-committed to any religious creed. How many people retain a general belief in God as the Creator is open to question. For those who do not, what meaning has the sanctity of life? If life is not bestowed by God, on what grounds is it sacred?

There can be no doubt that belief in the sanctity of life does survive the death or absence of religious belief. Taking life is as reprehensible to many agnostics and atheists as it is to the Christian or the Jew. Indeed very many such people have been more consistent in upholding and fighting for the sanctity of life than have certain warmongering Christian priests or those 'Christians' who in America gather round the gaols to celebrate the death penalty's return.[3] But what for a secular society is the basis of the sanctity of human life? In fact for most people who are not philosophers the answer is simple. They share a deep and embedded instinct that taking human life is wrong. Life is man's most precious possession. All other possessions, all potential joys, depend upon his continued existence. An attack on one individual's right to life which goes unchecked threatens us all. Our autonomy is undermined. Our security becomes precarious. The move away from a concept of life as God-given, however, has certain consequences. If at the basis of belief in the sanctity of life is a perception of the freedom of the individual, of the joy that life can bring, then the quality of life comes into account. The right of the foetus to come into possession of his own life, his own freedom, must be balanced against his mother's rights over her own life and body. When pain and handicap cause an individual to cease to wish to live, then he may be free to end that life. It is his to do with as he wishes. Individual choice becomes central to applying the concept of the sanctity of life. No one must interfere with an adult's choices on continued life. Whether any other adult can be compelled to assist a fellow to end his life raises more difficult questions. And the concept of freedom of choice offers little guidance where an individual is incapable of making a choice. Nevertheless this uncertain position commands a fair degree of generous support. People have an intrinsic right to life. Life is sacred, but not 'absolutely inviolable'.[4] This is the view which occupies the 'middle ground'.

Sanctity of life: a different perception[5]

The latest stage in the debate on the sanctity of life involves an attack on the whole idea that 'taking human life is intrinsically wrong'. Life is seen as having no inherent value. Life has value only if it is worth living. Taking life is wrong because 'it is wrong to destroy a life which is worth living'.[6] Side by side with a move to concentrate attention on the quality of life alone comes a redefinition of human life deserving of protection. It is *persons*,[7] not all human animals, whose lives have value. Unless there is capacity for self-awareness, for the individual to recognize himself as a functioning human person able to relate to other persons, he has no life of the quality and kind which must be preserved. Certain consequences follow. A person who can reason must be allowed to judge for himself whether continued life is worth it. A human who cannot reason for himself, who is not a person, may have that judgment made for him by others. Providing painless release for a person who considers his life not worth living, or an individual whose capacity for self-awareness has gone so that he has ceased to be a person, becomes a moral action. The unborn are not persons. They have no rights against their mothers who are persons. Abortion is moral and it may even be considered immoral not to abort a seriously damaged foetus. Research on embryos to benefit existing persons, whether by improving treatment for infertility or seeking a cure for congenital disease, is not only morally permissible but almost a moral imperative. Euthanasia of the hopelessly brain-damaged with no hope of recovery is entirely acceptable and may, in strictly controlled circumstances, be involuntary.

Sanctity of life and the medical profession

No doubt the disparity of views among the general population is reflected in the personal views of many doctors. Doctors, however, actually have to take decisions on the sorts of matters others debate. How far and in what fashion is the sanctity of life a central medical ethic? The Declaration of Geneva[8] includes the following undertaking:

I will maintain the utmost respect for human life from the time of conception; even under threat, I will not use my medical knowledge contrary to the laws of humanity.

When the Declaration was first formulated in 1947, 'the utmost respect for human life' no doubt imported to most doctors a prohibition on abortion, at any rate where the mother's life was not in danger, and a complete ban on any form of euthanasia. The Declaration was amended and up-dated in Sydney in 1968. By 1968 abortion on grounds other than immediate danger to the mother had been legalized in Britain and parts of the U.S.A. Within a decade debate was to flourish within respected medical circles as to whether keeping alive all handicapped babies was right, and whether prolonging the life of the sick and elderly had not been taken to extremes by modern medicine. What then does the utmost respect for human life entail?

What it does not entail, and what has never existed in any code of medical ethics, is an injunction to preserve life at any price.[9] The prevention of suffering is as much the doctor's task as the prolongation of life. Alas, the two cannot always be complementary. The doctor struggling to interpret and apply his obligation to respect life faces a number of quandaries.

The beginning and end of life

An admonition to respect human life would be easier to adhere to if there was uniform agreement as to when life begins and ends. Few biologists now see the fertilization of the woman's egg as the beginning of a new life. They argue that egg and sperm are living organisms and point out that many fertilized eggs fail to implant. The fertilized egg may still split into two, and in rare cases grow not into a baby but a cancer threatening the woman's life. Fertilization, it is said, is just one further step in a continuing process. Acceptance of that view renders acceptable use of contraceptive devices, including the 'morning-after' pill, which prevent implantation. At what stage then does life begin and attract respect? We have noted the argument that the foetus has no status because it is not a person. This appears from observation of medical practice to attract little support among doctors. A growing view appears to be that the foetus as potential life attracts greater and greater status as it grows to full human likeness.[10] On this sort of rationale certain organizations representing doctors have backed embryo research, but not beyond the first fourteen, at most seventeen, days of growth. They include the Royal College of Gynaecologists, the Medical Research Council and by the narrowest of majorities the British Medical Association. The Royal College of General Practitioners and the Royal College of Nursing remain adamantly opposed to any form of research on embryos.

The end of life too has no definite marker any more. It can no longer be equated with the cessation of breathing and heartbeat. Resuscitation techniques to restart the heart still enthrall the press, with tales of the 'man who came back from the dead'. The development of life-support machines to replace heart and lung functions during surgery or after traumatic injury demonstrate that life can go on although the heart has stopped. When then does death occur? A definition of death as the irreversible cessation of all activity in the brain-stem[11] is generally accepted within the medical profession although some doctors now expess public doubts. For the lay public the decision to agree to switch off the life-support machine of a relative causes individual anguish, and anxiety occasionally surfaces that a desire for organs for transplantation might prompt too swift a pronouncement of death. These are problems solved by procedures designed to ensure that no anticipation of death is allowed, by reassurance and sympathy offered by medical staff to waiting relatives. The moral dilemma relating to dying arises a stage before brain-stem death. A person may suffer irreversible brain damage, be irreversibly comatose and yet still show signs of some activity in the brain-stem. He is not dead according to the current definition of death. Some argue that this definition should be extended to include the irreversibly comatose. For those who regard human life as of value only where the individual can recognize himself as a person, loss of consciousness is equated with physical death.[12] But is such a move really euthanasia by the back door? The question of continuing to keep alive the unkindly named 'human vegetable' will not go away. It must be faced, not by a surreptitious moving back of the moment of death but by addressing ourselves to the question of whether the doctor may ever kill.[13]

Killing and letting die

We noted earlier that codes of medical ethics have never commanded the doctor to prolong life at any cost. Caring for a patient as he dies in peace and dignity may be the last service his doctor can perform for him. Doctors and nurses tending the terminally ill in hospices are accorded the highest respect. The doctor's obligation to relieve suffering may on occasion cause him to refrain from prolonging life. Asked whether a doctor should invariably invoke every weapon of medical progress to prevent death, people of every shade of opinion would answer, no. For the Roman Catholic the test would be whether 'extraordinary means' must be resorted to in order to prolong that life. Extensive surgery on a dying cancer patient offering him only weeks more life would be ruled out. Antibiotics to cure a sudden, unrelated infection pose a more difficult moral dilemma. Nevertheless for most of us, religious or irreligious, this satirical rhyme sums up our attitude:

> Thou shalt not kill; but needst not strive
> Officiously to keep alive.

We revolt at the thought of a doctor killing a patient directly. We accept and are content to leave to the medical profession a liberty to refrain from further treatment in a hopeless case.

Scratch the surface of this popular attitude and problems and doubts emerge. What amounts to 'officiously' keeping alive? Is the doctor alone to judge when a life is worth living, for example to decide when a patient with kidney disease qualifies for dialysis? Lawyers and philosophers enjoy the endless argument these issues generate. Doctors on the whole do not. They have to provide answers.[14] Where a patient is sane, conscious and an adult, the dilemma, albeit no less distressing, has today a relatively easy answer. The patient should decide whether treatment continues.[15] Indeed the doctor, if he has been frank with the patient, has little choice but to leave it to the patient. He cannot lawfully give treatment without the patient's consent. Once a patient has decided to reject further treatment the doctor must normally desist. Suicide, if refusing treatment can be so classified, is no longer a crime. The freedom of the individual to make his own moral choices where he is able is largely unquestioned.

A more acute dilemma arises where the patient cannot make his own decision. Here the distinction between killing and letting die takes a central role. Asked if a doctor, or anyone else, should be allowed to smother a brain-damaged patient, the average man recoils in horror. But when a parent at the end of his tether does the same to his dying handicapped child he may attract public sympathy and understanding. Public attitudes to what the press call 'mercy killing' are not consistent.[16] Not surprisingly then, the distinction between killing and letting die has not been allowed to go unchallenged. It is subject to a three-pronged attack. (1) New technology makes the distinction between letting die and killing difficult if not impossible to put into practice. (2) It is argued that there is no valid moral distinction between killing and letting die. (3) Some writers have maintained that directly and painlessly killing a patient may be a morally superior decision to leaving him to a slow undignified death.

The problems posed for the doctor by the technology at his disposal cannot be sidestepped. An accident victim rushed into hospital is put on a life-support machine. All that can be done is done for him. He proves to be irreversibly brain-damaged but not brain-dead. If he had never been put on a machine, then failing to put him on the machine would be allowing him to die. Disconnecting the machine, a positive act, may be seen as killing him,[17] though comatose patients disconnected from life-support machines have lived on for several years in some cases.[18] Into which category, killing or letting die, does not feeding the patient fall? A newborn baby grossly handicapped may never demand food, may be unable to feed naturally from breast or bottle. Is omitting to tube-feed the baby killing or letting die? What about failing to operate to remove a stomach obstruction? Into which category falls failure to perform delicate and painful surgery to relieve hydrocephalus (water on the brain)? The difficulties of applying the distinction in practice can be enumerated endlessly.

So, why not abandon the distinction altogether? In favour of such change of direction are several apparently persuasive arguments.[19] The conception of the value of human life as dependent on self-awareness and the quality of life renders it moral to end a life once self-awareness has gone, or, as in the case of a newborn baby, where it has never developed. A patient still able to reason but living in pain, distress and handicap retains the right to make his own judgment on his quality of life. Otherwise the decision may be taken from him. Once quality of life, not life itself, is the determining factor, it follows that directly killing the patient may be a moral imperative. For if the patient's quality of life is such that life has ceased to have any intrinsic value, is it not kinder to end that life painlessly than let him drag on for more days, weeks or months in undignified 'sub-human' misery? If one accepts the basic premise that the value of human life is solely dependent on life being objectively 'worth living', then in pure logic progress to acceptance that a doctor may sometimes kill his patient must follow.

Pure logic does not, however, govern most human reactions. Voluntary euthanasia, assisting a patient who desires to die, has a number of committed proponents. Involuntary euthanasia, the doctor directly killing patients whose prospects are hopeless, has very, very little support and virtually none among doctors themselves.[20] The arguments against are dismissed with some scorn by the philosopher proposing a change of attitude. Suggestions that doctors are 'playing God' ought to cut little ice unless you believe in God. Fear that powers to kill may be misused could be alleviated by proper controls. Instinctive revulsion is seen as an uninformed response.

The distinction between killing and letting die will not go away. Three factors militate against any introduction of involuntary euthanasia at least. First, the conception of life as in some sense 'sacred' in itself has a greater hold on the population as a whole than its detractors appreciate. Few may now subscribe to belief in the God of the Bible, the Talmud and the Koran. Belief in a Creator of sorts is more widespread. Belief that men must set limits on what man may do is deeply ingrained. Killing those who cannot speak for themselves remains taboo. Second, the vision of the slippery slope to euthanasia for the unfortunate and the dissenter operates to deter acceptance of involuntary euthanasia. Today the hopelessly brain-damaged, tomorrow the mentally handicapped, the day after opponents of the government is the fear of many. No elaboration of controls devised by lawyers and politicians will drive away the fear. Finally, and practically most importantly, even if the exercise of judging objectively quality of life is carried out in all good faith, how can it be achieved? Who will sit in judgment? Occasionally that task falls even now to certain doctors. There is insufficient provision for treatment of kidney failure within the N.H.S. Not all patients who need it can be offered dialysis. Some are left to die. The doctors decide. In Oxford doctors decided to terminate dialysis for a mentally handicapped patient. His quality of life did not justify continuing to treat him while denying others treatment. The public outcry was overwhelming. The doctors responsible were branded as 'murderers' and 'barbarians'. How much greater would that outcry have been had the decision been to kill the patient instantly? And that despite the fact that on one view killing him quickly and painlessly might be seen as 'kinder' than leaving him to die as his system was slowly poisoned by blood which his failed kidneys could not purify.[21]

Sanctity of life and the law[22]

Legislating on moral and ethical issues created fewer problems for the Victorian parliamentarian. Applying the common law posed no dilemma for the judge. He knew what was right and what was wrong. The Victorian was unperturbed by doubt, unconcerned by any feeling that his decision should mirror the moral attitudes of society as a whole. Women and the 'lower classes' were deemed incapable of making moral judgments in any case. Additionally the divisions in moral attitude, although they did exist, were not as deep as those pertaining today. Nor were the problems of medicine as complex. Death remained then an independent agent largely beyond the doctor's skill to combat.

Yet the law remains relatively unchanged on its face despite advances in medicine and medical technology and the problems attendant on those advances. Only the Abortion Act 1967 stands out as a piece of legislation specifically designed to tackle the improvements in medicine rendering abortion safe and the change of attitude making abortion in certain circumstances acceptable to part of our society. The history of the Abortion Act will not encourage legislators to hasten to new fields of law reform. The compromise in attitude it represents pleases few today, be they pro- or anti-abortion. Governments of all political colours flinch from entering the battlefield on sanctity of life. Debating Enoch Powell's Bill to ban research on embryos the House of Commons dissolved in uproar. The divisions in the House were not those of normal party loyalty. They were more bitter and more emotional than the most highly charged Government versus Opposition set-piece.

The regulation of the medical profession on issues of life and death has been left then to the profession itself within the framework of the common law. In drawing up and applying codes of practice on the treatment of the handicapped newborn, the brain-damaged and the dying, the medical profession acts within the constraints of the criminal law of murder and manslaughter. The doctor's exposure to the law can be brutal. The law holds its hand from laying down the code of practice within which he works. Struggling to decide on whether treatment should continue he acts within guidelines agreed within his own profession but lacking any statutory force. Ninety-nine times out of a hundred he can comfort himself with the thought that no one will question his decision in these grey areas between living and dying. On the hundredth occasion he may face the spectre of prosecution for murder or attempted murder. The distinction between killing and letting die does not operate in the criminal law to debar a charge of murder. Allowing a patient to die when it was the doctor's duty to treat him, when the doctor knew that and intended that death would ensue, is as much murder as stabbing the patient to death.

The crucial issue once more is what is the content of the doctor's duty? When is it his obligation to prolong life? Left to decide that issue according to conscience and professional opinion most of the time, doctors not unnaturally are resentful that intervention when it comes may take the form of criminal prosecution for murder. Doctors do not see themselves as murderers. Even the most vehement and passionate member of Life, believing as he will that medical decisions as to the care of the newborn are frequently wrong, err too often on the side of

29

withholding treatment, would not place the doctor on the same moral plane as the man murdering in the course of robbery.

The reaction of the medical profession has in the main been that the law should keep out of medical ethics. Proposals to replace the existing and hazy common law with detailed legislative rules attract little enthusiasm.[23] Procedural rules about consultation, reference to codes of practice and the keeping of records of decision-making appear more acceptable. What doctors might really welcome is such legislation which additionally promises immunity from prosecution to the doctor following the correct process. Such legislation would check the maverick. It would ensure that no one doctor whose standards deviate markedly from his fellows could pursue a course of treatment or non-treatment of patients unacceptable to the majority. But it would enshrine in the law a principle that such decisions are for the doctors alone. The rest of us would be excluded from any right to a say on these matters of life and death.

'The ultimate decisions about life and death are not simply medical decisions.' This was the view expressed in an editorial in the *British Medical Journal* in 1981.[24] I concur wholeheartedly. The meaning and application of the sanctity of life is not a matter to be left for the doctors to decide and for the philosophers to argue over. The law's involvement to ensure that society's expectations are met is inevitable. The law is very far from perfect in its operation. Reform in a society divided in its moral judgments is hard to formulate. And indeed, detailed legislation is probably undesirable even if such legislation were to be agreed on. The variation in the circumstances confronting the doctor is too great. Rules that would meet every possible medical and social dilemma the doctor may face cannot be invented. The doctor's judgment cannot and should not be excluded. What can be done, if there is a will to do so, is to stimulate greater debate on the codes of practice under which the doctor works. Greater legal and lay involvement in their development should be encouraged. The gap between lawyer and doctor needs bridging. Perhaps amendment of the law of homicide should be considered, so that a doctor alleged to have stepped beyond the bounds of the acceptable in his professional sphere remains subject to the judgment of his fellow men but avoids the horrors of an inappropriate murder trial. Doctors complain that laymen do not understand the full implications of the problems presented by the handicapped and the dying, do not appreciate the complexity of modern medical technology. Only greater openness and a greater willingness to involve those outside the medical profession in decision-making will bring about better understanding. Only better understanding of the problems of medicine will bring about better law-making.

I said earlier that governments had backed away from issues of medicine and morals. Now they are being forced to act. The prospect of research on embryos and the host of questions surrounding new reproductive techniques is compelling the government to legislate. They have started by acting to prevent commercial exploitation of surrogacy via the Surrogacy Arrangements Act 1985. Legislation on more sensitive issues such as embryo research itself is to follow soon. The government must act swiftly or they will have created a 'no-go' area where medical and scientific opinion alone determines the moral status of the embryo. They will have moved a step down the path to granting ultimate power to the doctor. And that power will rest in the hands of an unrepresentative group within the profession, a group of ultra-high-technology specialists. If legislation is not agreed on, or is unclear and ineffective, then we will to some extent have forfeited the right to complain if we do not like what develops from present research. The common law has no role to play. The embryo has no status there. Legislation must be hammered out, not just so that society maintains its role in deciding on matters of life and death, but also to ensure that those who work in this sensitive field in good faith for the good of humanity as they see it can ensure that their work is kept out of the hands of those who would put their knowledge to evil ends. The debate on embryo research is vitriolic. Much name-calling has taken place. While those who oppose any research on embryos attack the scientists wanting to conduct research as 'mini-Hitlers', some real 'mini-Hitler' may be muscling in on the research. While scientists seeking limited and controlled research attack their opponents as relics of the Dark Ages, their work may be taken away from them and perverted towards ends to which they would never assent. I consider that embryo research at any stage is entirely and utterly morally unacceptable. But I would rather see the introduction of legal controls falling short of a complete ban than no controls at all. That may be the choice that has to be made. The middle ground is never fought over, but it may be where the law has to settle on embryo research and indeed on many of the issues where what is contested is essentially the sanctity of human life.

Chapter 3
A Relationship of Trust and Confidence

Whatever, in connection with my professional practice, or not in connection with it, I see or hear in the life of men, which ought not to be spoken of abroad, I will not divulge, as reckoning that all such should be kept secret.

The Hippocratic Oath

I will respect the secrets which are confided in me, even after the patient has died.

Declaration of Geneva (as amended Sydney 1968)

Doctors, like priests and lawyers, must be able to keep secrets. For medical care to be effective, for patients to have trust in their doctor, they must have confidence that they can safely talk frankly to him. An obligation of confidence to patients lies at the heart of all codes of medical ethics, but comparison of the two quotations above shows that the obligation is not always absolute. The Ancient Greek physician undertook not to divulge that which ought not to be spoken of abroad. He presumably judged what fell into that category. The Declaration of Geneva is much more stringent. *Any* information given by a patient in confidence must be kept secret for ever. A moment's reflection reveals the problems inherent in both absolute and relative obligations of confidence. An absolute obligation leaves the doctor powerless to do anything but try and persuade his patient to allow him to take action when a patient tells him he has A.I.D.S. but is still sleeping with his wife, when a mother tells him of her violent impulses towards her baby, when examination reveals that a patient may be a rapist sought by the police. Examples could be elaborated endlessly. On the other hand a relative obligation, which leaves the doctor free to breach confidence when he judges that some higher duty to another person or to society applies, may disincline patients from seeking necessary treatment. This may damage not only the patient but also those very people vulnerable when the doctor treats and does not 'tell'. The wife whose husband goes untreated for A.I.D.S. and the baby whose mother seeks no counsel may be more at risk if fears of breach of confidence prevent the husband

and the mother getting any help at all than if the doctor treats them in confidence.[1]

I look at the law on confidentiality as it affects doctors and adult patients, and I examine the role of the medical profession itself in enforcing the ethical obligation of confidence. The special problems affecting confidentiality and parents and children are considered in Chapter 14. The vagueness of the law may surprise some. The number of occasions when the law compels the doctor to breach confidence may shock many. Finally we examine what the patient is entitled to be told. From the patient's viewpoint the doctor's obligation of confidence exists to prevent the doctor passing on information about the patient to third parties. A relationship of trust requires that this should not happen. It also requires that the doctor be frank with the patient. Information about the patient should generally not be withheld from him. How far is the patient entitled to frankness from his doctor? When may he have access to his records? It has been suggested that medical confidentiality has as much to do with preserving relationships of trust and confidence between doctors themselves[2] as between doctors and patients. I do not enter into the historical or philosophical debate. I do attempt to see what role the law plays in defining the doctor/patient relationship.

Breach of confidence: the law[3]

The present law on breach of confidence has developed in a rather haphazard fashion. The precise legal nature of any obligation of confidence is uncertain.[4] What is clear is that the judges have shown themselves willing to act to prevent the disclosure of confidential information in a wide variety of circumstances. A duty to preserve confidences has been imposed in settings as diverse as trade or research secrets confided to employees,[5] marital intimacies[6] and Cabinet discussion.[7] Very often the obligation of confidence arises as an implied term of a contract, as is the case with the employee bound by his contract of employment to keep his master's business to himself. But the obligation of confidence can equally arise where no contract exists, or has ever existed, between the parties. The basic general principles of the law on breach of confidence amount to these. The courts will intervene to restrain disclosure of information where (1) the information is confidential in nature and not a matter of public knowledge, (2) the information was entrusted to another person in circumstances imposing an obligation not to use or disclose that information without the consent of the giver of the information, and (3) protecting confidentiality of that information is in the public interest. As well as acting in advance to prevent the disclosure of confidential information, the courts may where appropriate award compensation after information has been improperly disclosed. Finally, once an obligation of confidence is created it binds not only the original recipient of the information but also any other person to whom disclosure is made by the recipient when that other person knows of the confidential status of the information.

Applying the general law to the specific issue of medical confidentiality, no problem arises from the requirement that the information given by the patient himself or that deduced by the doctor on examination is confidential in nature. Most people do not broadcast their medical problems from the rooftop. Equally it is unchallenged that the relationship of any doctor with any patient, N.H.S. or private, imports an obligation of confidence. In a very early case action was taken to prevent publication of a diary kept by a physician to George III.[8] Much later, in 1974, a judge put the doctor's duty thus: '. . . in common with other professional men, for instance a priest and there are of course others, the doctor is under a duty not to disclose, [voluntarily] without the consent of his patient, information which he, the doctor, has gained in his professional capacity, save . . . in very exceptional circumstances'.[9]

The problematic area of medical confidentiality comes, not in establishing a general duty of confidence, but in determining what amounts to 'very exceptional circumstances' justifying breach of that duty. First, disclosure will always be justified legally when the doctor is compelled by law to give the confidential information to a third party. This may be by way of an order of the court to disclose records in the course of some civil proceedings, or may be under some statutory provision such as those Acts of Parliament requiring specified diseases to be notified to the health authorities. We shall return to this later. Second, it is clear that the doctor may voluntarily elect to disclose information in certain circumstances. The general law on confidence, as we saw, required that preserving confidentiality be in the public interest. In early judgments the public interest 'defence' tended to concern disclosure of crime; 'there is no confidence in the disclosure of iniquity'.[10] It is clear now, though, that it is not limited to crime or even misconduct, not amounting to crime, alone. In *Lion Laboratories Ltd* v. *Evans* (which considered the disclosure of confidential information suggesting that a breathalyser device, the Intoximeter, was unreliable), Griffiths L. J. said:

I can see no sensible reason why this defence should be limited to cases where there has been wrongdoing on the part of the plaintiffs . . . it is not difficult to think of instances where, although there has been no wrongdoing on the part of the plaintiff, it may be vital in the public interest to publish a part of his confidential information.[11]

The exact ambit of the public interest defence as it affects doctors has not been fully considered by any English court. It raises a host of questions. Should, or rather may, the doctor inform on any patient whom he suspects of any crime, however trivial? What other circumstances justify the invocation of the public interest to override the patient's interest in confidentiality? The guidance received by doctors in this awkward area comes largely from the General Medical Council and I shall consider and assess their rulings. For despite the underlying authority on the law of confidence, the enforcement of the obligation of confidence in practice rests largely with the G.M.C. This is because the action for breach of confidence has as yet been little used in a medical context, nor is it likely to be. The civil action for breach of confidence is an excellent weapon for restraining threatened breaches of confidence. It is less effective in compensating the victim of a breach of confidence except in a commercial setting. If a trade secret is revealed by an employee and the employer loses profits his loss can be measured by the courts and appropriate compensation ordered. A breach of a medical confidence results usually not in any monetary loss but in indignity and distress for the patient. It is not clear whether damages for mental distress can be awarded in an action for breach of confidence. The Law Commission has recommended reforms which would allow the award of such damages.[12] Even so such damages may be costly to obtain, and complaining to the G.M.C. is likely to remain in general the preferred remedy in cases of breach of confidence. The role of the law is this. The G.M.C. is not the sole arbiter on issues of confidence. A patient dissatisfied with the findings of the G.M.C. has no appeal from the G.M.C. decision. What he does have is a concurrent right to take the matter to the courts by way of an action for breach of confidence. In this way the G.M.C.'s definition of the duty of confidentiality is on every occasion potentially susceptible to review by the courts. In the case of children under 16 Victoria Gillick has forced just such a review. We shall later see in Chapter 14 that at the end of the day the views of the G.M.C. were confirmed by the Law Lords.[13] We shall see in this chapter that the ethical standard set by the G.M.C. does not always exactly match legal principles. We shall see that there are occasions when the ethical

35

obligation may properly be the more stringent. That the relationship of professional ethics and law in this country needs much more careful review is the outstanding lesson of the present confusing picture.

Breach of confidence: the G.M.C.

A patient aggrieved by a breach of confidence on the part of his doctor will normally choose to pursue his grievance by way of a complaint to the G.M.C. Any improper disclosure of information obtained in confidence from or about a patient can constitute serious professional misconduct on the part of the doctor. Again the crucial issue is: when is disclosure improper? The G.M.C. gives further detailed guidance.[14] The doctor's duty is to maintain confidentiality strictly save in eight specified circumstances. The death of the patient does not absolve the doctor from this duty.[15] In this respect the doctor's ethical obligation is stricter than his legal duty. The law of confidence probably does not protect the patient's secrets after death. Doctors may disclose information in the following cases.

(1) The patient or his legal adviser gives written consent.
(2) Information is shared with other doctors, nurses or health professionals participating in caring for the patient.
(3) Where on medical grounds it is undesirable to seek the patient's consent, information regarding the patient's health may sometimes be given in confidence to a close relative.
(4) When in the doctor's opinion disclosure of information to some third party other than a relative would be in the best interests of the patient, the doctor must make every effort to get the patient's consent. Only in exceptional circumstances may the doctor go ahead and impart that information without the patient's consent.
(5) Information may be disclosed to comply with a statutory requirement, for example notification of an infectious disease.
(6) Information may be disclosed where it is so ordered by a court.
(7) 'Rarely, disclosure may be justified on the ground that it is in the public interest which, in certain circumstances such as, for example, investigation by the police of a grave or very serious crime, might override the doctor's duty to maintain his patient's confidence.'
(8) Information may also be disclosed if necessary for the purpose of a medical research project approved by a recognized ethical committee.

The exceptions to the duty of confidentiality as detailed by the G.M.C. leave a fairly large degree of discretion in the hands of the individual doctor to determine when a breach of confidence is warranted. This is unavoidable if any exceptions to the duty of confidence are to be permitted. What we need to consider is how far the categories of exceptions set out by the G.M.C. conform to the likely response of the courts if the issue were to be litigated rather than referred to the G.M.C.

The first two exceptions to confidentiality raise no problematic issues of law. There can be no breach of duty when a patient expressly consents to disclosure or when, as in the case of necessary communications with other doctors and nurses, consent can be implied.[16] Exceptions (5) and (6) again raise no awkward legal problems. The doctor must be justified in law in revealing information when the law compels him to do just that.

Disclosure in the patient's interests

Difficulty is first encountered when we look at exceptions (3) and (4). The essence of both is that the doctor should be free to speak with a relative, or, very exceptionally, with some other person, when he judges that the patient is too ill to make decisions as to his own treatment. He may act in the patient's best interests. Two points must be made clear. Relatives of an adult patient have no special status as regards his treatment. Acting in the patient's best interests is not in itself a defence to a breach of confidence. The legal justification for talking to third parties without consulting the patient is that generally he may be presumed to give his consent to such discussions. When a patient is unconscious, or cannot communicate at all, the doctor may reasonably infer that if able he would agree to his family and friends being consulted. Where a patient is very ill indeed, albeit still able to talk, the doctor may again usually assume that he will be prepared for the doctor to speak with his family to obtain their advice and to reassure them. Most people would be only too ready to agree and let their family take part in their treatment. But if a patient places a ban on communication with any third party, the doctor must respect that ban. The patient is entitled to confidentiality and entitled to require that it be maintained even when it is contrary to his interests. The doctor may seek to persuade him to change his mind. He may not override his decision.

Disclosure in the public interest

Exceptions (7) and (8) relate to the general 'public interest' defence available in any action for breach of confidence. The G.M.C. provides in exception (7) for a general exception of disclosure in the public interest, giving the example of informing the police about grave crime but not limiting the exceptions to disclosure of crime alone. They stress that disclosure should be resorted to rarely. Exception (8) concerns a special instance of the public interest disclosure as part of a properly approved research project. We shall leave consideration of this issue until the chapter on clinical research.[17]

We will look now at the circumstances in which a doctor is justified in informing the police about criminal conduct on the part of a patient. He is generally under no obligation enforced by the criminal law to contact the police. Unless a statute specifically so provides, the doctor does not himself commit any offence by failing to tell the police of any evidence he may have come across professionally which suggests that a patient may have committed or is contemplating some crime.[18] A criminal offence is committed only when a doctor or anyone else accepts money to conceal evidence of crime.[19] The major exception to this general rule is section 11 of the Prevention of Terrorism (Temporary Provisions) Act 1984. Section 11 makes it an offence for any person having information which he believes may be of material assistance in preventing terrorism or apprehending terrorists to fail without reasonable excuse to give that information to the police. In the light of the threat posed by terrorism today, the duty of confidence between doctor and patient is unlikely to be seen as a reasonable excuse for failing to go to the police.

In the case of most crimes then, the choice is the doctor's. The criminal law will not penalize him for not informing the police. Will he be in breach of confidence if he elects to do so? The judges early this century were divided on the issue of whether a doctor was justified in going to the police after attending a woman who had undergone a criminal abortion. Hawkins J. condemned such a course as a 'monstrous cruelty' and doubted whether such a breach of confidence could ever be justified,[20] where Avory J. saw the doctor's duty to assist in the investigation of serious crime as always outweighing his duty to his patient.[21] Recent judgments appear to support Avory J.'s view although they deal with confidential relationships outside the medical field. Lord Denning has suggested that the public interest justifies disclosure of any crime or misdeed committed or contemplated.[22] Within the doctor/

patient relationship freedom to disclose in the public interest should be more limited in scope. Unless commission of any crime disentitles the criminal from normal standards of medical care, disclosure should be strictly limited. Doctors who reasonably suspect that some other person is at risk of physical injury at their patient's hands must be free to act to protect that person. Doctors who discover that a crime of violence has been committed *may* be lawfully entitled to breach the patient's confidence. That is less clear. But in cases of child abuse,[23] rape, and serious violence the risk that the crime may be repeated will generally ensure that the doctor who breaches confidence acts with legal impunity. What the doctor may not do is hand over to the police information on each and every patient who transgresses the law. Parliament has legislated in a number of cases to compel breach of medical confidence. The courts should not be over-zealous to add to that list.

The inherent anomaly in this view may be that a doctor found to be in breach of confidence for disclosing a crime will be condemned by a court for taking steps to combat crime, a moral duty cast on every citizen. The doctor is distinguished from other citizens by the presence of a positive legal duty to his patient. Enforcing his duty to his patient benefits the public as well as the patient. Medical confidentiality is at the root of good health care. Should the courts, however, find that as upholders of the law they cannot condemn those who help bring lawbreakers to justice, the alternative solution is to rely on the ethical standard of the G.M.C., that breach of confidence is justified only in case of grave or serious crime. The doctor may not break the law if he discloses details of petty crimes. He may be punished for professional misconduct. The legal and ethical standards do not need to be exactly the same. The relationship between them does need careful thought.

Next arises the question of disclosure where crime is not an issue. The law no longer limits the concept of public interest disclosure to crime alone, nor does the G.M.C. in its ethical guidance to doctors. Defining exactly when the doctor may disclose on this more general basis is exceptionally difficult. Can he report a patient's epilepsy to the D.V.L.C. (Driver and Vehicle Licensing Centre) if the patient refuses to give up driving? May he tell a wife that her husband has A.I.D.S.? What about the problem of the patient whose genetic counselling reveals a risk that her sister too may be a carrier of genetic disease? In all cases the doctor must first do his utmost to obtain the patient's consent to disclosure. If persuasion fails, what may the doctor do? He must balance his duty to the patient against the risk threatening other individuals. It seems clear then that he may in an appropriate case inform any relevant public body.[24] So he may contact the D.V.L.C. concerning an epileptic patient. It is less clear whether he may communicate directly with an affected individual. In defamation a defence of qualified privilege protects any communication which the maker has a duty to impart and the recipient a legitimate interest in receiving. No defence of qualified privilege as such exists in breach of confidence.[25] The defence is that the public interest demands disclosure. Private interests alone are not enough. But where a genuine risk of physical danger, of injury or disease is posed to any third party then the public interest in individual security may be sufficient to justify disclosure to that person so that he may protect himself appropriately. When the doctor reasonably foresees that non-disclosure poses a real risk of physical harm to a third party he should be free to warn that person, especially if that person too is his patient. And the courts should not be over-zealous to prove him wrong. Similarly, in such cases, if the doctor thinks it more appropriate to contact the third party's G.P. he should not be condemned. But risk of harm must be established. A simple belief that someone else, spouse or relative, is entitled to information is insufficient. So a husband has no 'right to know' if his wife asks to be sterilized. Parents have no 'right to know' if their daughter of 16 or above seeks an abortion. They clearly have an interest, a legitimate and not merely prurient interest, in the matters at stake. That is not enough. The balance of public interest in confidentiality should be displaced only by danger of physical harm.

The doctor must not forget that at the end of the day the law determines when overriding interests justify a breach of confidence. The law should be generous in deciding whether an individual judgment by a doctor within a recognized category of disclosure is correct. It cannot abdicate responsibility for the overall framework of medical confidentiality. And the role of the law of defamation must not be overlooked. Disclosure of any confidential information, albeit every word is true, may be the subject of an action for breach of confidence. But if the doctor is mistaken and some of the information disclosed by him proves to be untrue, he may face a further action for defamation. Any statement causing responsible citizens to think less of a person or to avoid his company may be defamatory. Diagnoses of alcoholism, venereal disease and A.I.D.S. are all examples of possible defamatory remarks. Suspicion of child abuse is another. In defamation the doctor has a complete defence if what he has stated is true. Additionally he has a defence of qualified privilege if (1) he reasonably believed his state-ments to be true, and (2) he communicated with a person with a legitimate interest in the relevant information. Informing the police of suspected violence to a child is clearly privileged even if the doctor's suspicions prove to be unfounded. Informing an employer that an employee is an alcoholic is probably not. The issue of whether com-munication was justified is one and the same in the law of confidence and defamation.

In this most sensitive area of doctor–patient relationships, striking the balance between confidence and concern for others is of the utmost difficulty. One interesting suggestion[26] made to help strengthen the patient's position is that doctors ought in advance to give patients notice of the circumstances which they consider may warrant a breach of confidence. The framework of their future relationship would then be set by the parties involved. The weakness of the proposal lies in the difficulty of predicting circumstances calling for a breach of confidence in advance. And the danger exists perhaps of criminally inclined patients shopping around for a doctor who promises never to 'grass'. That would be scarcely edifying for the profession or the public.

Breach of confidence and negligence

I have suggested that on occasion the doctor's duty of confidence to his patient may be overridden by his duty to safeguard a third party from physical harm. If he mistakenly decides the question of this conflict of duty in the patient's favour, and the risk of harm to someone else materializes, is the doctor at risk of a lawsuit by the injured party? He may well be. For normally where risk of injury is readily foreseeable and a person has the ability to eliminate that risk, or at any rate to minimize it, a duty to take the necessary action will arise. An education authority which failed to ensure that small children could not get out of their nursery school and on to a busy main road were found liable, not just to any child injured on the road, but to a lorry driver injured in an incident caused by a straying child.[27]

In California the student medical centre at the University of California actually faced an action[28] in the courts for failing to warn a young woman of the risk posed to her by one of their patients. The girl's rejected lover sought psychiatric help at the centre. He told staff there of his violent intentions towards the girl and that he had a gun. The staff warned the police, who decided to take no action. The medical centre said nothing to the girl. She was murdered by their patient soon afterwards. Her family sued the University for negligence. The medical centre was found liable for failing to breach their patient's confidence and warn the girl of the threat to her life.

On similar facts an English court would be most unlikely to find a doctor negligent. First the court would have to determine whether in the special circumstances of medical confidentiality a duty to breach confidence could be countenanced. In the case of the education authority held liable for the escape of the infant, their duty to child and to lorry driver was one and the same. The doctor is faced with a stark conflict of duty. At the highest the doctor's duty may be set as an obligation to consider and assess the risk to the third party. The Californian medical staff did their best. They informed the police. The extent of the doctor's duty to third parties in England would appear to be this. He must not ignore any risk to other people created by his patient. He must weigh his duty to his patient against his duty to society and other individuals. If he acts reasonably on the evidence before him in this most awesome of dilemmas, the court will not penalize him if he ultimately proves to be wrong.

Breach of confidence: law reform

In 1981 the Law Commission, a body appointed to review the current state of the law and recommend reform, published a report on *Breach of Confidence*[29] proposing detailed reforms. As yet the government has not acted on the report. The proposals are to some extent technical and will have more impact in the field of commercial confidences than medical confidentiality. Those proposals relevant to doctors and patients include the following. The action for breach of confidence will lie in the form of an action for a tort, a civil wrong. An obligation of confidence will attach both to information entrusted by the patient to his doctor and to information about the patient confided to the doctor by a third party, for example reports to a general practitioner from a consultant to whom the patient has been referred. Compensation ordered where an action for breach of confidence is successful should include damages for mental distress and any consequent physical or mental harm. The Law Commission rejected arguments that the doctor's duty of confidence should survive the patient's death. They took the view that a law protecting the individual's interest in information entrusted by him to his doctor could not be stretched to embrace his family's privacy and freedom from distress after that person's own death. The ethical obligation imposed by the G.M.C. might properly be more stringent than the legal obligation enforced by the law on confidence.

Compulsory disclosure

The circumstances in which the doctor may choose to disclose information about his patients may concern some patients and certainly creates difficult problems for their doctors. The doctor's dilemma is to some extent solved when the law compels him to disclose information. The number of instances in which this is the case is worryingly high.

First, a doctor must give any information required by a court of law. Privilege, in the sense of being free to refuse to give evidence relating to professional dealings with clients, is something usually enjoyed by lawyers alone and not shared by any other professional colleagues. A doctor can be subpoenaed to give evidence just like anyone else. Nor can he withhold anything from the court. He does not have to volunteer his views or expertise but whatever questions he is asked he must answer. Just as he can be called to the witness box, so his records can be called up before the courts. The only protection for medical confidentiality lies in the judge's discretion. Judges will try to ensure that confidence is breached only to the extent necessary for the conduct of the trial in progress. The doctor may be unhappy at having to break trust with his patient. He can at least be reassured that he is at no legal risk. Any breach of confidence made as a witness in court will be absolutely privileged against later action by the patient.

One further emergent area of protection of confidentiality should be mentioned. In *D.* v. *N.S.P.C.C.*[30] the plaintiff sought to compel the N.S.P.C.C. to disclose who had mistakenly accused her of child abuse. The court refused to make the order. The public interest in people feeling free to approach appropriate authorities to protect young children outweighed the plaintiff's private interest in unearthing her accuser. Thus there will be some cases where the courts may refuse to help a party seeking to discover who gave damaging information about him to the police or some other body. The courts may find that the public interest outweighs the private rights of the affected party. A similar balance of public versus private interest may also apply where the doctor is not a potential defendant but merely a witness. Particularly sensitive information may be allowed to be withheld from the court in the public interest. The decision is always a matter for the judges, not the doctor. Again the doctor's protection depends on the judge's discretion.

Next, the doctor may be compelled to hand over information to the police or other authorities before any trial commences. We have seen that under the Prevention of Terrorism (Temporary Provisions) Act 1984 the doctor must take the initiative and go to the police. This is unusual. But what a number of statutes demand is that the doctor answers questions if the police come and ask him. If a statute imposes a duty on 'any person' to answer police questions, any person includes a doctor.[31] Again, his profession confers no exemption or privilege upon him. Where no specific statutory power aids the police in their investigation of a crime the question becomes whether, if they believe a doctor holds records or other material constituting evidence of a crime on the part of a patient, they can search the doctor's premises and seize the relevant material. The Police and Criminal Evidence Act 1984 grants police access to medical records but imposes certain safeguards. A search warrant to enter and search a surgery, hospital or clinic for medical records or human tissue or fluids taken for the purposes of medical treatment may be granted only by a circuit judge[32] and not, as is usually the case, by lay magistrates. The judge is directed to weigh the public interest in disclosure of the material against the general public interest in maintaining confidentiality.

Beyond the scope of the criminal law several further examples of compulsory disclosure must be noted.[33] Provision is made for notification of infectious diseases and of venereal disease. Accidents at work and instances of food poisoning are notifiable. Abortions must be reported. Details of drug addicts are required under the Misuse of Drugs Act. Births and deaths have to be notified by doctors as well as registered by families.

Finally, a number of bodies concerned with health administration may require information in the course of performing their functions. These include the Health Service Commissioner (Health Ombudsman), the D.H.S.S. and regional and district health authorities. Examining the individual items on the long list of circumstances when a doctor can be forced to hand over information concerning his patients, many can be justified on grounds of public interest. The trouble is that the list just grows haphazardly. What is needed is a review of medical confidentiality to examine all instances of compulsory disclosure and clarify when the public interest overrides the general benefit of preserving confidentiality. Legislation compelling disclosure should be express rather than simply including the doctor in a general requirement that any person gives information. Parliament should address the problem directly and not leave it to the judges to interpret ambiguous statutory provisions.

Patients' access to records[34]

We turn now to the opposite side of the coin. Patients are entitled to expect their doctors to keep their secrets. Can the doctors have secrets from their patients? The law of confidence prevents doctors from improperly disclosing information from or about their patients. But what if it is the patient who seeks information about himself? Extraordinarily, he has at present no right as such to demand information or to demand access to his records.

Let us take first the patient wishing to compel a doctor to give him information or let him see his records. The doctor must clearly give him any information necessary to ensure that the patient has adequate health care. Should a doctor fail to give the patient sufficient details of his condition or treatment to enable the patient to take care of himself, he may be found to be negligent. If he makes physical contact with the patient, for example administers an injection, and entirely misleads the patient as to the nature of the injection, this might even in an extreme case amount to assault. That is the limit of the doctor's obligation. He need not communicate every detail of his examination and diagnosis if such communication is not essential for proper treatment.

Next, can the patient demand to see his records? We will assume for the moment that the records are manual, not computer records. The answer now is probably no. In law the issue turns on ownership of the records. In the case of a *private* doctor the physical material on which the records are made belong to the doctor. He owns them and may decide what to do with them. But does the information contained in the records not belong to the patient? Much of what is in the records will be information given to the doctor by the patient, or discovered by the doctor as a result of examination of the patient's body. Unfortunately, ownership of information is at present a concept undeveloped by the law. And legislating to grant ownership of information would not help much, nor would an innovative judge developing the common law to the same end. In medical records much of the information clearly emanates from the *doctor*, the result of his observation and skill. As for information passed on by the doctor to other doctors, for instance letters of referral to consultants, to whom does that belong? Not to the patient, and additionally the doctor may argue that whatever *he* says in the letter is protected by the law of confidence. He wrote to the consultant in confidence. Thus, even if the consultant wishes, he may be unable to reveal the contents of the letter to the patient.

This complex picture gets even more complicated when we look at the position of records of N.H.S. patients. Medical records kept by N.H.S. general practitioners are made on forms and so on supplied by the Family Practitioner Committee and stated expressly to remain their property. The G.P. at least has control of his records while a patient remains on his list. Medical records made by hospital doctors are again made on N.H.S. property. Additionally, as hospital doctors, unlike general practitioners, are employees of the health authorities, records made by them in the course of their employment belong in law to their employer. The health service administrators control the fate of the records.[35] This has two implications for patients. First, a coach and horses may be driven through the traditional concept of medical confidentiality. A health service administrator may decide when to allow police or other authorities access to patients' records. Second, a health service administrator may allow the patient himself access to his records. Both courses infuriate the doctors. They argue that records made by them belong to them or should at least be controlled by them.

For patients the dispute as to who owns records is largely irrelevant.[36] What they may want is access to those records. This can be obtained if legal proceedings against a doctor or health authority are begun.[37] Earlier limitations to ensure that medical records if disclosed in litigation were handed over only to the patient's medical advisers have been removed, as we shall see. Should medical records be kept on computer, the patient may be able to obtain access to those records under the Data Protection Act 1984. That Act has several consequences for patients if medical records are computerized. First, it will enable data from those records to be transferred in secret from one computer record to another without the knowledge of doctor or patient. So data might be transferred with the agreement of an administrator, not a doctor, from a hospital computer to police computer records. Attempts by the B.M.A. to incorporate provision for doctors to control computerized health records failed. Second, however, the Act does impose controls on the transfer of computerized information and grants remedies in cases of unauthorized disclosure. Finally, the Act could from November 1987 give the patient, the 'data subject', the right to be given a copy of any information held on him within computer records. When medical records were computerized, then patients under the Act might acquire a right to know what their records contain. That right may not materialize. For section 29 of the Act grants power for a Minister to exclude any provisions of the Act providing subject (patient) access to health records. He has been urged to do so.

The present confused and anomalous state of the law has prompted a group of M.P.s and peers to campaign for legislation to grant individuals access to all personal files including medical records. A Bill to effect this proposal was presented to the House of Commons in October 1985 and concurrently introduced in the House of Lords. Its implications go far beyond medical confidentiality. The Bill would allow access to many sensitive government files. The government vigorously opposed it and the Bill failed. The issue of access to medical files remains controversial. The Campaign for Freedom of Information who backed the Bill will try again. Doctors in general oppose any move to grant patients an un-limited right of access to their records. They argue that patients might misunderstand technical details. Their ability to be totally frank with colleagues would be diminished. A chance remark placed on the record in exasperation such as 'Mrs B. in neurotic mood again!' might destroy a patient's trust. There are some good reasons for arguing that access to records may not be entirely beneficial, but equally some of the reasons advanced lack any merit. The benefits of access in reinforcing the patient's right to control his own life, in improving medical care by enabling the patient to play his part as an equal partner in his medical treatment, and in strengthening trust between doctor and patient by abolishing secrecy must be weighed in the balance.

N.H.S. procedures

Unless the law relating to medical confidentiality and patient access to records is clarified, control of these sensitive issues will continue to depend largely on medical and health service practice. We have already examined the role of the G.M.C. in enforcing the ethic of confidential-ity. Their jurisdiction is limited to medical practitioners. Day-to-day control of the records of N.H.S. patients, in particular hospital records, rests in the hands not of the doctors or other medically qualified staff but of health service administrators. Doctors as well as patients have expressed concern that a patient's notes are seen by an unnecessary number of persons. They complain that decisions as to when to disclose records, for example to the police in cases of suspected crime, are taken too often by administrators. Administrators are not subject to the control of the G.M.C. Doctors fear they may be less concerned about confidentiality. Medical staff are outraged too that administrators have been known to let patients see their own records without consulting the patient's doctor.

N.H.S. staff are of course subject to the law on confidence. Information confided by the patient to his doctor remains legally confidential when passed by the doctor to N.H.S. clerks for filing and preserving in N.H.S. files. But the undeveloped and uncertain state of the law makes it a dubious safeguard for the patient's privacy. In the last few years a number of committees[38] have addressed the problem. A draft Code on confidentiality within the health service has been proposed. The Code asserts the fundamental principle of confidentiality between doctor and patient and declares that that principle binds the health authority. Disclosure within the service is justified only if required in the context of the patient's health care. Disclosure to third parties outside the service is permissible only with the patient's consent save in exceptional cases. The exceptions, for example where disclosure is required by law or in case of serious crime, correspond closely to the exceptions sanctioned by the G.M.C. The innovation in health service practice introduced by the code is that prima facie the decision on disclosure shall always be taken by a medically qualified person and where possible it should be the doctor caring for the patient. The Code will be enforced by the sanction of disciplinary action or even dismissal against staff members who break it. A Working Party on Confidentiality[39] has recommended that in every staff contract an express clause on confidentiality should be included, and has advised that several other practical measures be taken to ensure that rules on confidentiality be respected.

Turning to the reverse side of the coin on confidentiality, when may a patient see his own records, the Data Protection Act has forced action on this issue too. It has been recommended, sensibly, that the rules on patient access to records should not differ depending on the chance of whether a particular set of records are kept on a computer or are manual records. Unless the Health Minister expressly exempts medical records from the Data Protection Act, patients will have an automatic right to see any computer records. The Minister is being asked to make such an exemption. Health service committees and professional bodies are agreed that there should not be an unrestricted right of access to one's own medical files. It has been proposed[40] that a distinction should be made between (1) information provided by the patient and (2) diagnostic and treatment information originated by medical staff. The patient should have unrestricted access to that information he himself provided. 'Personal health data' originating from professionals should generally be released to him unless, in the opinion of medically qualified staff, releasing that information would either (1) harm the patient, or (2) cause a breakdown of trust between doctor and patient, or (3) inhibit the keeping of full and frank records. A patient refused access to his records would have the right to have that decision reviewed. These proposals represent a compromise. Patients would be denied full and unrestricted access to their records. They would be granted 'limited access'. Sadly, even 'limited access' has been opposed by the B.M.A. The B.M.A. voted in 1986 to urge the Health Minister to exempt health records from the Data Protection Act. Patients would be denied any right of access to any information about themselves.

The cumulative effect of the assorted proposals concerning health service practices is this. Control of records is returned to the hands of the doctors. Decisions on disclosure to third parties become theirs. Determining what the patient himself may see becomes a medical decision. Even under the proposals for 'limited access', the criteria proposed to justify refusing patient access are wide. They negate any effective 'right to know'.

The problem throughout the area of medical confidentiality and professional secrecy is this. The issues arising within the doctor/patient relationship are unique. The law seeks to force medical confidentiality into the general framework of the law of confidence, privacy and ownership of records. It simply does not fit. The matters at stake are too important for these questions to be left fuzzy and unpredictable. Doctors and patients need to know where the law stands. It may well be that at the end of the day the ethical standard of confidentiality will diverge from the requirements of the law. For example, the profession itself may elect to enforce a higher degree of confidentiality in respect of suspected crime and to maintain the obligation of confidence even after a patient's death. The crucial importance of the continuing ethical debate[41] among doctors themselves must never be forgotten. For that debate to be fruitful, the legal framework within which the profession may properly act must be changed. If the G.M.C. is left to operate its concept of confidentiality in the present state of legal complexity and confusion, we outside the profession must not complain if we do not like their conclusions.

Part II

Medical Malpractice

Introduction

In this Part, I examine what general remedies the law affords a patient who is dissatisfied with the medical care which he has received. He may feel that he has not been fully consulted or properly counselled about the nature and risks of the treatment. He may have agreed to treatment and ended up worse, not better. Consequently a patient may seek compensation from the courts. Or he may simply want an investigation of what went wrong, and to ensure that his experience is not suffered by others.

The law relating to medical errors, commonly described as medical malpractice, operates on two basic principles. (1) The patient must agree to treatment. (2) Treatment must be carried out with proper skill and care on the part of all the members of the medical profession involved. Any doctor who operated on or injected, or even touched an adult patient against his will, might commit a battery, a trespass against the patient's person. A doctor who was shown to have exercised inadequate care of his patient, to have fallen below the required standard of competence, would be liable to compensate the patient for any harm he caused him in the tort of negligence.

In short, to obtain compensation the patient must show that the doctor was at fault. And if he sues for negligence he must show that the doctor's 'fault' caused him injury. Three overwhelming problems are inherent in these two simple statements.

First, how do courts staffed by lawyer-judges determine when a doctor is at fault? We shall see that the judges in England defer in the most part to the views of the doctors. Unlike their American brethren, English judges will rarely challenge the accepted views of the medical profession. Establishing what that view is may cause the court some difficulty though. Each side is free to call its own experts and a clash of eminent medical opinion is not unusual.

Second, as liability, and the patient's right to compensation, is dependent on a finding of fault, doctors naturally feel that a judgment against them is a body blow to their career and their reputation. Yet a moment's reflection will remind the reader of all the mistakes he has made in his own job. A solicitor overlooking a vital piece of advice in a conference with a client can telephone the client and put things right when he has a chance to check what he has done. A carpenter can have a second go at fixing a door or a cupboard. An overworked, overstrained doctor may commit a momentary error which is irreversible. He is still a good doctor despite one mistake.

Finally, the doctor's fault must be shown to have caused the patient harm. In general, whether a patient is treated within the N.H.S. or privately, the doctor only undertakes to do his best. He does not guarantee a cure. The patient will have a legal remedy only if he can show that the doctor's carelessness or lack of skill caused him injury that he would not otherwise have suffered. So if I contract an infection and am prescribed antibiotics that a competent doctor would have appreciated were inappropriate for me or my condition, I will be able to sue the doctor only if I can show either (1) that the antibiotic prescribed caused me harm unrelated to my original sickness, for example brought me out in a violent allergy, or (2) that the absence of appropriate treatment significantly delayed my recovery. And in both cases I must prove that had the doctor acted properly the harm to me would have been avoided.

We shall see therefore that the law is a remedy only for more specific and serious grievances against a doctor. It is in any case an expensive and unwieldy weapon. Many patients have complaints, particularly about hospitals, which do not amount to legal grievances. They complain about being kept waiting, inadequate visiting hours, or parents not being allowed to stay with their children. I shall look in this Part at extra-legal methods of pursuing complaints against a hospital or a doctor, and in particular I shall investigate the role of the National Health Service 'Ombudsman'. Nor do we limit our examination to faults alleged against medical practitioners. Many medical mishaps arise from the dangers inherent in certain drugs. I consider the liability of the drug companies and attempts by government to ensure that available medicines are safe. Finally I ask whether the whole basis of the present law of negligence as it applies to medical practice is due, or overdue, for radical reform.

Chapter 4
Agreeing to Treatment

Every adult has an inviolable right to determine what is done to his or her own body. We shall look at the law in relation to children later. A person who intentionally touches another against that other's will commits a trespass to that person just as much as coming uninvited on to the person's land is a trespass to his land. The tort of battery is committed. Where a person consents to a contact no battery is committed. So a boxer entering the ring cannot complain of battery when he is hit on the chin by his opponent. Battery is any non-consensual contact.

How does this tort relate to doctors? Any doctor examining, injecting or operating on a patient deliberately makes contact with that patient's body. Normally he commits no wrong because he does so with the patient's agreement. Should he fail to obtain a patient's agreement at all, should a doctor force himself on a patient, then clearly he commits a battery. But that is extremely unlikely. However, what of the surgeon who correctly decides to treat cancer of the bone of the right leg by amputating that leg and by error amputates the wrong leg, the left leg? Once the error is discovered the poor patient has to endure a further operation to remove the right leg. One patient's notes are mixed up and a woman who was scheduled for and consented to an appendectomy is given a hysterectomy. Both unfortunate victims can sue the surgeon in battery. They did not consent to the operation performed. In a Canadian case a woman who expressed her wish to be injected in her right arm was injected by the doctor in her left. She sued in battery and succeeded.[1]

Of course in all these examples the surgeon or some other member of the hospital staff has been careless. So the patient could normally sue in negligence too. But there are certain differences between the two torts. First, in battery, a patient need not establish any tangible injury. The actionable injury is the uninvited invasion of his body. This is important. A doctor may on medically unchallengeable grounds decide that an operation is in the patient's best interests. He goes ahead. The patient's health improves. Yet if it was done without consent a battery has still been committed. A doctor who discovered that his patient's womb was ruptured while performing minor gynaecological surgery was held liable to her for going ahead and sterilizing her there and then. She had not agreed to sterilization.[2] A woman who underwent a hysterectomy when all she had agreed to was curettage similarly recovered for battery.[3] The essence of the wrong of battery is the unpermitted contact.

The second difference between negligence and battery affects the doctor more than the patient. Where battery is proved, the surgeon's defence union will foot all the bill. Where negligence is proved, the bill will be apportioned between the health authority and the doctor's union.

Two other points should be noted. Battery may be alleged by a patient who says he did not consent. On whom does the onus of proof lie? It used to be argued that it was for the defendant, the doctor, to prove that the patient consented. Now a High Court judge has said that the onus of proof lies on the patient. He must establish that he did not agree.[4] And what sort of compensation will a patient receive? In negligence we shall see that a defendant is only liable for the kind of damage which he reasonably ought to foresee. In battery the test may be more stringent. The defendant may be liable for all the damage which can factually be seen to flow from his wrongdoing. A doctor who injected a patient in the 'wrong' arm would be liable in battery or negligence for any unwanted stiffness in that arm, for any adverse reaction which he ought to have contemplated in view of the patient's history. He would not be liable in negligence for a 'freak' reaction. In battery he may well be so liable. But judges in England seem eager to limit the scope of battery when it overlaps with negligence. They may strive to avoid subjecting any surgeon to liability in battery.[5]

What is meant by consent?

The key to the whole issue is consent. What is meant by consent? It need not be written, although as a matter of practice a consent form will always be provided before surgery. Consent may often be implied from the circumstances. If a patient visits his general practitioner complaining of a sore throat and opens his mouth so that the doctor can examine his throat, he cannot complain that he never expressly said to the doctor: 'You may put a spatula on my tongue and look down my throat.' A patient visiting casualty with a bleeding wound implicitly agrees to doctors or nurses cleaning and bandaging the wound. In an American case an immigrant to the U.S.A. complained that he had not consented to vaccination. It was found that he had bared his arm and held it out to the doctor. His action precluded the need for any verbal consent.[6]

A patient for whom surgery is proposed will be asked to sign a consent form. A standard form has been agreed between the Department of Health and Social Security, the B.M.A., the Medical Defence Union and the Medical Protection Society. It reads as follows:

CONSENT FOR OPERATION

.... Hospital

I .... of

hereby consent to undergo

the operation of ....

the nature and purpose of which have been explained to me by

Dr/Mr ....

I also consent to such further or alternative operative measures as may be found necessary during the course of the above-mentioned operation and to the administration of general, local or other anaesthetics for any of these purposes. No assurance has been given to me that the operation will be performed by any particular practitioner.

Date .... Signed ....

I confirm that I have explained the nature and purpose of this operation to the patient.

Date .... Signed ....

Deletions, insertions or amendments to the form are to be made before an explanation of the proposed surgery is given and, of course, before the patient is asked to sign the form.

The form is some evidence of the patient's consent to the proposed surgery and further authorizes the surgeon to perform 'such further or alternative measures as may be found necessary'. This would not affect liability in the cases discussed earlier of the doctor who sterilized a patient, or the doctor who performed a hysterectomy in the course of minor gynaecological surgery. Neither measure was immediately necessary to preserve the woman's health. The doctor is only authorized to carry out further surgery without which the patient's life or health will be immediately at risk. So the doctor discovering advanced cancer of the womb while performing a curettage may be justified in performing an immediate hysterectomy. Delay might threaten the woman's life. A doctor discovering some malformation, or other non-life-threatening condition, must delay further surgery until his patient has the opportunity to offer her opinion.

The use of the standard form is not compulsory within the N.H.S. In private hospitals and clinics a different form may well be used. What would be the effect of a form within which the plaintiff consented to the proposed operation and any further surgery which the surgeon saw fit to embark on? In the absence of the clearest evidence that the patient fully understood the 'blank cheque' which he handed to his doctor, such a form will be virtually irrelevant. Any consent form is no more than one piece of evidence that the patient did, in fact, consent to what was done to him. If the patient can show that despite the form he did not give any real consent to the procedure carried out, the surgeon will be liable to him.

How much must the doctor tell the patient?

We have seen that for consent to be real the patient must be told what operation is to be performed and why it is to be done. As the standard consent form puts it, the nature and purpose of the operation must be explained by the doctor to the patient. What else must the doctor explain? All surgery under general anaesthetic entails some risk. Many forms of surgery and medical treatment carry further risk of harm even if they are carried out with the greatest skill and competence. Patients have argued that if an operation entails an inherent risk then they cannot be said to have given a real consent to that operation if they were not told of the risk. They had inadequate information on which to make a proper decision. They could not give an 'informed consent'. Therefore an action in battery should lie. Alternatively they argue that if an action in battery does not lie, they ought to be able to sue for negligence. The doctor's duty of care encompasses giving adequate information and advice. If he has given the patient inadequate information and the patient consequently accepted a risky procedure and damage did ensue, then the doctor, it is argued, is responsible for that damage. How have such claims fared? So far, in England, the answer is not well!

Let us look first at the argument that if risks or side-effects inherent in an operation are not disclosed then the patient has not really consented at all, and the surgeon is liable for battery. A Miss Chatterton pursued such a claim in 1981. She suffered excruciating pain in a post-operative scar. Dr Gerson proposed an operation. The operation failed to relieve her symptoms. A second operation was carried out. Miss Chatterton was no better and subsequently lost all sensation in her right leg and foot with a consequent loss of mobility. She claimed that while Dr Gerson was in no way negligent in his conduct of the surgery, he failed to tell her enough for her to give her 'informed consent'. Her claim in battery failed. The judge said that a consent to surgery was valid providing that the patient was 'informed in broad terms of the nature of the procedure which is intended'.[7]

By contrast, a patient who agreed to an injection which she understood to be a routine post-natal jab but which was in fact the controversial long-acting contraceptive Depo-Provera succeeded in her claim for battery. Her doctor failed the test set in *Chatterton* v. *Gerson*. He obtained her agreement to the injection leaving her totally unaware and indeed misleading her, albeit in good faith, as to the nature of what was being done to her.[8]

Subsequent attempts to claim in battery have, where the nature of what was to be done was explained but the risks of the procedure were not, failed just as Miss Chatterton's claim failed. In 1983 another High Court judge deplored the bringing of such claims in battery. He viewed the proper cause of action, if any, as lying in negligence.[9] And in 1984 the Court of Appeal too added its voice. The Master of the Rolls said:

> It is only if the consent is obtained by fraud or misrepresentation of the *nature* [my italics] of what is to be done that it can be said that an apparent consent is not a true consent.[10]

The House of Lords unanimously endorsed his views.[11] The Canadian courts too see battery as an inappropriate remedy for inadequate counselling. The Canadian Chief Justice has said:

> I do not understand how it can be said that the consent was vitiated by failure of disclosure of risks as to make the surgery or other treatment an unprivileged, unconsented to and intentional invasion of the patient's bodily integrity . . . unless there has been misrepresentation or fraud to secure consent to the treatment, a failure to disclose the attendant risks, however serious, should go to negligence rather than battery.[12]

So the proper cause of action, the courts have said, lies in negligence. But English plaintiffs have fared little better in negligence. The courts have held that the doctor's duty of care to his patient includes a duty to give him careful advice and sufficient information upon which to reach a rational decision as to whether to accept or reject treatment. The problematic issue has been when the doctor is found to be in breach of that duty. Mr Bolam agreed to electro-convulsive therapy to help improve his depression. He suffered fractures in the course of the treatment. The risk was known to his doctor. He did not tell Mr Bolam. Mr Bolam alleged that the failure to warn him of the risk was negligent. The judge found that the amount of information given to Mr Bolam accorded with accepted medical practice in such cases and dismissed Mr Bolam's claim.[13] He added that even if Mr Bolam had proved that the doctor's advice was inadequate he would only have succeeded if he could have further proved that given better information he would have refused his consent to the treatment. The test of negligence was the test of generally accepted medical practice. Other cases in the 1950s were even more favourable to the doctors. Lord Denning held it to be entirely for the individual doctor to decide what to tell his patient.[14] It was a matter for his discretion. Another patient was partially paralysed in the course of an aortagram. A court in 1975 found that the risk was real but remote, and as the patient never inquired about risks the doctor had no obligation to enlighten him.[15]

The underlying trend in the English courts was that 'doctor knows best'. Across the Atlantic matters took a startlingly different turn. The doctrine of 'informed consent' was born. In *Canterbury* v. *Spence*[16] an American court said that the 'prudent patient' test must be adopted. Doctors must disclose to their patients any material risk inherent in a proposed line of treatment.

A risk is thus material when a reasonable person, in what the physician knows or should know to be the patient's position, would be likely to attach significance to the risk or cluster of risks in deciding whether or not to forgo the proposed therapy.

The Canadian Supreme Court too rejected the 'professional medical standard' for determining how much the doctor must disclose. Emphasis was laid upon 'the patient's right to know what risks are involved in undergoing or forgoing certain surgery or other treatment'.[17] The Canadian court did allow though that a particular patient might waive his right to know, might put himself entirely in the hands of his doctors. And they said that cases might arise where '. . . a particular patient may, because of emotional factors, be unable to cope with facts relevant to the recommended surgery or treatment and the doctor may, in such a case, be justified in withholding or generalizing information as to which he would otherwise be required to be more specific'.

The 1980s brought the issue once again before the English courts. Backed by the transatlantic doctrine of informed consent, lawyers tried again to breach the walls of medical silence. Miss Chatterton, who as we saw lost in battery, failed too in negligence. The doctor, the judge said, did owe her a duty to counsel her as to any real risks inherent in the surgery proposed. He did not have to canvass every risk and in deciding what to tell the patient he could take into account '. . . the personality of the patient, the likelihood of misfortune and what in the way of warning is for the particular patient's welfare'. This standard Dr Gerson had met.

The issue after *Chatterton* v. *Gerson* was who judged what amounted to 'a real risk of misfortune inherent in the procedure'. The English courts have generally rejected the 'prudent patient' test and opted for the professional medical standard. The case that eventually went to the House of Lords concerned Mrs Sidaway. For several years, following an accident at work, Mrs Sidaway had endured persistent pain in her right arm and shoulder. Later the pain spread to her left arm too. In 1960 she had just become the patient of Mr Falconer, an eminent neuro-surgeon at the Maudsley Hospital. An operation relieved the pain for a while. By 1973 Mrs Sidaway was once again in constant pain. She was admitted to the Maudsley Hospital in October 1974 and Mr Falconer diagnosed pressure on a nerve root as the cause of her pain. He decided to operate to relieve the pressure. Mrs Sidaway gave her consent to surgery. As a result of that operation Mrs Sidaway became severely disabled by partial paralysis.

Mrs Sidaway sued both Mr Falconer and the Maudsley Hospital. She did not suggest that the operation had been performed otherwise than skilfully and carefully. Her complaint was this. The operation to which she agreed involved two specific risks over and above the risk inherent in any surgery under general anaesthesia. These were (1) damage to a nerve root, assessed as about a 2 per cent risk, and (2) damage to the spinal cord, assessed as less than a 1 per cent risk. Alas for Mrs Sidaway, that second risk materialized and she consequently suffered partial paralysis. She maintained that Mr Falconer never warned her of the risk of injury to the spinal cord. Throughout the long and expensive litigation Mrs Sidaway's greatest handicap was that Mr Falconer died before the action came to trial. The courts were thus deprived of vital evidence as to exactly what the patient was told by her surgeon and what reasons, if any, he had for withholding information from her. The case had to proceed from the inference drawn by the trial judge in the High Court that Mr Falconer would have followed his customary practice, that is, he would have warned Mrs Sidaway in general terms of the possibility of injury to a nerve root but would have said nothing about any risk of damage to the spinal cord.

Mrs Sidaway's lawyers argued in the High Court that the failure by the surgeon to warn his patient of the risk to her spinal cord invalidated her consent to the operation. This claim in battery failed. The judge endorsed the views discussed earlier that a lack of full information will not render an operation a battery provided the patient understood the general nature of the surgery proposed. The judge dismissed her claim in negligence too. Against his judgment on the issue of negligence Mrs Sidaway appealed and lost again in the Court of Appeal.

Thus ten years after the unfortunate operation which left Mrs Sidaway paralysed, and seven years after Mr Falconer's death, the case reached the highest court in the land, the House of Lords.[18] The paucity of evidence as to what actually happened when Mrs Sidaway and Mr Falconer discussed the proposed surgery rendered the case, as Lord Diplock put it, 'a naked question of legal principle'.[19] What principle governed the doctor's obligation to advise patients and to warn of any risks inherent in surgery or treatment recommended by the doctor? The majority of their Lordships endorsed the traditional test enunciated in the case of Mr Bolam nearly thirty years before. The doctor's obligation to advise and warn his patient was part and parcel of his general duty of care owed to each individual patient. Prima facie, providing he conformed to a responsible body of medical opinion in deciding what to tell and what not to tell his patient he discharged his duty properly. There being evidence that while some neuro-surgeons might warn some patients of the risk to the spinal cord many chose not to, Mrs Sidaway's case was lost.

The *Sidaway* judgment must not, however, be seen as a total endorsement of the view that providing a doctor follows current medical practice in deciding on the advice to give his patients he will be immune from legal attack. The courts retain ultimate control of the definition of the doctor's obligation. First, for Lord Bridge and Lord Templeman the crucial issue in Mrs Sidaway's case was that the risk of which she was not advised was a less than 1 per cent risk, and all the medical expert witnesses were agreed that it was a risk which many responsible neuro-surgeons elected not to warn patients of. Where experts disagree, the courts remain the ultimate arbiter of their difference of opinion. Even where the overwhelming body of medical opinion accepted non-disclosure of a particular risk, Lords Bridge and Templeman asserted the judicial right to intervene where disclosure was obviously necessary to an informed choice on the part of the patient. Lord Bridge gave as an example '. . . an operation involving a substantial risk of grave adverse consequences, for example [a] ten per cent risk of a stroke from the operation'.[20] Second, for Lord Diplock and Lord Templeman a further vital question in the case was that Mrs Sidaway had not expressly inquired of Mr Falconer what risks the surgery entailed. For Lord Diplock the case is concerned solely with what information the doctor must volunteer. Lord Templeman said Mr Falconer could not be faulted for failing to give Mrs Sidaway information for which she did not ask.

The majority judgment of the Lords is by no means the end of the controversy over how much the doctor must tell. Indeed, all that this prolonged litigation may have achieved is that the transatlantic test that what the patient should be told should be judged by what the reasonable patient would want to know was rejected by the majority in the House of Lords. Only Lord Scarman rejected current medical practice as the test of what a patient needs to be told. He dissented, and in a powerful judgment asserted the patient's right to know. The patient's right of self-determination, his right to choose what happened to his body, was the factor which to Lord Scarman made the issue of advice given to the patient distinct from other aspects of medical care. The doctor should be liable '. . . where the risk is such that in the court's view a prudent person in the patient's situation would have regarded it as significant'.[21] But, albeit the patient's right of self-determination distinguishes advice given from other stages in medical care, advice before treatment cannot be totally separated from the doctor's general duty to offer proper professional and competent service. Thus the doctor, in Lord Scarman's view, should be to a certain extent protected by a defence of 'therapeutic privilege'. This would permit a doctor to withhold information if it can be shown that 'a reasonable medical assessment of the patient would have indicated to the doctor that disclosure would have posed a serious threat of psychological detriment to the patient'.[22] Lord Scarman recognized the right of a patient of sound understanding to be warned of material risks save in exceptional circumstances. But still he too found against Mrs Sidaway. He held that she failed to establish on the evidence put forward by her counsel that the less than 1 per cent risk was such that a prudent patient would have considered it significant. And the death of Mr Falconer deprived the court of evidence of his medical assessment of her condition and her state of mind.

The future of 'informed consent'

The *Sidaway* case may simplistically be hailed as a victory for the 'doctor knows best' school of thought. It will not, as I have said, mark the end of the debate. The underlying issue in the debate is complex. How do you reconcile the right of every adult to control his own life with the doctor's obligation to offer proper, personal care to each and every patient? Each patient will have a slightly different attitude to his medical condition and to the doctor. Some will happily place themselves entirely in the doctor's hands, leaving all decisions to him. Others will vociferously demand information. Very many may desire to be told kindly and with tact the options before them. Of this number some may be too shy, over-awed or frightened to ask questions. Others may find that in the atmosphere of a busy N.H.S. clinic, knowing that the doctor may be overworked and that other patients are waiting anxiously for their turn, asking too many questions seems selfish and inappropriate.

The atmosphere engendered by litigation, with an individual doctor with his back to the wall so to speak, is not the best means of investigating such a complex issue. All the courts could hope to do was to offer a formula which would guide the medical profession in their dealings with patients. The legal formula could be no more than a starting point. The majority of the House of Lords rejected the prudent patient test as damaging to the doctor–patient relationship and as uncertain in its application. But the test they set is little better on either criterion. The law endorses current medical practice as the usual touchstone for what the doctor must tell. This may please the doctors. But in emphasizing the judicial right to intervene in exceptional cases they lay open the field for patients to continue to go to law over informed consent, alleging that theirs is the exceptional case. No doctor wants to be sued. Limiting liability to exceptional cases of non-disclosure only very loosely defined in *Sidaway* will not stem the flood of litigation. It will make litigation more acrimonious. For the patient will have to allege not that his doctor and he have a difference of opinion as to what he, the patient, might reasonably have wanted to know, but that his doctor's conduct was so out of line with what was reasonable for the patient to make an informed choice that liability must ensue. The graver the allegation, the harder the doctor will feel obliged to fight the case.

As to the uncertainty of the prudent patient test, the emphasis placed by Lords Diplock and Templeman on Mrs Sidaway's failure to seek information about the risks of surgery leaves open the issue of what test governs the doctor's duty of disclosure to the expressly curious patient. Must he then be given whatever information the reasonable patient would require to answer his queries? *Sidaway* leaves the law unclear on this issue. Do we have a dual test on disclosure? What is the test for the curious patient? Such a dual test could have serious implications. The private patient, the middle-class patient, who may have met the consultant socially, is much more likely to ask questions than the working-class man who has snatched a morning off work to attend a busy impersonal clinic. That does not mean he is any less concerned about his treatment nor that his right to know is any less important to him than his more articulate fellow. Mrs Sidaway, who left the courts uncompensated, can be little cheered by what she has contributed to legal principle.

After Sidaway what next?

Judgments, at first instance, subsequent to *Sidaway* show that the legal debate on 'informed consent' continues. In *Blyth* v. *Bloomsbury A.H.A.*[23] a woman who suffered prolonged bleeding after receiving the long-term contraceptive Depo-Provera recovered compensation for her ordeal. Despite asking questions, she was not told of the drug's potential side-effects. Later Mrs Gold[24] won substantial damages when she gave birth to a child after nature had reversed her surgical sterilization. The surgeon had not warned her of that risk, nor did he canvass the safer option of a vasectomy for her husband. The judge held that he was not bound to follow *Sidaway*. The sterilization was not carried out in a therapeutic context, for medical reasons, but purely for convenience. *Sidaway* applied only in purely medical cases. Any sensible woman (prudent patient) would regard the information not offered to Mrs Gold as crucial to her decision to consent to sterilization, and failing to give Mrs Gold that information rendered the surgeon liable to her.

Does it matter who operates?

As important to many patients as what the operation entails may be the question of who operates. If a patient agrees to surgery believing eminent consultant X will operate on him, is his consent invalidated if registrar Y operates? Where he contracts with consultant X that he will operate, the consultant is in breach of contract if he substitutes someone else. Within the N.H.S. he would, in the abstract, have to show that his consent was conditional on X operating. He would not have agreed to the surgery if anyone else proposed it. In practice, the standard consent form used within the N.H.S. provides that no assurance is given that any particular doctor will operate. He cannot complain if the registrar operates. Of course if the registrar lacked the experience to perform a particular operation he will be able to sue him and the consultant if harm ensues. He can sue the registrar for his lack of competence. He can sue the consultant for his failure to provide proper supervision and for allowing an inadequately qualified member of the team to operate.

Every now and then suggestions have appeared in the press that medical students are being allowed to carry out minor operations. A story that hit the headlines in 1984 told of a vet who was allowed by a surgeon friend to remove a patient's gall bladder. A patient operated on by a vet will have a claim against the vet however competent he may have proved to be. He agreed to a qualified doctor operating on him. He no more agreed to surgery by a vet than to surgery by the author of this book. If the vet proves not up to the job, the patient can recover too against the surgeon who allowed him into the theatre and the hospital that permitted such an event. His action against them will lie in negligence. An operation performed by a medical student will give rise to a claim in negligence if the student is not competent. A claim in battery may also lie if the patient was not informed about the proposal to allow a student to operate. He consented to an operation and accepted, if he signed the standard form, that no particular practitioner undertook to operate. But he consented to surgery performed by a practitioner, not an 'apprentice'. Teaching hospitals play a vital role. The public interest requires that medical students train on real people. Nevertheless, any contact with a patient on the part of a medical student requires the patient's consent.

Emergencies

So far in this chapter we have made the assumption that the patient is in a fit state to give his consent. But when the patient is unconscious, treatment may have to be given immediately, before the patient can be revived and consulted. He may have been wheeled into Casualty after an accident. He may have agreed to operation X, in the course of which the surgeon discovers a rampaging tumour needing immediate excision. Surprisingly there is no modern English case in point. In a nineteenth-century case a woman agreed to the removal of a diseased ovary but told the surgeon that she was soon to be married and that he should not deprive her entirely of her ability to bear children. In the course of the operation he discovered both ovaries to be diseased and removed them both. Her claim against the surgeon failed on the grounds of her 'tacit consent'.[25] Despite her express statement prior to her operation, the court found that had she been in the shoes of the surgeon and seen the state of her organs she would be presumed to have agreed to the further surgery.

This idea of 'tacit consent' is still sometimes invoked to justify emergency surgery. The patient, it is said, can be assumed to consent to what the medical staff do to save him. Where the patient has agreed to one operation and signed the standard consent form then this idea has some validity. The patient has in truth authorized further necessary surgery. Where the patient is brought into Casualty unconscious the idea of 'tacit consent' is unreal and unwieldy. In other areas of law the courts have recognized a defence of necessity. Applied to medical cases, it can fairly safely be said that the doctor is justified in taking any necessary action to save life and '. . . proceeding, without consent, with any procedure which it would be unreasonable, as opposed to merely inconvenient, to postpone until consent could be sought'.[26]

Very often when a patient is unconscious or otherwise incapable of consenting to treatment himself the response of the hospital staff is to consult, when possible, with the patient's relatives or friends. What legal validity has a consent given by the relatives of an adult? The answer is none at all. The crucial factor when surgery is performed on an unconscious patient is whether what was done was immediately necessary. We have seen that further surgery in the course of an authorized operation was not justified when it was not immediately necessary to save the patient's life, albeit it was objectively in her long-term interest.[27] Similarly, treatment carried out on a patient brought unconscious into hospital must be shown to be medically necessary before the patient can be expected to regain his senses. Consulting relatives is courteous, but is legally significant solely in that as a matter of evidence it establishes that the doctor's attitude was reasonable, and may indicate the patient's own attitude. Only if the patient dies and his dependants seek to sue the doctor for performing the operation do their views become directly relevant.

One difficult problem arises in this sort of case. A patient is wheeled in unconscious and needs an immediate blood transfusion. His wife says, truthfully, that he is a Jehovah's Witness and would thus refuse a transfusion. Can the doctor lawfully give a transfusion? The procedure is necessary but the doctor knows the patient would be likely to refuse it. The doctor's defence would have to be that in the absence of knowledge of the patient's own wishes in the actual predicament he found himself in, it was not for the doctor to assume that he would refuse immediately necessary treatment. When it came to the crunch the patient might prefer to be saved. By contrast, if a Jehovah's Witness agrees to operation X and expressly instructs the surgeon that he will not accept a blood transfusion if one is called for, the surgeon cannot justify administering a transfusion. The patient has anticipated the emergency and refused the treatment.

Conclusions

The law relating to consent to treatment remains unhelpfully vague. The core of the problem, unsolved by the House of Lords decision in *Sidaway*, remains the extent to which the law will compel doctors to volunteer information about, and explanations of, proposed treatment. The most dismal prospect is that litigation will proliferate, with judges, in what *they* see as deserving cases, finding exceptions to the rule that the standard of accepted medical practice governs how much the doctor must disclose. Already, as we have seen, the distinction has been drawn between medical treatment required to cure illness, *therapeutic* treatment, and sterilization carried out as a convenient means of permanent contraception.

Doctors justifiably complain that to the lawyer, and the academic lawyer in particular, the issues discussed in this chapter are simply fascinating points of debate. For the doctor they are his daily diet. The influence the law can ever have is minimal. The law cannot improve the conditions in which doctors meet patients. It cannot and should not lay down a code of detailed guidance for pre-treatment counselling. What it should do is create a framework in which patients' rights and doctors' duties are defined with clarity. The uncertainty of the law does medicine a disservice. Encouragement of further litigation will not help the growth of public confidence in the medical profession or doctors' confidence in the law. Patients, doctors and lawyers meet in court as adversaries. They need to meet as colleagues. The issue of informed consent needs investigation by a body combining legal, medical and lay experience. The case for a Commission to examine medico-legal and ethical issues is made out in part by the unsatisfactory approach the law on its own has shown to the matter of consent to treatment.

Chapter 5
Medical Negligence

The civil law of negligence is designed to provide compensation for one individual injured by another's negligence. Gross negligence may occasionally also be punished by the criminal courts. And we will consider any possible criminal liability incurred by doctors later. A person seeking compensation for negligence has to establish (1) that the defendant owed him a duty to take care, (2) that he was in breach of that duty, that he was careless, and (3) that the harm of which the victim complains was caused by that carelessness. He must satisfy all these tests to succeed. A widow succeeded in establishing that a hospital doctor was careless in not coming down to Casualty to examine her husband. He was admitted to hospital in an appalling state which eventually proved to be caused by arsenical poisoning. He died within hours. She failed to recover any compensation from the hospital in respect of her husband's death because the evidence was that even had he been properly attended he would still have died.[1]

The bare bones of the law of negligence outlined above are general to everyone, in the conduct of their everyday activities and in carrying out their job. They are not special to doctors. But certain special factors about medical negligence claims need to be introduced here. I have already mentioned the factual difficulty of proving negligence where there is a clash of medical opinion, and the effect that the need to prove fault has on the medical profession's reaction to claims against them. They become, not unnaturally, highly defensive. For a long time the judges too were most unwilling to find against a medical man. A brotherly solidarity bound the ancient professions of law and medicine together. This attitude is changing somewhat. But three very real fears still haunt the courts.

(1) Medical malpractice claims in the U.S.A. are big business. Patients leaving English hospitals often return with a box of chocolates for the staff. Patients leaving American hospitals are as likely to return with a writ! Doctors and lawyers alike look across the Atlantic and shudder.[2] Whether their fears are exaggerated we examine later. (2)

Increased legal action against doctors may make them practise defensive medicine. They will opt for the treatment most legally safe, which may be expensive and time-consuming. So as actions in the U.S.A. against obstetricians became prevalent, alleging that the baby had suffered injury in the course of labour, so the rate of Caesarian sections increased to nearly one in three in some states. (3) Finally the ultimate defendant in most claims in England is the N.H.S. An award to compensate an individual patient must come out of funds which might otherwise be used for an extra consultant, a new neo-natal unit, or committed to a programme of preventive medicine.

Duty of care

A patient claiming against his doctor or a hospital usually has no difficulty in establishing that the defendant owes him a duty of care. A general practitioner accepting a patient on to his list undertakes a duty to him. A hospital and all its staff owe a duty to patients admitted for treatment. If the patient is an N.H.S. patient the duty derives from the law of tort, which imposes a duty wherever one person can reasonably foresee that his conduct may cause harm to another. Where the patient is a private patient the duty arises from his contract with the doctor or the hospital. It is the same duty regardless of its origins. We will look later at the circumstances in which the private patient is owed duties other than that of care.

Difficulty arises where a person has not been accepted as a patient. The law of negligence does not oblige anyone to be a Good Samaritan. If a man has a coronary attack on an Inter-City express, and a doctor fails to respond to the guard's call 'Is there a doctor on the train?', the doctor incurs no liability to the victim who dies for lack of medical treatment. Indeed, the law almost discourages the Good Samaritan. For if the doctor comes to the sick man's aid he undertakes a duty to him and will be liable if his skill fails him.

A practical problem today arises from the increasing practice of health authorities to centralize casualty facilities in the larger hospitals. More and more hospitals have notices on their gates stating that they do not accept emergencies and accident victims. The notice refers the injured to another named hospital. An accident victim whose injuries worsened because of the delay in reaching a casualty department is unlikely to succeed in a claim against the hospital which refused him admission. It never assumed any duty to him. A hospital which operates a casualty department, by contrast, is responsible for the patients who come within its doors regardless of whether they have been formally admitted to hospital. By running a casualty department an N.H.S. hospital undertakes to treat those who present themselves and will be liable in negligence if any failure on the part of their staff causes the patient to be sent away untreated.[3] Similarly a G.P. owes a duty to emergency patients as well as to those on his own list. His contract with the N.H.S. provides that he will treat visitors to his district falling suddenly ill. Like the hospital with the casualty ward he undertakes to treat the genuine emergency as much as his regular patients.

The medical standard of care

The second matter that any claimant in negligence has to prove is that the defendant was careless. The onus of proof is on the plaintiff. He must show that the defendant fell below the required standard of care. The basic standard is that of the reasonable man in the circumstances of the defendant. So a professional man must meet the standard of competence of the reasonable man doing his job. A woman who went to a jeweller to have her ears pierced developed an abscess because the jeweller's instruments were not aseptically sterile. The jeweller had taken all the precautions that any jeweller could be expected to take. The woman's claim failed. The defendant had done all a jeweller could reasonably be expected to do.[4] If she wanted the standard of care a surgeon could offer she should have consulted a surgeon.

The standard of care demanded of the doctor, then, is the standard of the reasonably skilled and experienced doctor. In *Bolam* v. *Friern H.M.C.*[5] the judge said:

The test is the standard of the ordinary skilled man exercising and professing to have that special skill. A man need not possess the highest expert skill; it is well established law that it is sufficient if he exercises the ordinary skill of an ordinary competent man exercising that particular art.

The defendant doctor will be tested against the standard of the doctor in his particular field of medicine. The general practitioner must meet the standard of the competent general practitioner; the consultant gynaecologist the standard of the competent consultant in that specialty. As Lord Scarman put it: '. . . a doctor who professes to exercise a special skill must exercise the ordinary skill of his speciality'.[6]

So a patient who attends his general practitioner complaining of an eye disorder cannot require him to have the skill of a consultant ophthalmologist. But he can complain if the G.P. fails to refer him on to a consultant when his condition should have alerted the reasonable G.P. to the need for further advice or treatment.

No allowance is made for inexperience. The Court of Appeal has consistently rejected the idea that standards of care should vary to allow for the degree of experience possessed by the defendant. They held an L-driver liable where, although she had done the best that could be expected of a learner, she fell short of the standard of the reasonably competent and experienced motorist.[7] The appeal court recently considered the liability of junior hospital staff.[8] A premature baby was treated and probably saved in a specialized baby unit. He needed extra oxygen to survive. Sadly, junior doctors made an error in readings of the oxygen levels in the baby's bloodstream. Excess of oxygen rendered the baby blind. Argument by the defendants that staff concerned did their best in view of their inexperience was rejected. The law requires all medical staff in such a unit to meet the standard of competence and experience society expects from those filling such demanding posts. Their Lordships recognized the need for medical staff to train 'on the job'. They stressed that the judgment of negligence on one occasion did not imply incompetence. The court canvassed two further ideas for future cases. (1) Should patients' recourse be not against individual junior staff but directly against any health authority using junior staff for tasks for which they were not yet experienced? (2) Would a junior doctor who, recognizing his inexperience, sought advice from his consultant have discharged his duty? Responsibility in law might then move to the consultant.[9] Just as no allowance is made for youth so none will be made for age. The eighty-year-old G.P. must meet the same standard of alertness and dexterity as his thirty-year-old colleague.

Ascertaining the standard of care

How does a court ascertain the standard of skill which the doctor should have met? As I have said earlier, they have to ask the doctors. Let us consider the case of Mr Bolam again. He was given electro-convulsive therapy and sustained fractures. He argued that the doctor was negligent (1) in not giving him relaxant drugs, (2) as drugs were not given, in failing to provide adequate physical restraints, (3) in not warning him of the risks involved in the treatment. We have seen that he failed in his argument that he should have been warned. As to the absence of relaxant drugs or restraints, the evidence was that while some doctors would have thought them necessary many others did not. The judge found that the doctor was not guilty of negligence for he acted:

. . . in accordance with a practice accepted as proper by a responsible body of medical men skilled in that particular area . . . a man is not negligent, if he is acting in accordance with such a practice, merely because there is a body of opinion who would take a contrary view.[10]

The test of 'accepted medical practice' is firmly entrenched in English law. It applies to all stages of medical treatment. In *Whitehouse* v. *Jordan* a woman of 4ft 10ins was in great difficulty in labour with her first child. The doctor attending her summoned the senior registrar, Mr Jordan. He attempted to deliver the baby by forceps. He pulled six times. He then abandoned the attempt and moved swiftly to deliver the child by Caesarian section. The baby was severely brain-damaged. The mother claimed that the excessive force in using forceps caused the damage. He should have pulled less often. Lord Denning in the Court of Appeal said that if Mr Jordan was at fault it was at most an error of clinical judgment for which a doctor could not be held liable.[11] The House of Lords too found that Mr Jordan was not liable. They found that the original trial judge's inferences from the expert evidence that Mr Jordan was negligent were wrong. (We will return to this aspect of the case in a later chapter.) But their Lordships were scathing about Lord Denning's suggestion that errors in clinical judgment were immune from question. Lord Edmund-Davies said, quoting the *Bolam* case:

'The test is the standard of the ordinary skilled man exercising or professing to have that special skill.' If a surgeon fails to measure up to that standard in *any* respect ('clinical judgment' or otherwise), he has been negligent . . .[12]

The case of Staff Nurse Maynard illustrates the strength of the accepted medical practice test. She consulted a consultant physician and a surgeon with symptoms both thought might well be tuberculosis, but she also displayed symptoms which might indicate Hodgkin's disease. The doctors decided on a diagnostic operation, mediastinoscopy. It carried a risk of damage to the vocal cords and Mrs Maynard's vocal cords were in fact damaged. And in fact she proved to have tuberculosis. She alleged that the doctors were negligent in subjecting her to the operation. The plaintiff's expert witness, Dr Hugh-Jones, argued that the operation should never have been done. He would have regarded her condition as almost certainly a case of tuberculosis. The defendants called a formidable number of experts who testified that the fatality rate for Hodgkin's disease if treatment was delayed justified the defendants in exposing Mrs Maynard to the risk of the mediastinoscopy. The original judge preferred Dr Hugh-Jones's evidence. The Court of Appeal and the House of Lords overruled him. Lord Scarman said:

> . . . a judge's 'preference' for one body of distinguished professional opinion to another also professionally distinguished is not sufficient to establish negligence in a practitioner . . . [13]

Accepted professional practice is not a test uniquely applied to doctors. It is applied to all skilled men. The judge is no more an expert in plumbing, or carpentry, or accounting practice than he is in medicine. But in relation to other professions the courts are ready to challenge accepted practice as unsatisfactory. We have seen Lord Scarman's attitude to Mrs Maynard's claim. He would not adjudicate between the two schools of opinion. The Court of Appeal recently asserted that there could be cases where the courts would think it appropriate to intervene. The Master of the Rolls, Sir John Donaldson, has said that a practice must be '. . . *rightly* accepted as proper by a body of skilled and experienced medical men'.[14]

In an appropriate case a judge may reject a medical view shown to be manifestly wrong. But this has very rarely happened in England. In one case a patient attended a physiotherapist for a course of treatment. He was severely burned in the course of that treatment. The defendant had warned him of the danger in the manner approved by the Chartered Society of Physiotherapists. The judge held the warning to be inadequate to safeguard the patient.[15] It is worth noting, too, that Sir John Donaldson's statement was made in the light of a claim relating to the amount of information a surgeon gives his patient. The judges may be readier to intervene in such cases as opposed to claims relating to such matters as diagnosis or choice of treatment.

'Accepted practice' means current practice

It is, of course, no defence for a practitioner to say that a practice was widely accepted when he was at medical school and is therefore accepted once informed medical opinion has rejected the practice.[16] The practitioner must keep us up to date with new developments and incorporate them in his practice. But there is an inevitable 'time-lag' between the making of new findings by researchers and the percolation of their ideas through to doctors in the field. The doctor will be judged by the standard of awareness and sophistication to be expected of a doctor in his sort of practice. Great emphasis is placed on the professional position and the specialty of the defendant.[17] A patient who suffered from brachial palsy as a result of his arm being extended in a certain position while he was given a blood transfusion in the course of a bladder operation brought a claim against the anaesthetist. Six months before the operation an article had appeared in the *Lancet* condemning this practice because of the risk of brachial palsy. The claim failed. Failure to read one recent article was not negligent.[18] Another doctor made a mistaken diagnosis of cancer of the bladder. If he had used a cystoscope he would not have made such a mistake. But at that time cystoscopes were not freely available. The defendant did not have one. Few doctors outside the major teaching hospitals did. He was not negligent.[19]

All doctors are not expected to have the level of awareness or sophisticated equipment available to a professor in London. They must be judged on what is to be expected of a doctor in regular everyday practice. The Department of Health and Social Security in London issues a flow of circulars to hospitals updating doctors on new developments. One, for example, outlines procedures to protect against surgical accidents.[20] Failure to take a precaution outlined in the circular would be strong evidence of negligence. This is material readily available to all hospital doctors of which they might reasonably be expected to take note and advantage. Being unaware of materials made available by the medical defence unions might similarly be negligent.

It must be stressed that the relevant date to judge current practice must be the date of the operation or treatment and not the date the claim comes to trial. In *Roe* v. *Ministry of Health* a patient had become permanently paralysed after an injection of the spinal anaesthetic Nupercaine, administered in 1947. His claim against the doctors and the hospital came to trial in 1954. Before the operation the drug had been kept in glass ampoules in a solution of phenol. The accident to the patient occurred because phenol percolated through invisible cracks in the ampoules and contaminated the Nupercaine. No one had ever known this to happen. The claim in negligence failed. Lord Denning said: 'We must not look at the 1947 accident with 1954 spectacles.'[21]

Once a tragic incident of this sort has occurred and been attended by publicity then of course a further incident would easily be proved to be negligence. Current practice would have been shown to be wanting.

Departing from 'accepted practice'

A doctor is legally 'safe' when he conforms with existing practice. Does he put himself 'at risk' if he departs from that practice? If liability in negligence automatically followed once harm resulted from the adoption of a novel method of treatment, medical progress in England would be stultified. Doctors would be fearful to challenge orthodox views, which might be mistaken, and could be wary of any innovation. It would be a brave man who would risk the blow of a finding in negligence to his career and reputation. This does not mean that I think that the patient should go uncompensated. I discuss in Chapter 9 schemes that would provide compensation more readily and effectively in this sort of case than the present law of tort.

The judges at present adopt a compromise. This is illustrated by the case of *Clark* v. *MacLennan*.[22] The plaintiff suffered from stress incontinence after the delivery of her first child. Early attempts at conservative treatment made her no better, One month and eleven days after the birth, the defendant operated to repair the weakness in her bladder and muscles. The plaintiff haemorrhaged and the repair broke down. Two further operations failed to repair the damage. The plaintiff was left permanently affected by stress incontinence. The operation performed on the plaintiff was a common procedure. But most gynaecologists delayed such an operation for at least three months after the birth to minimize the risk of haemorrhage and breakdown. The plaintiff's experts satisfied the judge that this was the orthodox view of treatment, the general practice. The judge held that while it was for the plaintiff to prove negligence, once she had shown a departure from an accepted practice, designed to guard her from the very sort of harm which she suffered, the burden moved to the defendants to justify their departure from accepted practice. This they failed to do.

A doctor who departs from orthodox views is thus not automatically branded as negligent. It is for him to justify his course of action either by indicating features of the individual case which call for a different mode of treatment or by showing his novel method to be superior or at least equal to the general practice.

We look now at some examples of decided and settled cases to see how the accepted practice test actually works.

Diagnosis

A wrong diagnosis is by itself no evidence of negligence on the part of the doctor. As a Scottish judge has said:

> In the realm of diagnosis and treatment there is ample scope for a genuine difference of opinion and one man is clearly not negligent merely because his conclusion differs from that of other professional men . . .[23]

A patient alleging that a wrong diagnosis was negligent must establish either that the doctor failed to carry out an examination or a test which the patient's symptoms called for, or that his eventual conclusion was one that no competent doctor would have arrived at. While the myth of total infallibility of 'clinical judgment' has been exploded, a patient who relies solely on an allegation that the doctor's conclusions were mistaken will rarely succeed. Not surprisingly a doctor who failed to diagnose a broken knee-cap in a man who had fallen 12ft on to a concrete floor was found to be negligent.[24] Other examples are hard to find.

The courts are readier to find negligence when a patient and his experts can point to a specific failure on the part of the doctor. A casualty doctor, who failed to examine or X-ray a drunken patient admitted with the information that he had been seen under a moving lorry, was found to be negligent when after his death next day he was discovered to have eighteen fractured ribs and extensive damage to his lungs. It was no defence that the patient never complained of pain. The doctor should have known that alcohol would dull the patient's reaction to pain.[25] The doctor must be alert to the patient's background. A G.P. who failed to test for and diagnose malaria in a patient who had recently returned from East Africa was held liable for the patient's death. The doctor was consulted nine days after the patient's return to this country, and a relative suggested malaria but the doctor diagnosed 'flu. Six days later malaria was diagnosed in hospital, where the patient died that day.[26] A too hasty diagnosis of hysteria has led to settlements by the Medical Defence Union in 1982[27] and 1983.[28] The physical symptoms should have been investigated.

In all the above examples the doctor was negligent because he failed to act on information available to him and to perform routine tests. Where a diagnostic procedure is not routine, is costly, or painful, or risky, an additional factor has to be considered. Do the symptoms displayed by the patient justify subjecting him to the procedure? The doctor faces a legal as well as a medical dilemma. If he does not arrange for the test and the patient does suffer from some condition which the test would have revealed, the doctor may be sued for that failure. If he does arrange the test and an inherent risk of the test harms the patient, the patient may sue if the test reveals that the doctor's suspicions were groundless. We saw that that is what happened with Staff Nurse Maynard.[29] The defendants were found not to be liable to her because they had followed accepted practice in going ahead with the test despite its dangers. Doctors argue forcefully that alacrity to pin liability on them for every diagnostic error may cause patients to be submitted to more expensive and potentially risky procedures than may be strictly medically desirable.

Treatment

A claim in respect of negligent treatment may be based on an allegation that the treatment chosen was inappropriate, or that while the treatment embarked on was correct it was negligently carried out. In the case of the first sort of allegation, nothing more can be said than that the test will be whether the chosen method of treatment conformed with accepted practice. It is examples of the latter sort of case which we will now examine.

First, all doctors involved must act on adequate information and supply each other with adequate information. A G.P. prescribing drugs must check what other medication the patient is on. So in 1982 the Medical Defence Union settled a case where a prescription of a powerful painkiller for pain in the wrist and fingers of an elderly patient reacted with long-term anti-coagulants also prescribed for the patient and caused neurological problems.[30] Doctors must be alert to common drug reactions and actively seek relevant information from patients. A clinic which injected a woman with penicillin was held liable for her death an hour later.[31] Had they inquired of her, or examined her records, they would have been aware of her allergy to penicillin. A G.P. arranging for the admission of a pregnant patient to hospital while he was treating her for a septic finger was found negligent in not so informing the hospital. She contracted septicaemia. Had the hospital known of the state of her finger they would have put her on antibiotics straight away.[32] But doctors must be wary of relying entirely on information supplied by their colleagues. In 1984 the Medical Defence Union settled this claim. A patient was admitted for a gynaecological operation. The gynaecologist asked a general surgeon to remove what he said was a ganglion from the patient's wrist. Thus the patient would be spared two separate operations. It was not a ganglion. Surgery of that sort was inappropriate and the patient's hand was permanently paralysed. The M.D.U. settled because the general surgeon should have made his own pre-operative assessment and not relied on a colleague from another specialty.[33]

Once the doctor is properly informed and has selected his course of treatment he must ensure that he carries it out properly. He must check the dosage of any drug. Prescribing an overdose will readily be found to be negligent.[34] He must be sure that his handwriting is legible. The M.D.U. issues frequent pleas for legible prescriptions after settling, for example, a claim where a pharmacist read a prescription for an antibiotic as instructing him to dispense a quite different and potentially dangerous drug. And he must advise his patient properly and unambiguously as to dosage.[35]

Where surgery is called for, the risk of injury is increased. Especially risky for any patient is the administration of the anaesthetic. Nearly 3 million Britons undergo an anaesthetic every year. Between 250 and 300 will die. The anaesthetist will be found to be negligent if he failed to make a proper pre-operative assessment of the patient, failed to check his equipment, failed to monitor the patient's blood pressure and/or heartbeat in the course of surgery or if, an inevitable accident having occurred, the anaesthetist fails to invoke adequate resuscitation measures. Some specific failure on the defendant's part must be pinpointed. An anaesthetic tragedy of itself is no real evidence of negligence. An anaesthetist who failed to check equipment and ended up administering carbon dioxide instead of oxygen was put on trial for manslaughter in New Zealand.[36] An anaesthetist who injected cocaine instead of procaine was found negligent in this country,[37] as was the junior doctor who injected pentothal into an anaesthetized patient, causing his death.[38] If the wrong drug, or the wrong dosage, or a contaminated drug, is used, the patient's claim will generally be made good. The exception will be where the error cannot be laid at the anaesthetist's door. So, as we saw, in *Roe* v. *Ministry of Health*[39] a patient who was paralysed because a then unknown risk of phenol percolating into the ampoules of local anaesthetic materialized, recovered no compensation.

Surgery itself must be performed with the utmost care. One judge has suggested that the more skilled the surgeon the higher the standard of care.[40] Some errors advertise their negligence. Leaving swabs and equipment inside the patient is a good example. And the surgeon must accept responsibility for such matters and not rely on nursing staff.[41] Nor does the surgeon's responsibility end with the careful completion of surgery. He must give his patient proper post-operative care and advice. A surgeon performed a cosmetic operation just below the eye. He told his patient to inform him if bleeding occurred within 48 hours. It did and the patient tried to telephone the surgeon and got no reply. The surgeon was held to be negligent.[42]

I have done no more here than to outline a few examples of decided and settled claims. I go on in the next chapter to the practical problems of medical litigation. In a claim for negligence it helps to pinpoint some specific failure by the doctor. In the next chapter we will see how that may be done.

Relating the injury to medical negligence

So far the majority of the cases we have looked at involved something going wrong as a result of a medical mistake. The patient's problem has been to prove that what was done, or not done, amounted to action-able negligence. But, as I said at the beginning of the chapter, proving negligence by the doctor does not conclude the case in the patient's favour. He must also show that his injury, his worsened or unimproved condition, was caused by the doctor's negligence. What happens when the evidence is that had the patient been properly treated he *might* have avoided certain injury, disease or deterioration in his condition? The chance of recovery was there with proper treatment, but even with first-class care the patient might have been no better. This problem is acute where the negligence alleged by the patient is in essence that adequate treatment was unjustifiably delayed.

Such a case came before the High Court in *Hotson* v. *Fitzgerald*.[43] The plaintiff, a schoolboy of 13, fell heavily from a rope on which he had been swinging to the ground 12ft below. He was taken to hospital. His knee was X-rayed and revealed no injury. No further examination was made and the plaintiff was sent home. Five days later the boy was taken back to the same hospital and an injury to his hipjoint was diagnosed and subsequently swiftly and correctly treated. But the injury had traumatic consequences. The boy suffered a condition known as avascular necro-sis. This condition, caused by a restriction of the blood supply in the region of the original injury, leads to misshapenness of the joint, disability and pain, and later in life almost certainly brings on osteo-arthritis in the joint. The plaintiff's disability might have ensued from the accident in any case. But there was a 25 per cent chance that given the correct treatment immediately the plaintiff might have avoided disability and made a nearly full recovery.

The defendant hospital admitted negligence in failing to diagnose and treat the plaintiff's injury on his first visit. Both parties agreed that prompt treatment would have offered a 25 per cent chance of avoiding permanent disability. The defendants argued that as that chance was less than 50 per cent the plaintiff had not made out his case. He had not shown that it was more likely than not that injury could have been avoided with proper care because there was a 75 per cent chance that the plaintiff would have been disabled even with proper treatment. The judge rejected that argument. He said that the plaintiff had to prove negligence. This he had done. The hospital admitted their breach of duty. That breach of duty caused the plaintiff to lose a substantial chance of full recovery. It was totally different from the case where a hospital negligently failed to treat a victim of arsenical poisoning where the poison would inevitably have killed the man. The hospital's delay in treating the schoolboy caused him a definite and ascertainable loss. The issue was not whether the hospital was liable but what compensation they should pay the boy. Having by their breach of duty deprived the boy of a 25 per cent chance of recovery, the judge ordered that they should pay compensation amounting to 25 per cent of the sum the boy would have received had his disability been a certain and inevitable consequence of the defendants' negligence. The judge's approach to the skilfully argued but excessively technical defence advanced was vigorous. He said that once negligence was proved or admitted, the courts should as a matter of policy be wary of accepting arguments to negate liability and deprive the plaintiff of compensation. He described the defence as in essence a 'heads I win, tails you lose' attempt.

Overtired, overworked doctors

Any account that lists the claims which succeed against, or are settled by, doctors distorts the true picture and appears unfair. The proportion of claims in relation to visits to G.P.s, hospital admissions and successful surgery is low. And no account is taken of the hours doctors work. Many junior hospital doctors work more than 80 hours a week. Some are forced to put in 100 hours. Who would not occasionally make a mistake faced with such pressure? If such a doctor makes a mistaken diagnosis because he is intolerably weary, or makes a surgical error because his dexterity fails him, will the patient's rights be in any way affected? No. The courts will not accept any argument that the doctor's duty is fulfilled if he provides an adequate service generally and only occasionally falls below the required standard of competence.[44] Judges sympathize with hard-pressed doctors. But a doctor who carries on beyond the point when fatigue and overwork impair his judgment remains liable to an injured patient. The fact that the doctor was required by his employer to work such hours will not affect the patient. The patient might, though, more appropriately proceed too against the doctor's employers, the hospital authority. He would allege that the hospital undertook to provide him with adequate care.[45] Requiring their doctors to work to the point of utter exhaustion is a breach of that duty. Should the patient choose to sue the doctor alone, the doctor may bring the hospital authority into the action. He could ask them for a contribution towards the plaintiff's claim on the grounds that it was their breach of duty as much as his which resulted in harm to the patient.

Liability of nursing staff

Nurses, as well as doctors, may sometimes make mistakes. All that has been said in relation to doctors applies equally to them. A nurse will be judged in accordance with the standard of skill and carefulness to be expected of a nurse in this position and speciality with this seniority. A midwife must show a midwife's skill. It is not enough, for example, to display only the standard of an S.R.N. who has done 13 weeks obstetrics. The midwife holds herself out as a specialist. There are a few decided cases relating to nurses. A nurse who either failed to note or act on evidence of a lump in a patient's breast when she examined her at a Family Planning Clinic was held to be negligent. She should have taken steps to ensure that the patient's incipient cancer was properly investigated.[46] The more independent the nurse's function, the greater the risk of a finding of liability. Where she is in the front line with some responsibility for diagnosis and choice of treatment, her responsibility equates with that of her doctor colleagues.

Within hospitals nurses may find themselves liable for negligence if they fail to take careful note of instructions given to them, or if they fail to provide adequate nursing care or attention. A patient was prescribed thirty injections of streptomycin for boils. The sister failed to note on the treatment sheet when the prescribed course was completed. An additional four injections were given before the error was discovered. Damage to a cranial nerve resulted. The sister was found to be negligent.[47] Failure to make or record routine tests required by medical staff or failure to ensure that these are properly carried out can result in liability resting on the nurse. Where nurses and doctors work together, as in the operating theatre, liability for an accident may be shared. The theatre sister should check that all swabs are removed; so should the surgeon. They are jointly liable. A swab marker was inadvertently not removed from an elderly lady after exploratory surgery. The patient developed complications. An X-ray was taken. A consultant radiologist missed the swab marker on the X-ray. Fifteen months later the lady was admitted to hospital with an intestinal obstruction. The error was discovered. A settlement was reached. Liability was shared in equal proportions between the surgeon, the consultant radiologist and the hospital on behalf of the theatre sister.[48]

Private patients

A patient who pays for his treatment enters into a contract with his doctor. They are free to set the terms of that contract, save that the doctor cannot exempt himself from liability for any injury to his patient arising from his negligence.[49] There is rarely a written contract between them. The terms will be implied from their relationship. This usually means that the doctor undertakes a duty of care to the patient. His duty of care to his private patient is indistinguishable from his duty to his N.H.S. patient.

In private practice could a doctor be found to have contracted to *guarantee* the desired result of treatment? This can never happen in the N.H.S. The doctor can only be liable in tort for a failure in care. Only rarely however will a private doctor be found to have guaranteed a result in contract either. Where a patient is ill and seeks a cure, unless the doctor foolishly and expressly promises success in his treatment, no court will infer any term other than that the doctor will exercise skill and care. And, so far, claims by patients who have undergone private sterilization have ultimately failed in attempts to argue that the surgeon guaranteed permanent sterility.[50]

Criminal liability

Negligence is pre-eminently a matter for the civil, not the criminal, law. However gross, however culpable an act of negligence, it will generally not be criminal in England unless made so by an Act of Parliament, as in the case of careless driving. The picture changes if the victim dies. Gross negligence causing death can lead to a conviction for manslaughter. Much more than ordinary negligence, of the sort which would found a civil action for negligence, must be proved. Convictions are rare to say the least. Usually the negligence will be seen to derive from some morally disgraceful conduct – say, a doctor operating while drunk or under the influence of drugs. In *R.* v. *Bateman*[51] the Court of Appeal overruled a conviction for manslaughter of a doctor whose ignorance and failure to send a woman to hospital resulted in his patient's death. The judge at the trial had failed to direct the jury properly. Criminal liability required more than the degree of negligence needed to establish civil liability. The doctor must be shown to have '. . . showed such disregard for the life and safety of others as to amount to a crime against the State and conduct deserving of punishment'.

Hence convictions for manslaughter will fortunately be few and far between in the absence of some personally disgraceful conduct on the part of a doctor. But recklessly unwise courses of action widely condemned in the profession may engage criminal censure. A dentist was convicted of manslaughter when a patient died in the dental chair.[52] He had extracted a tooth and administered a general anaesthetic entirely alone. This dual role of surgeon and anaesthetist had led to perhaps 100 deaths in the U.K. over the past twenty years. The General Dental Council had campaigned vigorously against it. The unfortunate dentist was the first to be convicted of manslaughter. But he did not go to prison. He was fined £1,000 and given a suspended sentence. His more unfortunate patient was dead. The case may serve as a warning to others.

Conclusions

The principles of the law of negligence as they apply to the medical profession have been criticized as leaning too far in favour of rubber-stamping professional practice. Yet in the last decade judicial attitudes have changed. Courts are more ready, albeit reluctantly, to find against the doctor on occasion. Two problems bedevil medical litigation. First, the medical profession becomes increasingly resentful of what they see as judicial interference and the damage done to medical careers. While compensation for injured patients depends on proof of fault on the part of medical staff, judicial 'interference' is inevitable and likely to increase. A judgment that a doctor on one day was liable for actionable negligence is not a finding that that doctor is a bad or incompetent doctor. It is merely a decision that in one isolated instance his conduct was such as to give a fellow citizen a claim for compensation. But that is not how the doctors may see it. Second, the issue of judging when a doctor falls below an acceptable standard remains a thorny problem. If it is not to be judged by responsible medical opinion, how is it to be decided? The real problem is ascertaining the content of responsible medical opinion. The rules of litigation in England allow each side to call its own experts. The trial becomes a trial of strength between opposing experts. Investigation of what actually happened to the patient becomes nigh on impossible. In the next chapter we go on to examine this issue and to see how in practice the rules on negligence are applied in the courtroom and outside.

Chapter 6
Medical Litigation

In Chapters 4 and 5 we examined the principles governing liability for medical malpractice. Now we look at the actual process of litigation. Formidable practical problems confront the patient plaintiff.[1] Whom should he sue? How quickly must he act? How do you prove negligence? What level of compensation is available? Is it worth it? These are some of the issues this chapter attempts to cover.

Whom should the patient sue?

One of the first practical matters which the patient and his legal adviser must consider is whom they should sue. The legal doctrine of vicarious liability is important here. This provides that when a person who is an employee commits a tort in the course of his employment, his employer too is responsible to the victim. The employer will often be better able to pay compensation than an individual employee.

Let us look first at a claim by a patient who alleges that he suffered injury in the course of treatment as an N.H.S. patient in an N.H.S. hospital. If he can identify a particular individual as negligent he may, of course, proceed against him, be he consultant, anaesthetist, houseman, nurse, physiotherapist or hospital porter. And he may also sue that person's employer. Should it be a hospital doctor who is sued personally, payment of any award of compensation is guaranteed. The hospital doctor's contract of employment requires him to be fully insured against professional liability. So the doctor is obliged to belong to a medical protection society, usually the Medical Defence Union or the Medical Protection Society. Once an award of damages is made or a settlement agreed, the protection society will pay promptly. The Royal College of Nursing, and the other nursing unions, offer similar facilities to their members, but nurses are not obliged to be insured against liability. Patients may want to ponder the wisdom of proceeding personally against even an insured defendant. The doctor who sees his reputation on the line may fight the case tooth and nail, backed by his protection society. His employer may be more prepared to accept responsibility and settle swiftly.

The employer to sue, as vicariously liable, in the case of N.H.S. treatment will normally be the district health authority.[2] But as privatization creeps into the health service this must be examined carefully. Take this example: an elderly, confused patient slips and falls on a highly polished floor. Who, if anyone, is responsible? The relevant negligence may be that a nurse failed to supervise the patient, or it may be that cleaners were careless. The nurse will be employed by the health authority. The cleaner these days may be the employee of a private contractor. If the patient can rely only on the doctrine of vicarious liability to make someone other than the individual nurse or cleaner liable, he may have difficulty in selecting the correct defendant. Health authority and contractor may each blame the other's employee.[3] And what too of the case where an N.H.S. patient is treated in a private hospital by virtue of an arrangement between the health authority and the private hospital? Who then, other than the responsible individual, may the patient sue if things go wrong?

What we need now to examine is the direct, primary liability of the health authority to an N.H.S. patient. First, the authority will be liable for any failure of its own. A patient may suffer injury not because any particular doctor or nurse is careless but because the system provided by the authority is inadequate. There may be insufficient medical staff to cope swiftly enough with injured patients admitted to the casualty ward. Lack of experienced staff on night duty may cause injury to a patient whose condition deteriorates rapidly, and whom the staff on duty cannot, with the best will in the world, treat sufficiently promptly. For such faults an action may lie directly against the health authority.[4]

Lord Denning, however, would take the direct responsibility of health authority to N.H.S. patients an important step further. He has argued thus.[5] When a patient is admitted for treatment under the N.H.S. the health authority undertakes to provide him with reasonably careful, competent and skilled care and treatment. Should any aspect of his care and treatment fall below that standard, the authority is directly, and not just vicariously, responsible to the patient. So if an elderly patient falls on a slippery floor, and had proper care been taken that would not have happened, the authority is liable. It matters not whether a nurse employed by the authority or a cleaner employed by a contractor was the individual personally at fault. The authority undertook to care for the patient. It failed and it is directly liable. A patient offered a hip-replacement on the N.H.S. need not be concerned if the operation is contracted out to a private hospital. The health authority undertook to provide the care and treatment. If anything goes wrong through negligence the authority is liable. The patient can lie back and enjoy the trimmings of the private hospital.

The importance of Lord Denning's view of direct liability in today's health care conditions can clearly be seen. Most commentators back his view.[6] It has not been tested because until recently it hardly ever mattered whether the authority was sued vicariously or directly. Practically everyone working in N.H.S. health care was a N.H.S. employee. Now that is no longer the case, Lord Denning's view should prevail.

Our next concern is the private patient. A private patient who engages a pay-bed in an N.H.S. hospital generally contracts individually with his surgeon and anaesthetist for the surgery and the administration of the anaesthetic, and contracts separately with the health authority for nursing and ancillary care. Even if the surgeon and the anaesthetist are employed by the health authority when caring for N.H.S. patients, when they act for a private patient they are acting on their own behalf and not in the course of their N.H.S. employment. So if an error by surgeon or anaesthetist causes the patient injury he can sue only the responsible individual. If the carelessness is that of nursing or other medical staff he may sue the health authority. As we shall see, this may cause problems of proof of negligence.[7] Identifying who was the responsible individual may be nigh on impossible, leaving surgeon and authority to blame each other and the patient to go uncompensated.

A patient entering a private hospital needs to consider carefully the exact nature and scope of his contract. The usual arrangement is similar to that entered into by a private patient taking a pay-bed within the N.H.S. The patient engages his own surgeon and anaesthetist who will not be employees of the hospital. The hospital contracts to provide other medical and nursing care. Like the private patient within the N.H.S., the patient must proceed against the surgeon for any error of his, and against the hospital for errors by their staff. But some private hospitals and clinics will contract to provide a whole 'package' of care and treatment. When the hospital undertakes to provide total care, the operation, anaesthetic, post-operative care, etc., then it is liable for any failure to meet the required standard of care. They are in breach of contract.[8] It is irrelevant that the surgeon, anaesthetist, or anyone else is not an employee of the hospital. The hospital is not vicariously liable for any fault of a particular person. It is directly responsible for its own breach of contract.

What, now, of claims against general practitioners? First of all, general practitioners are not employees of the health authority. A claim relating to negligence by a G.P. operating a single-doctor practice lies against that G.P. alone. And general practitioners are not obliged to belong to a medical protection society. The vast majority, of course, do, but a slight risk remains that a G.P. sued may be personally impecunious and professionally uninsured. Where a G.P. is a member of a partnership his partners may be sued as jointly responsible for any negligence. If it is not the doctor himself who is at fault but a receptionist or nurse employed by the practice, then the G.P. and his partners are vicariously liable as employers. So if a receptionist refuses to allow a home visit, refuses to allow the patient to speak to a doctor, and fails to pass any information on to the doctor with the result that a seriously ill patient becomes sicker or even dies, the doctor, while he may be personally blameless, will be vicariously at fault and liable to the patient or his family.

The thorny question of whom to sue in relation to general practice arises out of the use of locums and deputizing services. Locums and deputies are not employed by the regular general practitioner as a hospital doctor is employed by the health service. Therefore the general practitioner is not vicariously liable for any and every act of negligence on their part.[9] Of course, he may be liable for any personal carelessness of his in selecting a locum or deputizing service. Failing to check the qualifications of a locum, engaging a deputizing service notorious locally for its incompetent doctors, will be negligence on the part of the G.P. It is arguable too that engaging a locum or deputy without checking whether he carries professional indemnity insurance may equally be a breach of duty to the patient. It would be an extension of the present law. But I would suggest that a G.P. selecting another to care for his patients must consider not only the stand-in's medical skill but his ability to meet any claim against him. Doctors know all too well that such a claim can arise out of the occasional error made by even the most skilled practitioner.

But once again we must return to Lord Denning's view of direct responsibility for health care to see if the patient is inevitably to be left to sue the locum or deputy alone. When a G.P. accepts a patient on to his list he undertakes to provide for that patient health care of a standard and nature to be expected of a competent G.P. If the health care provided falls below that standard, the patient's own G.P. should be liable regardless of whether he or a locum or deputy is the one at fault. By analogy with Denning's view of the obligation of the health authority to an N.H.S. patient in hospital, the G.P. is directly responsible to the patient for his general health care. The arrangements the G.P. makes to provide care at night or when he is on holiday are beyond the patient's control and not his concern. Such a solution is fairer to patients and not unfair to the G.P., who is free and able to arrange appropriate insurance cover and whose subscription to a medical protection society will be reimbursed as expenses by the Family Practitioner Committee.

When must proceedings be started?

A patient contemplating an action for medical negligence must act relatively promptly. The general rule is that all actions for personal injuries must be brought within three years of the infliction of the relevant injury. This is known as the limitation period and is laid down in the Limitation Act 1980. A writ must be served on the doctor or hospital authority no later than three years from the date of the alleged negligence. But sections 11 and 14 of the 1980 Act provide that where the patient originally either (1) was unaware that he had suffered significant injury, or (2) did not know about the negligence which could have caused his injury, the three-year period only begins to run from the time when he did discover, or reasonably should have discovered, the relevant facts. Where the patient knew all the relevant facts, but was ignorant of his legal remedy, the three-year limitation period runs from the time when he was or should have been aware of the facts.

All is not quite lost for the patient who delays beyond three years or who is ignorant of the law. A judge may still allow him to start an action later. Section 33 of the 1980 Act gives to the court a discretion to override the three-year limitation period where in all the circumstances it is fair to all parties to do so. The courts will examine the effect of allowing the action to go forward on both parties, taking into account, among other things, the effect of delay on the cogency of the evidence, the conduct of the parties, and the advice sought by and given to the patient by his lawyers and medical advisers. The three-year (or longer) limitation period applies only to *starting* legal proceedings. Once started, an action may drag on for years before it is settled or finally decided.

Access to records

When considering whether he has a claim in respect of negligence and whom he should sue, the patient and his legal advisers will clearly benefit by gaining access to the patient's notes, reports and X-ray and other test records. Disclosure of records benefits the public interest too. A claim may be seen to be fruitless or a particular individual exonerated. Money and effort will be saved. Before 1970 the patient usually had to go ahead in the dark and ask at the trial for a subpoena ordering the health authority and the doctor to produce their records. Legislation in 1970 introduced a right to pre-trial access to records.[10] That original legislation has now been replaced by the Supreme Court Act 1981.

The effect of section 33 of the 1981 Act is this. A patient may apply for a court order requiring the doctor or the authority whom he plans to sue to disclose any records or notes likely to be relevant in forthcoming proceedings. Section 34 goes further. The court may order a person *not* a party to proceedings to produce relevant documents. So if the patient has started proceedings against the doctor but believes that the hospital authority or clinic holds notes of value to his claim, the authority or clinic can be made to hand over the notes. This will help the private patient in a dilemma as to whether he should properly proceed against doctor or hospital. And it may of course lead to the hospital being brought into the proceedings.

Once legislation compelling disclosure of documents was enacted, hospitals and medical protection societies reluctantly became prepared to hand over documents voluntarily. They feared a spate of fishing expeditions by aggrieved patients. But they preferred to disclose records to the patient's medical adviser alone, and not to the patient or his lawyers. Indeed, they sought to argue that this was the limit of their obligation. The House of Lords disagreed.[11] Under the 1970 statute, they said, the patient himself was entitled to see the documents produced. Pleas that patients would be unduly distressed and fail to understand medical data cut little ice with their Lordships. The 1981 Act is less favourable to patients. A court may limit disclosure to (a) the patient's legal advisers, or (b) the patient's legal and medical advisers, or (c) if the patient has no legal adviser, to his 'medical or other professional adviser'. It is up to the court to decide whether the patient sees the records. But as long as he has retained a lawyer, his lawyer must be permitted to examine the documents. Hospitals and medical protection societies offering voluntary disclosure often still try to keep records even from the patient's lawyers. Lawyers in the medico-legal field advise against accepting such an offer: a lawyer may spot relevant material in support of a claim which even the most experienced medical advisers could miss.

Three final matters on disclosure need a mention. First, the intention to bring proceedings and the likelihood that they will go ahead must be real before the court will order disclosure. The patient must have some solid ground for thinking he has a claim. He cannot use an application for disclosure as a 'fishing expedition' on the off-chance that some evidence of negligence will come to light.[12] Doctors are advised to say nothing and disclose no records without consulting their protection society. The protection society will require evidence of a bona fide claim before advising disclosure, and a court asked to compel production will not be satisfied with less. The difficulty a patient faces in obtaining access to 'his own' notes may surprise some. They feel that they have an automatic right to see their medical records, regardless of whether or not they are in dispute with the doctor or hospital. But, as we saw in Chapter 3, at present it appears to be the case that patients have no such right. The records belong not to them but to the health authority or the doctor.

Second, will the patient be able to see notes of any inquiry ordered by the health authority into his misadventure? The position is complex. If the inquiry was held mainly to provide the basis of information on which legal advice as to the authority's legal liability is based, then the records are protected by legal professional privilege. But if the dominant purpose of the inquiry was otherwise, for example to improve hospital procedures or to provide the basis of disciplinary proceedings against staff, then the patient may be allowed access to the notes of the inquiry.[13] That is the legal position. The Court of Appeal has expressed its disquiet about the effect such claims of legal professional privilege may have on the patient's claim. Claims of privilege can be and are used to frustrate the patient's attempt to find out what happened, what went wrong. In *Lee* v. *South West Thames R.H.A.*[14] a little boy, Marlon Lee, suffered a severe scald at home but he should have recovered completely. He was taken to a hospital run by health authority A and then transferred to a burns unit controlled by health authority B. The next day he developed breathing problems, was put on a respirator, and still on the respirator was sent back to A in an ambulance provided by health authority C, the South West Thames R.H.A. When three days later the boy was taken off the respirator he was found to have suffered severe brain damage, probably due to lack of oxygen. In her attempts to find out what went wrong, the child's mother sought disclosure of records and notes on her son prepared by staff of all three authorities. Health authority A asked South West Thames R.H.A. to obtain a report from their ambulance crew. South West Thames R.H.A. complied and forwarded the report to A. It was this report which the plaintiffs went to court to obtain access to. South West Thames R.H.A. had revealed its existence but refused to hand it over to the family. They claimed it had been prepared in contemplation of litigation and to enable legal advice to be given in connection with that litigation. So it had, but it had been prepared on the request of health authority A to obtain advice as to A's liability to the child. Reluctantly the Court of Appeal held that the privilege attaching to the document was enjoyed by health authority A. South West Thames could not be ordered to disclose the report. Even had they been prepared to do so they could not have handed over the report without A's agreement. The principle was that defendants or potential defendants should be '. . . free to seek evidence without being obliged to disclose the result of his researches to his opponent'.

So a child was damaged for life in circumstances pointing to negligence on someone's part, and the law was powerless to help his mother find out what exactly caused his brain damage. The Court of Appeal expressed their disquiet and called for reform of the law. Within the doctor–patient relationship Sir John Donaldson said there was a duty to answer questions put before treatment was agreed to.[15] Why should the duty to be frank with the patient be different once treatment was completed? The president of the Court of Appeal suggested some new action for breach of the duty to inform might develop. But it was too late for Marlon Lee and that suggested development seems unlikely to materialize. Practically there is a further difficulty. Doctors and nurses who can see notes of the inquiry being used in evidence against them in court may refuse to give evidence to the internal inquiry. We shall return to this unhappy state of affairs in Chapter 8.

Lastly, the court retains the power to refuse to order disclosure where to do so would be injurious to the public interest.[16] This is unlikely to be the case where what is asked for is the plaintiff's own medical notes.

Pre-trial medical examinations

One distressing but inevitable feature of a claim of medical malpractice is that the patient, who is presumably already unwell, has to submit to several further medical examinations and sometimes to painful diagnostic tests. I stressed at the beginning of this chapter the importance of expert testimony on the patient's behalf. What is so often at issue is whether the patient's present condition results from the normal progression of disease, or an inherent risk of surgery, or carelessness. The patient's own expert cannot advise him and testify for him without examining him. So first the patient must be examined by his own expert witness, or witnesses. But he must also agree to be examined by the defendant's experts. If he refuses, the defendant may apply to stay the action, to have it stopped from proceeding any further. The ability to call his own expert witnesses is a fundamental right of the defendant. The patient will not be allowed to frustrate that right by refusing an examination.

The courts have not been particularly sympathetic to patients unhappy about such 'compulsory' medical examinations. A patient sought to insist on the presence of her own doctor as a condition of agreeing to examination by the defendant's doctor. The court refused.[17] They did suggest that had she been confused or elderly, or the defendants' expert been known to be fierce or intimidating, then exceptionally a patient might be allowed the support of her own doctor. And of course a woman will be allowed to insist on the presence of another woman before undergoing examination by a male expert. Another patient sought to make disclosure of the defendant's expert's report to him a condition of agreeing to examination. He failed.[18]

That last example raises again the question of disclosure of reports. We saw above that disclosure will be ordered of notes and records contemporaneous to the treatment complained of. Disclosure of reports of examination by expert witnesses will not. The Court of Appeal[19] has held that in a medical negligence claim the expert reports are directed to the central issue of the trial. Ordering their disclosure, the court declared, was the equivalent of compelling a witness to give his evidence in advance.

It follows from the above that from the standpoint of the patient there is a great deal to be said for his lawyers attempting to agree on a joint medical examination and report with the defendants. But an English court cannot order such a course. Where the claim is hotly contested the defendants are unlikely to agree. The toll taken by our adversarial system of justice is a theme to which we shall return.

Proving negligence

We come now to the very heart of the problem. How does the patient prove negligence? The onus lies on him. He must demonstrate that it is more likely than not that his deterioration in health or injury resulted from the negligence of the defendant. Mrs Ashcroft underwent an operation on her left ear. In the course of the operation she suffered damage to the facial nerve and her face was left permanently partly paralysed. The judge found the evidence finely balanced. There was formidable evidence that this should not have happened if proper care was taken. There was equally formidable evidence that in such delicate surgery damage to the nerve might occur even where the utmost skill and care were used. The judge held that the plaintiff must fail.[20] There were, he said, 'no winners in such circumstances'.

How does the plaintiff discharge the onus of proof laid on him? In the majority of cases he will be heavily reliant on expert testimony. He will need to put forward medical evidence to demonstrate (1) that there was negligence on the part of the defendant, or a person for whom the defendant was responsible, and (2) that the relevant negligence caused the harm of which the plaintiff complains. Finding an expert to testify may not be easy. Doctors are unhappy about voicing public criticism of a colleague. Knowing that all men and women make mistakes, helping to condemn a fellow doctor who is unlucky enough to make a mistake with disastrous consequences is not a popular task. In practice the patient's expert witness will have to be found from a different area of the country. Colleagues in the same health authority simply refuse to testify against each other. To their credit, the Royal Colleges will offer assistance in finding expert witnesses, and A.V.M.A. (Association for the Victims of Medical Accidents) maintains a comprehensive list of helpful and reliable medical experts. Not only must the doctor chosen be impeccably qualified and substantially experienced, he must also be able to stand up to cross-examination by the defendant's counsel.

Once an eminent and helpful expert is found, the problems for the patient are only partly solved. For the defendant too will be free to call his own experts and will usually find it far easier to obtain supporters. The court will be faced with conflicting accounts of what the proper standard of care in the procedure in issue is, and whether the harm caused did result from anything done or not done by the defendant. A glance at a leading case highlights the court's dilemma. In *Whitehouse* v.

Jordan[21] (which we have already looked at in the context of principles of liability) a claim was brought on behalf of a baby born disastrously and irretrievably brain-damaged. His mother, who was aged 30 and 4ft 10ins, had refused to submit to any internal examination or to an X-ray of her pelvis. The consultant in charge of her pregnancy put on her notes that 'trial of forceps delivery' should be attempted. But when Mrs Whitehouse went into labour he was not there. He was ill with 'flu. The difficulty of the case caused the young doctor on duty to summon help. Mr Jordan, a senior registrar, came to his aid. He had never seen the plaintiff before. Mr Jordan had five or six attempts to deliver the baby by forceps. He then discontinued the attempt and proceeded swiftly and efficiently to deliver the baby by Caesarian section. The baby was born damaged. The mother alleged that this resulted from Mr Jordan's continued attempts to deliver by forceps and that he had persevered in those attempts beyond the point where a competent obstetrician would have desisted. He had pulled too hard and for too long. He was negligent, she said, in not proceeding sooner to delivery by Caesarian section. On the central issue of the extent to which it is correct practice to pursue an attempt to deliver by forceps, the trial judge was faced with a galaxy of 'stars' from the field of gynaecology and obstetrics. For the child, there appeared Professor Sir John Stallworthy (past president of the Royal College of Obstetricians and Gynaecologists) and Professor Sir John Peel (former gynaecologist to Her Majesty). For Mr Jordan, there lined up Professor Sir John Dewhurst (past president of the R.C.O.G.), Professor L. B. Strang, Professor J. P. M. Tizard, and Dame Josephine Barnes (past president of the R.C.O.G.). The plaintiff's witnesses put in a joint report, originally prepared by them but 'settled' by counsel, i.e. her lawyers prepared the final draft! Lord Denning in the Court of Appeal criticized the report as wearing 'the colour of a special pleading rather than an impartial report'.[22] Not surprisingly then, the opinions of the experts as to how far an attempt at forceps delivery could be pursued were miles apart. It is disturbing for the lay person to discover how large a gap can exist as to what constitutes proper obstetric practice.

Faced with the contradictions offered by the experts, the trial judge based his decision on a report by Professor Maclaren, the head of the unit, that the child's head had become impacted. The judge interpreted this as meaning that the head was in the pelvis and that Mr Jordan continued to pull with the forceps, thus subjecting the head to undue pressure. Professor Maclaren subsequently said that 'impacted' did not carry this meaning, and the defence experts supported him. And at the end of the day so did the House of Lords.

The claim in *Whitehouse* v. *Jordan* dragged on for eight years from the issue of the writ. The child was nearly eleven before his claim was finally dismissed. The cost of three Queen's Counsel, two junior counsel, the solicitors' and experts' fees must have been astronomic. Two questions in particular raise concern. Six experts appeared. Why are the numbers not limited? The courts seem adamant that parties be allowed to choose as many experts as they like, rather like football teams.[23] And is it right that lawyers should 'doctor' the doctors' reports? Finally, the curious laywoman will wonder why the original decision to go for trial of labour rather than an elective Caesarian was never questioned. After all, the mother was exceptionally small and her refusal to be examined meant that her doctors had no idea of her internal pelvic size. The answer is that although an action was started against Professor Maclaren, who had been in charge of her pregnancy, this was discontinued early on. Thus that issue was closed to the courts.

Let no one be misled. The function of an English court is not invariably to investigate the claim, to uncover the truth, and do abstract justice. The judge is too often the referee in a game whose rules are loaded against the plaintiff. But in few cases do the rules of the game in the long run do much for the defendant's peace of mind and reputation.

Furthermore, difficult though it may be to credit, the central issue of *Whitehouse* v. *Jordan*, the question of what is or what is not proper practice, may not be the most difficult matter on which conflicting expert evidence may be put to a judge. In *Whitehouse* v. *Jordan* the trial judge's finding that the brain damage was caused in the course of delivery was not questioned. Where whether the harm did actually result from the alleged negligence is in issue, the task of the courts is even more difficult. They will be deluged by technical data, submerged by medical debate. Two possible reforms need urgent consideration. First, on the issue of the factual cause of the harm suffered, has not the Continental practice of the court appointing one eminent and important expert much to commend it? And second, should the case for a judge occasionally sitting with medically qualified assessors to advise him be considered?

Where the burden of proof shifts to the doctor

While in the majority of cases the patient must prove negligence and the doctor is not called on to prove his 'innocence', we should now look at those occasions when that burden shifts to the doctor. There is a general rule of the law of negligence that where the defendant is in complete control of the relevant events, and an accident happens which does not ordinarily happen if proper care is taken, then the accident itself affords reasonable evidence of negligence. The defendant will be held liable unless he can advance an explanation of the accident consistent with the exercise of proper care by him. This rule is known as *res ipsa loquitur* (the thing speaks for itself).[24]

Res ipsa loquitur can be applied in medical negligence cases. At first it was argued that *res ipsa loquitur* applied only where everyone of reasonable intelligence would know that that sort of accident did not ordinarily happen without negligence. As most people are not medically qualified, how could they know whether the accident to the patient was one which could or could not happen if proper care was taken? The Court of Appeal said that expert medical evidence was admissible to establish what should and should not occur if ordinary care was exercised.[25] *Res ipsa* has proved to be a boon in straightforward cases. A typical example is where sometimes after an abdominal operation a swab or even a pair of forceps is discovered in the patient's body. *Res ipsa* is also of value to the N.H.S. patient who has clearly suffered because someone was negligent either in the theatre or in the course of post-operative care, but he cannot identify that someone. If every member of the staff who might be responsible is employed by the health authority then an inference of negligence is raised against the authority, who are necessarily vicariously liable for whoever may be the culprit.[26] So in *Cassidy* v. *Ministry of Health*[27] a patient was operated on for Dupuytren's contraction affecting two of his fingers. After the operation the patient's hand and lower arm had to be kept rigid in a splint for up to fourteen days. When the splints were removed the plaintiff's whole hand was paralysed. Upon finding that all the staff involved in Mr Cassidy's care were N.H.S. employees, the court held that there was evidence of negligence against their common employer. The onus shifted to the authority to explain how this disaster might have struck without *any* of its employees being negligent.

But what if one of the staff caring for the patient is not an employee of the health authority? For example, the theatre sister may be an agency nurse. Can the authority say, 'No inference of negligence is raised against *us* because the negligent actor may well have been that nurse for whom we are not responsible'? Once again it depends on whether the hospital's liability is solely vicarious, or whether Lord Denning is right and the hospital is directly liable for any failure to measure up to the required standard of skill and care.[28] As long as the Denning view is correct, which I maintain it is, it matters not to the patient who actually employs the negligent individual.

The private patient may be less fortunate. As we have seen, whether he enters an N.H.S. or a private hospital he will usually contract separately with the surgeon and the anaesthetist for surgery and anaesthetic. The surgeon and the anaesthetist will not be acting as employees of the hospital. If something goes wrong in the operating theatre or post-operatively and it is not clear who is to blame, *res ipsa loquitur* probably cannot be invoked. The hospital is not liable for any negligence on the part of the surgeon or anaesthetist. He can raise an inference of negligence against the hospital only if he can trace the relevant negligence to one of their staff. He can raise an inference of negligence against the surgeon or anaesthetist only if he can pin the relevant act on one of them personally. If surgeon and hospital are both sued, neither can be compelled to testify against the other. And in many cases they may refuse to give evidence. The patient's task is made even harder because of an agreement between hospital authorities and medical protection societies that generally neither will join the other as co-defendant. They will not engage in mutual accusations of blame which might offer evidence which could assist the patient. They will simply remain silent, leaving the patient in the dark.

Once again Lord Denning offers some hope to the patient who can show there has been negligence but cannot identify the negligent actor. He has said this:

. . . I do not think that the hospital authorities and [the doctor] can both avoid giving an explanation by the simple expedient of throwing responsibility on to the other. If an injured person shows that one or other or both of two persons injured him, but cannot say which of them it was, then he is not defeated altogether. He can call on each of them for an explanation.[29]

Thus robust common sense would force open any 'conspiracy of silence'.

Nevertheless, the value of *res ipsa loquitur* in a medical negligence claim must not be overstated. Very often expert medical evidence is needed to establish that what happened does not ordinarily occur if proper care is taken. Conflicting expert evidence on that issue can be just as confusing and just as contradictory as on any other issue related to proving medical negligence.

Departing from accepted practice

There is one recent development in the law which may assist patients seeking to prove negligence. We have already discussed the case of *Clark* v. *MacLennan*[30] in the context of principles of liability. There the defendant operated on the plaintiff to repair damage to her bladder caused during childbirth. He performed the operation just under six weeks after the birth. The repair broke down and the patient was left permanently afflicted by stress incontinence. The generally accepted practice was to delay such an operation for at least three months because of the risk of such a breakdown. The judge held that once the patient had established a departure from accepted practice, the defendant must justify his course of treatment. This he failed to do and was found liable in negligence.

Awards of compensation

Once a patient has overcome all the formidable hurdles in his path and has satisfied the court that there has been malpractice by the defendant as a result of which he suffered harm, what damages will he receive? There are no special rules governing medical malpractice awards. The patient's damages will be assessed to compensate him for any actual or prospective loss of earnings and for the pain, suffering and disability which he has and will endure. His compensation for loss of earnings will include a sum representing any period in which he would have expected to be alive and earning but because of his injuries he will be prematurely dead.[31] Additionally to these sums to represent what he has lost, the patient will be awarded an amount to cover extra expenses which he and his family will incur. So if he requires intensive nursing care, or his house needs adapting to his invalid needs, or he requires constant attendance so that his wife gives up her job, all these expenses will be reflected in the award of damages. If the patient himself is dead, the damages awarded to his family will reflect the loss to them of the moneys he regularly expended on them. They recover for their loss of dependency.[32] It takes little imagination to see that if the patient dies the burden of compensation will be reduced. Dead he suffers no pain. Dead he incurs no expenses.

Returning now to the living patient, certain thorny problems do bedevil the question of damages. The first is this. The patient must usually sue within three years.[33] At that stage a prognosis of his future health is very much speculative. All his medical advisers may be able to say is something like this. The patient has a degree of brain damage. He is mildly handicapped now. There is a 20 per cent chance he may deteriorate to a vegetable condition in ten years' time. Until 1985 the process of assessing damages for such a patient was ludicrous. The courts would work out what he should receive if he did deteriorate and award him 20 per cent of that sum! If the prospect of deterioration materialized, the patient was grossly under-compensated. If it never did, the doctor had paid out a sum to compensate for damage that had never happened. The Administration of Justice Act 1982, which came into force in July 1985, set out to remedy this absurdity. Section 6 provides that in such a case a provisional award can be made at the trial on the basis of what the plaintiff has suffered or will certainly suffer. If the prospect of further damage or deterioration materializes, the plaintiff can apply again to the court for the proper compensation. We shall have to wait and see how section 6 will work in practice.

Where the speculative nature of the patient's claim is not whether his condition admittedly and entirely caused by the defendant may or may not become worse, but is whether his condition was in fact caused by medical negligence, or might have arisen in any case from the natural course of the patient's original injury or disease, the court's approach is this. The plaintiff must first prove that the relevant breach of duty deprived him of a realistic and significant hope of avoiding his present disability or aggravated injury. Once this is established, it must be assessed what the chance of avoiding disability amounted to. The patient will receive the proportion of full compensation for his disability corresponding to the chance of recovery of which the defendant's negligence deprived him. So a schoolboy who would have had a 25 per cent chance of avoiding permanent disability after an injury to his hip, had he been promptly and properly treated, was awarded 25 per cent of full compensation for that disability when the hospital admitted that its negligent delay in treatment caused the boy to lose his chance of complete recovery.[34]

Another difficulty lies in claims for future expenses. This is especially acute where the patient is so damaged as to be unable to manage his own affairs. Large sums of money can be claimed to cover the cost of his future care in expensive nursing homes. But there is no guarantee that that money will be so spent. The patient may be consigned to the N.H.S., and the money deposited to grow with interest and eventually when the patient dies to form a windfall for relatives. The courts are alert to this danger. They will seek to ensure that the sum awarded is such as will be wholly exhausted by care of the patient, leaving no surplus as a bonus for relatives. Plans for care must be realistic. And one further change has recently been made. Section 5 of the Administration of Justice Act 1982 provides that 'any saving to the injured person which is attributable to his maintenance at public expense . . . in a hospital . . . or other institution shall be set off against any income lost . . .'

One final quirk in the law is that the plaintiff may be able to claim for the full cost of any private medical care he selects regardless of whether such facilities are available free on the N.H.S.[35] Even where exactly identical surgery to alleviate the patient's condition could have been performed without charge, the plaintiff may claim the full cost of the private care for which he opted.

Yet all the above issues are mere pinpricks compared to the main anxiety of medical protection organizations and health authorities, the escalating costs of personal injuries awards. As more malpractice actions are begun, lawyers become more astute at establishing the highest possible quantum of damages. Inflation pushes the costs spiral higher. The kind of injury suffered in medical accidents is often of the most dire, brain damage or paralysis. And the skill and dedication of doctors themselves have played their part. New medical techniques keep alive many damaged patients who would have died a decade earlier. Many now live but need constant and expensive care. And as we have said, the living gain and need much higher levels of compensation than the dead. Awards climb higher and higher.

In December 1985 record damages of £679,264 were awarded to Linda Thomas, whose life and marriage were wrecked when she suffered severe brain damage in the course of a routine tonsillectomy.[36] Three months later Caroline Turville's parents settled for £600,000 compensation for the disastrous consequences of their daughter's mismanaged birth.[37] Caroline's lawyers claimed that had they pursued the case to its end a judge might have awarded £1 million. The £1 million award is on the horizon. Dire warnings are issued that increased litigation and escalating awards will damage health care for us all. Concern about the effect on N.H.S. resources is justified. Sympathy for the unfortunate doctor whose momentary lapse results in disaster is deserved. Attempts to find a better way of compensating patients injured by medical mishaps should be commended. Some of the propaganda against medical malpractice claims must be dismissed. Whenever a claim hits the headlines the spectre of 'defensive medicine' is invoked. We are told that doctors will no longer give us the treatment appropriate to our condition but will opt for the practice most likely to keep them out of court. We will be subjected to a battery of unnecessary tests and X-rays. Certain patients may be refused treatment. In parts of the U.S.A. obstetricians refuse to treat female lawyers! The spectre must be firmly exorcised.[38]

First, it must be recognized that the size of an award of compensation bears no relation to the seriousness of the error giving rise to liability. In a civil claim for negligence the doctor's general reputation and competence are not in issue. Second, the cost to the N.H.S. and doctors' insurers is vastly added to by the legal costs of fighting and stalling claims for years, eight years in Linda Thomas's case and six in Caroline Turville's.

Who pays the compensation?

We have seen that in perhaps the majority of medical malpractice claims there are a number of defendants. The detailed rules by which the court works out who pays what, I shall not embark on. But certain features of apportioning liability are important.

First is an issue which need not concern the successful patient-plaintiff. Whoever he chooses to sue must pay in full. If one defendant cannot pay and another can, that other must pay in full. Once compensation has been recovered by way of a court award or a settlement, the party ordered to pay may seek a contribution from the others who share liability. Now generally today as between health authority and doctors this will take place behind closed doors. For health authorities and medical protection societies have agreed to settle such matters privately.[39] Neither will publicly blame the other.

What is of interest, though, about the rules governing sharing out liability in a medical malpractice claim is that certain of the difficulties which bedevil the patient's claim disappear at this stage. For example, we saw that for the private patient the fact that his surgeon's liability often lies in contract and the hospital's in tort may be an insuperable obstacle to proving negligence. Once liability is established it ceases to be a problem. If both are responsible, responsibility for paying compensation can be shared between them.[40] Liability will be apportioned on the basis of what is 'just and equitable'[41] having regard to each party's relative responsibility for the mishap.

And that is another interesting feature of the practice of apportioning liability. The courts at last make an effort to discover what really happened. The share a doctor is ordered to pay will depend on his real blameworthiness. So where a relatively inexperienced doctor made an error in administering an anaesthetic resulting in a patient's death, she was held to be very little to blame for that error. The major share of responsibility lay on the hospital authority. Lord Denning said:

> It would be in the highest degree unjust that hospital authorities, by getting inexperienced doctors to perform their duties for them, without adequate supervision, should be able to throw all the responsibility on to these doctors as if they were fully experienced practitioners.[42]

Conclusions

Medical litigation in England today bears close resemblance to a steeplechase. If the patient fails to fall at a fence, he will fall at the water jump. And indeed, in this chapter we have not touched on the preliminary issue of how the patient finances his action. To meet the full cost of litigation the patient will have to be extremely rich. To qualify for legal aid he has to be extremely poor. For those who do qualify for legal aid, they must first demonstrate to a committee run by the Law Society, the professional body of solicitors, that they have a case worth fighting with a realistic chance of success. So before a patient even reaches the starting point of the main race he must overcome formidable obstacles. Yet substantial criticism has been levelled at legally aided patients. It has been claimed that 75 per cent of medical malpractice claims are legally aided despite the fragility of some claims. The patient suing on legal aid is seen as having all to win and nothing to lose. If that were so perhaps the Law Society committees granting legal aid are not doing their job properly. Or is the better explanation that the vast majority of patients who fail to qualify for legal aid because they are 'too rich' just cannot afford the fees to pay lawyers to advise and represent them?

The tone of this chapter must necessarily at first sight appear 'anti' the medical profession. It is not meant to be. The adversarial nature of English civil justice is such that the doctor necessarily sees himself under attack. A cruel twist of fate turns his mistakes into disastrous tragedies. He has no opportunity to put right an error made when he is overtired and overworked, as a solicitor may next morning correct a faulty deed. Criticism should be directed at the law, not the doctors. There must be a better way to handle claims. I shall look at suggestions in Chapter 9. But the crucial question remains: even if there is a way is there the political will?

Chapter 7
Drug-induced Injuries

Not so long ago the pharmaceutical industry basked in the warm glow of public acclaim. The development of antibiotics, of drugs to combat high blood pressure and heart disease, to alleviate the pain of rheumatism, and later the invention of the contraceptive Pill, brought benefits to many and bought life itself for some.[1] The sixties were to change the drug companies' image. Starting with the thalidomide tragedy, a series of disasters taught us all the painful lesson that drugs can be dangerous and their use must be paid for. The list of drugs enthusiastically promoted in the first place and withdrawn from the market a few years later, amid bitter allegations that the drug in question caused injury and even death, is long. Debendox, Opren, and now junior asprin are but a random sample of the better-known cases. And in the same period allegations of gross profit-making by the multinational drug companies have proliferated.[2]

Thalidomide had been developed originally by West German manufacturers, Chemie Grunenthal.[3] A British company, Distillers, bought the formula and manufactured and marketed the drug here under licence from Chemie Grunenthal. The drug was promoted as a safer alternative to existing sedatives and was expressly claimed to be suitable for pregnant and nursing mothers. Thalidomide was alleged to be the cause of gross foetal deformity. All over Europe, wherever thalidomide had been available, babies began to be born suffering from startlingly similar deformities, notably phocomelia (flipper limbs). After a long and bitter campaign, Distillers and the children's parents reached a settlement to provide compensation for children recognized as damaged by thalidomide. Debendox, prescribed to alleviate morning sickness, is similarly charged with causing foetal deformities. Although a similar claim failed in the U.S.A., parents of British children fight on for compensation. They claim that the drug marketed in Britain had a component not present in the drug available in the U.S.A. The anti-rheumatic drug Opren, withdrawn here in 1982, is alleged to have caused kidney and liver damage, and even death, in some of its elderly users. At the time of writing, actions for compensation have been started by a number of those affected. They are suing not only the manufacturers but also the Department of Health and Social Security (D.H.S.S.) and the Committee on Safety of Medicines who gave Opren the product licence which permitted its sale in the United Kingdom. The Dalkon Shield, an intra-uterine contraceptive device, is said to have caused infection, infertility and death in some of the women fitted with it. A number of American women have already been awarded damages by courts in the U.S.A. British claimants are still battling again in the American courts.

The litigants here in England in the Opren claim face an uphill struggle. The history of earlier actions against drug companies is of protracted litigation ending in withdrawal of the claim or an out-of-court settlement which leaves the claimants bitter and dissatisfied.[4] However, as we shall see, Opren victims have achieved some success in preliminary legal skirmishes. The women resorting to American courts over the Dalkon Shield may have greater success. I shall examine the law as it is now. I shall look at provision for compensation for injury, at legislation designed to prevent injury, and briefly at when litigants can sue abroad and why they should want to. And finally I consider the changes in the law now proposed by the government and the European Community.

Product liability and drugs

First, though, it must be acknowledged that whatever scheme for compensation is in operation there are problems relating to drug-induced injury which will not go away. The law, here and in the U.S.A., now and under proposed reforms, treats drugs as just another product.[5] For legal purposes a defective drug is little different from a defective electric blanket or kettle. In practice there are vital distinctions affecting both user and manufacturer if litigation is even started. Defects in products can be of two sorts: in design, which means that every example of the product will prove defective, or in construction, which means that some but not all of the eventual products will be faulty simply because they have not been put together properly. Faults in electric blankets, kettles, and even aircraft are often construction faults. Defects in drugs are almost invariably design defects. That means that when a drug company faces a claim alleging their product to be defective they are facing a disaster. There are going to be not just one or two claimants but a whole host of embittered and injured users. The cost to the company may put it out of business. So the company fights back with equal vigour.

From the user's viewpoint, his greatest difficulty in any claim against the drug company is going to be proving that the drug caused his injury. Should a new brand of electric blanket suffer a design defect and within a week of purchase 5 per cent of users suffer an electric shock, the link between cause and effect will be clear. With a new drug the process may be nothing like so swift or sure. Consider the case of diethylstilboestrol, a drug prescribed over twenty years ago to women threatening to miscarry. Now evidence has emerged that young women, *in utero* when their mothers took the drug, are affected in disproportionate numbers by vaginal and cervical cancer.[6] Delay in effect is only one of the problems. There may be very real uncertainty as to whether injury resulted from the drug taken, the original disease, or some other natural cause. When a drug is alleged to cause foetal deformity this is a particular difficulty. Was the child's disability the result of the drug, or of some inherited disorder or disease in the mother, or one of a number of other possible causes? Then in all claims there is the problem of proving that the drug was taken by the patient in the proper dosage, and as very often the same drug is manufactured under different brand names it must be shown which brand the patient actually used.[7] Medical records are too often far from perfect, and memory is fallible. Finally, there is the intractable difficulty of personal idiosyncrasy. A drug beneficial to 99.9 per cent of us may be lethal to 0.1 per cent. Is that drug defective? Should the company, or anyone else, compensate the 0.1 per cent who suffer injury?

The drug companies rightly refuse to let government and legislators forget these special problems. They press other claims for special treatment too. Drugs are intrinsically dangerous. Patients should accept that there is a balance of benefit and risk. And the pharmaceutical industry argues too that laws which weighed too onerously on it would inhibit research. Medicine would be held back and British companies would suffer loss of competitiveness. Some view this claim sceptically. Today much of the competition appears aimed at producing new brands of the same basic drugs. The pace of innovation has slowed down.[8] Doctors are moving away from prescribing as freely as in the past. Any decline in the pharmaceutical industry is as likely to be due to these factors as it is to be the result of law reforms to help drug-injured patients.

The present law: contract

We start our examination of the present law with the law of contract, which provides substantial protection for the purchasers of defective goods. Two conditions are implied in every contract for the sale of goods. The goods must be merchantable.[9] This means they must be in a reasonable state to be sold at the sort of price charged. And the goods must be reasonably fit for the purpose for which they are sold.[10] When drugs are bought over the counter they must meet these conditions just like any other goods. To take a simple example, a patient buying a bottle of cough mixture suffers internal injury because the medicine is contaminated by powdered glass. That patient may recover full compensation for his injuries from the pharmacist who sold him the medicine. The pharmacist may be entirely without fault. The medicine may have been supplied by the manufacturer in a sealed, opaque container. That does not matter; the medicine was not fit to be sold and the pharmacist is in breach of his contract with the patient. This simple and effective remedy, from the patient's viewpoint, has a defect, however. It is available only when the person suffering injury from the defective drug bought it himself. Had the contaminated medicine of our example been purchased by a husband and taken by his wife, she would have had no remedy in contract. She cannot benefit from a contract to which she is not a party.

How useful then is the contractual remedy? Medicines sold without prescription are, after all, the least likely to cause harm. Drugs prescribed within the N.H.S. will not attract any conditions of merchantability and fitness for purpose, because there is no contract between the pharmacist and the patient into which such conditions can be implied, even though the patient will often have to pay for his prescription.[11] The pharmacist dispenses the drug as part of his obligation under his contract with the local Family Practitioner Committee to provide pharmaceutical services in the area. The patient pays a statutory charge. He does not buy the drug; he in effect pays a tax for N.H.S. services.

By contrast, when drugs are dispensed under a private prescription a contract does exist between the pharmacist and the patient. The patient pays the full cost of the drug directly to the pharmacist. It matters not whether the contract is one of simple sale or a contract of service under which the pharmacist provides a skilled service and incidentally supplies the drug. Now conditions of fitness are imposed in identical terms regardless of whether goods are supplied in the course of a service or in a straight sale transaction.[12] With the introduction of the 'limited list' of prescribable N.H.S. drugs the number of private prescriptions may well rise. The pharmacist is exposed on the front line of liability for defective drugs.

Once prescription drugs become the subject of conditions of fitness, certain problems of applying those conditions are likely. The question may arise as to whether a drug perfectly safe for all but pregnant women is fit to be supplied. First, if it is specifically aimed at pregnant women, for example a morning sickness preparation, then clearly if it damages the woman or her baby it is not fit for the purpose for which it is supplied. Second, if it is a general medicine, such as a hayfever remedy, it could be argued that if it carries risk to a substantial section of the community, pregnant women, then it is not merchantable, not fit to be on general sale. This immediately raises further issues. Did the manufacturer warn of the risk to pregnant women? Should the doctor have prescribed that drug? Should the woman herself be aware of the dangers of taking drugs and avoid drugs while pregnant? These are the sort of problems which plague the whole question of liability for defective drugs. At present it is the pharmacist who is vulnerable to litigation. It is scarcely surprising that pharmacists want to move the burden back to where they think it belongs, to the manufacturers.

The present law: negligence

For many patients suffering drug-induced injury their remedy, if any, at present must lie in the tort of negligence. An action in negligence arises where one person suffers injury as a result of the breach of a duty of care owed him by another. Such a duty, as we have seen, is owed by the doctor to his patient. The doctor may well be the first person too to whom the patient turns for a remedy when he believes a drug prescribed by that doctor has harmed him. The doctor will be liable for drug-induced injury if the drug caused damage because he prescribed an incorrect dosage, or because he ought to have appreciated that that drug posed a risk to a particular patient in the light of his medical history, or where drugs have been prescribed in inappropriate and harmful combination. The problem for the patient is that all he knows is that he is ill and he believes the drug to be the cause. He will initially have no means of knowing whether an inherently 'safe' drug was prescribed for him in an unsafe and careless fashion, or whether the drug is inherently defective and harmful however careful the doctor may be. Hence patients contemplating litigation for drug-induced injury probably have to start by suing the doctor *and* the manufacturer, and must hope that evidence of who was actually to blame will emerge in the course of the litigation.

Turning now to the liability of drug companies manufacturing drugs, the manufacturer of any product

> . . . which he sells in such a form as to show that he intends them to reach the ultimate consumer in the form in which they left him with no reasonable possibility of intermediate examination, and with the knowledge that the absence of care in the preparation or putting up of the products will result in injury to the consumer's life or property, owes a duty to the consumer to take that reasonable care.[13]

There is no doubt that this duty to take care attaches as much to the manufacturer of drugs as to the manufacturer of ginger beer or any other product. The duty covers the design and formulation of the drug as well as its construction. Nor is the duty limited to the original manufacturer. We saw that thalidomide was initially developed by a West German company and manufactured under licence here by Distillers. Distillers still owed a duty to test and monitor the formula before putting the finished product on the U.K. market. Even if they had imported the drug ready-made, if they had then sold it under their brand name they would have owed a duty to English patients to take steps to check on the safety of the drug.[14]

Establishing a duty to avoid negligence is not then the problem. Determining what amounts to negligence is a formidable task. The potential harm caused by a defective drug is such that a very high standard of care will be imposed on the manufacturer. This is generally acknowledged. However, in England no action for personal injuries against a drug company has yet resulted in an award of damages by a court. What are the obstacles confronting claimants, then? First, the drug company must be judged by the standards for drug safety and consumer protection pertaining at the date when the drug was put on the market, not at the date proceedings are taken against them. Drug companies, like doctors, must not be judged negligent on hindsight alone. Today the risk to the developing foetus of drugs taken by the mother is well known to all lay women. When thalidomide was first on the market it is far from clear that the dangers of drugs to the foetus were widely appreciated even by gynaecologists and scientists.

Consideration of the history of the thalidomide claim[15] leads us into the second area of difficulty for litigants. How does a claimant get hold of the hard evidence he will need to prove the company careless? The thalidomide story is instructive, albeit depressing. The charge against Distillers was that they should have foreseen that the drug might harm the foetus and therefore should have conducted adequate tests on it before promoting it as safe for use in pregnancy and/or that once adverse reports on the drug reached them they should have withdrawn it at once. In retrospect, the available evidence that Distillers were negligent falls into three categories. First, there was material available from 1934 onwards to suggest that drugs did pass through the placenta and could damage the foetus. Second, in the 1950s a number of drug companies marketing new products had carried out tests to check the effect on the foetus mainly by way of animal experiments. Such evidence would need to have been given by experts and might not have been conclusive. The burden of proof lies on the claimant. The defendant's experts would have argued that when thalidomide was developed it was by no means universally accepted that drugs could damage the foetus, the efficacy of animal tests would have been disputed, and it would have been strongly submitted that in any case such tests were not then current general practice.

The third and final category of evidence might have been more damning if the claimants could have got hold of it. Reports of the original testing of thalidomide in West Germany by Chemie Grunenthal suggest that it may have been a pretty hit and miss affair. Fairly early on, adverse reports on the drug and concern over risk to the foetus were in the hands of Chemie Grunenthal. Some considerable time elapsed before they withdrew the drug there. Distillers seem to have acted faster, taking the drug out of circulation soon after adverse reactions were reported to them. The contents of adverse reports on a drug, the sequence and exact dates on which those reports are received, are of crucial importance to a claimant. No drug company is going to hand the reports over voluntarily. The process of discovery, of compelling a defendant to hand over documents, was seen to be complex enough in a malpractice claim against an individual doctor. In a claim against a drug company the process may become an insuperable obstacle race.

One last general point on the law of negligence as it affects drug claims can be made by way of illustration from the thalidomide case. It may at the end of the day prove to be the case that there is insufficient evidence that the company were negligent when they originally marketed the drug. But there may be evidence, however hard to come by, that they were negligent in failing to act on adverse reports and recall the drug. Is that a breach of the manufacturer's duty? Two separate situations must be examined. Had it been proved that a child was injured by thalidomide when the drug taken was put on the market by Distillers after a date by which they should have known it to be dangerous, there is no problem. The drug that injured that child was negligently put into circulation. Difficulty would arise where the drug taken by the mother had been put into circulation before Distillers should have known it was dangerous but was actually prescribed to her and taken by her after that date. Although it is not as clearly established as the duty to manufacture a product carefully,[16] I believe that a court would hold that the manufacturer owes a further duty to monitor his product and to take reasonable steps to withdraw it if it proves unsafe. Proving breach of the duty could be a nightmare. Stories of doctors continuing to prescribe, and pharmacists retaining stocks of withdrawn drugs, recur. The patient suing in such a claim could falter and sink in a sea of allegation and counter-allegation between drug company, doctor and pharmacist.

The tort of negligence as a means of compensating for drug-induced injury simply does not work. Indeed, successive bodies who have examined the tort of negligence in relation to general product liability have concluded that the law as it stands is inadequate. Change must come. Doubts persist as to how beneficial changes proposed will be.

The present law: preventing injury

The horror of the thalidomide tragedy provided the impetus for one change unrelated to compensation for injury. Measures were taken to improve the monitoring of drugs before they were permitted to be marketed in the U.K. This was first effected by way of a voluntary scheme. The government set up a Committee on Safety of Drugs to examine and approve new drugs and to monitor those already on the market. Drug companies were not compelled to accept the scheme, but the majority complied.[17] In 1968 the Medicines Act 1968 introduced statutory compulsory vetting of new drugs. It is this statute which still largely provides for the licensing and monitoring of drugs in the U.K. today.

The 1968 Act entrusts the licensing of new drugs and the scrutiny of drugs already on the market to the Health Minister.[18] No medicine may now be manufactured, imported or marketed without a licence from the

Minister. When a new product is developed, a clinical trial certificate must be obtained before it can be tested on patients, and a product licence is required before the drug can be marketed.[19] The Minister acts on the advice of a body known as the Medicines Commission and its specialist committees. The Commission's powers are general in nature. It is directed to advise the Minister on (*inter alia*) the practice of medicine and pharmacy, and the operation of the pharmaceutical industry.[20] The Committee on Safety of Medicines (C.S.M.), one of three committees established by the Medicines Commission, has the more specific, central role in licensing new drugs. The C.S.M. is empowered to advise on the safety, quality and efficacy of drugs, and to promote the collection of information on adverse reactions and advise on action to be taken as a consequence thereof.[21] It is to the C.S.M. that applications for clinical trial certificates and product licences are first referred. The Minister cannot refuse a licence without first consulting the C.S.M.[22] In practice if not in law, in the overwhelming majority of cases the C.S.M. is the licensing authority.

When deciding whether to grant a licence the Minister and the C.S.M. are directed to consider:

(1) the safety of the drug to which the application relates;
(2) the efficacy of the drug for the purpose for which it is to be administered; and
(3) the quality of the drug, having particular regard to its method of manufacture, and arrangements proposed for its distribution.[23]

The C.S.M. is expressly *excluded* from taking into account any question of whether other existing drugs are equally or more efficacious for the purpose proposed.[24] So the C.S.M. cannot reject an application for a product licence for a new tranquillizer simply because it considers there are already sufficient effective drugs of that sort available. The C.S.M.'s remit is to protect the consumer from injury, and not from a plethora of expensive close-copy drugs. When the C.S.M. advises and the Minister agrees that a licence be granted, a product licence is operative for five years[25] and a clinical trial certificate for two.[26] At the end of those periods the manufacturer must apply again for renewal of his licence. The C.S.M., as we saw, is also responsible for monitoring adverse reaction to drugs in use. Section 28 of the Medicines Act 1968 empowers the Minister, on the advice of the C.S.M., to revoke an existing licence. Several grounds for revocation are established, of which the most important is where:

. . . medicinal products of any description to which the licence relates can no longer be regarded as products which can safely be administered for the purposes indicated in the licence, or can no longer be regarded as efficacious for those purposes . . .

The decision to withdraw a drug from the market is no longer solely a matter for the manufacturer.

A manufacturer aggrieved by the advice of the C.S.M. that a licence be refused, or an existing licence be revoked, may seek to have the advice of the C.S.M. reviewed by the Medicines Commission. A manufacturer whose product has been approved by the C.S.M. and/or the Commission but who is refused a licence by the Minister has a right to a further hearing. The Minister, the licensing authority in law, is obliged to consult the C.S.M. If he chooses, as he may, to reject their advice, he must set up an independent inquiry before which the manufacturer may state his case.[27] This has happened only once since the Medicines Act 1968 came into force. The Minister recently rejected the advice of the C.S.M. to license the injectable contraceptive Depo-Provera for long-term use. After receiving a report from the independent inquiry panel set up, the Minister licensed the drug under strict conditions. The details of the continuing row over Depo-Provera are dealt with in Chapter 16.

It can be seen then that an elaborate framework for licensing drugs in the U.K. now exists. We have only skimmed the surface of the scheme. Detailed provision is made for the submission of applications, and a great deal of work and manpower is expended both by the companies and by Health Ministry and C.S.M. staff. Lately the pharmaceutical industry has attacked the procedure. They claim it is over-burdensome and bureaucratic. Drug companies in the U.K. are suffering. They dare not innovate. They cannot compete. The drug companies' well-orchestrated self-pleading has been vigorously resisted. And with the spectre of several drug disasters hanging over us, today does not seem to be the time to weaken existing consumer protection laws which have not in themselves proved entirely adequate.[28]

Claims against the Minister and the C.S.M.

The possibility of governmental liability for drug-induced injury was aired even in the thalidomide days. The then Health Minister, Sir Keith Joseph, dismissed suggestions that the government could be liable. He argued further that even when the elaborate licensing provisions of the 1968 Act were in force, the legal liability for any defect in the drug rested on the manufacturer alone.[29] Now both the Health Ministry and the C.S.M. face a suit for negligence brought against them in respect of the original licensing and continued marketing of the anti-rheumatic drug Opren.[30] Is there any realistic prospect that the claim against them will succeed and establish a direct duty owed by the government and its agents to victims of drug disasters?

The nearest analogy to a claim against the Ministry and the C.S.M. can be found in cases concerning building regulations. In *Anns* v. *Merton L.B.C.*[31] the plaintiff's maisonnette was severely defective. The foundations of the block were alleged to be inadequate. The plaintiff sued the builder and the local authority. The local authority had powers to inspect all building operations and could stop the builder going ahead if foundations or other crucial works were found to be inadequate. The local authority said that they could not be legally liable if their inspection process had been ineffective. The House of Lords disagreed. They held that if it were found that the local authority had misused the power entrusted to them by Parliament they could be liable for the resulting damage suffered by the plaintiff. The same test of misuse of power is likely to govern the liability of the Health Minister and the C.S.M. They cannot be liable because events proved them wrong. Simple carelessness will not engage their responsibility. But were it to be shown that the Minister or the C.S.M. failed to exercise their powers on proper, relevant considerations, failed to act with due diligence, liability might follow.

Claims brought abroad

The majority of drug companies are multinationals. Drugs are not clearly confined within national borders. We have noted that British women claiming to have suffered injury as a result of using the Dalkon Shield I.U.D. are suing the manufacturers in the U.S.A. When can an injured patient resort to a foreign court and why should he want to?

Whenever a claim has a foreign element a set of rules known as the rules of private international law, or conflict of laws, come into play. These are excessively complex and we shall give only the barest outline of the relevant law. Essentially, when a claim for negligence is brought the claimant can sue in any country where a relevant act of negligence occurred.[32] There may be more than one such country. So in the case of a defective drug, negligence may have occurred both in the country where it was carelessly manufactured and in the country where it was carelessly marketed as safe[33] and injured the claimant. It is on the basis of the careless manufacture of the device in the U.S.A. that the women suing over the Dalkon Shield are able to go to court in America. Where there is a dispute over whether an action should be allowed to go ahead, the law of the country where the claimant is trying to sue determines whether it should do so. British women claiming in the U.S.A that U.S. formulated contraceptive Pills caused heart attacks and strokes won a substantial settlement.

Why should anyone want to sue abroad? After all, if they took the drug here and were injured here they can bring their action in their homeland on the basis of negligent distribution in the U.K. There are two main reasons for claimants to opt for the hassle of a foreign lawsuit. First, liability in the country of manufacture may be strict. This means negligence does not have to be proved. What has to be shown is that the drug was defective and injured the claimant. Strict liability of this sort exists in many states of the U.S.A. Second, there are powerful financial incentives to sue in the U.S.A. if you can. Not only is liability for drugs strict, but awards of damages are made by juries still and are generally much higher than English judge-made awards. Most important, though, is the contingency fee system. To start off with the claimant need pay his American lawyer nothing. If the case is won, the lawyer takes a share of the damages. Should the claimant lose, the lawyer may not get a penny. Claimants can afford to start an action unhampered by fears of the expense of their case.

Proposed reform: strict liability

The inadequacy of the tort of negligence as a means of compensating people injured by defective products has been recognized in every review of the state of product liability in England.[34] A move to strict liability for products is urged. In essence this means that, as is now the case in the U.S.A., the claimant will need to prove only (1) that the product was defective, and (2) that it injured him. Negligence will be irrelevant. Strict liability is seen as fairer to claimants because it is argued that liability for injury will thus be borne by the person creating the risk, and benefiting financially from the product, i.e. the manufacturer. The manufacturer too is in the best position to exercise control over the quality and safety of the product, and can more conveniently insure against the risk of injury posed by the product than may individual users. Strict liability has been supported too on the grounds that prolonged and complex litigation will be less likely than is common at present with the tort of negligence.[35] The arguments for change are impressive. The manner in which the government has chosen to implement reform causes us to doubt whether the proposed change to strict liability will in fact bring about the stated aims of such a reform.

The scheme of strict liability to be adopted is based on a European Community directive[36] issued by the Council of Ministers on 25 July 1985. The directive obliges all national states of the European Community to pass legislation making the directive part of their national law within three years. The first draft of this proposed European reform appeared in 1974. It was argued about for eleven years. Now a compromise has been agreed. States who so wish may deviate from the original plan for uniform rules throughout the Community by either adopting a development risks, 'state of the art' defence or imposing a financial limit on manufacturer's liability. The British government has opted for the development risks defence. I shall seek to show that the incorporation of such a defence in new laws will to a large extent undermine the whole purpose of the reform.

The European Community directive imposes liability for personal injury arising from defective products on all *producers* of goods. This includes the importers of drugs.[37] The imposition of liability on producers as opposed to manufacturers is important. Companies importing drugs into Europe will be liable as if they manufactured them here. Suppliers of drugs will be treated as producers if they fail to identify the source of their supply. The directive ensures that there will be a *producer* on whom liability must rest. No one will be able to hide behind a smokescreen as to his identity.

The next stage of a claim is where the claimant will meet his first obstacle. He must establish that the drug was defective. The European directive defines defective in Article 6.

1. A product is defective when it does not provide the safety which a person is entitled to expect, taking all circumstances into account, including:
(a) the presentation of the product;
(b) the use to which it could reasonably be expected that the product would be put;
(c) the time when the product was put into circulation.
2. A product shall not be considered defective for the sole reason that a better product is subsequently put into circulation.

Determining when a drug falls within that definition will be far from easy.[38] Drugs are by their nature dangerous. They are designed to do damage to the bacteria or diseased cell or whatever caused the original disease. What amounts to the safety that the patient is entitled to expect? Side-effects are often unavoidable. The court will have to try to balance the potential benefit as against the risk when deciding when an unwanted side-effect renders the drug defective. Distinctions may be drawn based on the condition the drug was designed to combat. A minor tranquillizer which carried an unforeseen 5 per cent risk of liver damage could be deemed defective when an anti-cancer drug carrying identical risk probably will not. Relief of moderate anxiety may be seen as insufficient to warrant the risk, whereas the battle against cancer may justify that degree of inherent danger. Anticipated risks raise different issues. Clearly an anticipated risk must be warned against. Will the tranquillizer be deemed not defective if its potential danger is outlined to doctors and patients, leaving this choice to them? Clearly the warning must be taken into account – it is part of the presentation of the product. An antibiotic harmful only to the foetus will almost certainly not be defective if a warning of its risk is clearly given. Less essential drugs may remain defective even if risks are detailed. The patient may never have the warning passed on to him after all. In such a case, though, a heavy share of liability would rest with the doctor prescribing the drug in contravention or ignorance of warnings from the producer.

Other problems in applying the definition of defective in the E.C. directive can easily be predicted. What of the patient who suffers injury because of an allergic reaction to the drug? The drug is perfectly safe and effective for you, but lethal to me. If risk to an individual or group is foreseeable and *not* warned of in the presentation of the product it is defective. Clearly an individual is entitled to expect that the manufacturer will not simply ignore an identified danger to however small a group. When the risk is not foreseeable, the size and predictability of the affected group will be crucial. A sedative which causes damage to the foetus or liver damage in 10 per cent of the over-seventies will be defective. Pregnant women and the elderly are large groups of potential consumers known to be vulnerable to drug-induced injury. But what if the sedative injured only a handful of users out of millions?

The difficulties that may arise in applying the E.C. directive definition of defective could be detailed at much greater length. For potential claimants the disturbing news is this. The 'new' test of defectiveness offers as much of a prospect of prolonged litigation as the 'old' test of negligence. And proving defectiveness is only the start of the claimant's difficulties. Causation remains as thorny a problem as ever. The onus remains on the claimant to prove 'the causal relationship between defect and damage', as Article 4 of the directive puts it. Liability comes entirely to an end ten years after the product is put into circulation. Drugs such as the anti-miscarriage drug which caused cancer up to twenty years later in some of the daughters *in utero* thus escape the regime of strict liability.

Finally, the effect of the development risks, 'state of the art', defence to be adopted in the U.K. must be examined. A development risks, 'state of the art', defence amounts to this. The manufacturer will not be liable if he can prove 'that the state of scientific and technical knowledge at the time when he put the product into circulation was not such as to enable the existence of the defect to be discovered'.[39] This means that if a drug manufactured in 1985 is in 1988 shown to be defective, but applying 1985 standards for the manufacture and testing of drugs the drug company did all it could be expected to, the company will not be liable for any damage done by their defective product. It will remain the case that the company can no more be judged by hindsight than it may under the present law of negligence. Of great value to the defendant will be the irrefutable evidence that the C.S.M. saw fit to grant him a product licence. Unless there is evidence that the defendant misled or was not frank with the C.S.M., a court may be reluctant to say that in their opinion the manufacturer failed to comply with the standards of the time when the experts, the C.S.M., had found he did.[40]

What benefits then, if any, will the proposed reform bring? A great deal will depend on how the judges interpret defectiveness. Otherwise the greatest material change will be this. While a producer able to raise the development risks defence will still be able to plead that according to current practice he could have done more than he did, the onus will lie on him to prove this. Once a claimant has shown that the product was defective and that it injured him, the ball moves into the defendant's court. Distillers, if sued over thalidomide under the proposed regime of strict liability, would have had to prove that current practice did *not* involve tests for effect on the foetus and to reveal what tests were conducted. They would have been forced to disclose all the material available to them to support their case. The greatest potential benefit of the reforms proposed at present is that defendants will lose the advantage of trying to keep as much as possible of the scientific and expert evidence available to them out of the hands of the plaintiff.

What must now be asked is why the British government is so insistent on the development risks defence. All the bodies who have previously investigated product liability reform have come out against such a reform. The Pearson Commission, which reviewed the whole of the law relating to personal injuries, said:

. . . to exclude development risks from a regime of strict liability would be to leave a gap in the compensation cover, through which, for example, the victims of another thalidomide disaster might slip.[41]

The government has been swayed by counter arguments from industry. They claim that innovation would be discouraged and that the cost of insurance against development risks would be crippling.[42] Their case has convinced only the government and was expressly rejected in all earlier inquiries. There is another disquieting feature of the acceptance of a development risks defence too. West Germany, which boasts a thriving pharmaceutical industry, has rejected the development risks defence specifically with regard to drugs while adopting it in relation to other products. West Germany does not want to become a testing ground for risky drugs. Does Britain? The government should think again.

Proposed reform: no fault 'liability'

The pharmaceutical industry itself remains apprehensive of strict liability despite the view of many commentators that its position regarding liability for injury will be little changed. The Association of British Pharmaceutical Industries (A.B.P.I.) appears to favour more radical reform, a move to a scheme of no fault compensation. This would differ from strict liability in this way. Under strict liability the claimant has to show that he was injured by a drug and that that drug was defective. A no fault scheme would simply require proof that the drug caused harm. Claimants would recover compensation from a state fund for injury without anyone having to be shown to be at fault in any way. No fault compensation raises several questions. Who will pay for it? Why separate out drug-induced injury for special treatment? Will such a scheme encourage irresponsibility by companies freed from the threat of court action? These are questions raised in relation to medical malpractice as well as drug injuries. We examine them in Chapter 9. We look now at the one example of a very limited no fault scheme in operation today, the Vaccine Damage Payments Act 1979. How successful has this well-meant scheme been?

Vaccine damage: a special case

Vaccine damage is a candidate for special treatment because of the distinction in social effect between vaccines and other drugs.[43] Generally the benefit and risk of taking a drug rests with the individual patient alone. No one else suffers directly if he does not take the drug. No one else benefits directly if he does. With a vaccine the position is different. If a child is immunized against contagious disease, the child himself benefits from the immunity conferred and his friends and schoolfellows benefit from the elimination of the risk that he will pass that disease on to them. Consequently vaccination of young children against tetanus, diphtheria, polio, measles and whooping cough is actively promoted by the Health Ministry. It is the whooping cough vaccine that has caused the greatest outcry and distress. A number of children healthy before vaccination have, their parents claim, suffered severe and lasting brain damage as a consequence of receiving the vaccine.

What remedies have the parents of a vaccine-damaged child? First, they may, as a number of parents of children allegedly damaged by whooping cough vaccine have done, seek to use the tort of negligence to obtain compensation. The advantage of this course is that if the claim was successful their children would receive full compensation for any handicap caused by the vaccine. The problem for the parents is whom to sue. The present vaccine is controversial. Doctors argue vehemently whether the risk of the vaccine to a child is greater than the risks posed by contracting the disease itself. An action against a doctor for negligently using the vaccine is likely to fail because although some doctors and experts condemn its use, a substantial body of informed opinion still backs the vaccine. A malpractice action is really only viable if some special feature of the child's history should have ruled out routine vaccination, or if symptoms at a first vaccination, indicating that further vaccination was unwise, were missed. Suing the manufacturers will run into the problem of the risk/benefit ratio of the product. The manufacturers dispute the level of risk from the vaccine and will argue that the overwhelming benefit to the community of vaccination outweighs any risk to a very few.

A claim against the D.H.S.S. has already been once before a court: *D.H.S.S.* v. *Kinnear*.[44] The D.H.S.S. argued that the case against them was totally untenable and should be struck out without a full hearing. The judge held that insofar as the claimants challenged the *policy* decision by the D.H.S.S. to promote vaccination their action would be stopped. But allegations that D.H.S.S. advice as to the circumstances and manner of vaccination was inadequate would be allowed to go forward. The attempt by the D.H.S.S. to have the claimants' case against them entirely blocked as untenable failed.

Whether parents sue their doctor, the manufacturers of the vaccine or the D.H.S.S., their prospects of success at the end of the day received a severe blow from a decision of the Scottish courts in August 1985. The court held that the Scottish claimants had not proved that their son's disabilities resulted from the vaccine. Proving that a drug caused the relevant injury is, as we have seen, the thorniest issue in any action for drug-induced injury. The Scottish decision will encourage the manufacturers to contest even more fervently this central issue of whether whooping cough vaccine does lead to brain damage.[45] In England the legal battle for full compensation for children allegedly damaged by the vaccine suffered a further blow. The *Kinnear* case, when it finally came to a full trial, collapsed. The boy's father lost his legal aid certificate when it appeared that the evidence in this particular claim was weak. The judge sought to salvage some of the lost time and expense by seeking to continue the trial on the *general* issue of whether the vaccine could ever cause brain damage to *any* child. His laudable efforts came to naught. In 1987 another set of claims by parents of other children are listed for trial together. The proceedings may take a year to conclude in the High Court alone.

The enormous problems of litigation for negligence may deter many parents from going to court. Successive reviews of the issue of compensation for vaccine damage have recognized that it is an example of injury where compensation via the tort of negligence may be totally inappropriate. There may at the end of the day prove to be no negligence on anyone's part because the benefit to the majority is held to justify the risk to a small minority. Yet it is scarcely fair that those who suffer damage should bear the whole burden of their handicap alone. On the recommendation of the Pearson Commission, Parliament enacted the Vaccine Damage Payments Act 1979 to provide for a no fault compensation scheme for vaccine-damaged individuals. The scheme is far from generous. It provided originally for an award of £10,000 only where a person suffers 80 per cent disablement as a result of vaccination against a disease to which the Act applies. In July 1985 the amount payable was raised to £20,000 but only for claims made after that date. Claims for payments under the Act are made initially to the D.H.S.S. If the D.H.S.S. official responsible is not satisfied that the claim is made out, the claimant may ask for the decision to be reviewed by an independent medical tribunal. The decision of the tribunal is final. The making of a payment under the 1979 Act does not debar a claimant from also suing for negligence in respect of the vaccination.

The most bitter criticism of the Act is that even the increased payment of £20,000 is woefully inadequate. The Act, it is said, is no more than a sop to public opinion. It has not replaced the tort of negligence with an adequate compensation mechanism. Other critics complain that the ever-present problem of causation of drug-induced injury is simply ignored in the Act. The claimant must establish on the balance of probability that his disablement resulted from the vaccine. Disputed cases go to the independent tribunals. Statistics seem to show that establishing cause and effect is not a precise science. It is difficult to see what factors account for a 39 per cent success rate in disputed cases before the Manchester tribunal in contrast to only a 12 per cent success rate in Belfast.[46] The finding of the Scottish courts that parents had failed to prove that the vaccine caused brain damage may throw even the minimal compensation scheme operated under the 1979 Act into disarray.

What of the future?

The introduction of strict liability on the lines proposed by the government does not appear to offer much comfort to patients damaged by defective drugs. Recent events do, however, offer patients a glimmer of hope. Claims by several people alleging that their general health was ruined by taking the anti-rheumatic drug Opren have yet to come to full trial. But already the case has made legal history. Acting under the umbrella of the Opren Action Group, claimants and their lawyers are co-ordinating their campaign. The judge who is to hear the case has held that the basic issue of whether the drug caused damage to health and whether the defendants (the manufacturers, the C.S.M. and the D.H.S.S.) were negligent will be decided at one trial. The patients may proceed with a 'class action', pooling their resources to pay lawyers and medical experts. The same judge has also resisted attempts by health authorities to refuse Opren patients their records, saying that he could see no case to deprive them of vital evidence. One request he did refuse. The claimants sought to have documents released not just to them and their lawyers but also to an expert chosen to co-ordinate the claim. The judge rejected their choice of a medical journalist. But he said that some other less partisan person might well be sanctioned to take on a task that he, the judge, recognized as crucial to the claimants' chance to present their case properly.[47]

Sadly, at the same time as judges and lawyers showed some signs of determination to ensure that the legal process to consider claims of drug-induced damage works efficiently and fairly, evidence of yet another drug disaster came to light. The C.S.M. warned of the risks of aspirin to children under twelve, and junior aspirin preparations were withdrawn from general use. What concerned many observers was how long it took the C.S.M. to act, nearly fifteen months from the time when concern was first expressed and U.S. authorities had acted.[48] No improvement or reform of the process to compensate drug-victims can ever be as important as ensuring that our procedures for testing and monitoring the safety of drugs are effective.

Chapter 8
Hospital Complaints Procedures

The bravest patient may well quail at embarking on litigation for medical malpractice. For litigation to be economically worthwhile it must offer some hope of substantial compensation. Moreover, money may not be the aggrieved patient's primary concern. Many simply want an explanation of what went wrong and perhaps an apology. Despite the clumsy and inadequate nature of a lawsuit as a means of investigating medical error, some patients sue just to try and find out what really happened. One such patient, a mother whose delivery of twins at a private hospital went disastrously wrong and one baby died, won £31,000 in damages. The money, she said, was much less important than finding out why her child died.[1] Going to court was her only remedy. Interestingly, private hospital organizations are now considering setting up complaints procedures.[2]

Within the National Health Service there is an assortment of complaints mechanisms. The Health Service Commissioner, district and regional health authorities and the Health Minister all have a role to play. Many of the procedures had no statutory basis until 1985. The number of complaints to the Commissioner has risen over the years. Handling of critical complaints will be seen to be poor and sometimes to aggravate patients' original grievances. In 1985 Parliament acted to initiate a review of complaints procedures.

Hospital Complaints Procedures Act 1985

This Act derives from the personal experience of Michael McNair Wilson M.P. while he lay in a series of N.H.S. hospitals acutely ill with renal failure. He was on the whole grateful for and impressed with the care he received. One or two things did go badly wrong though. For example, a stitch left in his leg went septic and he got septicaemia. Like many other patients, he asked himself: '. . . to whom do I complain? Who will offer me compensation? Who will listen to my problem?'[3]

125

When he returned to the House of Commons he introduced the Private Member's Bill which has now become the Hospital Complaints Procedures Act 1985. The Act is brief. The Health Minister already had power to give directions to health authorities.[4] Section 1 of the 1985 Act imposes a duty on the Minister to give directions to health authorities to ensure that in each hospital for which the authority is responsible arrangements are made for dealing with patients' complaints and that adequate publicity is given to those arrangements. The scheme to be followed by the authority must comply with the directions of the Minister. The Act did not become law immediately. It is to come into force on a date to be set by the Minister. The delay is so that the Minister can consult fully with the medical professions and N.H.S. administrators.

On its face this 1985 Act is a modest piece of legislation. Yet it has been opposed by some doctors led by the B.M.A. who see no need for further changes.[5] Indeed, it has been suggested that the Minister's directions under the 1985 Act should simply embody the present non-statutory 'code' for dealing with complaints. The importance of the Act is this. (1) It provides formal recognition of the crucial role effective complaints procedures play in the health service. (2) The Minister is now obliged to review and rationalize present procedures. (3) The Act offers an opportunity for change and places emphasis on dealing with complaints at source, in the hospital where the patient is being or has been treated. The scheme envisaged by Mr McNair Wilson would lead to the appointment in every N.H.S. hospital of a hospital 'ombudsman'.[6] He or she would be a senior member of staff, able to deal on equal terms with consultants, senior nurses and administrators. The details of such a scheme remain to be settled. A consultation paper was issued in June 1986. It has three key elements. A 'designated officer' to handle all complaints should be appointed in each N.H.S. hospital, in effect Mr McNair Wilson's 'ombudsman'. Health authorities should be obliged to monitor the handling of complaints regularly, and procedures should be well publicized to patients.

Initial complaints

Dissatisfaction with the way in which complaints were dealt with led the government in 1971 to set up a committee chaired by Davies J. to inquire into complaints procedures. The Davies Committee reported in 1973[7] and some, but not all, of their recommendations were incorporated into the code of practice issued to health authorities in 1981.[8] The only significant change likely to result from present proposals to implement the 1985 Act is that complaints will initially be addressed to 'the designated officer' in the actual hospital rather than to a more remote health authority official.

Informal and minor complaints are to be dealt with as they arise by the member of staff involved. Staff are counselled to listen sympathetically to any comments or misgivings voiced by patients, however trivial they may appear. Formal complaints must be addressed in writing to the administrator of the district health authority (or, soon, 'the designated officer'). He will refer the complaint to a senior member of staff for inquiry and a written response will be agreed upon by the administrator and the staff members looking at the complaint. The D.H.S.S. advises that (1) all complaints must be investigated thoroughly and promptly, (2) the patient must be kept informed of the progress of the investigation, and (3) any member of staff involved should be fully informed of allegations made against him and advised of his right to seek the advice of his professional association or trade union. It is of course entirely right that staff members be treated fairly. Some may consider, though, that protection of the staff member is on occasion the prime concern of the administrator handling the complaint. The D.H.S.S. warns prophetically: '. . . unsatisfactory handling of a complaint may become the cause of further complaint'.

The Health Service Commissioner

Patients and ex-patients unhappy with the reply to their complaint may next take the matter to the Health Service Commissioner. The office of Commissioner was created in 1973 and his powers are now set out in Part V of the National Health Service Act 1977.[9] The Commissioner is empowered to investigate any complaint where it is alleged that a failure in the health service or maladministration in the service resulted in injustice or hardship. His jurisdiction does not extend to all areas of the N.H.S. He may not, for example, investigate complaints about general practitioners.[10] Hospitals, ambulance services, clinics and district nursing services are among the bodies which he may review.[11] Even then important restrictions are placed on him. The two most central restrictions on his powers are these. The Commissioner may not pursue a complaint where the person concerned may have a remedy in the courts unless he is satisfied that it is not reasonable to expect the complainant to invoke that remedy. And he may not investigate any action taken as a result of the exercise of the professional, clinical judgment of doctors or nurses. What then is the extent of the Commissioner's power and influence?

Investigating a complaint

Complaints to the Commissioner must be made in writing, normally within one year of the incident giving rise to the complaint.[12] The complaint may be made by a patient personally or by some responsible person acting on his behalf.[13] The Commissioner has an unreviewable discretion as to whether to pursue a complaint.[14] His powers of inquiry are extensive. He and his staff investigate in private. They will contact all hospital staff involved with a complaint and seek their comments. The Commissioner has complete control of the investigation. If co-operation from hospital staff or administrators is not forthcoming, the production of records and documents may be ordered and staff may be compelled to testify to the Commissioner.[15] Exceptionally evidence can be taken on oath, but this has happened only once so far to my knowledge.[16] In that case the preliminary evidence from the parties had been totally irreconcilable. The Commissioner regretted this occasion. Successive Commissioners pride themselves on good relations with health service staff, rendering resort to powers of compulsion unnecessary.

On completion of an investigation the Commissioner reports to the complainant, the health authority, and any individual against whom allegations were made. The report will contain a decision as to whether the complaint was justified and recommend a remedy. In 1984–5[17] 47 per cent of complaints investigated were found to be justified. The most common remedy is an apology from the authority and the staff member involved. Increasingly he recommends too that the D.H.S.S. and health authorities make changes in practice to avoid a recurrence of similar complaints. For example, in 1984–5[18] on the initiative of the Commissioner steps were taken to review procedures for writing to G.P.s on the patient's discharge, to improve communication with relatives and to improve monitoring of complaints procedures. Very occasionally the Commissioner may additionally recommend the making of an *ex gratia* cash payment to a patient by way of compensation. These are usually small sums, arising from cases where maladministration has resulted in loss of patients' property or unnecessary expenses.

The Commissioner does not regard it as his function to grant monetary compensation for pain and hardship suffered by patients.[19]

Each year the Commissioner makes an Annual Report to Parliament published by H.M.S.O. and available to the public. Additionally in the course of each year he publishes two or three reports of the details of selected investigations with all the parties involved kept anonymous. His activities are monitored by a Select Committee of M.P.s who have, as we shall see, encouraged him in his work and spurred him on to greater efforts on behalf of patients. The issue of maladministration in the N.H.S. is thus brought firmly into the public eye. Improvements are constantly urged and generally implemented, yet the trend is that the number of complaints submitted to the Commissioner and the percentage he finds to be well founded continues to rise.[20]

The work of the Commissioner

The reports of the Commissioner from 1974 onwards make interesting, if somewhat depressing, reading. Certain sorts of complaints recur. Waiting lists, lack of communication by medical staff, inadequate liaison with G.P.s, delay in attendance by doctors, and unsatisfactory supervision of the elderly and vulnerable appear again and again. Maternity and geriatric care seem to generate a disproportionate number of complaints. Rudeness, lack of sympathy and even in extreme cases allegations of assault by staff cause the Commissioner much concern.

The Annual Report for 1984–5 identifies six topics which have caused the Commissioner particular concern. They are (1) care and supervision of the elderly and handicapped, (2) contents and use of medical records, (3) delay in doctors attending patients, (4) arrangements made for discharge from hospital, (5) recording and investigation of alleged assaults, and (6) the initial handling of complaints by hospitals. The care of the elderly is a matter for anxiety and occasionally outrage. The Commissioner can do little more than investigate and advise. The solution depends largely on resources and imagination and no legal reforms are likely to bring improvement.

The other five topics admit of greater hopes of change. Complaints about medical records included the startling case of the man who had undergone treatment in a teaching hospital and later discovered in a medical textbook a full face full frontal picture of himself naked.[21] The Commissioner insisted on procedures to require that illustrations involving patients (1) blanked out their face, and (2) had their consent.

Other complaints related to failures to record information about patients, especially when it came from the patient himself.[22] At the source of many complaints about records is the presumption that the patient's medical history belongs to the doctor. The patient's rights and role in his treatment need clearer acknowledgement.

Two other topics of 1984–5, delay in doctors attending and inadequate arrangements for discharge, again have a common and disturbing cause. Communication within the health service is not as it should be. One complaint concerned an elderly man admitted to hospital solely to control acute pain from terminal cancer which his G.P. and a visiting anaesthetist could no longer cope with at home. The Commissioner found a three-hour delay in getting a doctor to him. He commented that such a failure to provide basic medical care was profoundly disturbing and constituted a serious failure in the service. Health authorities were advised to issue clear instructions to nursing staff as to when to call an alternative doctor if the duty doctor had failed to respond.[23] Relating to discharge from hospital, an elderly woman was discharged after nine weeks' hospitalization for chest trouble. Earlier that week she had scalded herself and on the day of discharge she fell in the ward. The Commissioner found that inadequate arrangements were made to inform her G.P. of her state, and that her husband was given insufficient information as to how to care for her at home.[24]

The last two topics, recording and investigating assaults and handling complaints, are the prime candidates for immediate reform. Both spring from the unsatisfactory nature of the system for initial handling of complaints and from the defensive attitudes of the medical profession. Of the handling of complaints the Commissioner said, '. . . a very large number of complaints would never reach me if they were dealt with more thoroughly, accurately, promptly and sympathetically in the first instance'.[25]

The Commissioner's remarks are well illustrated by the following complaint. The complainant's daughter was referred by the G.P. to a consultant psychiatrist. She was admitted to hospital twice and diagnosed as suffering from manic depression. Her parents thought that her symptoms seemed to be related to her menstrual cycle. The consultant arranged for tests to be made by a gynaecologist colleague. The parents were not given the results of the tests until some seven months after they were available to the hospital. In the meantime they removed the girl to the care of a private doctor and complained to the health authority about the delay. The response was a letter from the consultant's solicitors threatening a libel action. At every further stage to which they pursued the complaint the parents were obstructed until the Commissioner found for them.[26]

No one would deny that a number of complaints are trivial and that distressing allegations are sometimes made against doctors and nurses with absolutely no basis. But complainants do not go away if they are ignored or even threatened. Very often a simple explanation is all that is called for. If that is not forthcoming, the complainant will simply progress to the next stage of the procedure. Investigation by the Health Service Commissioner wastes more valuable medical time, causes more anxiety and is more likely to damage the doctor's or nurse's reputation than a thorough prompt internal inquiry. For this reason it is to be hoped that the Hospital Complaints Procedures Act leads, as it was intended to, to an effective and uniform scheme based on the individual hospital ombudsman.

The concerns of the Commissioner in 1984–5 echo familiar themes from the previous eleven years. Other areas which have generated complaints of particular importance include failing to tell patients of their right to object to the presence of medical students,[27] inadequate explanations when obtaining consent to surgery,[28] failing to listen to the patient, and many others in a catalogue illustrating the importance to the patient of being treated as an intelligent individual. Other complaints arise from sheer mismanagement. Dentures get lost. Special diets are ignored, and so on. A number of disquiets arise from the lack of resources. Waiting lists for hip-replacements have been investigated by the Commissioner several times. He cannot wave a magic wand and end the waiting. He can ensure that maladministration does not extend the waiting time, that the lists are properly organized, and once again that patients are kept fully informed.

The Commissioner and the courts

Many of the complaints dealt with by the Commissioner would not be the subject of court action for a variety of reasons. The elderly gentleman left to suffer from acute pain and dying of terminal cancer died the next day. Claiming damages would not have been worthwhile for his widow. Imposing the presence of medical students or publishing photographs of a naked patient give rise to no legal remedy in England, where privacy is poorly protected by the law. Other investigations undertaken by the Commissioner are more likely subjects of a claim for malpractice, for example those cases where the Commissioner finds a lack of complete or voluntary consent to treatment. One notorious example concerned a woman of 23. She sought an abortion in 1970 and attended the hospital with her mother. The woman held a job but suffered from temporal lobe epilepsy and a degree of personality disorder. After discussion with the parents the consultant sterilized the woman with their consent. The first she learned of the operation was when some years later and married she was trying to have a baby. D.H.S.S. guidelines stated that sterilization of persons suffering from mental disorder should never be carried out without that person's consent unless the patient was unable to understand the nature and consequences of that operation. The Commissioner found no evidence that sterilization was necessary for the woman's health. He judged that acting in breach of D.H.S.S. guidance, which he had never read, the consultant was at fault.[29]

This example is by no means the only case where the Commissioner has inquired into lack of full consent, an issue which as we saw in Chapter 4 can give rise to litigation. The restriction on the Commissioner's power to investigate cases which might go to court is mitigated in two ways. He alone decides the matter, and he is directed to consider not whether a court case is technically possible but whether in all the circumstances it is reasonable to expect that complainant to go to court. Informed consent is a legal hot potato. Litigation could have been contested all the way to the House of Lords and resulted in relatively low compensation even if successful. The Commissioner rightly took on the complaint.

Other cases where a court remedy looks more straightforward sometimes come before the Commissioner. A Caesarian section resulted in injury to a patient who had had problems with anaesthesia in earlier surgery. The complainant alleged that records of her previous difficulties were not transferred to her obstetric records, that her own warnings were ignored, and that her complaint was badly and unsympathetically dealt with. Her first two allegations are of simple negligence. The Commissioner nevertheless agreed to investigate the case in return for an undertaking that the complainant would not take legal proceedings.[30] This has become a common practice.[31] The undertaking is not legally binding and there is nothing to stop a complainant assuring the Commissioner he will not sue and then launching proceedings on the basis of evidence uncovered by the Commissioner. Apparently this has happened only twice. Of course, if it was a regular occurrence the

Commissioner might feel bound to reject all cases where there was any possibility, however remote, of court action.

Is the restriction on dual access to the Commissioner and the courts justifiable? The Commissioner seems to think so. In 1980 he expressed his concern that he might be used to provide a free investigation service to enable potential litigants to decide whether or not to sue.[32] Is there anything wrong with that? We have seen the tremendous difficulties faced by patients in litigation. If negligence has resulted in injury, and investigation as opposed to adversary litigation discovers that negligence, the patient ought to get compensation. His only crime is that he has not played the game by the old English rules. The rules are wrong.

The Commissioner and clinical judgment

It is generally accepted, except by the medical profession, that the exclusion of clinical judgment from review by the Commissioner is the most serious limitation on his effectiveness. Public concern about errors of clinical judgment is illustrated by the fact that out of 446 complaints rejected as outside the Commissioner's jurisdiction, 150 related to clinical judgment.[33] The 1977 Act provides that the Commissioner may not investigate any '. . . action taken in connection with the diagnosis of illness or the care or treatment of a patient being action which, in the opinion of the Commissioner in question, was taken solely in consequence of the exercise of clinical judgment . . .'

Narrowly and literally interpreted, this limitation could have put senior doctors at least beyond the Commissioner's reach. Successive Commissioners have declined to follow that path. In the case discussed earlier, of the woman with epilepsy sterilized without her consent, the consultant first raised the 'defence' of clinical judgment. The Commissioner's finding that the consultant's decision was not founded on any decision that sterilization was necessary for her health enabled him to continue his investigation. In 1979–80 a complaint by a woman who had undergone mastectomy and was refused a breast prosthetic on the N.H.S. was investigated. The consultant argued that he never authorized prosthetics, that they were unnecessary and purely cosmetic. The Commissioner rejected his claim that the decision was arrived at in the exercise of clinical judgment. It had nothing to do with treating the complainant's illness; it was not a medical decision. The Commissioner condemned the refusal.[34] One final example: a consultant genuinely

133

concerned with the accessibility of records and X-rays refused to honour an appointment with a patient when the X-rays and records failed to be delivered. He would not even remove the plaster on his leg. The Commissioner found the doctor at fault. His concern for proper access to records was commendable. He may have been in the right in his dispute with the administration but he did not treat that patient properly. Nor could he claim that he acted in the exercise of clinical judgment. His course of action was not related to the care of the patient before him.[35]

Despite the Commissioner's activism in restricting clinical judgment to its proper sphere, strictly medical decisions on the treatment of the individual patient, the exemption of clinical judgment still causes concern. Drawing the line is very difficult. The Commissioner is, as we have seen, unhappy about arrangements for discharge. He cannot, however, question the original medical decision that the patient is fit for discharge. The case of the elderly lady discharged after having been scalded and after a fall exemplifies his problem. The essence of that complaint would seem to be whether she should have been discharged at all.

The Select Committee on the Health Service Commissioner has urged since 1978 that the Commissioner's jurisdiction be extended to cover clinical judgment.[36] Previous Commissioners have seemed less keen. The introduction of review of clinical judgment is seen as bringing radical change to the office. Senior medical staff would need to be attracted to the Commissioner's staff.[37] And the Commissioner has expressed fears of complainants using the investigation as a pre-litigation service. The Commissioner felt that investigation should only be allowed if a choice between the Commissioner and the courts could be made binding. If you went to the Commissioner, you would be barred from court.[38] I have already condemned this as a misguided view. The present Commissioner, Anthony Barraclough Q.C., has yet to give his personal views on the question. At present the debate on clinical judgment and the Commissioner is at stalemate. In 1981 the revised D.H.S.S. code introduced a new procedure for examining clinical judgment.[39] The Select Committee on the Health Service Commissioners gave it a cautious welcome.[40] The Commissioner when he rejects a complaint because it concerns clinical judgment will advise the complainant of this new procedure which we will now examine.

Professional review of clinical judgment[41]

The initial stage of dealing with a complaint raising a question of clinical judgment remains in the hands of the district administrator. Where the complainant remains unhappy, the complaint is referred to the regional health authority's medical officer. He will discuss the case with the consultant and attempt to conciliate. If this stage fails to resolve the matter the complaint becomes the subject of independent professional review.

Independent professional review is intended to deal with substantial complaints not likely to give rise to court action and not suitable for the formal inquiry procedures available to the health authority. For professional review two independent consultants in active practice in the specialty will be appointed. They will be nominated by the Joint Consultants' Committee, which represents the Royal Colleges and the B.M.A. One should be a doctor from a comparable hospital working in another region. These 'second opinions', as the circular calls them, are to have access to all clinical records, and to meet with the complainant, the consultant, and any other medical staff involved. Their meeting with the complainant is to explore his medical problems, and if they find the complaint unjustified they attempt to allay his anxieties and explain to him what happened. At the end of their investigation the 'second opinions' report to the regional health authority advising on any action to be taken. The complainant will not see the report. He will be told of any action to be taken. Action contemplated seems generally directed at preventing the recurrence of similar incidents. The 'second opinions' have no coercive powers and cannot award compensation. They can presumably recommend invocation of formal inquiry procedures. The 'second opinions' scheme has not yet been the subject of detailed analysis. At first sight it seems rather lacking in teeth and uncertain of its role. Is it an effective means of investigating patient complaints for the benefit of aggrieved patients? What rights have complainants? Controversy flared in 1986 when a consultant acting as a 'second opinion' refused to go ahead with a meeting with elderly parents complaining about their son's death because they wanted a community health council official to help them present their case.[42]

Health authority inquiries

Where at any stage in an investigation of a complaint further action is found to be necessary, the matter may be referred on to the regional health authority. The authority may appoint one or more of its own members to look into the complaint, or in serious cases may set up an independent inquiry.[43] The inquiry will be conducted by a small committee consisting usually of a legally qualified chairman and two medical practitioners, one from the same specialty as the person whose competence is in issue. All inquiring members will be unconnected with the hospital where the complaint originated. Copies of all documents are circulated to all parties. The complainant and the subjects of the complaint may be legally represented, and cross-examination of witnesses is allowed. Legal aid is not available, and no one can be compelled to attend the inquiry. The committee's findings of fact are then submitted to the staff concerned for further comment. Finally the committee reports its findings and recommendations to the authority.

The inquiry procedure can be effective. We shall see later that it can also be cumbersome and unfair. And if hospital staff refuse co-operation the procedure may break down altogether. In 1976 Elizabeth Shewin entered hospital for a gall-bladder operation. In the course of the operation she suffered irreversible brain damage. On the advice of their medical defence union, all ten doctors involved with Miss Shewin refused to give evidence to the inquiry. They finally agreed to appear on condition that the authority met any costs and award that might result if court action were later taken. The inquiry discovered that Miss Shewin's injury resulted from her being given nitrous oxide instead of oxygen because of an improvised and inadequate repair to anaesthetic equipment in the operating theatre. Miss Shewin's relatives sued the authority for negligence and won damages of £262,500. The authority in turn sued the manufacturers of the anaesthetic equipment.[44] The doctors were virtually exonerated.

In a second example, a 26-year-old man, David Woodhouse, entered hospital in 1981 for an appendectomy. He never regained consciousness and ten months later still lay in a coma. Pressure from M.P.s led the health authority to set up an inquiry. Again, on the advice of their defence union the doctors refused to testify. The inquiry was abandoned. The authority then asked three independent experts to examine the case. They reported on a series of disasters. For example, the anaesthetist's command of English was poor, he could not spell the names of basic drugs, and neither he nor the duty registrar knew how to use the ventilator. Mr Woodhouse was left without oxygen for 20 minutes. The health authority promised to tighten up procedures. An out of court settlement was reached to pay compensation to David Woodhouse and his family.

Inquiries by the Health Minister

The National Health Service Act 1977 section 89 empowers the Health Minister to '. . . cause an inquiry to be held in any case where he deems it advisable to do so in connection with any matter arising under this Act'. At such an inquiry all those involved may be compelled to attend, to produce documents, and if the person appointed to hold the inquiry sees fit all evidence may have to be given on oath. The Health Minister rarely uses his coercive power. M.P.s pressed him to do so in the David Woodhouse case. He refused. Inquiries by the Health Minister are at present limited to cases of national scandal, such as ill-treatment of mental patients or the conditions at Stanley Royde Hospital which led to an outbreak of salmonella food poisoning. Successive Ministers have argued that their power to order an inquiry was not intended for use in cases of individual error or even gross incompetence. His powers are to be invoked only to protect the public at large. Yet serious cases of accidents involving individuals may reveal dangers to the public. The Minister refused to order an inquiry in the Woodhouse case despite tremendous pressure in Parliament.[45] The authority's own endeavours revealed grave risks to anyone accepting anaesthesia in the area. Was it not in the public interest that this be revealed? Are prospective patients not entitled to know that their health authority may be employing doctors whose knowledge of English and resuscitation procedures may be lamentably and dangerously inadequate?

Evaluating inquiry procedures

At first sight the trouble with inquiry procedures is that the Health Minister's powers are reserved for national *causes célèbres* and that health authority inquiries have no teeth. Look more deeply at the problem and the cause lies partly in the defensive attitude of the doctors. Too often they will not co-operate. Advised by his insurer, if there is the slightest chance of litigation the doctor stays silent. Yet the Shewin case shows that an inquiry may exonerate the doctor and remove the taint of suspicion which might impede his career. What can be done?

Patients might well answer that doctors should be forced to co-operate. After all, within the N.H.S. they are the employees of the health authority. It is a strange situation where an employer cannot require his employee to explain conduct that has resulted in injury to the 'clients of the business'. Other people whose error may result in injury to persons are made to co-operate. After every rail accident involving casualties, an inquiry is held and every British Rail employee involved is required to give evidence. The inspector holding the inquiry then publishes a report giving his findings of fact and the name of anyone found to be negligent and responsible for the accident. Very often the inquiry report reveals not individual incompetence but some defect in the system or unforeseeable event.

Are doctors to be treated differently from railmen? An objection based solely on the distinction between an ancient profession and the artisan cuts little ice today. Real objections are three-fold: fear of baseless complaints, fear of litigation and fear of publicity. Baseless complaints do not evaporate. Refusal to attend an inquiry may generate more attention than co-operation with the inquiry. The Woodhouse case did. Any sensible person knows full well that doctors are vulnerable to unjustified attack. In grief, pain and bereavement some people will always turn on the doctor. Refusing to help in the investigation of complaints just makes matters worse. Where a doctor will not explain his action and help in discovering what went wrong, the general reaction may be that there is no smoke without fire. For the sake of every 'guilty' doctor protected by medical defensiveness from the consequences of an error, an 'innocent' and competent doctor is left tainted by suspicion.

Fear of litigation is a constant theme. Why should the doctor assist a patient to find evidence against him? Every hospital doctor, at least, is insured. Any compensation will not come out of his own pocket. He may find that eventually insurance premiums rise generally. But the risk of a cash award against him seems an unlikely reason for litigation phobia. Is it right to expose the doctor to double-jeopardy, to the inquiry and then to a suit for malpractice? The patient, some say, should choose. He should shut up or sue. More moderate voices urge a compromise: allow investigations but make access to investigations conditional on forfeiting the right to go to court for compensation. This compromise, we saw, has the backing of the Health Service Commissioner himself. I reject it. The root cause of disquiet is that in England we are just not accustomed to doing justice by way of investigation. The adversary game rules. The lawyers devise the rules. Doctors cannot be blamed for playing by them. Some doctors are beginning to reject them.[46]

Finally, what about the fear of publicity which is closely allied to fear of litigation? We have already said that refusing co-operation may not make publicity go away. Co-operation may clear the doctor. Perhaps that is a little naïve. The press may well latch on to the start of an inquiry. A story may appear on the front page detailing the complainant's allegation that Dr X amputated his left leg unnecessarily, while drunk and flirting with the nurses in the theatre. Two days later a sentence hidden away in the middle of the paper reports the doctor's exoneration. Doctors are vulnerable to bad publicity. Statistically they must be at far, far greater risk of baseless complaint after a medical accident than the railman after a rail accident. Their career can be put at risk. Their private practice will be threatened. Surely it is not beyond the wit of the lawyers and politicians to devise procedures with which all staff must co-operate but which protects their privacy up until the stage that findings and recommendations are made?

Who should judge clinical judgments?

Finally, any proposal for change must tackle this thorny problem. It is too early to evaluate independent professional review where the medical profession polices itself. The fact that the complainant never receives the 'second opinions' report and that no one other than a doctor is involved in the process may detract from the scheme's independence in the public eye. The ultimate answer lies in co-operation between the profession and independent opinion. The Select Committee continues to press for the Health Service Commissioner to be free to look into clinical judgment. He would need qualified medical staff. A formal post of Deputy Commissioner (Medical) could perhaps be created.

Any reform needs the goodwill of the medical profession. To call for reform is not to doubt the concern of the profession for their patients or their commitment to the highest standards of health care. Doctors must be persuaded to shed certain misconceptions and to abandon defensive attitudes to patients. Accountability for error cannot be avoided for ever. Thorough investigation is better than a strategic campaign to avoid inquiries. Avoiding inquiry may create damaging publicity for the profession as a whole. Co-operating with the inquiry may, as the Shewin case did, prove the doctors to be innocent of blame. Doctors must be more open to inquiry when things go wrong. Patients must learn that medical accidents, like any other accident, can happen without anyone being to blame. Above all, though, there must be a political will for change. The Hospital Complaints Procedures Act offers an unparalleled opportunity to act.

Ensuring, as is proposed, that complaints are initially dealt with swiftly in the hospital where the patient received treatment is a valuable first step. It does not go far enough. The whole maze of assorted complaints procedures should be reviewed and rationalized.

The Wendy Savage affair[47]

I have examined so far inadequacies of N.H.S. complaints procedures as perceived by patients. Events in 1985 highlighted aspects of health authority inquiry procedures profoundly disturbing to doctors. Tower Hamlets Health Authority suspended Wendy Savage, a consultant obstetrician and senior lecturer at the London Hospital. Allegations of incompetence were laid against her by her colleagues, and a health authority inquiry was launched. Charges against her focused on her handling of five maternity cases, accusing Mrs Savage of allowing sympathy for women wanting a natural birth to override her professional judgment and endangering mother and child. In only one of the cases cited against Mrs Savage had a patient complained. Two patients were outraged that their treatment was being used as evidence against a doctor whom they trusted and backed implicitly. They were also horrified when their confidential medical records were made public at the inquiry. The Savage inquiry was, in essence, not an inquiry into complaints of unsatisfactory treatment by patients, but a public ventilation of professional disagreements.

The procedure at the inquiry left much to be desired. The initiation of the complaint by colleagues of a doctor, rather than patients, cannot be faulted in principle. Protection of patients requires that procedures exist to allow practitioners to air their concern about the practices or competence of a colleague. Fundamentally there are *three* flaws in the inquiry procedure revealed by the highly publicized Savage inquiry. (1) Before the start of an inquiry immense power rests in the hands of the health authority chairman. The decision to suspend a doctor is his. Allegations have been made that health authority chairmen are over-free with the use of this power to suspend hoping that, unlike Mrs Savage, the suspended doctors will simply resign quietly.[48] (2) The inquiry is not an *investigation*. The procedure at the Savage inquiry resembled a criminal trial. A Q.C. engaged by the authority 'prosecuted' Wendy Savage. He called medical experts who saw her practices as unsound and leapt on any error they could discern. Mrs Savage's counsel 'defended' her. Experts favourable to her had their say. At no stage did an observer feel that a difficult problem of correct obstetric practice was being objectively investigated. (3) Mrs Savage was effectively 'on trial'. Yet she had no automatic claim to the support of her protection society as would have been the case had she faced a civil suit for negligence. The M.D.U. at first refused to fund Mrs Savage's 'defence' by the lawyers of her choice. They did eventually agree and assist her.

The Savage inquiry demonstrated once again that English legislators and lawyers seem incapable of devising a genuinely investigatory procedure. It showed too that a procedure designed to consider complaints by patients is ill-equipped for use either as a forum for debate on what constitutes good medical practice or to resolve difficulties between colleagues antipathetic to each other. Wendy Savage was acquitted of all charges of incompetence. Getting her back in her post against the continued hostility of some other doctors has proved a tougher battle for her and for the health authority now obliged to reinstate her.

Chapter 9
Radical Reform: An End to Fault Liability

In earlier chapters in this Part, I examined the present system for compensating injured patients and investigating patients' complaints and found both to be unsatisfactory. The medical profession perceives an action for negligence against a doctor as an attack on his professional integrity and a potential blight on his career. Backed by the medical defence societies, and aided by the skill of expensive lawyers, every opportunity provided by our adversary system of litigation may be invoked to defeat the patient's claim. Furthermore, the defensive attitude engendered by the law relating to malpractice actions carries over into the way in which the profession and health authorities react to any form of complaint. I have suggested that to some extent the doctors' fears are misplaced. The function of the tort of negligence is to compensate an individual injured by another's error, not to adjudicate on a defendant doctor's general competence. I have further sought to explain that complaints procedures as often exonerate the doctor as condemn him. Very often all a patient wants is an explanation of what went wrong; he is not gunning for the doctor. Better communication between lawyers and doctors might alter such medical attitudes. But what must be recognized is that there is reasonable cause for the doctors' concern. It is all very well to say that the action for negligence has little to do with blame. To the non-lawyer the term negligence itself connotes blame, neglect, carelessness and so on. The conduct of litigation creates an atmosphere of conflict. The patient may not start out with any intention of harassing the doctor. The rules of 'the game' of litigation ensure that at the end a 'me against him' mentality exists. The spectre of a malpractice action hangs over complaints procedures too. There the doctor is haunted by the risk that by co-operating fully he may provide incriminating evidence against himself.

The rules of the game cry out for reform. Certain changes to improve the present law have already been discussed. What I consider now is whether the time has come to change the game. Should the action for medical malpractice be replaced by an entirely new scheme to compensate for injuries arising out of medical misadventure? What is proposed, and now receives support from many doctors, is a system of no-fault compensation. Under such a system a patient who suffers injury in the course of medical treatment would receive compensation without any need to prove that the medical staff involved were at fault. We shall look at the arguments advanced in favour of such a scheme, consider how similar schemes operate abroad, and begin to examine the problems of implementing a no-fault compensation scheme.

An attack on tort

Criticism of the tort of negligence as a means of compensating for personal injury however caused, whether by medical error or in a road accident or any other area of human activity, is far from new.[1] The tort system has been condemned as unpredictable, expensive and unfair.[2] These criticisms are as valid today as they ever were.

The nature of the tort system is unpredictable. The injured person, on whom the burden of proving negligence falls, cannot know in advance whether he will receive any monetary compensation. This has damaging consequences. The claimant cannot plan his personal finances and put his life in order. For example, a person rendered paraplegic in an accident cannot know whether he will be able to afford to convert his house to meet the limitations imposed by his new disability. The uncertainty and delay as he fights his claim through the courts may even impede his recovery to health.

The tort system is expensive because of the enormous cost of pro-tracted litigation. A part of the cost is already borne by the state. Where the claimant is legally aided the state funds his claim, perhaps with nothing to show for it in the end. The cost of courts and officials to man the system comes again from the state. The prohibitive price of litigation may deter some claimants with a genuine case from pursuing it if they are not wealthy but are sufficiently well off to fall outside provision for legal aid. The expense of any no-fault scheme, often given as an argument against its introduction, must be measured against the existing total cost of the tort system. The National Consumer Council claims that for every £1 awarded as compensation 85p is eaten up by the costs.[3]

Most of all the tort system is not fair. First, the difficulties and cost of litigation place enormous pressure on a claimant to settle for less than full compensation. Second, the dividing line between negligence and no-negligence is paper thin. Think back to the controversial case of

Whitehouse v. *Jordan*,[4] discussed at length in earlier chapters. The experts were divided on whether Mr Jordan acted wrongly when delivering the child. The judges were divided. At the end of the day Mrs Whitehouse went away without a penny. Yet the opposite outcome would have been equally unfair to Mr Jordan. He came into the case late at night for the first time. He pursued a course many distinguished experts backed. Others disagreed. To condemn him on that basis would have been inappropriate. This feature of the law of tort, the need to apportion blame for medical accidents and the difficulty of doing so, has attracted criticism from the judiciary as well as from doctors and academics. Finally, the tort system has been attacked as unfair on the grounds that it lacks any proper moral basis. What is the justification for giving X, who can attribute his injury to human error, full compensation, and leaving Y, whose injury has some other cause, to struggle along on state benefits?

The Pearson Report[5]

Criticism of the operation of the law of tort and the introduction of alternative compensation schemes elsewhere in the world led to the creation in 1973 of the Royal Commission on Civil Liability and Compensation for Personal Injury chaired by a Law Lord, Lord Pearson. The Pearson Commission was set up to consider to what extent, in what circumstances and by what means, compensation should be payable in respect of death and personal injury. They were specifically instructed to examine the tort system in the light of other provision made for compensation, whether via insurance or social security benefits.

The Pearson Commission reported in 1978. They advised against wholesale abolition of the tort of negligence as a means of compensating personal injuries. They made a number of specific proposals for more limited reforms. We concentrate on the proposals which relate to medical and drug-induced injuries. The Commission decided against recommending a no-fault scheme for all medical injuries.[6] They did propose a scheme whereby the government would become strictly liable to victims of vaccine damage[7] and those conducting medical research would be strictly liable for injury caused to volunteers in the course of clinical trials.[8] The Report further recommended the introduction of strict liability against producers of defective drugs.[9] And they urged, too, the creation of new disability allowances for all severely handicapped children irrespective of whether their handicap resulted from anyone else's fault.[10] The Commission further said that although in 1978 they had decided against an overall no-fault scheme for medical accidents, some Commission members found the question difficult and saw the arguments for and against as finely balanced.[11] All agreed that circumstances might change, calling for review of the Commission's decision, and accordingly the progress of no-fault schemes elsewhere, particularly in Sweden and New Zealand, should be studied and assessed.

The Commission's Report has gathered dust ever since. Their major proposals in all fields have gone largely unheeded. In the medical field we have seen that a half-hearted attempt to create a compensation scheme for vaccine damage was made. No change has been made in the law on clinical trials, although we shall see that in practice drug companies are largely operating a no-fault scheme voluntarily. Strict liability for drug damage is on its way. The reform comes not as a result of the Pearson Report but because of pressure from Europe. The legislation to be enacted here contains the development risks defence expressly condemned by Pearson. Review of foreign 'no-fault' schemes is under way under the aegis of the British Medical Association and other doctors' groups, and by a Labour Party working group. No government action has yet been taken.

The case for a medical 'no-fault' scheme

The case for a no-fault scheme is made out in part by the manifest defects of the present tort-based system. It is beyond the scope of this book to consider whether a comprehensive no-fault scheme for all types of accidents should be introduced. We must concentrate on the specific issue of medical injury. One of the grounds on which the Pearson Commission rejected a *general* scheme for all medical accidents must be taken note of by subsequent champions of such a scheme. The Commission argued that the tort, fault-based system, served a valuable purpose in emphasizing the accountability and responsibility of *individual* medical staff. They could not hide behind a bureaucratic smokescreen. However, the major reason for the Commission's rejection of a general scheme was the problem of causation. The Commission felt that distinguishing between an injury arising from treatment given and the natural progression of disease or inescapable side-effects of treatment was just too difficult. They were anxious too about the overall cost of any no-fault scheme and the way in which it could be designed to cover public and private medicine. Moreover, the Commission seemed unimpressed by what they had seen of the no-fault scheme already operating in New Zealand.

The objections of the only official body to investigate a change to no-fault provision must be answered if the case for change is to stand up. I consider that although the Commission's concern about causation is valid the problem of causation is insufficient reason to rule out a change to no-fault compensation. Causation presents just as much of a problem within the present system. Reform of the law introducing the no-fault principle would have the following benefits. A greater number of claimants would obtain compensation to help them adapt their lives to their disabilities or to meet the financial loss resulting from death of a breadwinner. The damage done to relations between the medical profession and the public by bitter and protracted litigation would be removed. The link between compensation for the patient and blame for the doctor would be broken. The patient would obtain compensation because he suffered as a result of treatment going wrong. The issue of *why* it went wrong and the doctor's competence as a doctor would be for completely separate investigatory procedures. The problem of causation would still be there. Nevertheless, distinguishing between injury and the progression of disease or whatever would be made easier in one sense. The issue of causation would be *investigated*. It would not be part of a battle between the patient and the doctor, with the doctor having a vested interest in finding experts to deny that the patient's condition was caused by the treatment.

The overall cost of a no-fault scheme is difficult to judge. The Commission did not go into this in detail, and before any new scheme could be finally agreed detailed costings and projections would be necessary. Any cost-benefit analysis must take into account the costs of the present system. The Commission's final concerns, the operation of a scheme to cover public and private medicine and the difficulties they had noted in New Zealand, are important points to which we attempt later to provide some response.

The Pearson Commission recognized that the case for a no-fault scheme for medical injury was sufficiently strong for it to be likely that at some later stage the issue might be reviewed again. Since 1978 when their Report was published and shelved, medical litigation has increased markedly. The courts are being pushed to extend the boundaries of the existing fault-based system. In general judges refuse to do so, backing, as the patient sees it, the doctor against the patient. This does nothing to improve public confidence in the courts or the medical profession. A marked change in judicial attitude, a willingness to extend the concept of negligence to embrace a greater number of medical errors, has equal if different dangers. The risk of the practice of defensive medicine as happens in the U.S.A. is real if sometimes exaggerated. Take once again the example of *Whitehouse* v. *Jordan*. Had Mr Jordan been found liable, what would have been the likely reaction of his colleagues? The legally 'safe' option would become to resort to Caesarian section at the least hint of a problem. Thousands of women who since 1981 have enjoyed normal if difficult deliveries would have been subjected to surgery.

As litigation increases, so does the dissatisfaction of the medical profession with the present state of the law. This is scarcely to be wondered at. The immediate consequence has been a sharp rise in the doctors' insurance premiums, although doctors' premiums are still lower than those paid by many other professionals. The doctors' unhappiness with the present system is not based on pure self-interest. Any no-fault scheme would be likely to draw at least part of its resources from the doctors' pockets. Despite this, doctors increasingly back a change in the system. The B.M.A. set up its own internal working party to investigate no-fault liability and has now initiated talks with the lawyers. For many doctors, the fear of ever-expanding medical litigation here, and the spectre of American-style extensions in liability, convince them that '. . . progress towards a full no-fault system could be much preferable'.[12]

Experience abroad[13]

A growing number of no-fault compensation schemes operate abroad. I outline only two, the New Zealand accident compensation scheme, which covers medical injury within comprehensive provision for compensation for personal injury from all causes, and the Swedish Patients' Insurance Scheme, designed specifically for medical injuries. Review of New Zealand's and Sweden's experience will highlight certain problems of no-fault liability. They are problems which should be taken as instruction in mistakes to avoid rather than as indication that the whole idea of no-fault liability should be avoided. In this brief review of both schemes I concentrate on how the basic principle of no-fault liability works. Space does not allow me to consider in detail the funding and administration of either scheme. I believe that what must be accepted initially is the principle of change. How it is to be effected can then be investigated in a positive spirit lacking in earlier reviews.

The New Zealand scheme[14] is administered by the Accident Compensation Corporation. About 130,000 claims a year are made to the Corporation, whose remit is to award compensation to anyone who has suffered 'personal injury by accident'. Personal injury by accident is defined as including 'medical, surgical, dental or first aid misadventure'. Damage caused exclusively by disease, infection or the ageing process is specifically excluded. The distinction between damage caused by medical misadventure and that resulting from disease poses the Commission its first problem *re* medical injuries. The distinction has also been criticized as unfair. There may be two elderly women side by side in a hospital ward. One has suffered a stroke in the course of minor surgery and is awarded compensation for medical misadventure. The other suffered hers by Act of God and gets nothing. The New Zealand Commission, whose report led to the implementation of the accident compensation scheme, hoped that eventually the scheme would embrace disease as well as accident.

The second difficulty for the Commission in claims for medical injury lies in applying the concept of accident and the term 'misadventure' to damage suffered when something goes wrong with medical treatment. Failure to give treatment at all has not generally been classified as misadventure. The birth of a child after a failed sterilization has not led to compensation unless the claimant can point to some specific error in the surgery itself. Misadventure has been defined, in the course of a report rejecting a claim for compensation for failure to arrange adequate treatment, as:

. . . injury or damage . . . caused by mischance or accident, unexpected and undesigned in the nature of medical error or medical mishap.

Applying this definition to three cases in England where the plaintiff failed to win compensation, it is clear that one at least of the claimants would have failed also in New Zealand. In *Ashcroft* v. *Mersey A.H.A.*[15] the surgeon accidentally cut into a nerve in the course of delicate facial surgery. He was acquitted of any negligence. A claim in New Zealand would have succeeded because although the surgeon could not be blamed, the patient's injury was unexpected and undesigned, an unfortunate mischance. Mrs Whitehouse,[16] had she claimed in New Zealand in respect of the brain damage suffered by her son, would have faced no less acute difficulty in establishing that his injuries resulted from Mr

Jordan's use of forceps. Moreover, as everything Mr Jordan did was by design, the issue of whether the baby's injury resulted from misadventure might again turn on whether Mr Jordan's course of action was medically proper or not. Faced with catastrophic injury the Corporation has tended to be generous, and might have found that although Mr Jordan's attempt at normal delivery was in no way erroneous, the ultimate outcome was beyond what was expected and designed and qualified as medical mishap. The third of our trio of unsuccessful English plaintiffs, Mrs Sidaway,[17] would have failed in New Zealand as she failed here. She complained of her surgeon's failure to warn her of a well-known, albeit slight, inherent risk of the surgery to which she consented. The risk materialized and she suffered injury but there had been no accident, no misadventure. Everything went as the surgeon planned.

Medical misadventure has proved a difficult concept to apply in New Zealand. It has excluded from compensation some claimants, for example patients suffering from failure to treat, who might succeed in the tort of negligence. The tort of negligence is not entirely dead in New Zealand. Where his claim constitutes 'personal injury by accident' he must seek redress only through the compensation scheme. If his claim falls outside that scheme he may sue. Experience of the restrictive interpretation of medical misadventure may in future prompt more claimants to elect for the old common law remedy.

The Swedish Patients' Insurance Scheme[18] is expressly designed to provide compensation for medical injuries. How does the basis of no-fault liability then differ in Sweden from the New Zealand scheme? Compensation is payable in respect of any injury or illness resulting from any procedure related to health care. Injury arising from any diagnostic procedure, inappropriate medication, medical treatment or surgery thus falls within the ambit of the Swedish scheme. But compensation for such injury is subject to three important provisos. As in New Zealand, the injury must be proved to result from the procedure in issue, and not from the original disease. Injury resulting from a risk taken by the doctor to save life or prevent permanent disability is excluded. Most crucially, the claimant has to show that the procedure causing his injury was *not medically justified*. The test of whether the procedure was medically justified often re-introduces the question of negligence. Had Mrs Whitehouse claimed in Sweden, the central issue would have been whether Mr Jordan's delay in proceeding to Caesarian surgery was justified. Faced with balancing the risk of surgery against the risk of vaginal delivery, did he take the correct medical decision?[19] Certain claimants who lose in England will obtain compensation in Sweden. Mrs Ashcroft, who suffered injury to a facial nerve when the surgeon accidentally cut the nerve, would recover. The surgeon was not to blame, but cutting the nerve was not medically indicated.[20] Mrs Sidaway once again would probably lose in Sweden as she would in New Zealand and did in England.[21] The limitation in the Swedish scheme to injury arising from acts not medically justified is as restrictive as, if not more so than, the term 'medical misadventure' in New Zealand. What the Swedish scheme does embrace where New Zealand's does not is injury arising from failure to treat if the failure is not medically justified.

Examination of the deficiencies of the schemes operative in New Zealand and Sweden must not obscure their advantage. Patients uncompensated by a tort-based system benefit in those countries. The investigation of the cause of a medical mishap may still involve issues as to the doctor's negligence. But it is an investigation. The patient will discover what happened. The opportunities for scoring points, seeking to disclose as little as possible about what went wrong, and the advantages to be gained from having the best advocate rather than the best case, just do not exist in New Zealand or Sweden.

The way ahead for the U.K.

The experience of New Zealand and Sweden must be considered carefully and learned from. The basic structure of any scheme would be to redirect claims for compensation for medical injury away from the courts and towards an independent tribunal. Tribunal staff would initially investigate each claim. They would have access to all relevant records. Provision for hearings and appeal against an unfavourable initial decision would have to be made. Care would need to be taken to prevent the lawyers taking over the process and adding to its expense, formality and technicality. The underlying problems confronted in Sweden and New Zealand of defining the criteria for compensation would have to be faced. The basic premise of any British scheme would be the same. Compensation claims for personal injury would be made not in the courts against the doctor but to an administrative tribunal. Tribunal staff would examine medical notes and see the parties involved. There would be no adversarial hearing. Provision would need to be made for the grant of a hearing to the claimant where appropriate and for appeals by claimants dissatisfied by the initial decision. The distinction between injury resulting from disease and injury resulting from medical treatment is a problem we must probably live with. Ideally a system would be devised whereby the healthy provided funds to alleviate the discomfort and disadvantage of disability and disease, however caused. This is at present an ideal unlikely to be realized, and reform must have a more limited aim by replacing the tort of negligence by a fairer and less destructive system of compensation for medical injury.

The scheme proposed should embrace two categories of medical injury. (1) Injury or illness arising from an absence of, or delay in, appropriate medical treatment[22] provided that (i) treatment would have prevented that injury or illness, and (ii) a reasonable request for medical care from a person or authority under an obligation to provide care has been made by the patient or some other person acting on his behalf. (2) Injury or illness resulting from medical treatment provided that (i) the injury or illness is not caused by the natural progression of disease or the ageing process, and (ii) the injury or illness is not the consequence of an unavoidable risk inherent in the treatment of which the patient has received proper warning.

Category 1 would cover injury arising from failure to treat, both in circumstances where the present tort of negligence would operate and where it would not. For example, today a request for treatment might be made and not acted on by the G.P. because at the time he acted reasonably in thinking an immediate visit was not necessary. Events prove him wrong. They do not render him negligent. Under this proposed no-fault scheme the patient would recover because he did in fact suffer as a result of lack of treatment, albeit no one was to blame.

Category 2 is more difficult to define. Very careful drafting of any legislation will be called for, and I do not attempt that formidable task. The intention of category 2 is that it should extend to any damage to the patient which is neither the result of the natural progression of his original disease or condition nor a consequence inherent in that treatment and unavoidable if that treatment is to be successful. Under that last limitation the side-effects of certain surgery and therapy would be excluded. At one level the patient could obviously not recover compensation for pain and suffering ordinarily attendant on surgery. At another level unpleasant and dangerous side-effects, for example the patient's hair falling out during chemotherapy or the risk of a stroke in some forms of brain surgery, would have to be excluded if they were inescapable in the pursuit of proper treatment. One important proviso is attached to the exclusion of unavoidable side-effects from compensation. The patient must have been properly warned. Failure to give proper warning, which results in injury unexpected and unconsidered by the patient, would remain a ground for compensation. What amounts to proper warning may remain a ground for controversy.

Ways and means

My emphasis on principle rather than detail does not mean I am blind to the problems inherent in setting up a no-fault scheme or to its potential cost. But until the impetus for reform is sufficiently cogent, any examination of ways and means may be an exercise in attempting to find insuperable problems.

The means adopted in Sweden to provide finance and to administer the scheme, however, recommend themselves. An insurance-based scheme would draw on resources already employed in making compensation payments and fighting compensation claims. Funds in Sweden are drawn from the authorities maintaining public health facilities and from doctors and clinics operating in the private sector. Similar provision could be made here for levying premiums on the regional health authorities and private care organizations. The need for resources here is likely to be greater than in Sweden. Benefits paid in Sweden are limited to what is needed to 'top up' their already generous social security system. A levy on individual practitioners would almost certainly be required. This should be no greater than their present contribution to professional insurance premiums. The financial equation to be worked out is this. Total compensation payments under a no-fault scheme will increase. Will that increase be greater than the total now spent on compensation and expensive, protracted litigation?

Drugs and medical injuries[23]

Finally, we must look at the relationship between drug-induced injury and medical injury. We have seen how the distinction operates at present, often denying a patient any remedy because he cannot establish whether he was damaged because the doctor prescribed negligently or because there was some inherent defect in the drug. Present plans to introduce strict liability for defective drugs have been shown to be somewhat defective themselves. How would a no-fault scheme for drugs operate and how would it relate to the medical injury scheme?

Under a no-fault scheme for drugs, the first benefit to ensue would be an end to the kind of unproductive expensive lawsuits discussed in Chapter 7. A patient injured by a drug would receive compensation without need to prove the company negligent, or the drug defective. It would be no answer to a claim that the damage to the patient resulted from some condition peculiar to him. Question of whether risk to a particular group was sufficiently great to be taken into account would cease to be relevant. The drug companies could save a great deal of money which they now spend on lawyers. Compensation would be paid even where the manufacturer cannot be identified, for example where the patient took a generic drug and records to trace the manufacturer are unavailable. Issues of the balance of risk versus benefit of a drug would be removed from the courts. A dilemma posed by some drugs is this. They benefit 99.9 per cent of us and damage 0.1 per cent. Under no-fault the 0.1 per cent would get proper compensation. And the issue of whether they should ever have been exposed to that risk is properly and impartially investigated, not submitted to the adversary atmosphere of a court. Causation remains an inescapable problem. But as with medical injury, I believe that investigation of a claim for no-fault compensation is more likely to reveal the truth than a battle in court with the drug company having a vested interest in disclosing as little as possible.

The central problem to be tackled in implementing a no-fault scheme will be whether it should be separate from or incorporated within a medical injuries scheme. My preference would be for incorporation and a definition of medical treatment including drug-induced damage. That way, resources for the unified scheme could be maximized, with the drug companies contributing. Against unification lies the argument that inclusion of drug-induced damage, and so potentially another thalidomide disaster, would impose too great a strain and imbalance on the scheme's resources. But some relationship between medical and drug-induced injury must be worked out to ensure that no future patient falls between the two stools, ending up admittedly injured but unable to get himself into the right scheme to obtain compensation.

Compensation and blame

One of the prime aims of a no-fault compensation scheme is to separate compensation and blame. One of the fears expressed by opponents of no-fault is that the removal of the element of blame will lead to a decline in standards of competence and care. This must not happen. Any reform of the compensation system for medical and drug-induced injuries must be matched by a thorough review of complaints procedures. Detaching fault from compensation is necessary because, in the medical field at least, the finding of fault in a negligence action has little to do with ascertaining the doctor's real competence. The fault system damages medical care and doctors' relationships with patients. Doctors must accept though that freeing them from a fault-based compensation system must be paid for by the establishment of thorough *investigatory* procedures to deal with allegations of incompetence or want of care.

Part III

Matters of Life and Death

Chapter 10
Pregnancy and Childbirth

Conception to birth

Today medical care begins long before a baby is born. Research into the growth of the foetus in the womb has established the crucial importance of good ante-natal care. The thalidomide tragedy highlighted the vulnerability of the developing foetus. The drug thalidomide was prescribed to a number of pregnant women to help them sleep. It was described as non-toxic and safe for use by pregnant and nursing mothers. It was not safe. Many children were born without limbs and with other awful disabilities. The drug company denied negligence. A settlement was eventually reached, but not all the children received compensation because of dispute as to whether their disabilities did relate to the mothers' taking the drug.[1] A further difficulty for the children was that at the time of the birth of children deformed by the drug thalidomide, the courts had never decided whether doctors, or drug companies, or anyone at all, could be sued by children for injuries suffered by them before their birth.[2] So Parliament enacted the Congenital Disabilities (Civil Liability) Act 1976. The Act governs the child's rights only.

Can parents sue?

The parents of damaged children may be able to recover for their loss at common law. The doctor caring for the mother in pregnancy owes her a duty not only in relation to her own health but also to care for the health of the developing embryo. The damage which she will suffer if she bears a disabled child, the emotional trauma[3] *and* the financial burden of the extra expenses such a child brings with him, are readily foreseeable and recoverable. But will she be able (1) to prove negligence, and (2) to prove that the child's disability resulted from that negligence? Proving negligence is, as we have seen, no easy task in any malpractice claim. A claim in relation to the birth of a damaged child has two special problems of its own. First, if the claim lies against the doctor, it has to be established that he should have been aware of the risk posed to the embryo by drugs he prescribed or treatment he gave. Second, where a mother becomes ill in pregnancy or the pregnancy itself is complicated, the interests of mother and child may conflict. An ill or injured pregnant woman may need drugs or surgery known to carry some risk to the child. For example, a woman injured in an accident may need surgery which can only be carried out under general anaesthetic. The anaesthetic may harm the baby. The doctor's duty to the mother, his patient, is this. (1) He must consult and advise her, giving her sufficient information as to her needs and the risk to her baby. If she chooses to reject a particular course of treatment for the sake of her baby he cannot impose it. (2) He must in any case aim at a course of action which will benefit the mother with minimum risk to the child. Even if it can be shown that the doctor has failed in his duty to the mother, that he was negligent, establishing that the infant's disability resulted from that negligence is likely to be even more difficult.[4] Despite immense advances in knowledge concerning the development of the embryo, pinpointing the exact cause of a birth defect is extremely difficult. Success in a claim for negligence depends on proof that it is more likely than not that the relevant negligence caused the injury. All a claimant with a damaged child is likely to be able to prove is that a drug she took or treatment she received may have caused the defect in the baby. But equally it may be some inherited disease, some problem that she suffered in pregnancy, or some other unknown cause. So she may well fail to satisfy the burden of proof.

Congenital Disabilities (Civil Liability) Act 1976

This Act, passed to give rights and a remedy to children born disabled as a result of some human fault, is ambitious, complex, and now largely irrelevant. It is ambitious in that it sought to provide a scheme to protect children not just against negligence, such as drugs wrongly prescribed to mothers in pregnancy, but against any act at any stage of either parent's life which might lead ultimately to a disability affecting a child. Its complexity I will outline in succeeding sections. It is irrelevant because it fails to address the central problem in this type of claim. How do you prove that the disability resulted from an identifiable act of negligence? Just as his mother's claim is likely to founder for lack of proof of the cause of the disability, so is the child's. If Parliament intends and desires to give children disabled by human act a remedy, it must consider whether retaining the normal burden of proof in actions by mother and child is possible and workable.

We move on now to the complexity of the Act. The Act applies to all births after 1976, and purports to provide a comprehensive code of liability for disabled children in respect of damage caused to them before birth. Under the Act the child's mother[5] is generally exempt from any liability to her child. The father is offered no such immunity. The Act entirely replaces the common law and it would not be possible for a child unable to recover under the Act to argue that liability exists at common law. So, for example, a child seeking to sue his mother, exempt under the Act, must fail, however reckless her conduct in pregnancy and however clear it might be that she caused him to be born disabled.

The scheme of the Act is this. The child must be born alive.[6] He must establish that his disabilities resulted from an 'occurrence' which either (1) affected the mother or father in her or his ability to have a normal healthy child (pre-conception event), or (2) affected the mother during her pregnancy, or (3) affected mother or child in the course of its birth. At this first hurdle, proving the cause of the disability, many claims will fail. Where proof of cause is forthcoming the child faces further formidable obstacles. It is not enough to show that the person responsible for the occurrence was negligent. The child must prove that the person responsible for the occurrence was liable to the affected parent. The child's rights are derivative only. Of course the likelihood is that the occurrence at the time caused the parent no harm. Thalidomide's original effect was to sedate anxious mothers-to-be. So the Act provides that it is no answer that the parent affected suffered no visible injury at the time of the occurrence providing there was '. . . a breach of legal duty which, accompanied by injury, would have given rise to the liability'. The breach of duty is the negligence of the defendant in relation to the affected parent's reproductive capacity. Sandra Roberts recovered £334,769 in compensation for catastrophic damage she suffered during her mother's pregnancy.[7] A blood transfusion administered to her mother seven years before her birth rendered her parents rhesus incompatible, creating danger for any child of theirs. The hospital knew of Mrs Roberts's condition. They failed to act to prevent or minimize the risk to Sandra. This was negligent care of the mother and thus created a right to compensation for mother and via her for Sandra. Other cases are less straightforward.[8]

Drugs[9] and damage to the embryo

Let us take first what appears to be a simple case, the sort of case the Act was intended to remedy. A pregnant woman takes a drug which damages her baby and he is born disabled.

The drug was prescribed for her by her doctor. The child can prove that his disability results from the effect of the drug on the foetus. He will have to show that the doctor was negligent towards his mother. It must be proved that (1) the doctor knew or ought to have known that she was pregnant, and therefore was in breach of duty to her in prescribing a drug which might damage her baby, and (2) that he ought to have been aware of the risk posed by the drug. It will be no defence for the doctor to answer that far from injuring the mother the primary effect of the drug benefited her by, for example, ameliorating the symptoms of some common ailment, or helping her to relax or sleep. The doctor's responsibility to her embraces taking care to avoid harm to the child she carries. Two real difficulties arise. First, a general practitioner is judged by the standard of the reasonable, average G.P. He is not expected to be an expert on embryology or drug-related damage. Proving that he ought to have been aware of the risk of the drug may be awkward. Second, the doctor may be aware of the risk to the baby but argue that the risk to mother and child of not prescribing the drug is greater. This was the case, many English doctors suggested, with the drug Debendox, once commonly prescribed for morning sickness. Now it is alleged that it caused deformities in children whose mothers took the drug. A number of doctors (a) are still not entirely convinced by the available evidence that it caused deformities, and (b) argue that any slight risk was justifiable because of the danger and acute distress caused by continuing severe morning sickness. The drug has now been withdrawn in this country, but an action against a G.P. for prescribing it earlier would seem doomed to failure.

The doctor, of course, is not the only potential source of compensation for a drug-damaged child. Could the child sue the drug company? In such an action the central issue is whether the manufacturers ought to have been aware of the risk posed to unborn children. An extremely high standard of care will be demanded, and clinical tests on drugs must include research as to the effect of the drug on the foetus. A disabled child who overcame the enormous difficulties of proving that his disability resulted from the drug and that the drug was marketed as safe for use in pregnancy would be likely to succeed in any claim against the drug company. They would be shown to be negligent either in originally promoting the drug or in failing to withdraw it once evidence was available as to its inherent dangers. Of course the company must be judged on the state of knowledge at the time that the drug was made available to the mother, but unless a very long time elapses between the mother taking the drug and tests conducted by experts acting for the child, I would suggest that if a year or so later expert tests can demonstrate the drug's dangers, then the drug company's tests ought to have revealed those dangers earlier.

Having said all that, the essential problem remains actually proving that the drug caused the damage. In America negligence need not be proved in an action against a drug company. What a claimant need prove is that the drug did in fact cause damage. This is called product liability and I discuss it in detail in Chapter 7. An action was brought in the United States by disabled children whose mothers had taken Benedictin, a morning sickness drug manufactured by the same company which marketed Debendox in England. The action failed. They failed to prove that Benedictin caused their disabilities. The English parents, who allege that Debendox damaged their babies, fight on. They claim that Debendox, although much the same drug as Benedictin, had an extra component. That was the component, they argue, which caused the deformities in their babies. Parents and children face an uphill struggle.

Finally, an increasing number of medicines are now available without prescription. What is the responsibility of the drug company in such cases to an unborn child damaged because his mother took such a drug in pregnancy? First, ought the company to have known that the drug posed risks to unborn children? A high standard of care in testing drugs on general sale to the public will be demanded of the company, and the tests on the drugs must include tests for its potential effect on the foetus. But very many common medicines now carry a warning to the effect that pregnant women should not take them. Does that discharge the company's duty to an unborn child? The difficulty is that damage to a developing foetus may be caused before a woman knows that she is pregnant. It might be thought unreasonable to ban all preparations for coughs and colds and stomach upsets because of slight risk to the child of an unknowingly pregnant mother. If the risk is substantial, the court would have to determine whether the benefit to the community at large balanced the risk to the few.

A drug marketed without a warning to pregnant women and posing a substantial risk to the foetus may thus give rise to a claim by the baby.

The company's defence may be that section 1(7) of the Act provides that where the 'parent affected', the mother in this case, shares responsibility for the child being born disabled, damages may be reduced by an amount representing the extent of the mother's responsibility. The drug company may argue on these lines. A number of doctors strongly advise pregnant women, and women who think that they may be pregnant, to abstain from all medicines save those specifically prescribed for them. So can it be said that a pregnant woman who takes a proprietary medicine is partially responsible for any damage it does a baby? I think it unlikely. Women today are aware that many medicines do carry a warning against use in pregnancy. A medicine lacking such a warning may well be assumed to be safe. As for general warnings on drugs and pregnancy, medical advice is not consistent. As many doctors as those who would bar all medicines in early pregnancy advise that everyday preparations such as aspirin are quite safe. To reduce the child's damages because the mother was bemused by conflicting advice would seem entirely unfair.

Suing a doctor

I have already briefly mentioned the potential liability of the mother's G.P. in prescribing drugs for her. She will no doubt meet other doctors during ante-natal visits. One special feature of suing a doctor under the Act needs note: section 1(5) of the 1976 Act, 'the doctors' defence'.

The dilemma posed by drugs like Debendox and the differences of opinion that exist in the medical profession as to the management of pregnancy and childbirth are responsible for the inclusion of section 1(5). Inserted after pressure from the doctors, this sub-section says:

> The defendant is not answerable to the child, for anything he did or omitted to do when responsible in a professional capacity for treating or advising the parent, if he took reasonable care having due regard to the then received professional opinion applicable to the particular class of case; but this does not mean that he is answerable only because he departed from received opinion.

The aims of those who sought the inclusion of those words 'then received professional opinion' were probably twofold. First, they quite reasonably wanted it made clear that hindsight as to the effect of a drug or course of treatment should not prejudice a doctor, and second, less reasonably, they did not want the courts to adjudicate on the adequacy of received opinion. As the defendant's standard of care will always be tested by what was expected of the competent practitioner at the time of the alleged breach of duty, that first objective was met at common law and, as to the second, we have earlier seen that no court as yet has challenged in any medical negligence claim the received opinion of the profession. The final phrase of section 1(5), that the doctor is not to be answerable 'only because he departed from received opinion', might appear to the cynical to be an attempt by the medical profession to have their cake and eat it. Its practical importance is limited to this. In *Clark* v. *Maclennan*[10] (a claim relating to negligent treatment of a post-natal complication), Peter Pain J. said that where there is but one orthodox course of treatment and the doctor chooses to depart from that he must in effect provide evidence to justify that departure. Could a doctor defending a claim by a disabled child under the Act maintain that that approach is outlawed by the Act in such claims? One hopes not. All that is said is that the doctor cannot be answerable *only* because he departs from received opinion. The words of the Act are satisfied so long as the doctor is offered an opportunity to explain and justify his conduct.

Amniocentesis

Brief mention must be made at this point of the use of amniocentesis to diagnose foetal abnormalities. A needle is inserted through the mother's abdomen and the uterine wall into the sac surrounding the foetus. A small amount of the amniotic fluid surrounding the baby is removed. Tests on the fluid will indicate whether a number of abnormalities are present, including spina bifida and Down's syndrome (mongolism). Cultures from the fluid may be grown which will disclose the child's sex. A mother who underwent amniocentesis and was told that she carried a spina bifida or Down's syndrome baby could then opt for an abortion. A mother who knew she was a carrier of haemophilia and learned that she carried a male child might similarly seek a termination. But there are medical problems with amniocentesis. It cannot be performed before the 14th week of pregnancy and is usually delayed until the 16th week. It carries about a 1 per cent risk of causing a miscarriage. It sometimes causes the mother an acute if short period of discomfort. And it is an expensive procedure, reserved largely at present for mothers at special risk of producing a disabled infant, in particular those over 35 or women whose routine blood tests suggest some abnormality in the baby.

What are the legal implications of amniocentesis? First, it involves an invasion of the mother's body. Her consent is essential and should be obtained expressly and in writing. Second, the risk that a healthy baby may be lost should be communicated to the parents. The duty of the gynaecologist caring for the mother must embrace offering her the information on which to make such a crucial decision. But the major implications of the development of amniocentesis are these. If amniocentesis is indicated and not carried out, or if tests on the amniotic fluid are carelessly conducted so that a mother continues her pregnancy and gives birth to a disabled child, can the child sue the doctors who negligently allowed him to be born? If a mother refuses amniocentesis when it is indicated, or rejects an abortion after amniocentesis has revealed abnormalities, will the child's rights when born against any person whose negligence caused the abnormality be affected? Both these questions are discussed throughout the rest of the chapter.

Wrongful life claims

The examples we considered earlier arose where the defendant's negligence caused a foetus normal at conception to be affected by disabilities in the course of its mother's pregnancy. What of the case where the baby was damaged from conception by, for example, genetic disease, and tests that should have revealed the disease failed to do so? Or where German measles damages the baby but is not detected? *McKay* v. *Essex Area Health Authority*[11] recounts such a tragedy. Such claims are often called claims for 'wrongful life'. The plaintiffs in *McKay* were a little girl, born disabled as a result of the effect of German measles suffered by her mother early in pregnancy, and her mother. When Mrs McKay suspected that she had contracted German measles in the early weeks of her pregnancy, her doctor arranged for blood tests to establish whether she had been infected. As a result of negligence by either her doctor or the laboratory staff employed by the Area Health Authority, Mrs McKay was wrongly informed that she had not been infected by German measles. So she continued with the pregnancy. Had she known the true position she would, as her doctor was well aware, have requested an abortion under the Abortion Act 1967. The little girl was born in 1975 before the Congenital Disabilities Act was passed. The Court of Appeal had to decide the position at common law. They said that no action lay where the essence of the plaintiff's claim was that but for the negligence of the defendant she would never have been born at all. The child's claim was thrown out, although her mother's claim is still proceeding. But the case is not solely of historical interest. The judges further said that under the Act no child born after its passing could pursue such a claim.

In the view of the Court of Appeal, the Act[12] can never give rise to a claim for 'wrongful life'. Ackner L.J., considering section 1(2)(b) of the Act, said that the relevant 'occurrence' has to be one that affected the mother in pregnancy 'so that the child *is born* with disabilities which would not otherwise have been present'. Clearly under the Act, then, where the breach of duty consists of carelessness in the conduct of the pregnancy or the birth the claim must relate to disabilities inflicted as a result of the breach of duty by the defendants. Where the essence of the claim is that the child should never have been born at all, it lies outside the scope of section 1(2)(b). Thus a claim by the child that amniocentesis should have been performed, or that subsequent tests were negligently conducted so that the pregnancy continued and he was born disabled, will fail.

Children damaged by pre-conception events

Let us move on now to look at claims by children born disabled as a result of events affecting a parent before conception. This could happen, for example, where the father or mother is affected by radiation or drugs so that the sperm or ovum carries a serious defect. Or the child may be damaged if doctors mismanage a previous pregnancy, for example if they fail to take note of and treat Rhesus incompatibility in the mother and the second child is born brain-damaged.[13] The Act obviously intended to cover such cases, providing as it does that the relevant occurrence may be one which affected either parent in his or her ability to have a healthy child. But it may be argued that if the claim is that the child was born disabled because one of his parents is incapable of creating a healthy infant, his claim is essentially that he should never have been born at all, and that it is an action for 'wrongful life' and is barred under the Act. I think this is a mistaken view of the Act. The child's claim in the case of a pre-conception occurrence rests on the hypothesis that *but for* that occurrence he would have been born normal and healthy, and that his actionable injury is therefore the difference between the life he might have had and the life he must now perforce endure. In *McKay* the infant plaintiff sought to maintain that her actionable injury was life itself, and as such her claim was not and would not be sustainable. What *McKay* does clarify in cases of pre-conception injury is that a doctor, not responsible for that original injury, cannot be liable under the Act if he fails to diagnose the child's deformities in pregnancy and so fails to perform an abortion in such circumstances.

165

What if a parent realizes the risk?

Further problems confront the child plaintiff whose claim is based on pre-conception injury. Section 1(4) of the Act provides that in such cases if the affected parent is aware of the risk of the child being born disabled the defendant is not answerable to that child. Responsibility for knowingly running the risk of creating a disabled baby is placed with his parents, and whatever the degree of his fault, the original creator of the risk is relieved of any liability to the child. There is one exception to this rule. Where the child sues his father, the fact that the father is aware of the risk of begetting an abnormal child will not defeat the child's action as long as his mother is ignorant of the danger. This raises a nice question. A young man suffers contamination by some chemical at work through the negligence of his employers. He is warned that his reproductive capacity has been damaged, that he is likely to beget abnormal offspring, and is strongly advised never to have children. He ignores the warning, marries, and tells his wife nothing. A disabled child is born to them. The child cannot sue his father's original employers. Even if they were in breach of duty to his father, 'the affected parent', the father's knowledge of the risk is a complete defence. But can the child sue his father? The answer has to be no. The child, like the infant plaintiff in *McKay*, can only claim against his father that he should never have been born at all. His father's condition at the time of the relevant 'negligence', begetting the child, was such that he could not beget a normal child. The father's 'negligence' was in creating him, not in inflicting a disability which but for some act or omission on his part would not have been present.

The question that arises now is whether a father can ever be liable to his child under the Act? Unlike the mother he is not granted any express immunity. If he assaults the mother during her pregnancy and damages the child in the womb, he will be liable in battery to her and through her to the child for its injuries. But it is difficult to envisage any other example of paternal liability. Other examples, such as that which we discussed above, or the father who knows he has syphilis, all fail to result in liability because the father's essential negligence is in creating a child at all, not in inflicting disabilities which the child could have been born without.

Must a mother consider abortion?

The partial defence that the affected parent shared responsibility for the child being born disabled, which may result in the child's damages being reduced, raises the final difficulty where the child sues in respect of pre-conception injuries. The child's disabilities may be diagnosed, perhaps when the mother has an ultrasound scan, or through amniocentesis, well before his birth. Blood tests may cause the doctor to recommend amniocentesis but the mother refuses. This may also happen with a child damaged in the course of its mother's pregnancy. Once the mother knows of the damage or potential damage to her child, she will under the 1967 Abortion Act be entitled to an abortion on the grounds that there is a substantial risk that the child if born would be seriously handicapped. Assuming that it is the mother who is the affected parent, does she 'share responsibility for the child being born disabled' if she refuses an abortion? No court has yet had to face that unhappy dilemma. But in *McKay* v. *Essex Area Health Authority*, refusing to allow the infant plaintiff's claim that she should have been aborted, Ackner L. J. said that he could not accept:

. . . that the common law duty of care to a person can involve, without specific legislation to achieve this end, the legal obligation to that person, whether or not in utero, to terminate his existence. Such a proposition runs wholly contrary to the concept of the sanctity of human life.[14]

Applying Ackner L. J.'s proposition to a submission that the mother should have accepted abortion advanced by the defendant responsible for inflicting the disabilities suffered by the child, such a submission must fail. To impose an *obligation* on a mother to undergo an abortion would appear if anything even more repugnant to the concept of the sanctity of human life than to impose an obligation to abort on a doctor.

However, at least one High Court judge has exhibited an attitude to abortion dramatically different from that of Ackner L. J. In *Emeh* v. *Kensington, Chelsea and Fulham Area Health Authority*[15] the plaintiff underwent sterilization. The operation was carried out negligently by the first defendant and she became pregnant again. She claimed damages for the cost of bringing up the child. In the course of this unexpected and unwanted pregnancy the plaintiff had been offered but had refused an abortion. She said she was afraid of putting herself in the hands of the doctors again. The judge held that once she elected to continue the pregnancy the pregnancy ceased to be unwanted, and that the birth of the child was the result of her own actions and not a consequence of the defendant's negligence. He said that in the circumstances the plaintiff's refusal to consider an abortion was so unreasonable as to eclipse the defendant's wrongdoing.

The Court of Appeal overruled him.[16] Mrs Emeh did not become aware of her pregnancy until it was about 17–18 weeks advanced. Refusing an abortion at that stage in pregnancy could not be considered unreasonable. Whether the Court would have taken a different view had the pregnancy been less advanced remains open to question. Waller L. J. laid great stress on the increased risk, discomfort and hospitalization entailed in abortion at 12 weeks plus.[17] Slade L. J. was emphatic that abortion should generally never be forced upon a woman. He said:[18]

Save in the most exceptional circumstances, I cannot think it right that the court should ever declare it unreasonable for a woman to decline to have an abortion in a case where there is no evidence that there were any medical or psychiatric grounds for terminating the particular pregnancy.

Three further matters must be weighed in deciding whether a mother who refuses abortion once her baby's disabilities are diagnosed shares responsibility for him being born disabled. (1) There is, of course, a difference between such a mother and Mrs Emeh. The defendant may argue that foetal abnormality presents a medical ground for termination, and Slade L. J.'s dictum condemning 'forced' abortion excluded cases where medical grounds for termination were present. On the other hand, the Court of Appeal in *McKay* pronounced against obliging the doctor to abort where medical grounds should, had care been taken, have been diagnosed. Why should a mother be less favourably treated? (2) The issue in a child's claim under the Act is rather different from a mother's claim for a failed sterilization. The child's damages are to be reduced if a parent 'shares responsibility for the child being born disabled'. The mother who refuses an abortion may share responsibility for the birth but she does not share responsibility for the disability. The original purpose of this partial defence appears to have been the sort of case where a mother ignores medical advice and worsens her child's condition by drinking, smoking or failing to take precautions advised by her doctors. She contributes to the disability. That is very different from refusing abortion. (3) Even where a court is prepared to entertain the defence, how will they assess the mother's decision? Is it to be what the hypothetical reasonable woman in 1987 would do, a totally objective test? Or are the mother-to-be's own moral views and religious affiliation to be considered? Whatever a court decides, controversy will follow.

Pre-pregnancy advice and genetic counselling

It is becoming increasingly common for women planning a child to seek medical advice before allowing themselves to conceive. For a healthy woman this may be simply a check that she is immune from German measles, a disease which if contracted in early pregnancy can damage the nervous system, causing the child to be born with severe disabilities. Another may seek reassurance that pregnancy will not damage her own health, for example if she has a history of cardiac or kidney disease. Finally, couples in whose family hereditary disease or defects have appeared, or couples who already have a damaged child, may need specialized genetic counselling.

In all these cases, the doctor counselling the woman undertakes a duty to her in relation not only to her own health and welfare as it may be affected by the course of pregnancy and childbirth but also in relation to the birth of a healthy child. If she is given the green light to go ahead with a pregnancy and suffers at the end of it the trauma and financial burden of a damaged child, she may have an action in negligence. Once again, proving negligence may not be easy. Not only must she show that the doctor failed to take into account factors relating to her medical history or genetic background, or failed to conduct tests that would have alerted him to the danger, but she must show that a reasonably competent doctor would have discovered the risk. If a woman today requests a test for immunity from German measles, is brushed aside, and subsequently contracts the disease in pregnancy, her claim will succeed. The enormous publicity given to the D.H.S.S. campaign to eradicate the risk to the unborn child posed by German measles is such that any G.P. must be aware of and guard against that risk. If the sister of a haemophiliac consults her doctor and explains her brother's condition, and he fails to refer her for counselling with the result that she bears a haemophiliac son, she too should succeed. But beyond these obvious examples of want of competence the medical profession is much divided on the value of pre-conception advice. Some doctors run special clinics and advise special diets and total abstinence from alcohol when attempting to conceive. Greater evidence of the relationship of such regimes to the reduction of risk to the child, and their acceptance by the profession at large, will be needed before a claim based on the lack of such detailed guidance could succeed.

A woman claiming damages for the birth of a disabled child may face two further obstacles. (1) She will have to establish that had she received proper advice she would not have allowed herself to become pregnant when she did. (2) If the defect in the child is diagnosed in pregnancy and she is offered and refuses an abortion, she may face the argument that in refusing an abortion she becomes the author of her own damage. I have already expressed my view that such an argument should not prevail. However, should the woman elect to undergo abortion then she should receive compensation for the suffering, physical and emotional, that that operation entails.

Has the damaged child himself a remedy? We must distinguish three types of cases where negligent pre-pregnancy advice results in the birth of a disabled child. (1) The relevant negligence may be that the woman was encouraged to become pregnant when, had proper care been taken, she could have been advised never to contemplate pregnancy because of the risk to any child she might bear. The child's action in such a case will fail because the essence of his claim is that he should never have been born at all. It is once again a claim for 'wrongful life' and excluded by the Court of Appeal in *McKay*. (2) The negligence may have been in failing to counsel the mother properly on precautions to take, or the timing of pregnancy. Such a claim may raise an awkward problem. For example, a woman is not tested for immunity to German measles or the test is negligently conducted. She is wrongly told that she has immunity. She becomes pregnant, contracts the disease and the child is damaged. Had she been properly advised, she would have been vaccinated against the disease and advised in the strongest of terms to delay pregnancy for three months after the vaccination. The actual child born would thus never have been born. The particular set of genes in the ovum (egg) and sperm that went to create him would never have met. A literal interpretation of *McKay* would deny the child a remedy on the grounds that that unique individual would never have been born had the mother had proper advice. It would seem a harsh result, but the conclusion that it follows from the interpretation of the Act by the Court of Appeal in *McKay* is difficult to resist. Examples of this sort could be multiplied endlessly. There could be a parent who is undergoing treatment for venereal disease. He or she is carelessly advised that pregnancy is now safe. It is not. Treatment was not complete. The child born disabled would not have been born had proper advice been given. A woman knows a little of a family history of genetic disease affecting the males in her family. She seeks counselling. She should have been advised of the risks to male children and been offered amniocentesis in pregnancy, so that she could if she wished have terminated a pregnancy had the tests shown that she carried a male child. A male child born disabled cannot sue under the Act, for had amniocentesis been offered and accepted that male child would not exist. (3) And so there is only one very limited class of case where the child's action based on allegedly careless pre-pregnancy advice may succeed. That is where the advice omitted, or inadequate in content, would have enabled that very child to be born hale and hearty. Realistic examples are difficult to think of. Perhaps one topical example concerns the relationship between the maternal diet before conception and spina bifida. There is some evidence that a special treatment with multi-vitamins may reduce the likelihood of that terrible disability. A child might argue that had his mother been advised to follow that regime his disability would not have developed. He would have been born but not disabled. Such a child claims for his disabilities, not wrongful life. He overcomes the first problem in his claim against medical staff, but will he be able to prove that the treatment if given would have prevented his disability? It is a matter for controversy among doctors. We shall see in Chapter 18 that the question of how to test the theory has aroused other controversy.

What I should make clear is that in the first two classes of case, while the child's claim may fail as a 'wrongful life' claim, the parents' claim may still succeed. In *McKay* no decision was reached on the mother's claim. But there seems no reason why such a claim should fail. Genetic advice and other pre-pregnancy counselling has as its purpose enabling a woman, if possible, to bear a healthy child, and, if not possible, to save her from the trauma of bearing a disabled child. If through negligence a disabled child is born, is there any reason to deny the parents compensation for the very damage that the defendant should have protected them from? Arguments of public policy may be advanced. (1) The essence of this sort of claim is that the child was allowed to be born. Should the birth of a child ever be seen as a matter calling for compensation? The Court of Appeal see no objection to compensating a mother who bears a healthy child after a negligent sterilization operation.[19] The birth of a disabled child, which care should have prevented, calls even more strongly for compensation. (2) Will awarding compensation put undue pressure on doctors to abort, a circumstance deplored by the Court of Appeal in *McKay*? A distinction needs to be emphasized here between the nature of the claim of mother and child. Abortion would entirely dispose of any claim by the child. The mother will still have a claim for discomforts of the pregnancy, so far as it was endured, and for the trauma of the abortion even if she agrees to abortion. True, damages for the upkeep of the child will usually be greater, but a doctor pressuring a patient to abort may end up with a heavy bill for the possible emotional consequences of that decision. It seems in any case a slight on an honourable profession to suggest that to protect 'their own' they would put pressure on a pregnant woman. (3) If the 'wrongful life' of a child cannot form a cause of action for the child, is it fair to give the parent a remedy? Again the distinction must be clearly drawn. The Court of Appeal in *McKay* said that the difference between existence and non-existence was incapable of measurement by a court. The difference between the cost of bringing up a healthy child and the cost of bringing up a disabled child can be measured with some degree of accuracy. The suffering caused to the parents is visible. (4) But what of the child's welfare; may he not suffer over and above his disability by the public branding of his existence as unwelcome? Similar arguments were raised and failed in respect of the birth of a child after negligent sterilization. The provision of adequate money to retain paid expert help, to adapt the family house and relieve the burden on his parents is in fact likely to increase the chance that the child will be loved and cared for within his own family.

Genetic counselling and confidentiality

The genetic counsellor's legal problems are not confined to his obligations to the woman seeking his advice. If he discovers that she is, or is likely to be, the carrier of congenital disease, then he will be well aware that any sisters of hers are also at risk as carriers, and so to a lesser degree are other female relatives. Obviously he will ask her permission to inform her sister or her sister's doctor. What if the woman refuses permission? She will argue that the counsellor owes her an obligation of confidence. But if the sister later bears a damaged child, the consequences to her are dreadful and she might sue the counsellor. The sister could contend that the risk to her was readily foreseeable and the counsellor had a duty to warn her. I would suggest that in such circumstances the counsellor may be justified in breaking his obligation of confidence. The Court of Appeal[20] have held that information obtained in a confidential relationship may be disclosed if disclosure is in the public interest. The interest in preventing the birth of damaged children is sufficient to merit disclosure.

Childbirth

How much choice?

Our grandmothers gave heartfelt thanks if they survived the perils of childbirth. Our mothers were the first generation to have general access to hospital confinement and skilled attention if things went wrong. Today medical technology offers a whole range of sophisticated devices to monitor mother and baby and ensure safe delivery. But increasingly groups of women reject the panoply of machinery found in many hospital labour wards. Accepting the necessity of 'high-tech' birth for a minority of difficult cases, the natural childbirth movement has campaigned for the medical profession to be more willing to let nature take its course. For a number of women the ideal would be delivery of their baby at home in the comfort of familiar surroundings. The debate is largely medical and social. Gynaecologists in many areas of the country have accepted the ideas propounded. Hospital birth in 1987 is probably substantially less interventionist and impersonal than in 1977. But home delivery is more difficult to obtain. Few general practitioners will now deliver babies at home. There are insufficient community midwives to meet demand. Progress is being made, but the overall impression which a layman is left with is that while doctors will make considerable efforts to meet women's demands for more natural childbirth in hospital, all but a few in the profession are opposed to home delivery.

What role does the law play in this debate? Childbirth is a medical monopoly. The law effectively denies a woman, unable to persuade a doctor or midwife to attend her at home or a hospital to comply with her wishes concerning the birth, the choice of seeking alternative help. She may either give birth alone or fall in with medical requirements and accept medical help. For it is a criminal offence for a person other than a registered midwife or a registered medical practitioner to attend a woman in childbirth.[21] An offender faces a maximum fine of £500. And any person means any person. On 6 August 1982 a husband was convicted of delivering his own wife and fined £100.[22] Nor is the unqualified attendant the only potential 'criminal'. The mother herself, if she procures the other's services, in ordinary English if she asks for their help, may be guilty of counselling and procuring a criminal offence. So her choice as delimited by the law is to accept the medical help available or give birth alone. Giving birth alone is not a very encouraging option and is itself not free of legal hazard, not to speak of medical risk. For if the baby dies the mother may face prosecution for manslaughter. Gross negligence by attendants in the delivery of a baby has resulted in criminal conviction where the baby died.[23] The issue where an unattended mother was on trial would be whether refusing medical attendance was sufficiently culpable negligence in relation to the safety of her child.

The rationale for the legislation which makes medical attendance at childbirth compulsory appears self-evident. If a person refuses to seek medical help for any other life-threatening condition he physically harms himself alone. A woman refusing medical attention in childbirth puts her baby at risk. Yet she can lawfully refuse attention for the nine months up to delivery. Proposals that maternity grants and benefits should be made dependent on ante-natal visits have been made. Nobody has yet suggested that it should be a criminal offence to fail to attend the ante-natal clinic. The truth is that there is no express and considered policy on the respective rights and liberties of mother and baby. The legislation originally enacted to require professional attendance at childbirth was intended to outlaw the 'Sarah Gamps', the elderly and often not entirely clean local women who made their living as unqualified midwives.[24] Today's legislation has moved a long way from that point. It may by chance be correct, but it needs proper consideration whether a husband delivering his wife, or a mother her daughter, should be branded as criminal when all goes well and mother and baby thrive.

Hospital birth

Entering hospital, the mother puts herself into the hands of the doctors and the midwives. She consents to all the inevitable invasions of her body that delivery of her child must normally entail. So such acts will not be a battery. The extent of the mother's consent to treatment in childbirth has been put in this way.

Apart from any express prohibition she might make, if she receives substantially that form of treatment, a lack of explicit consent to particular details will not make it unlawful, providing that those details relate reasonably to the treatment according to the prevailing professional standards.[25]

Let us apply and test this statement of the law. One of the most controversial issues of hospital birth is the use of episiotomy. Episiotomy is the procedure whereby a small cut is made in the vagina to assist delivery and prevent tearing. One of its advantages is said to be that the deliberate cut will heal better than a random tear. But it has been alleged that episiotomy became routine. It was performed regardless of any necessity for it. And since those allegations were discussed in the press the number of episiotomies has fallen. The law, as the statement quoted makes clear, will render such a procedure unlawful if the woman *expressly* bans it. Many women will enter the labour ward confused and a little overwhelmed. They will give no express instructions. On the statement quoted, episiotomy on them is lawful without express consent, providing the procedure conforms to 'prevailing professional standards' in obstetrics. The Wendy Savage inquiry showed that obstetricians do not agree on what constitutes 'prevailing professional standards'.[26] I would regard episiotomy without express consent as unlawful. For it is not an inevitably necessary invasion of the mother's body, as are for example the contacts by the midwife as she feels the abdomen and assists the baby's exit. Episiotomy is a greater invasion of the body than the contacts implicitly authorized simply by seeking professional aid. The skin is cut. A wound, however small, is made. The law should uphold the mother's right to control what happens to her. The controversy over whether the law should compel medical attendance in childbirth would be much less substantial if the woman's rights in hospital were fully protected.

It goes without saying that a mother suffering injury as a result of carelessness in the management of childbirth is entitled to compensation for negligence. Applying the principle may be more difficult. For the medical staff have duties to both mother and child. In 1985 a horror story surfaced to strike terror into mothers facing Caesarian births. Mrs Margaret Ackers was awarded more than £13,000 compensation when the Wigan Health Authority accepted that although an anaesthetic given to her in the course of a Caesarian rendered her paralysed and unable to speak, it was not adequate to prevent her feeling pain. She remained conscious and suffered appalling pain as the incision was made. Several similar claims are now going to court. They raise an awkward issue. Anaesthesia for Caesarian surgery is very difficult. The mother should be given enough anaesthetic to render her totally unconscious. Too much anaesthetic may knock the baby out and risk brain damage. Clearly when the balance is wrong the damaged party, be it mother or child, deserves compensation. The danger of the action for negligence is that if anaesthetists are to be dragged through the courts they may become unwilling to assist in Caesarian surgery. The threat of negligence actions too led many mothers to find their complaints of awareness during surgery dismissed as fantasy or blocked entirely by the health authority. Such cases are clear examples of the need for 'no-fault' compensation. Then the issues of whether any lack of skill or care contributed to the mother's distress could be properly investigated. And free of threats of constant legal action, anaesthetists could strive to find and issue guidelines on the correct medical solution to this difficult dilemma.

A mother who succeeds in proving negligence on the part of her obstetrician will receive damages for her own pain and suffering and for the shock and grief she suffers if the baby dies as a result of negligence by medical staff. Damages will also include the effect of the mismanaged delivery on her prospects of future childbearing.[27]

The child's rights

So far in this section we have concentrated on the mother's choices. What of the child's rights? Has he a remedy if the doctors or midwives are incompetent and he suffers injury? What are his rights if his mother refuses a course of action that will benefit him and thus causes him injury?

The child's rights are now governed by the Congenital Disabilities (Civil Liability) Act 1976. For that Act covers not only injury to the child in the womb but also any occurrence which affected mother or child in the course of its birth. It is quite clear that the common law recognized a duty to a child in the course of delivery.[28] It has been argued that the 1976 Act, which replaces the common law, reduces the child's rights.[29] For liability under the Act arises only where the defendant would have been liable in tort to the affected parent. Where the failure by the defendant attending the mother, failure to proceed quickly enough to Caesarian section or whatever, is in no way the responsibility of the mother, no problem is caused to the child. I have argued before that the duty to the mother embraces care of her child. A breach of duty to her which injures the child creates rights in both her and her child.

The thrust of the argument that the Act reduces the child's rights lies in these sorts of circumstances. The child is believed to be at risk. Doctors recommend Caesarian section. The mother refuses and the child is born suffering from brain damage. The child will not be able to sue the doctor. The doctor is clearly not liable to the mother. The child cannot sue his mother, for the Act grants immunity to mothers.[30] More seriously than that, it is argued[31] that if there is no duty directly to the child a doctor cannot after the 1976 Act advance his duty to the child as a defence to acts done to the mother. Were there still a direct duty to the child, the doctor might contend that in exceptional circumstances he could, for example, proceed to Caesarian section without consent in order to save the baby.

Two points should be made on this argument. First, as the authors of the argument themselves say, a doctor who can establish the necessity of a battery against the mother to save the child may still have a defence of necessity to an action by her, regardless of the absence of a *direct* duty to the child. Second, it may perhaps be doubted whether in relation to damage done in the course of delivery the 1976 Act does negate a direct duty to her child. Section 1(1) of the Act speaks of an occurrence affecting 'mother *or child* in the course of its birth'. The later provision in section 1(3) that the defendant must be liable in tort to the affected parent does not make sense if the occurrence is one which the Act applies to because it has affected the child. It is another example of the inadequacy of that Act. But interpreting the Act to give a limited direct duty to the child in the course of its birth would not solve the basic problem of conflict between rights of the mother and duties to the child. When does the 'course of its birth' begin? The position could be reached where a direct duty to perform a Caesarian was owed under the 1976 Act to the child in distress whose mother was already in labour, but *not* to the child whose mother's condition indicated that an immediate Caesarian was called for but who had not yet gone into labour.

What is the solution to this dilemma? An American court has made an unborn child a ward of court and compelled the mother to submit to Caesarian section.[32] I believe that the law must at the end of the day affirm the mother's sovereignty over her own body. I recognize the injustice to the child and I reach my conclusion tentatively and with some reluctance. The evils are plain to see. On my conclusion, in theory the law may allow a child to die or be damaged without hope of compensation. On any other conclusion, every woman would lose her right to control the most important physical event of her life. Any objection to intervention, be it episiotomy, forceps, Caesarian, would be met by the answer that the doctor must in law decide what is best for the baby. The woman's only recourse would be, after the event, to pursue a long and expensive legal claim. The relationship between women and their doctors would scarcely be improved. More women might opt out of medical help and in the end more babies might be damaged. The pro- and anti-natural childbirth debate is bitter enough without heavy-handed legal intervention compelling women to undergo surgery.

Chapter 11
Problems of Infertility

We move on now to examine the legal problems affecting procedures to relieve infertility. It is estimated that as many as one in ten couples, and maybe more, have difficulty conceiving naturally and seek medical help. The technical ability of the doctors to give that help has made incredible progress in the last decade. The birth of the first 'test-tube' baby, Louise Brown, in 1978 gave hope to thousands of childless couples. The advent of surrogacy offered the chance of a child even to the woman who had undergone hysterectomy. Yet for every man or woman who rejoiced at what the doctors could now do, there were as many who condemned the technical advances as unnatural and contrary to the will of God. And much publicized though these new techniques have been, they have brought heartbreak too, for the success rates are still low as we shall see. Such was the furore created that the government established a Committee under Dame Mary Warnock (now Baroness Warnock) to consider:

. . . recent and potential developments in medicine and science related to human fertilization and embryology; to consider what policies and safeguards should be applied, including consideration of the social, ethical and legal implications of these developments; and to make recommendations.

The Warnock Report was published in the summer of 1984.[1] It fuelled rather than stilled the controversy. I shall examine the present state of the law and the Warnock proposals. At issue are not only the questions of a doctor's responsibility if things go wrong, but fundamental areas of family and criminal law. I would hope too to show how the law can operate in this field and to demonstrate its limitations. The public debate on the Warnock Report has sometimes been vitriolic. Accusations that doctors and scientists are 'mini-Hitlers' have been countered by allegations that opponents of new techniques are 'living in the Dark Ages' and are uncaring about the misery of infertility. Such deep divisions in society make it extremely difficult to legislate on the crucial problems now posed by new treatments for infertility.

Artificial insemination by donor (A.I.D.)

Where it is the man who is infertile, a couple may be offered the opportunity to have a child by another man, by artificial insemination by donor (A.I.D.). As a procedure, A.I.D. is far from new and is so simple that it can be, and has been, performed without medical assistance. The problems are legal and ethical, not medical. Let us look first at A.I.D. in its most favourable setting. A couple are happily married. They are carefully counselled. The husband fully and freely consents. Still in law today the resulting child remains the illegitimate child of the wife and the donor. The consequences of this are in theory dire. Should the marriage break down before the child's birth the husband has (1) no obligation to maintain the child, and (2) no rights of custody or even access. The donor, on the other hand, may be subject to affiliation proceedings brought by the wife. As the child's father, the donor may be obliged to maintain him. Once the child is born and treated as the husband's child then the husband will acquire obligations to and rights in respect of that child as a 'child of the family'. But even so, on the husband's death if he dies intestate the child has no rights in his estate, whereas he may have a claim on the donor's estate.

Many doctors dismiss these nightmares. They say that the stability of the marriage is thoroughly investigated before A.I.D. is offered, so as to eliminate the risk of a couple parting before the birth. Once born, an A.I.D. child is usually registered as the husband's child. All is done in secrecy and no one will ever know of the child's origins. As for the donor, his identity will be carefully concealed. Most donors are young medical students, whose sperm is stored in sperm banks maintained by the teaching hospitals. They donate (or sell) sperm on the understanding that absolute secrecy will be preserved. Two flaws exist in the doctors' confidence. First, a parent who registers an A.I.D. child as the husband's commits a criminal offence, perjury contrary to section 4 of the Perjury Act 1911. Second, the possibility of a jealous sibling or another relative discovering the A.I.D. child's origins and seeking to keep him out of an inheritance can never be entirely dismissed.

Proposals to change the child's legal status

It may not be very likely that the full theoretical horror of an A.I.D. child's legal limbo will materialize. Nevertheless, both the Law Commission[2] and the Warnock Committee[3] recommend the following changes in the law. A child born by A.I.D. to a married couple should be deemed to be the legitimate child of husband and wife providing that the husband consented to the procedure. The husband would be presumed to consent and the onus would be on him to prove the contrary. All links with the donor would be severed. He would cease to have any parental rights or duties in relation to the child. In other words, in law the A.I.D. child should be put in exactly the same position as any natural and legitimate child of the couple.

A.I.D. and unmarried mothers

The original guidelines issued by the Royal College of Obstetricians and Gynaecologists (R.C.O.G.) restricted the availability of A.I.D. to married couples.[4] This has been criticized as unduly restrictive and paternalist, and some doctors are clearly willing to offer A.I.D. to unmarried women. Couples living in a stable relationship without benefit of clergy may desire children. There are women who want children without the encumbrance of a male partner. Nature does not limit the provision of children as the R.C.O.G. seeks to do. On the other hand, society via legislation imposes even more stringent tests before permitting a couple to adopt a child not theirs. We must examine the legal implications for an A.I.D. child born to a woman who is not married.

If a child is born by A.I.D. to a couple living within a stable relationship but not married to each other, that child will not have and never will have, unless the couple later marry, any legal claim on the male partner, his apparent father. The 'father' will have no obligation to maintain him, nor will he have any rights in respect of such a child. Should the couple part, however fond and caring a father he may have been, he will, if the mother wishes, be entirely cut off from the child they agreed to create. The only remedy open to him would be to seek to make the child a ward of court and hope that the court might of its discretion award him custody or access.

A.I.D. and the husband's consent

Another condition placed by the R.C.O.G. on the provision of A.I.D. is that where the woman is married her husband's consent must invariably be obtained. The Warnock Committee backed this view emphatically.[5] The need for the woman's husband to consent to A.I.D. can be seen as an unjustifiable restriction on her rights over her own life and body, and it is not a restriction imposed by the law. No claim lies against the doctor if he performs A.I.D. without the husband's agreement. The woman alone is competent to give consent to the physical invasion of her body. Nor does the woman commit adultery by accepting A.I.D.,[6] though to go ahead with A.I.D. against a husband's wishes will almost certainly give grounds for divorce based on the wife's unreasonable behaviour. The child is the vulnerable party. For if the mother goes ahead without her husband's full support he may leave her in pregnancy. The child will be left with no claim on the husband and if the donor cannot be identified, any legal link with him will be worthless.

Both R.C.O.G. 'rules' cease to be supportable if society is prepared to accept that artificial aid should be offered by the medical profession to assist women to give birth to a child who will be, or could be, effectively fatherless. If that is now acceptable, then single women should also have access to A.I.D. That raises the question of lesbians who want children but deplore the prospect of intercourse with a man. At present doctors alone decide on these matters. The Warnock Committee considers this right. They recommend that A.I.D. should always be given under the supervision of a registered medical practitioner. If that limitation on A.I.D. is accepted, no doctor should ever be *compelled* to use his skill to aid the conception of a child in circumstances which he considers unethical or unfavourable to the child's prospects of a secure childhood.

What should an A.I.D. child be told?

Should an A.I.D. child be told of the manner of his conception? An adopted child has at 18 a right to access to his original birth certificate and so has the opportunity to trace his natural parents.[7] At present it is most unusual for an A.I.D. child to be told of his origins, and if he is, he is probably going to meet with no success if he tries to discover his father's identity. The Law Commission's proposal to deem an A.I.D. child born to a married couple to be the child of that couple would continue and strengthen the trend towards concealment of A.I.D. origin. The Warnock Committee too recommends that the donor retains his personal anonymity.[8] Two major reasons support this trend. First, the apparent father will very likely not wish his infertility to be known even to the child. The object of A.I.D. is to give a couple a child as near to their own as possible. Second, donors may well be unwilling to come forward if many years after they donated sperm they face the prospect of being confronted by their 'children' and consequent possible disruption of the families they may by then have founded.

Against these arguments is mounted a powerful case that knowledge of an individual's genetic history is more than just a matter of curiosity and personal concern. The health of the A.I.D. child's own children may be at stake. Consequently the Warnock Committee, while preserving the anonymity of the donor, do propose that at 18 the child should have access to basic information about the donor's ethnic origins and genetic health and that this limited 'right to know' should be enforced by legislation.[9]

Liability of the doctors

No responsible doctor would ever ignore the legal implications of A.I.D. just outlined, but in what circumstances might a doctor incur liability for malpractice as a result of performing A.I.D.? Where A.I.D. is performed within the N.H.S. there is of course no remedy if no pregnancy results. Even where the patient contracts with a doctor to receive A.I.D. privately, the obligation undertaken by the doctor is to perform the procedure competently – not to guarantee a pregnancy. But what if pregnancy results and a damaged child is born? This might happen where the donor transmits some congenital defect to the child. I would suggest that the obligation undertaken to the mother includes a duty to take care in the selection of donors and to exclude potential carriers of genetic disease or defect. Negligence in performing that obligation should result in liability to the mother. Liability to the child is more difficult. The child must sue under the Congenital Disabilities Act, and must show that his injuries result from an occurrence that either affected one or other parent in his or her ability to have a healthy child, or affected his mother in the course of pregnancy. The relevant negligence of the doctor did not affect either the donor-father, who was, before he ever donated sperm, already damaged in his reproductive capacity, or the mother, who was herself perfectly normal. Nor is the mother injured in the course of her pregnancy unless we can say that injury in the process of artificial inducement of pregnancy will satisfy that requirement. Even then the child's action must fail on another ground: but for the negligence of the doctor in not selecting fit donors he, that individual, would never have been born at all. The doctor's negligence did not inflict the disabilities. The child of that father could not but be born disabled. The doctor's negligence causes him to be born, and like the infant plaintiff in *McKay*, such a child has no remedy.[10]

Artificial insemination by husband (A.I.H.)

There are some rare cases where although the husband is fertile he cannot beget a child because he is incapable of normal intercourse. His sperm may be used to impregnate his wife by artificial means. The child will be just as much the legitimate child of the couple as if it were conceived naturally. If the marriage has never been consummated, the acceptance of A.I.H. will not prevent the wife from petitioning the court to annul the marriage,[11] although on policy grounds the court may refuse a decree if they consider that in having the child the wife approbated the marriage. The child will in any case remain legitimate even if his parents' marriage is later annulled, for they were married when he was conceived and non-consummation only renders a marriage voidable by the court. It does not mean that the marriage was never valid at all.

The facility to store sperm by freezing may cause further problems if a husband banks sperm for later insemination of his wife. He may choose to do so before undergoing vasectomy or treatment that might damage his fertility, or that might pose a risk to children later conceived. To whom do the sperm belong when the husband dies? May the wife ask for insemination then, and if so, what is the child's status? This has already happened in France, when a court ordered a sperm bank to release a dead man's sperm to his widow. In England, at present, it would seem that the husband's frozen sperm forms part of his estate, to be disposed of according to his directions. If the sperm bank permits the insemination of the widow, the child, although the child of her dead husband, will be technically illegitimate because he is not the issue of a marriage in being. But even an illegitimate child can claim on the intestacy of its reputed father. Whether, if a widow bears her husband's child years after his death, his estate would have to be re-divided to give that child a share provides one more illustration of the overwhelming need to legislate to provide for the variation on normal family relationships science now has to offer. The Warnock Committee came down firmly in favour of the view that a child born by A.I.H. who was conceived after the father's death should be disregarded for the purposes of inheritance from the latter's estate.[12] Indeed, the Committee seemed rather unhappy about allowing A.I.H. after the husband's death at all.

In Manchester in 1985 a more awkward question still was raised. A widow first requested A.I.H. from sperm collected from her husband before his death and stored in a sperm bank under the control of the health authority. Then it emerged that she would probably not be medically fit to carry any child to term. She asked the hospital to inseminate her sister with the husband's sperm. Her sister would carry the child as a surrogate mother and hand it over at birth. In the legal vacuum on A.I.H. after death and surrogacy, doctors and officials referred the matter to the hospital ethical committee. One proposal was to release the sperm but not to permit insemination of the sister in the N.H.S. hospitals under their scrutiny. The health authority now appear to have left the initiative in the woman's hands. She has been advised to go to court and ask the court to order the authority to release her husband's sperm. Thus it is hoped that questions of ownership and control of donated sperm after the donor's death may be resolved.

Regulating artificial insemination

The intervention of a third party, the donor, to give a child to a married couple offends a number of religious people. The Warnock Committee were not swayed by this sense of offence. They regarded A.I.D., and A.I.H., as ethically acceptable but saw all too clearly the potential for abuse. For example, we saw that if things go wrong the child is unlikely to have a remedy, and the mother's legal rights will be worthless if an unscrupulous practitioner is insolvent. If a single donor is used to inseminate several women, the possibility of unwitting incest by his numerous offspring rears its head. Preventing damaged children result-ing from A.I.D. and preventing brother and sister unknowingly marrying is much better than picking up the pieces later. Accordingly Warnock recommended[13] that A.I.D. should be put on a properly organized basis and be subject to licensing arrangements, as should all other forms of infertility treatment. Specifically in relation to A.I.D. it was further proposed that no single donor should be used for more than ten inseminations and that the practice of paying for sperm should be phased out.

Female infertility

Female infertility has always posed a much greater medical problem. Test-tube babies and the potential for surrogacy are just two of the many recent advances of medical science in this area. I go on now to look at these and other techniques. All were primarily designed to overcome female infertility, but some have also proved useful where it is the man who is sub-fertile.

Test-tube babies

A woman who ovulates normally, but whose Fallopian tubes are absent or damaged, will never conceive naturally because the ova (eggs) that she produces cannot travel to meet sperm and be fertilized. The test-tube baby procedure (*in vitro* fertilization or I.V.F.) offers such women the chance of their own child. Ova are removed from the woman and fertilized in the laboratory with sperm taken from the woman's husband or partner. The embryo, or embryos, thus created are carefully tested and then implanted in the mother's womb. No issue of family law arises. The child has the same status and relationship to its parents as if it were naturally conceived. Providing the parents are married at the date of fertilization or marry before the birth, the child is legitimate. The R.C.G.O. has said, in its submission to the Warnock Committee, that it is prepared to offer *in vitro* fertilization to any couple living together in a stable heterosexual relationship outside marriage. The child of such a couple will be illegitimate but will suffer no greater disadvantage than any normally conceived brother. The technique may also be used where the woman is fertile but her partner has a very low sperm count. Fertilization in the laboratory in such cases appears more successful than fertilization by normal means. When a woman and her partner are both infertile it is perfectly feasible to fertilize the woman's ova with sperm from a donor. A child so created would be the subject of all the legal difficulties afflicting an A.I.D. child born to a normally fertile mother.

Liability of the doctors

A doctor suggesting an attempt at *in vitro* fertilization does not guarantee a successful pregnancy. Success rates are still low, with one report showing only about a 14–15 per cent chance of conception.[14] The doctor's legal obligation and that of all the other persons involved in the process is to exercise proper care and skill. If something goes wrong and an abnormal baby is born, can parents or child claim compensation? We are concerned solely with an abnormality arising from the process of *in vitro* fertilization. Any negligence relating to the doctor's management of the pregnancy will be determined according to the principles discussed in Chapter 10.

I have earlier argued that once a woman is accepted for treatment in an N.H.S. hospital, the hospital undertakes a duty of care towards her.[15] If she enters a private clinic the clinic contracts that she will be treated with proper care and skill. Should *she* suffer personal injury, for example in the course of the removal of ova, the hospital or clinic would be liable and she need not identify the responsible individual. Similarly, if the hospital or clinic is liable to her for damage to the child she need not pinpoint the actual wrongdoer, which is important because it may be extremely difficult to know exactly when the embryo was damaged. But that is the central issue. Is there a duty to the parents in relation to the condition of the child? I suggest that there is. The woman undergoing treatment expects from the hospital the exercise of proper professional judgment in relation to the 'production' of the child as much as in their treatment of herself. It is readily foreseeable that she will suffer damage if she bears a damaged child. She will suffer an emotional trauma which may well have physical consequences affecting her health. She and the child's father will suffer financial loss in the form of the extra expense of bringing up a disabled child. Such negligently caused losses will be recoverable.

One obstacle may confront the parent's claim. Test-tube pregnancies are carefully monitored. Any abnormality in the child will be likely to be discovered well before it is due to be delivered. The mother will be offered an abortion. If she refuses the defendants may argue (1) that the birth of the child therefore results from her act, her decision, and not from their original negligence, and (2) that in refusing an abortion the mother has been contributorily negligent. That first argument was rejected by the Court of Appeal in *Emeh* v. *Kensington, Chelsea and Fulham Area Health Authority*[16] in relation to a claim arising from a negligently performed sterilization. I have earlier expressed my view that neither argument is generally legally acceptable. But in this context the doctors may further argue that acceptance of monitoring and possible abortion was part and parcel of agreeing to I.V.F. Thus they may seek to distinguish the decision in the *Emeh* case.

Any remedy the child himself may have is governed by the Congenital Disabilities (Civil Liability) Act 1976. The child has to establish that the defendants were responsible for an occurrence which:

(a) affected either parent of the child or his or her ability to have a normal healthy child, or

(b) affected the mother during her pregnancy . . . so that the child is born with disabilities which would not otherwise have been present.

Parliament envisaged two sorts of cases. First, cases where one parent was damaged in his or her reproductive capacity, and second, cases where the embryo was damaged after conception. In the case of the negligent conduct of *in vitro* fertilization the child is damaged in the course of 'conception'. Unless it can be argued that *in vitro* fertilization is in essence treatment of the mother and so, if negligently performed, affects her in her ability to have a normal, healthy child, a claim by the child must fail. If that argument should succeed the child will succeed. For the defendants are liable in tort to the mother, and the child is clearly born with disabilities which but for their negligence would not have been present.

Freezing embryos

It is now possible to create an embryo in the laboratory, freeze it, and implant it in the original mother, or some other recipient, at a later date. Doctors in Australia were the first to use a frozen embryo to establish a pregnancy in a woman when the first attempt, using a fresh embryo, had ended in an early miscarriage. British doctors held back for some time, but in March 1985 a baby was born in Manchester who had begun life as a frozen embryo. Several difficulties still surround the freezing of embryos.

First, until a child has been born who began life as a frozen embryo and has grown to adulthood it will be impossible to know whether the freezing process damages the human embryo. If damage caused by the freezing process became apparent later in life, could the child seek compensation from the doctors who created him? Two obstacles confront him. We have seen that the child's claim for any damages caused in the process of artificial conception appears to be outside the bounds of the 1976 Congenital Disabilities Act. If he were still dependent on his parents they might have a claim. But more crucial than that, how would child or parent prove negligence? The allegation of negligence may essentially amount to this. The freezing process was itself at fault and should never have been used on embryos. The legal outcome of such a claim several years hence is entirely unpredictable. A parent or child seeking compensation through the tort of negligence takes a terrific gamble. If the law is to sanction physical risks to the child it should provide for compensation if those risks materialize. The damaged child should not have to attempt the obstacle race represented by an action for medical negligence.

The potential liability of the doctor is just one legal issue surrounding the freezing of embryos. A more immediate question is, who owns the embryo? Who determines its fate? Do its 'parents' have parental rights and duties? The relationship between the 'parents' may break down or one partner may die. Can the 'mother' insist on implantation to give her a child after the death or divorce of its father? What if both parents die? In Australia this dilemma is very real. A millionaire couple arranged for the wife to undergo I.V.F. with donated sperm. Some of the resulting embryos were frozen. A little while later both man and wife died in an air crash. Children of the husband's first marriage wanted the embryos destroyed. They were afraid that if they were 'given' to other infertile women and developed to maturity, the embryos, having become children, might have a claim in the parents' estate. The State of Victoria is legislating on the embryos' fate. This case is complicated by the fact that the embryos were genetically related to the wife only, but would full sisters and brothers be any less worried about the threat to their inheritance?

One can only speculate as to the present state of English law. If a frozen embryo is regarded as property (which is far from clear), it presumably passes into any deceased parent's estate. Where 'parents' divorce, any existing frozen embryos would need to be considered in the property settlement made or agreed. Legislation in England should be enacted before a real problem is created and legislation has to be hurried through in an emotive atmosphere.

Warnock makes several sensible proposals[17] on the freezing of embryos and family relationships. First, there should be no rights of ownership in frozen embryos although prima facie the 'parents' would have the right to determine the use and disposal of the embryo. Where one partner dies rights over the embryo should pass to the survivor. Where both die, or they cannot agree on how to use or dispose of the embryo, rights should pass to the storage authority. Finally, an embryo not implanted in the mother until after the father's death would have no claim on his estate. Warnock leaves two problems untackled. Both have overlaps with other controversial areas of the advances made in medicine. Once rights over the embryo pass to the storage authority, what may they do with the embryo? If a frozen embryo is implanted in another woman, other than its genetic mother, will it when it develops to maturity have a claim on the genetic mother's estate?

All the above presupposes the acceptability to society of freezing embryos. Several objectors do not find it acceptable. There is the risk that the child may later show signs of damage from the process itself. And there is also the question of disposal of eventually unwanted embryos. To those who believe that human life begins at fertilization, the eventual destruction of the unwanted embryos is not to be contemplated.

Spare embryos and embryo research

We have seen that extra, spare embryos may result from freezing embryos for future use. Whether freezing is to be used or not, the creation of spare embryos is an inevitable result of refinements to the original I.V.F. procedure. Doctors seek to improve the chance of establishing a successful pregnancy by giving the woman drugs to induce her to produce several ova at once. All are then fertilized, and between two and seven re-implanted. Doctors argue fiercely about how many can be with safety implanted at one time. A number of multiple pregnancies have already resulted. But what should be done with embryos not implanted? They could of course be frozen. They may be destroyed. Scientists believe that there is enormous potential in allowing the embryos to develop further in the laboratory so that they may be monitored, and be the subject of experiments. Three apparent benefits are said to follow from the latter course. (1) Monitoring embryos which will be identical to that growing in the mother would enable doctors to detect immediately any defect in the embryo in the womb. (2) Experiments on embryos might assist scientists to understand and cure congenital disease. (3) Embryo tissue is thought to be usable in a number of ways in the cure of existing disease. But at what cost would these benefits be bought?

For anyone who believes that life begins at fertilization, the use of embryos for experiments, or as storage banks for live 'medical supplies', is unthinkable. But then so is the destruction of embryos. If this is the generally held view, then the simple and only solution is to prohibit the fertilization of more embryos than can be safely re-implanted in the mother. Thus there will be no 'spare' embryos. The prevalent view among those working in this field appears to be that experiments are ethically permissible until the embryo's neural system begins to develop, which happens about seventeen days after conception. But this deadline is pushed much further by some, and the neural system could itself be removed. The spectre of brainless zombies plundered for their organs casts a very real shadow. Society must swiftly decide where it will draw the line. At the moment no legal restrictions attach either to experiments upon or the destruction of embryos. They are not capable of independent life, so fall beyond the scope of homicide or offences against the person. Killing an embryo cannot be counted in law as criminal abortion, for the offence of abortion requires an act done to procure the miscarriage of a woman. The test-tube embryo left in the laboratory has never been carried by a woman.

Warnock came down in favour of limited permission to experiment on embryos.[18] Research should be permitted on human *in vitro* embryos only by specially licensed persons. Unauthorized use of a human embryo should be a criminal offence. The couple from whom the embryo originates must consent where possible. And most importantly, research would be allowed only up to fourteen days after fertilization. Research on an embryo at any later stage of development should be a criminal offence.

Warnock satisfied few of its audience. A number of doctors and scientists felt a limit of fourteen days would inhibit valuable research. Far more laymen were appalled at the concept of embryo research at all. Enoch Powell M.P. introduced a Private Member's Bill to ban research and eliminate the production of spare embryos. The Bill received massive support on its second reading. But the government refused it support or time and the Bill did not pass. The Bill would have required the permission of the Secretary of State to create an embryo *in vitro*. Such permission was only to be given '. . . for the purpose of enabling a named woman to bear a child by means of embryo insertion, and not for any other purpose'. The permission to create and handle the embryo would last until the procedure of embryo insertion was completed or four months as a maximum.

The Bill had certain dangers. Doctors were appalled at the thought of having to name their patients and seek government consent to what they saw as a medical procedure. The Bill would probably have meant that the practice of creating a number of embryos would have had to cease. And the Bill had loopholes if it was to carry out its author's intent. We shall see that in the U.S.A. doctors can now develop an embryo in the normal manner in a woman's womb, remove it, and 'transplant' it into another woman. Such an embryo created *in utero* might instead be removed and used for research. Embryos created *in utero* fall beyond the ban proposed by Mr Powell's Bill and the limitations proposed by Warnock.

Legislation is badly needed. It will not be easy. The moral positions are too far apart. Legislation must be carefully considered and not rushed. The opponents in the debate must recognize each other's sincerity, and be honest themselves. Those seeking a total ban must accept the price, namely that I.V.F. will be less effective, and that research into disease may take longer. Doctors supporting research should recognize that their opponents do not dismiss the benefits which research might bring. But set against the sanctity of life, such benefits cannot for many tip the balance in favour of research. The divide between the two sides is such that at the moment no legal controls at all limit embryo research. In the interim, doctors and scientists have acted to set up a voluntary licensing authority with a number of lay members, which will monitor embryo research in this country. The Medical Research Council has called for a national ethical committee to monitor embryo research on a formal basis.

Ova donation and embryo transplants

Some women, by reason of congenital defect or as a result of disease, do not ovulate at all. And so they can never conceive naturally. Intensive hormone treatment has helped many such women to start or re-start ovulation, but for a number that treatment proves fruitless. Techniques now exist whereby a fertile woman (the donor) can donate ova to the infertile woman (the recipient), so enabling the recipient to carry and give birth to a child. In Australia, surgeons removed an ovum from a donor via a minor surgical operation, fertilized it in the laboratory with the recipient's husband's sperm, and successfully implanted the embryo in the recipient's womb. A healthy baby was born in November 1983. In California a slightly different method was used. The donor was artificially inseminated with sperm taken from the recipient's husband, and five days later the fertilized ovum was transferred to the recipient's womb. A baby was born. We will refer to the first method as ova donation and to the second as embryo transplant. British doctors were well aware of, and capable of carrying out, both ova donation and embryo transplants. The legal and ethical implications of these techniques caused them to await the Warnock Report before offering this treatment for infertility here. What are the legal implications?

First, in both ova donation and embryo transplant, minor surgery involving a physical invasion of the donor's body is necessary to remove the ovum. Her free consent is essential if the doctor is to avoid liability for a trespass upon her. Clearly she must be fully aware of what is to be done to her, and in a state of mind where a rational and considered decision can be expected of her. The Royal College of Obstetricians and Gynaecologists suggest in their evidence to the Warnock Committee that ova might conveniently be collected from a donor undergoing sterilization or hysterectomy, or investigation of her own fertility. I would suggest that to collect ova in such circumstances is of dubious legality. Of course it has the advantage of avoiding an additional surgical interference with the donor, but this is now minimal in any case. The legal risk is that, should the donor later regret her decision to give away 'her child', she may contend that in circumstances where she was receiving other medical treatment from the doctor (and in at least two of the examples used by the R.C.O.G. the donor was on the point of giving up her own hopes of further children), she was not in a proper state of mind to give full and free consent. Ova donation should be independent of other medical treatment of the donor and only be embarked on after careful counselling of the donor.

Warnock saw no ethical objection to ova donation, which they regarded as the female counterpart of A.I.D. They properly laid great emphasis on counselling. Limitations similar to those imposed on A.I.D. were recommended.[19] Licensing and controls on ova donation should be introduced. The number of children born from the eggs of any one donor should be limited to ten. And, subject to the child's right to information as to his genetic origins, the anonymity of the donor should be protected.

Embryo transplants raise a slightly different issue. Suppose the donor consents to insemination but then refuses to agree to the removal of the embryo. The doctors can go no further. The courts will be unlikely to intervene. In a case where a couple persuaded a girl to conceive and carry the husband's child and she later went back on her agreement to hand over the baby, the courts refused to order her to do so and left the child in its natural mother's custody. The courts are even less likely to order a donor to submit to the removal of her child from her womb.

The Warnock Committee expressed no view on this matter. They were not satisfied with the safety of the technique of embryo transplant and recommended that it not be used at present.[20]

Next let us assume that after successful ova donation or embryo transplant the recipient gives birth to a child. What is the status of the child? Who is, in law, its mother? The donor may be said to be its genetic mother. The recipient is the carrier mother. A straight analogy with A.I.D. would force us to the conclusion that the donor was the mother. The following results would ensue. The child would be the illegitimate child of the donor and the recipient's husband. The donor would have a prima facie right to custody of the child and would be under an obligation to support the child. The recipient would have rights to custody of the child and duties in relation to its care and maintenance, providing she was married to the child's father, because she would have treated it as a child of the family. But if she were not married (and the R.C.O.G. envisages offering such treatment to couples in a stable relationship outside marriage), her only hope of obtaining the care of, or even access to, the child would lie in making it a ward of court. If the donor died intestate the child could claim from her estate. If the recipient died intestate the child would have no claim, and indeed, if the recipient's will gave legacies to 'my child' or 'my children', rather than naming the child, once again the child would be excluded. Perhaps the analogy with A.I.D. is inexact. After all, the infertile husband plays no part in the procreation of an A.I.D. child. The carrier mother is responsible for the transformation of the child from an embryo of a few cells to a viable child. It may be that the common law would declare her to be the mother. But this cannot be predicted with any certainty. Regarding the carrier mother as the mother has its drawbacks too. The child and society lose access to the child's genetic background. The child would be free to marry the donor's own children, its half-siblings, and prohibited from marrying any naturally conceived children of the recipient, with whom it would have no genetic relationship. Furthermore, while to designate the woman who bears the child as its mother would assist women who receive ova donation, it would frustrate the purpose of other infertile women who seek a 'surrogate' to carry the child for them.

The frequently heard reply that the legal niceties as to the child's status are irrelevant, because the carrier and the father will simply register the child as theirs, is inadequate. In so registering the child the 'parents' commit perjury. The child's origins remain shrouded in secrecy, in stark contrast to the statutory rights of the adopted child to discover the identity of his parents. The immediate family, certainly the father and probably any naturally conceived siblings, cannot be kept in the dark. If these methods of artificial conception are ever widely used, who can guarantee that a family dispute will not persuade some member of the family to invoke the dubious status of the special child in a fight for custody or a vicious inheritance claim? Legislation is imperative to control the use and the consequences of ova donation and embryo transplants.

Warnock, too, expressed this view. Legislation was recommended in relation to ova donation so that the carrier should be in law for all purposes the child's legal mother.[21]

Surrogate mothers

Finally we approach what has become the most emotive issue of all, surrogacy. Surrogacy may take a number of forms. The most common arrangement so far is this. A surrogate agrees to artificial insemination with the husband's sperm. She agrees to carry any resulting child and to hand the child over to the father and his wife immediately it is born. But I.V.F. may offer a couple where the wife does ovulate, but cannot safely carry a child to term, the chance of a baby who is genetically theirs. Ova are taken from the wife, fertilized in the laboratory with sperm from the husband, and the embryo implanted in the surrogate. The surrogate once again carries the child and agrees to hand it over at birth. The surrogate is in effect merely a 'hostess' for the couple's embryo. Surrogacy in all its forms has attracted almost universal condemnation in Britain. The greatest outcry is against commercial surrogacy, where the couple approach and pay an agency who find the surrogate and make all the necessary arrangements. 'Buying babies' is seen as repugnant and distasteful. And the government has introduced legislation to ban commercial surrogacy.[22] Warnock goes further, and would prohibit any third party, commercial agency or doctor, from assisting a couple to arrange a surrogate pregnancy. Warnock proposed to ban both forms of surrogacy, whether the child is genetically the child of the surrogate or of the couple.[23]

What are the legal issues arising out of surrogacy at the moment? There are three. Can it ever amount to a crime to arrange a surrogate pregnancy? What happens if the surrogate changes her mind and refuses to hand the baby over? Where the baby is genetically that of the wife and implanted in the surrogate via I.V.F., who is in law the child's mother?

Surrogacy where no money changes hands is perfectly lawful in the sense that no crime is committed. Once payment is made to the surrogate or an agency, however, an offence is committed. The Surrogacy Arrangements Act 1985 makes it a criminal offence for anyone to play any part in setting up a surrogacy arrangement on a commercial basis. Advertising or compiling information to promote or assist surrogacy arrangements are also made criminal. Offenders face a punishment of a fine and/or up to three months in prison. Under the Act, no offence is committed by a woman herself seeking to become, or becoming, a surrogate, nor is any offence committed by the man or the couple who persuade her to carry his child. The Act is limited to banning the activities of any commercial agencies or individuals aiming to make a profit out of surrogate motherhood. Under the Act, a gynaecologist who helps an infertile couple choose a suitable surrogate to carry a child for them incurs no criminal liability as long as he does not charge for his services. The Warnock proposal that *any* third party intervention, including professional help from a doctor, which was intended to set up a surrogacy arrangement should be made illegal has not been acted on. The 1985 Act does, however, embrace all forms of surrogacy regardless of whether the surrogate is the genetic mother or merely the 'hostess' for an embryo created from the ova and sperm of the infertile couple.

Although the surrogate and the couple engaging her services do not commit any offence under the 1985 Act even if she is paid for what she does, all three involved may be guilty of an offence under the Adoption Act 1958.[24] For it is a criminal offence, punishable by a fine or up to six months in prison, to give or receive any payment in relation to the adoption of a child, the grant of consent to adoption, or the handing over of a child with a view to its adoption. In order to make the baby born to the surrogate certainly and legally theirs, at any rate where the surrogate is the child's genetic mother, the infertile couple must ultimately adopt the child. If the fee paid to the surrogate is found to include a sum in payment for her agreement to the adoption and handing over the child, the surrogate and the prospective adopters may face prosecution. Moreover, the 1958 Act further provides that the court may order the infant to be removed to a place of safety 'until he can be restored to his parents or guardians or until other arrangements can be made for him'. So the child could in theory be removed from all those involved in the surrogacy arrangements and given in the end to fresh adopters. So far the Act has not been invoked in a surrogacy case. The dilemma of what to do in such cases faced Barnet Social Services early in 1985. A baby girl was born in their area amid great publicity. Her mother had agreed to carry her for a childless couple from abroad. She was artificially inseminated with the husband's sperm. The arrangements were made through an agency who were paid £13,000 by the father, of which the surrogate received £6,500. The baby was born and the mother prepared to hand her over. Barnet Social Services stepped in. Eventually the little girl was made a ward of court. Latey J.[25] had to decide on her fate. He said that the crucial issue before him was what was best for this baby. The methods used to create the child and the commercial aspects of the case raised delicate problems of ethics, morality and social desirability. They were not for him to decide. Careful inquiries showed that the father and his wife were eminently suitable to be parents. The judge granted them custody of the baby and permission to take her abroad with them to their home.

Barnet Social Services were criticized for intervening at all. But what else could they do? Had the child later figured in a child abuse case, opprobrium would have been heaped on Barnet. At a time when surrogacy is neither effectively prohibited nor properly regulated, making any baby so born a ward of court is probably the only option.

In the Barnet case the baby was genetically the child of the surrogate and the husband. Would it make any difference were the child genetically that of the husband and his wife? The case for allowing them to have the child might be seen to be stronger. And no criminal offence might even theoretically be committed. Surrogate and couple might argue that the child was the legitimate child of the couple. They would not then need to adopt. Handing the baby over and receiving a fee would not be making a payment with a view to adoption but simply paying for the surrogate's service in incubating the baby. 'Rent a womb' would literally be the case.

In the Barnet case, the mother went through with her agreement and relinquished the baby. What would have been the legal position had she changed her mind? It is clear that where there can be no doubt that the surrogate is the child's mother, where she is the genetic mother as well as the carrier, any agreement to hand over the child is unenforceable. Sections 1(2) of the Guardianship of Minors Act 1973 and 85(2) of the Children Act 1975 specifically so provide. The father is of course free to apply to court for custody of the child, but he is unlikely to succeed. In A. v. C.[26] a girl agreed to have a man's child by artificial insemination and to hand over the baby to its father and his woman friend in return for payment of £3,000. The mother changed her mind when the baby was born. The father sought care and control of the child. A judge refused him care and control but granted him limited access. The

Court of Appeal rejected his appeal and denied him access, expressing abhorrence at the arrangement that led to the child's birth.

Had the surrogate in *A.* v. *C.* been a carrier only, the issue once again would have arisen of who was in law the child's mother. If the genetic mother is regarded as the mother, the legislation rendering an agreement giving up rights in the child unenforceable would not apply. But at common law would the courts demand that a woman who has carried a child in her womb and nurtured it and risked, however minimally today, her life and health for it, give it up?

The possible legal issues arising from surrogacy are endless. If a carrier is negligent, drinks and smokes in pregnancy, can she be sued? If so, by whom? If the baby is born disabled, can the father and his wife be forced to take it or at least maintain it? Warnock expresses no views on these matters, nor on the crucial issue of who the mother is when surrogacy and I.V.F. are used together. They would outlaw surrogacy. The government's ban is limited to commercial surrogacy. And is surrogacy as unacceptable as seems now to be thought? Is a complete ban the best approach?

Conclusions

Research on embryos and surrogate motherhood are the most emotive issues that the advances in reproductive medicine have created. Agreement on either question is still far off. The government obviously regards the Warnock proposals as a hot potato they would rather not pick up. Legislation is essential, (1) to safeguard children born as a result of new procedures, particularly by a Family Law Act to give them a secure status in the family in which they are growing up, and (2) to set limits on what society considers permissible. If debate on that second stage is still too divisive for the government to take action, at least the issues of family law and liability to the child should be settled quickly.

Chapter 12
Abortion

No medico-legal issue has caused as much bitter public controversy as the debate on abortion. To those who believe that life given by God begins at conception, abortion is a grave sin, equivalent to murder, justifiable, if ever, only when the mother's life is at stake. To others, the right to abortion is part and parcel of a woman's sovereignty over her own body. The present law, the Abortion Act 1967, is unsatisfactory to both groups and is seen as an out-dated attempt at a compromise. We shall see too that the Act is far from clear in its provisions. The operation of the Act in 1987 has departed significantly from the intentions of those who framed the legislation twenty years earlier.

Criminal abortion

The present law relating to criminal abortion is to be found in section 58 of the Offences Against the Person Act 1861. This statute makes it a criminal offence punishable by a maximum of life imprisonment (1) for any woman, being with child, unlawfully to do any act with intent to procure a miscarriage, and (2) for any other person unlawfully to do an act with intent to procure the miscarriage of any woman. Self-induced abortion by the woman herself is therefore criminal only if the woman is in fact pregnant. Any act by a third party is criminal regardless of whether or not the woman can be proved to be pregnant. This limited protection afforded to the woman extends only to cases where she acts entirely alone. If she seeks help from a doctor, or any other person, she may be charged with aiding and abetting that person to commit the offence of criminal abortion[1] or of conspiracy with him to commit that offence.[2] The law embodied in the 1861 Act was applied rigorously up to 1967. In one case in 1927, a girl of 13 was prosecuted for attempting to induce an abortion on herself by taking laxative tablets and sitting in a hot bath. The rigour of the law was tempered only by a defence to a charge of criminal abortion by a doctor, that he acted to preserve the life or health of the mother.[3] Some doctors interpreted this defence liberally as including the mother's mental health and even happiness. Others would intervene only to prevent a life-threatening complication of pregnancy endangering the woman. Illegal abortion flourished. And several thousand women were admitted to hospital for treatment after back-street abortions. The Abortion Act 1967 was introduced to bring uniformity into the law, to clarify the law for the doctors, and to stem the misery and injury resulting from unhygienic, risky illegal abortions.

The Abortion Act 1967

This Act provides that abortion may be lawfully performed under certain conditions. A pregnancy may be terminated by a registered medical practitioner if *two* registered medical practitioners are of the opinion, formed in good faith, that grounds specified in the Act are met. These grounds are (1) that the continuance of the pregnancy would involve risk to the life of the pregnant woman, or of injury to her physical or mental health, or that of the existing children of her family, greater than if the pregnancy were terminated, and (2) that there is a substantial risk that if the child were born it would suffer from such physical or mental abnormalities as to be seriously handicapped. In assessing any risk to the health of the woman or her children, account may be taken of the woman's actual or reasonably foreseeable environment. Exceptionally one registered medical practitioner may act alone when he is of the opinion that an abortion is immediately necessary to save the life of the woman or to prevent grave permanent injury to her physical or mental health. Section 4 of the Act provides that no person shall be under any duty to participate in the performance of an abortion if he has a conscientious objection to abortion, save where immediate treatment is necessary to save the life of the woman or to prevent grave permanent damage to her health.

The furore surrounding the 1967 Act intensified rather than abated after the Act became law. Clinics offering abortions proliferated, and there was suspicion that some clinics were scrupulous neither about observing the conditions laid down by the Act, nor in their care of their patients. A committee was set up, headed by a woman judge, Dame Elizabeth Lane. She reported in 1974,[4] and certain changes were made relating to the approval of clinics operating outside the N.H.S. Critics of the Act were not satisfied. Clear evidence was emerging that women could obtain an abortion on demand from some gynaecologists. On the other hand claims were made that there were also, and still are, areas of the country where the Act is so restrictively interpreted that abortions are not much easier to obtain than before the Act was passed. In the latter case the only legal remedy would be for a woman to sue if she did suffer damage to her health as a result of the continuance of a pregnancy and successfully persuaded a court that the refusal of the abortion was negligent and unreasonable.[5] Unless her request for abortion was on the ground of foetal handicap, her hopes of success in legal action would be slim.

Abortion on demand or request

Gynaecologists who admit that they are prepared to perform an abortion simply on the request of the pregnant woman rely on statistics which appear to show that statistically the risk of abortion in the first 12 weeks of pregnancy is always less than the risk of childbirth. Therefore any abortion performed in that period meets the requirement of the Act that the continuance of the pregnancy poses a greater risk to the health of the woman than does termination. The medical profession itself is divided on the validity of the statistics. The issue has never been tested in court. Doctors performing abortions have to make a return to the D.H.S.S. stating the grounds for the operation. Some returns simply stated 'pregnancy' as the grounds. The D.H.S.S. changed its forms in 1982 in an attempt to tighten up on rules for legal abortions. The new form demanded to know the main *medical* condition justifying abortion. Pro-choice doctors continued to return 'pregnancy' as the grounds justifying an operation. No prosecutions have been brought in these cases. A successful prosecution against a doctor performing an abortion on demand would have to establish (a) that the statistics indicating that abortion posed less risk than childbirth were invalid, and (b) that the doctor on trial did not believe them to be valid and so failed to act in good faith. In view of the fact that only one successful prosecution has ever been brought against a doctor for performing an abortion purportedly under the 1967 Act in bad faith,[6] such a course would appear a clumsy means of regulating or eliminating abortion on demand or request. Frequent attempts by Private Members' Bills to amend the Act to require the risk of pregnancy to be *substantially* greater than that of abortion have also failed.

Post-coital birth control

The 1967 Act envisaged that once a diagnosis of pregnancy had been made, the doctor faced with a request for an abortion would then consider and weigh any risk to the woman or the child. But now a drug has been approved for general use which will, if taken by a woman within 72 hours of intercourse, ensure that any fertilized ovum will not implant in the womb. This 'morning-after' pill is not the only means by which a fertilized ovum (egg) may be disposed of at a stage before pregnancy can be confirmed. An intra-uterine device (I.U.D.) fitted within a similar time after intercourse will have the same effect.[7] And finally, if more than 72 hours elapse after unprotected intercourse before the woman seeks help, menstrual extraction can be used at or just after the due date of her next period. By this technique, an instrument attached to a vacuum is used to remove the whole of a woman's monthly period within a few minutes, including, if it exists, the product of any unwanted conception.

Are such methods lawful? They raise the question of where the line is to be drawn between contraception and abortion. A distinction must be made between the 'morning-after' pill and the I.U.D. on the one hand, and menstrual extraction on the other. The first two operate at a time before the fertilized ovum can implant in the womb. By the time menstrual extraction is utilized, the ovum will have become an implanted embryo. The action taken to remove that embryo by the vacuum clearly constitutes an induced abortion. The crucial legal issue then, in relation to the use of the 'morning-after' pill and the I.U.D., is whether a procedure which prevents implantation is an act done to procure a miscarriage so as to make the doctor liable for criminal abortion. The woman herself will not be able to be proved to be with child. She will thus not be guilty of an offence herself, but could, as we have seen, be prosecuted for conspiracy with her doctor. The argument that prevention of implantation is no offence runs thus. There is no carriage of a child by a woman before implantation takes place, and so to prevent that event even occurring cannot be an act done to procure a miscarriage. Many fertilized ova fail to implant naturally and no one then suggests that a miscarriage has occurred. The opponents of post-coital birth control reply that the fertilized ovum is present within the body of the woman; she carries it within her. Therefore there is carriage of a child, and any act removing that child from her womb is an act done to procure a miscarriage. Up to 40 per cent of *implanted* embryos also abort spontaneously. Thus arguments based on spontaneous loss of fertilized ova are irrelevant. The battle rages on. At its heart lies an unbridgeable disagreement as to the nature and sanctity of human life.

For the moment, the 'morning-after' pill and the I.U.D. will not be the subject of prosecutions. A challenge to the legality of the 'morning-after' pill by Life led the present Attorney-General to express his view that before implantation there is no pregnancy.[8] He will presumably intervene to stop any prosecution brought. And indeed, should the police think to prosecute, their obligation to inform the D.P.P. before proceeding[9] means that they are likely to be advised to desist. But it does not follow that successive Law Officers will take the same view, and specific legislation on the issue would be preferable.

I have so far assumed that the 'morning-after' pill or the I.U.D. is simply given to the woman without any attempt to meet the conditions laid down by the Abortion Act. It seems unlikely that such an attempt is ever made. But what if it is? And what of menstrual extraction, where the arguments relating to implantation and the start of pregnancy would be of no avail? Prima facie, any person participating in the procedure commits a criminal abortion unless the conditions laid down in the 1967 Act are met. The Act, as we said, appears to assume a positive diagnosis of pregnancy. It is possible, though, that two doctors could act on a supposition of pregnancy and then seek to apply the criteria in the Act to that hypothetical pregnancy. One doctor admitted to this practice, and regularly carried out menstrual extraction up to 18 days after a missed period. Again, the Attorney-General of the day gave his opinion that this was lawful.[10] The Lane Committee recommended that the Act should be amended to make this clear. Something should be done. For menstrual extraction can be carried out by a woman alone. Criminal liability may thus be avoided, because it will be impossible to prove whether she was ever in fact pregnant. But the procedure could harm her, and lack of medical advice could lead her to regard a missed period as a pregnancy when it may be a symptom of disease. The area of post-coital birth control is riddled with ambiguities. Full debate on it will be painful and rancorous, but needs to be faced. Leaving the issues to a court to decide when some determined person manages to force an issue to litigation in an over-charged emotional atmosphere is not a happy solution.

From foetus to baby

The Abortion Act itself sets no limit as to the time when abortion may lawfully be performed. It provides instead that nothing in the Act should affect the provisions of the Infant Life (Preservation) Act 1929 (protecting the life of a viable foetus). The objective of the law is to protect any baby born alive and any foetus which but for improper intervention could have been born alive. The 1929 Act created the offence of child destruction. That offence is committed when any person with intent to destroy the life of a child capable of being born alive causes the child to die before it has an existence independent of its mother. Evidence that a woman had been pregnant for 28 weeks or more is prima facie proof that she was pregnant with a child capable of being born alive. No offence is committed if the destruction of the child was done in good faith for the purpose only of preserving the life of the mother. Effectively, then, an outside limit of 28 weeks is placed on abortions in England and Wales. Any later abortion will constitute the offence of child destruction unless the doctor can show either that the child was not capable of being born alive, or that the act was done to save the mother's life. Yet the popular press still regales us with tales of babies who survive abortions only to be left to die on a slab in the sluice room. Let us examine the law more closely in the light of modern medicine.

Today in special care baby units babies of only 24 weeks' gestation and very occasionally less than 24 weeks can survive, and increasingly such babies survive without mental or physical handicap. The 1929 Act talks of a baby capable of being born alive and then presumes this to be so if the woman had been pregnant for 28 weeks. Child destruction is still committed when the aborted foetus was capable of live birth, even if of less than 28 weeks' development. But the burden of proof lies on the prosecution in such cases. Moreover, the phrase 'capable of being born alive' itself causes a difficulty. Very few, if any, babies born at less than 28 weeks would survive unless delivered with the utmost care and transferred swiftly to a special unit. One eminent lawyer once argued that such children are not 'capable of being born alive' within the meaning of the 1929 Act.[11] The Act protects only the child capable of surviving natural childbirth and living with no more than normal maternal care. The argument has the advantage of clarity and simplicity; nevertheless I disagree with this interpretation. 'Capable of being born alive' means, in my view, a child who has reached a stage of development where he can survive independently of his mother albeit requiring the support of medical science. Any other interpretation would have at least one undesirable and ludicrous consequence. Any child (of whatever stage of development even beyond 28 weeks) whose own, or whose mother's, condition prevented natural birth would be in theory beyond the protection of the law on child destruction. But my view presents its own contradictions. The rapid development of technology to keep premature babies alive allows very tiny babies of 22–24 weeks to survive for a while, at least in centres of excellence. No doubt the limit may be pushed back further. Is a 22-week foetus capable of being born alive because he might be kept alive for a few days in the most advanced neo-natal unit? Will the law distinguish between hospitals, saying foetus X, aborted in a small town, is not capable of being born alive but Y, aborted at University College Hospital, London, is? Of course not. Wishy-washy though it is, a general test of what could reasonably be expected with average facilities can be the only answer to the question of whether the foetus is a child 'capable of being born alive'.

The central dilemma of the doctors, apart from the uncertainty of the law, revolves around their own ability to save children at an earlier and earlier stage. It cannot be pleasant for a doctor on the same day to be required to use all his care and skill to save one baby whose mother has gone spontaneously into premature labour at 24–26 weeks, and then to destroy another baby at exactly the same stage of development. A joint working party of the Royal College of Obstetricians and Gynaecologists and the British Paediatric Association recommended that the limit for abortion should be set at 24 weeks.[12] But those who opposed the proposal argued that a 24-week limit would result in the birth of more handicapped babies. A survey of late abortions in 1982 indicated that out of 1,000 abortions *post* 24 weeks in that year, about 26 related to severely handicapped foetuses.[13] The force of the objection depends on (1) the degree of emphasis to be given to attempts to prevent the birth of handicapped babies as against the interests of healthy babies who may be aborted, if the limit is not reduced, and (2) acceptance of the view that the handicapped child's rights are less than those of his normal brother. It would now appear to be the case that the consensus of medical opinion and the guidance issued to gynaecologists by their Royal College has imposed *de facto* a limit of 24 weeks on the performance of abortion, with provision exceptionally for abortion of a grossly handicapped foetus at a later stage. Attempts to amend the law to give legal force to this veto on late abortions will continue to be resisted. It is argued that if the law made 24 weeks the outer limit for abortion, doctors, to ensure they were legally safe, would refuse to perform any abortion after 20 weeks. At present, diagnosis of foetal handicap is still performed mainly via a test, amniocentesis, carried out at 16–18 weeks into pregnancy. Allowing time for the tests to be processed, a woman may well be over 20 weeks pregnant before she is offered an abortion if the foetus is shown to be damaged. Trials are now in progress to test a new method of detecting handicap much earlier in pregnancy. Should amniocentesis be abandoned in favour of this at present experimental procedure to test for handicap at 8–12 weeks into pregnancy, the medical profession may be content to see the law fall into line with their present practice and ethical standards.

So far we have looked only at the child destroyed by the abortion itself. But whatever the foetus is subjected to, a child may survive and be born alive. Hence the horror stories I referred to of children left to die on a slab. The child once born alive is protected by the law of murder. Any positive act to destroy it is murder. Indeed, if the child survives the attempt at abortion but later dies as a result of the acts constituting that attempt, the doctor may be guilty of murder.[14] Failure to offer the child proper care *with the intention that it shall die* on the part of persons with an obligation to care for the child is once again murder. In 1983 a consultant gynaecologist was charged with attempted murder. The prosecution was brought after pressure from anti-abortion campaigners. Police had been informed that a baby had been left on a slab to die for some time before being transferred to a paediatric unit. The allegation against the doctor was that he performed an abortion on the basis of an estimate of 23 weeks' pregnancy and, when the baby proved to be of 34 weeks' gestation, left it without attention intending it to die. The prosecution was dismissed by magistrates for lack of evidence.

Failure to offer the child proper care out of incompetence or carelessness is manslaughter. The theory is clear. Reality is more problematical. A doctor who embarks on an abortion undertakes the care of the mother and undertakes to relieve her of her unwanted child. Yet the criminal law imposes on him an obligation to the child. His position nonetheless is clearly distinct from that of the doctor undertaking safely to deliver a mother of a desired child. And what of the child born handicapped? The doctor sets out to abort on the grounds of the substantial handicap to the child, but if it survives must he then use all his efforts to save it? This leads us into the whole issue of medical care of the defective newborn baby, its rights and those of its parents, a minefield we enter in the next chapter.

Nurses and abortion

Many nurses naturally find abortion distasteful and distressing. Many have exercised their right of conscientious objection to refuse to participate in abortions. Some complain that doing so has prejudiced their career. And some doctors have complained of 'disloyalty' by nurses reporting irregularities in performing abortions, particularly late abortions. But the nurses' greatest concern relates to a change in the manner of performing abortions in the middle months of pregnancy. The Abortion Act provides for circumstances when a pregnancy may lawfully be terminated by a registered medical practitioner, a doctor. In 1967 all lawful abortions were carried out by surgical means. The surgeons removed the foetus and ended the pregnancy. By 1972 medical induction of abortion was introduced as the standard method of terminating pregnancies in the middle months of pregnancy. Nurses play the leading role in this treatment. A doctor inserts a catheter into the woman's womb. Later, a nurse attaches the catheter via a flexible tube to a pump, which feeds the hormone prostaglandin through the catheter and induces premature labour. The nurse administers another drug via a drip in the woman's arm to stimulate her contractions. The immature foetus is born dead. The substances that cause the abortion are administered by the nurse. She in effect terminates the pregnancy.

The Royal College of Nursing became concerned about the legality of medical inductions of abortion. They argued that a pregnancy terminated by a nurse was not lawfully terminated. Nurses might face prosecution for conducting criminal abortions. The Department of Health and Social Security issued a circular upholding the legality of medical inductions of abortion. The Royal College of Nursing went to court for a declaration that the circular was wrong in law. The College lost in the High Court, won in the Court of Appeal and finally lost by 3–2 in the House of Lords.[15] A total of five judges out of nine agreed with the College. But it is the House of Lords' judgment that counts. The majority of their lordships held that the Act must be construed in the light of its social purposes, first, to broaden the ground on which abortions may lawfully be obtained, and second, to secure safe and hygienic conditions for women undergoing abortion. The Act contemplated the participation of a team of hospital staff involved in the overall treatment of the woman, and exonerated them all from criminal liability if the abortion was carried out within the terms of the Act. It was not necessary for a doctor to perform every physical act leading to the termination of the pregnancy. Provided a doctor accepts full responsibility for every stage in the treatment, a nurse acting under his instructions and in conformity with accepted medical practice does not act unlawfully when she administers the drugs which terminate the pregnancy in an induced abortion.

Fathers and abortion

Has the father of the unborn child any say in whether or not the child be aborted? In 1978 in *Paton* v. *British Pregnancy Advisory Service*,[16] a husband tried to prevent his wife having an abortion. She had been concerned about her pregnancy and consulted her doctor, but did not consult her husband. She obtained a certificate from two registered medical practitioners that the continuance of the pregnancy would involve risk to her health. So an abortion could lawfully proceed. Her husband intervened. He went to court to ask for an injunction (an order) to prevent the abortion from being carried out without his consent. The court refused an injunction. The judge said that the 1967 Act gave no right to the husband to be consulted. In the absence of such a right under the Act, the husband had 'no legal right enforceable at law or in equity to stop his wife having this abortion or to stop the doctors from carrying out the abortion'.

The abortion went ahead. The husband went to the European Commission on Human Rights, arguing that the Act and the judge's decision infringed the European Convention on Human Rights. He argued that his right to family life and the unborn child's right to life had been infringed. The Commission dismissed his claim.[17] They said that where an abortion was carried out on medical grounds, the husband's right to family life must necessarily be subordinated to the need to protect the rights and health of the mother. The unborn child's right to life was similarly subordinate to the rights of its mother, at least in the initial months of pregnancy. The Commission's decision suggests that a rather different view might be taken of abortions performed later in pregnancy and of abortions performed other than to protect the mother's health.

One final issue remains open. The father in *Paton* reluctantly accepted that the doctors' certificate as to the need for the abortion was issued in good faith. Had he challenged the certificate, could he have asked for an injunction to prevent an unlawful abortion taking place? The judge in *Paton* did not have to decide this point. He expressed the view that an injunction would not be granted. The supervision of abortion and the issue of the doctors' good faith is left to the criminal law and a jury. A remedy that consists of the prosecution of the doctor after the event is not one to bring much comfort to fathers.

Girls under 16

The Abortion Act makes no special provision for abortion on girls under 16. The much disputed issue has been whether in the case of such a girl her parents must consent to the abortion. In 1981 a sad case was reported.[18] A 15-year-old girl who already had one child became pregnant again while in local authority care. She wanted an abortion. Her doctors believed that the birth of a second child would damage her mental health and endanger her existing child. The girl's father objected. Abortion was contrary to his religion. The local authority applied to have the girl made a ward of court and thereby seek the consent of the court to the operation. Butler-Sloss J. authorized the abortion. She said that while she took into account the feelings of the parents she was satisfied that the girl's best interests required that her pregnancy be ended. Her decision was approved by the House of Lords in *Gillick* v. *West Norfolk and Wisbech A.H.A.*[19] Indeed, the result of that notable case would appear to be that as long as the girl is old enough to understand what abortion entails physically and emotionally, the doctor may go ahead on the basis of her consent alone. If the girl is insufficiently mature to make a decision for herself, the doctor must act in her best interests. Should her parents refuse consent to abortion, then like the local authority in the case discussed above, the doctors should seek to make the girl a ward of court[20] and ask a judge to decide on the conflict between medical and parental opinion. A doctor who ignores parental views will not be guilty of an offence of criminal abortion though. He may face legal action by the girl's parents in the civil courts, or, in an extreme case, prosecution for an assault on her.[21]

Conclusions

The debate on the morality of abortion continues. Pro- and anti-abortion campaigners shift ground from issue to issue. The 1967 Act was an attempt to delimit the operation of the law in a morally divided society. It has proved too full of ambiguity to meet its task. The Act has created as many opportunities for disagreement as the common law before it. Another attempt to provide a clear and enforceable statement of the law is overdue. The pattern of legislation in Europe and the law enforced by the Supreme Court in the U.S.A. has been to permit abortion on request in the first three months of pregnancy, to restrict abortion in the second three months, and to prohibit abortion in the final trimester. Such a pattern has the advantage of clarity, and represents the views of those who accept a woman's right to choose in the early weeks of her pregnancy but see the foetus as acquiring increasing rights as it develops into a recognizable person. It has nil attraction to the devout Roman Catholic or adamant 'pro-choice' campaigner. Nevertheless, the difficulty in framing new legislation must not deter lawmakers from a fresh attempt to clarify the law.

Chapter 13
The Handicapped Newborn:
Whose Rights? Whose Decision?

The birth of a severely handicapped baby is a human tragedy that most of us prefer to imagine will never happen to our family. The joy of normal childbirth is replaced by fear for the infant's and the family's future. Until relatively recently, two factors to some extent mitigated the parents' dilemma. Very little could be done for such a baby. Many handicapped babies survived only a few weeks or months from birth. Their parents suffered the pain of their loss, but they were spared anxiety as to the child's future. In any case, whether the child lived or died, the decision was made by 'God or nature'. The parents could do nothing about it. Advances in the care of the newborn and in neo-natal surgery have changed the picture. Doctors are now able to prolong the lives of the majority of handicapped infants. At first they applied their skills to the maximum possible number of damaged babies. Today some paediatricians voice publicly their doubts as to the wisdom of that original policy. It is even argued by some authors that in extreme cases the most gravely handicapped babies should be actively put to death. The parents of a badly handicapped baby today may be faced with agonizing decisions as to the treatment of their baby within hours of the trauma of birth.

Euthanasia and neonaticide

It is not only in relation to the handicapped newborn that doctors have begun to question the wisdom of *always* applying the full range of available modern treatment to prolong life. The problem arises equally acutely in relation to the terminally or chronically ill adult, or an adult or older child desperately and irreversibly injured in an accident. I deal with these topics in Chapter 20. I treat the subject of the handicapped newborn separately from the general question of adult euthanasia for the following reasons. First, the conscious adult patient can speak for himself. The decision as to any continuation of treatment may be his. Even if unconscious, he may earlier have expressed his wishes should the question arise. The baby cannot express any preference. His parents may give their views. The issue is then joined as to whether society and the law should regard those views as paramount. The *British Medical Journal* sees the parents as the instrument through which the baby accepts or rejects treatment.[1] Their wishes are therefore decisive. Parents' views are crucial, but children have rights too. Second, the baby's plight is very different from that of a newly handicapped adult. He does not move from full health to handicap. He does not endure a dramatic drop in his expectations of life. A life of handicap is all he can know. Third, a clear body of opinion has developed among doctors, philosophers and lawyers that the problems of the treatment of damaged or sick adults and the handicapped newborn raise separate if related issues. The term neonaticide[2] has been coined to cover the latter. Somehow the life of a newborn infant has come to be regarded in certain circles as having a lesser value. Proposals have been made for specific legislation on neonaticide. One feature of the debate and the proposals, though, is a distinct lack of agreement as to when the period after birth when neonaticide might be seen as permissible should end.

All in all, a tremendous shift in the climate of opinion has occurred among the professions. It may be doubted whether their views command wide popular support. What has brought about this shift? (1) For paediatricians one major factor must be that the universal application of sophisticated medicine and surgery to all damaged babies has had disappointing long-term results. This is best illustrated by the example of babies born suffering from spina bifida. The development of surgery to effect external repairs, and of 'shunts' to drain water from the brain where the frequent complication of hydrocephaly was present, was hailed as a landmark in the treatment of spina bifida. Virtually all affected babies were operated on within hours of birth. Research has shown[3] that barely 41 per cent of the children treated reach their tenth birthday. Of the survivors, only about 7 per cent can hope to lead something approximating to a normal, adult life. All the children underwent repeated painful surgery and long stays in hospital. (2) The Abortion Act permits the termination of pregnancy when there is a substantial risk that the child, if born, will be severely handicapped. Amniocentesis is increasingly used to test mothers at risk for spina bifida or Down's syndrome. At present it is carried out at 16 weeks into pregnancy, and if the results are positive the pregnancy is ended at about 20 weeks. The child is very real to a mother at that stage. She may find it difficult to understand why a child who could have been actively destroyed if his handicap had been diagnosed in pregnancy must be the subject of intensive life-saving measures if his handicap goes unnoticed until his birth. (3) The concept of the sanctity of each and every human life is under attack. Forceful arguments are advanced[4] that the value of life lies in its quality and the contribution possible to society, rather than in any intrinsic merit in life itself. Such arguments are equally forcefully rebutted, but seem to have commanded a measure of support among the medical profession as far as severely damaged babies are concerned.

1981: Baby Alexandra

The debate as to the treatment of the handicapped newborn reached the English courts in 1981 in a blaze of publicity. First, there occurred the case of Baby Alexandra; this little girl was born in 1981 suffering from Down's syndrome and an intestinal obstruction. In a normal child, simple surgery would have been carried out swiftly with minimal risk to the baby. Without surgery the baby would die within a few days. The baby's parents refused to authorize the operation. They agreed that God or nature had given their child a way out. The doctors contacted the local authority and the child was made a ward of court. A judge was asked to authorize the operation. He refused to do so. The authority appealed, and the Court of Appeal[5] ordered that the operation go ahead. Counsel for the parents submitted that in this kind of decision the views of responsible and caring parents must be respected and that their decision should decide the issue. The Court of Appeal rejected the submission, holding that the decision must be made in the best interests of the child.

Templeman L.J. said:

It is a decision which of course must be made in the light of the evidence and views expressed by the parents and the doctors, but at the end of the day it devolves on this court in this particular instance to decide whether the life of this child is demonstrably going to be so awful that in effect the child must be condemned to die, or whether the life of this child is still so imponderable that it would be wrong for her to be condemned to die. There may be cases, I know not, of severe proved damage where the future is so certain and where the life of the child is so bound to be full of pain and suffering that the court might be driven to a different conclusion, but in the present case the choice which lies before the court is this: whether to allow an operation to take place which may result in the child living for 20 or 30 years as a mongoloid or whether (and I think this brutally must be the result) to terminate the life of a mongoloid child because she also has an intestinal complaint. Faced with that choice I have no doubt that it is the duty of this court to decide that the child must live.

213

1981: the trial of Dr Arthur

In October of 1981 the Director of Public Prosecutions announced that he would not proceed against a doctor who had been reported as taking no action to preserve the life of a spina bifida baby.[6] Then, in November, Dr Leonard Arthur, a distinguished paediatrician from Derby, faced trial for murder.[7] A baby boy was born in the hospital where Dr Arthur was consultant paediatrician. He suffered from Down's syndrome. His parents did not wish him to survive. He died 69 hours after his birth. The prosecution alleged that Dr Arthur ordered nursing care only and prescribed a drug which would suppress the baby's appetite and so starve him to death. They claimed that apart from being a Down's baby the baby was otherwise healthy, and that his death resulted from lack of sustenance and the effect of the drug causing him to succumb to broncho-pneumonia. Defence evidence established that (1) the baby suffered from severe brain and lung damage, (2) Dr Arthur followed established practice in the management of such an infant, (3) that in the first three days of life normal babies take in little or no sustenance and usually lose weight (which the dead baby had not done). The baby patently did not starve to death. The judge directed that the charge be altered to attempted murder. Summing up on the law for the jury, the judge stressed that there is '. . . no special law in this country that places doctors in a separate category and gives them special protection over the rest of us . . .' He emphasized that however severely handicapped a child may be, if the doctor gives it drugs in an excessive amount so that the drugs will cause death then the doctor commits murder. He highlighted the distinction between doing something active to kill the child and electing not to follow a particular course of treatment which might have saved the infant. Considering the ethical arguments on terminating newborn life, the judge reminded the jury that if ethics and the law conflict, the law must prevail. But his lordship concluded:

> . . . I imagine that you [the jury] will think long and hard before deciding that doctors of the eminence we have heard in representing to you what medical ethics are and apparently have been over a period of time, you would think long and hard before concluding that they in that great profession have evolved standards which amount to committing crime.

The jury acquitted Dr Arthur.

A confused picture emerges from 1981. The baby girl with Down's syndrome was ordered to be saved. The D.P.P. implied that no crime was committed in withholding treatment from a spina bifida baby. Dr

Arthur was not guilty of a crime in relation to his treatment of a severely damaged Down's infant. A tentative attempt is made to rationalize these three decisions. I recognize that my conclusions will provoke considerable disagreement among doctors and lawyers.

Deliberate killing

Neither doctor, nor parents, nor any other person may do any *act* intended *solely* to hasten the death of the handicapped baby. The deliberate killing of any human being is murder. The moment that the child has an existence separate from his mother,[8] the moment he has independent circulation, even though the afterbirth may not yet fully have been expelled from the mother's body, he is protected by the law of murder. It has on occasion been faintly argued that a grossly malformed child, 'a monstrous birth', should not be regarded in law as human.[9] No court is likely to accede to such a view. Defining humanity, other than by virtue of human parentage, would be an impossible and unacceptable task. Does 'monstrous' refer to appearance, in which case an intelligent infant of appalling mien could legitimately be destroyed? Does it cover lack of intelligence, lack of a brain? Both are almost impossible to measure at birth.

One area of doubt does exist. What of the doctor who administers drugs, or large quantities of a drug, with the primary intention of relieving a baby's suffering but in the knowledge that the drugs may shorten the baby's life or weaken his capacity to survive? In *R.* v. *Adams*[10] a doctor was charged with the murder of an elderly patient by means of excessive quantities of pain-relieving drugs. He was acquitted. Directing the jury, Devlin J. said:

If life were cut short by weeks or months it was just as much murder as if it were cut short by years.

He went on to say:

But that does not mean that a doctor aiding the sick or the dying has to calculate in minutes or hours, or perhaps in days or weeks, the effect on a patient's life of the medicines which he administers. If the first purpose of medicine – the restoration of health – can no longer be achieved, there is still much for the doctor to do, and he is entitled to do all that is proper and necessary to relieve pain and suffering even if measures he takes may incidentally shorten life.

Two conditions, then, limit the administration to a baby of medicines that may in themselves, or in the quantities administered, as a secondary effect shorten his lifespan. (1) His handicap or congenital defect must be of a kind that will in the course of nature lead to his death early in infancy. If he is handicapped but has a lifespan measurable in years, even though significantly less than that of a healthy child, the use of such drugs must be avoided. This proposition then begs the question as to the case of a child suffering from a defect that could kill him swiftly but whose life could be prolonged by active treatment. I consider this in the next section, taking the view that if the doctor may lawfully withhold treatment then he may lawfully do all he can to mitigate the suffering of the untreated baby. (2) The drugs must be shown to be necessary to relieve suffering in the baby. It may be that the main threat of the charge of murder against Dr Arthur was blunted once the defence showed that the drug he prescribed was given not to an uncomplicated Down's baby but to a severely damaged and probably suffering infant. The jury may have reasoned thus. The child's condition killed him in the end. His doctor was entitled to make his hours on earth comfortable.

Withholding treatment

To what extent, then, does the law require parents and doctors to provide treatment to prolong the baby's life? The bare bones of the law can be stated quite simply. Before any failure to treat a child can engage criminal liability, it must be established that a duty to act was imposed on the accused. Parents are under a duty to care and provide for their dependent children. Failing to provide proper care, including medical aid where necessary, will result in a conviction for wilful neglect of the child, provided that the parent was aware of the risk to the child's health.[11] Should the child die, the parents may be convicted of manslaughter.[12] Parents who are well aware of the danger to a child's health but who do not seek medical aid because of religious or other conscientious objection to conventional medicine have no defence to criminal prosecutions for neglect or manslaughter.[13] Parents who deliberately withhold sustenance and care from a child intending him to die may be guilty of murder.[14] Finally, a range of other legal remedies is available to local authority social services departments. Failure to provide medical aid is a ground for taking a child into care,[15] or the child may be made a ward of court.[16] What of the doctor? If he is under a duty to treat a baby then, like the parent, should the child die, he may be prosecuted for manslaughter if his omission resulted from neglect, or for murder if he intended the infant to die. Once the doctor accepts the baby as a patient he assumes a duty to that baby to give him proper medical care. Nor is it likely that a paediatrician could, should anyone ever want to, evade responsibility by refusing to accept the child as a patient after his birth. His contract with the N.H.S. imposes on him an obligation towards the children born in his hospital or area, giving rise to a duty to the individual infant.[17]

Parents and doctors, then, have a duty to provide medical aid, but what is the scope of that duty? Where a baby is born suffering from gross handicap, may proper medical care be defined as keeping the baby comfortable but deliberately withholding life-prolonging treatment? It is now that we have to attempt to reconcile the 1981 series of cases. Two factors play a vital role in the decision as to whether to treat a handicapped newborn infant. What do his parents desire? What is the practice of the medical profession in the management of this kind of handicap? The answer to the second question is that in a number of cases many doctors will explain the treatment available, give a prognosis as to the child's future, and then abide by the decision taken by the parents. That practice does not entirely accord with the view of the Court of Appeal in the case of Baby Alexandra, when they ordered that a Down's baby undergo surgery to remove an intestinal blockage. But, say some, it is supported by the decision not to prosecute doctors who omitted to operate on a spina bifida baby, and by the acquittal of Dr Arthur. The conditions of the children in issue were somewhat different. Baby Alexandra suffered from the mental and physical handicaps attendant on Down's syndrome. If treated, she could expect the same quality of life as any one of the other many, many Down's babies born each year. She would suffer no pain from her handicap, and the evidence suggests that if properly cared for such children are within themselves reasonably happy. The surgery needed to save her was simple and without risk. The spina bifida baby faced an operation leading to a series of further operations with a less than 50 per cent chance of his survival beyond ten years old. His life would be one of pain and lived mostly in hospital. Dr Arthur's infant patient was severely damaged over and above his condition as a Down's baby. The issue of whether Dr Arthur should have actively intervened to save him once he developed broncho-pneumonia was never properly examined at his trial.

Perhaps one can, very hesitantly, suggest that from the general law on medical care and from those cases in 1981 the following points emerge.

(1) Any decision in relation to the treatment, or non-treatment, of a handicapped newborn baby is to be taken in the best interests of the child. He is to be accorded no lesser value because he is newborn than if he were 5, 15, or 50. And his parents' wishes, while relevant, are *not* paramount. (2) When surgery is called for if the child's life is to be prolonged, the surgery necessary may be withheld if the child's handicap is so severe and crippling that even after the operation his life, however well he is cared for, will be 'demonstrably awful', will be dominated by pain and suffering for *him*. (3) If the surgery necessary is extensive and entails risk to the child, and has a relatively low rate of success, it may be more readily withheld. (4) Non-surgical treatment, such as antibiotics should the child develop an infection, need not be given to a child already in the process of dying within a few weeks or months. A child whose handicap will disable him, but not within the foreseeable future kill him, must be treated exactly as a healthy child would, save in the most extreme and painful of cases where the child's present and future life is one of known suffering. (5) No child who demands food should have it withheld. A child who makes no demands should be tube-fed or otherwise nourished, just as an otherwise normal but premature baby would be, unless once again his handicap will inevitably cause his death in weeks or in months, or his life, if he survives, offers no prospect of anything but suffering.

Two features predominate if this analysis of the law is correct. First, the interests of the child are assessed on the basis of an assumption that he receives proper care in his future life. It has been argued that handicapped children rejected by their parents enjoy such a low quality of life in institutions and foster-homes that death must be in their best interests. If this is so, it is an indictment of our society and not of the state of the law. Second, to put it brutally, the result of the application of the points outlined above represents the present law as this. The child with gross spina bifida must be afforded general nursing care, and fed if he demands food. A considered decision by doctors and parents conforming to proper paediatric practice that no other steps be taken to prolong his life will not expose the doctor to criminal liability. The baby suffering from Down's syndrome, or other mental handicap, plus some other minor defect requiring surgery, must be operated on. If he contracts an infection, he must be treated. Mental handicap is more horrifying to some than physical defect. A mentally handicapped child creates a heavy burden for his family. But no one would, I hope, deny that careful thought must be given before judges or society decide that the mentally handicapped should deliberately be left to die for want of routine treatment.

The overwhelming problem of the law at present is this. There is difficulty in reducing it to working principles. There is ample room for considerable disagreement with what is said. A doctor making a decision in conformity with his conscience, his ethical standards, and with what he believes to be the law of the land can face debate on that decision, not in academic journals but in court as he faces trial for murder. For if he falls short of the duty imposed by law and he intended the death of the child, that is the only appropriate charge to bring against him. And the only way in which paediatricians could protect themselves in cases of difficulty where parents objected to treatment would be to apply to have each and every affected child made a ward of court.

Proposals for legislation

Legislation on neonaticide has been proposed on three grounds. (1) The law should be clarified. No other doctor ought to face, as Dr Arthur did, a test case in an uncharted area charged with the offence of murder. (2) The law should more readily permit doctors to withhold treatment, where parents concur, from children whose objective quality of life is low. (3) In extreme cases the law should sanction active measures to end the child's life. This is seen by some as more humane than leaving the child to a lingering death.[18] Proposals for legislation have met with a lukewarm to hostile reaction from the medical profession. We will examine two such proposals.

The first is a detailed draft 'Limitation of Treatment Bill' proposed by two lawyers, Diana and Malcolm Brahams.[19] Their Bill proposes that no criminal offence would be committed where a doctor refused or ceased treatment of an infant under 28 days, provided that (1) the parents gave their written consent, and (2) two doctors, both of at least seven years' standing and one of them being a paediatrician, certified in writing that the infant suffered from severe physical or mental handicap which was either irreversible or of such gravity that after receiving all reasonably available treatment the child would enjoy no worthwhile quality of life. The Bill directs the doctors to consider a number of factors in assessing the child's likely quality of life. They must consider (*inter alia*) the degree of pain and suffering likely to be endured, the child's potential to communicate, and also the willingness of the parents to care for him and the effect that that may have on *their* physical and mental health.

A doctor/lawyer team, Professor Mason and Dr McCall Smith of Edinburgh University, suggest a much shorter, single-clause piece of legislation.[20] The Bill would read:

It will not be an offence if two doctors, one of whom is a consultant paediatrician, acting in good faith and with the consent of both parents, if available, arrange within the first 72 hours of life for the termination of the life of an infant because further life would be intolerable by virtue of pain and suffering or because of severe cerebral incompetence; and the underlying condition is not amenable to reasonable medical treatment.

Both proposals apply only to the more severely damaged of babies. The baby must have 'no worthwhile quality of life' under the first; his prospect of life must be 'intolerable' under the second. Thus neither would seem to excuse non-treatment of a Down's baby with no additional defect or deformity likely to lower his quality of life. The term 'severe cerebral incompetence' in the second proposal suggests a total inability to appreciate one's surroundings or communicate with others. As it stands, it is a phrase which could cause endless difficulties of interpretation. The differences between the two proposals highlight the difficulties in the path of any legislator. The Brahams' proposal is the wider, in that the latitude offered to doctors lasts for up to 28 days. It allows time for tests and diagnosis, and time for parents to recover from the trauma of birth and make a considered decision. It takes into account the interests of the parents and the family, thus permitting a greater degree of parental control over the final decision. It stops short of sanction for any active measures to end the baby's life. The Mason/McCall Smith proposal allows only 72 hours for any decision to be made, and essentially the decision will be that of the doctors. The parents must consent. They may require the doctor to treat the child but they cannot oblige him to withhold treatment. It is in this sense a much more child-centred proposal. The child's life may be terminated if and only if his life is medically likely to be intolerable. The parents' ability and willingness to care for him are not to be a factor in the decision. The controversy inherent in the Mason/McCall Smith Bill is that it does sanction active measures to kill the baby. This is an issue which must be faced. For the argument goes: if it is permissible to stand by and watch the baby die slowly, why is it impermissible to end his life swiftly and painlessly? The intention in both cases is the same, that the baby should die. It is an issue which must be faced again in relation to euthanasia and adults, and I can suggest no solution to it that will not be deeply disturbing to many members of society.

Neither proposal has met with much favourable response from the medical profession. The Brahams 'Bill' has been vigorously criticized by Dr Havard of the B.M.A.[21] He sees it as an attempt to confine and define medical discretion to an unacceptable degree. He also, and with some justification, fears a situation where the interpretation of such a statute could be argued through the courts at length. Dr Havard would prefer a statement by the Attorney-General to the effect that no doctor taking a decision relating to a severely handicapped baby would face prosecution if he made the decision in a suitable paediatric unit. If necessary he would support legislation to that effect. Such a course will not commend itself to lawyers. It would be in effect an abdication by the law and society from all decision-making in this sensitive area.

If legislation is to be enacted in this field, society must take a series of deeply difficult and divisive decisions. Do we accept some distinction in the value of the life of the newborn, and the older child or adult? If so, where is the line to be drawn? Is it 72 hours, or 28 days, or later still? The Abortion Act has altered our perception of the sanctity of life. But debate has ebbed and flowed for centuries as to the status and humanity of the unborn. Abortion, although severely punished, was never equated with murder. Birth is a clear dividing line. No other distinction can be as clear. Do we regard the parents as standing proxy for their child in any decision as to treatment? If so, why draw the line at 28 days? Older children develop chronic disease, are disabled in accidents, are discovered to suffer from gross handicap later in childhood. We have as a next stage to determine whether parents are to be given the power of life or death over all their minor children.

The enormity of the moral and legal problems facing an intending legislator makes the prospect of legislation remote. The experience of attempts to legislate on the related area of voluntary euthanasia does not make encouraging reading for intending legislators.[22] Before giving up on any attempt to introduce reform, one question needs answering. The doctor attending a handicapped baby has an awesome responsibility. If, with entirely honest motives, he makes a decision out of line with a law which is far from clear, he may be punished as a murderer. It may be that the decisions taken by the doctors, the responsibility we entrust to them, are of such importance that the awfulness of the penalty for misjudgment is justified. But we must be satisfied that this is so before engaging too readily in criticism of the profession for attempts to protect its members.

Chapter 14
Doctors and Child Patients

The previous chapter considered the effect of criminal and civil law regulating the treatment, or non-treatment, of severely damaged new-born infants. In this chapter we move on to examine generally the impact of the law on the doctor's relationship with his child patients and their parents. Victoria Gillick's campaign to prevent girls under 16 being prescribed the Pill without their parents' knowledge thrust the issue of parental rights into the limelight. At the end of the day the House of Lords ruled against her. But the Gillick saga illustrates the many legal problems concerning parents, children and doctors.

We look at the decision in *Gillick*[1] and consider its impact on the medical treatment of children generally, not just on the question of contraception for teenage girls. Where does the law stand on the question of blood transfusions for the children of Jehovah's Witnesses? May a doctor insist on administering a transfusion against the parents' wishes? Are there limits to treatment to which a parent may agree on behalf of the child? For instance, may a mother, learning that her 4-year-old daughter is a likely carrier of haemophilia, have the child sterilized at 4? What role does the law play in limiting damaging or mutilating surgery on children, for example the ghastly practice of female circumcision? These are just some of the issues addressed now.

Family Law Reform Act 1969

The Family Law Reform Act 1969 reduced the age of majority from 21 to 18. For the purposes of medical treatment, however, children attain adult status at 16. When the 1969 Act was before Parliament it was unclear as to what effect, if any, a consent to medical treatment given by a minor, a person under the age of majority, might have. Numbers of 16 and 17-year-olds live, or spend considerable periods of time, away from their parents. Some are married and parents themselves. Section 8 of the 1969 Act clarified the law concerning 16 to 18-year-olds and empowered them to consent to their own medical treatment. Sub-sections (1) and (2) of section 8 are clear. They provide:

(1) The consent of a minor who has attained the age of 16 years to any surgical, medical or dental treatment which, in the absence of consent, would constitute a trespass to his person shall be as effective as it would be if he were of full age: and where a minor has by virtue of this section given an effective consent it shall not be necessary to obtain any consent for it from his parent or guardian.

(2) In this section 'surgical, medical or dental treatment' includes any procedure undertaken for the purposes of diagnosis, and this section applies to any procedure (including, in particular, the administration of an anaesthetic) which is ancillary to any treatment as it applies to that treatment.

So far, so good; once a person is 16 he can decide for himself on matters of medicine and surgery. But section 8 went on in sub-section (3) to provide:

(3) Nothing in this section shall be construed as making ineffective any consent which would have been effective if this section had not been enacted.

The majority of lawyers and doctors interpreted section 8(3) in this way. The common law had never directly determined the issue of when, if at all, a child could give effective consent to medical treatment. The assumption acted on was that the law gave effect to consent by a minor provided she or he was sufficiently mature to understand the proposed treatment or surgery.[2] Sixteen was the *average* age at which doctors judged patients to be old enough to give consent without consulting parents on every occasion. At 16, too, a person may choose his own doctor,[3] and at 16 a person may without reference to his parents seek voluntary treatment in a mental hospital.[4] Nevertheless, many doctors regarded themselves free to treat children *under* 16 without parental approval if the individual child appeared sufficiently intelligent and grown up to take the decision on treatment alone. The issue before 1969 in *every* case turned on the doctor's assessment of the particular child in his surgery. The 1969 Act freed the doctor from doubt and risk where the patient was over 16. He no longer had to consider the maturity of a patient over 16. He could assume adult status and capability. Sub-section (3), then, it was argued, simply preserved the status quo for the under-16s. Doctors could continue to treat a child under 16 as long as the child was mature enough to make his own judgment. This assumption, that there had always been a limited freedom to treat children under 16 without parental consent, and that what sub-section (3) did was preserve that freedom, was the issue at the heart of the Gillick saga.

The Gillick case

The Gillick saga has its origins in a circular issued by the D.H.S.S. in 1974, outlining arrangements for a comprehensive family planning service within the N.H.S. Section G dealt with provision for the young. Statistics on the number of births and induced abortions among girls under 16 led the D.H.S.S. to conclude that contraceptive services should be made more readily available to that age group. The essence of the D.H.S.S. advice was that the decision to provide contraception to a girl under 16 was one for the doctor. He might lawfully treat, and prescribe for, the girl without contacting her parents. Indeed, he should not contact parents without the girl's agreement. In 1980 the D.H.S.S. revised its advice. The revised version stressed that every effort should be made to involve parents. But if the girl was adamant that her parents should not know of her request for contraception, the principle of confidentiality between doctor and patient should be preserved. The parents must not be told.

This amended advice from the D.H.S.S. did not satisfy critics appalled at the prospect of young girls being put on the Pill in their parents' ignorance. Victoria Gillick, then the mother of four daughters under 16, wrote to her local health authority seeking an assurance that none of her daughters would be given contraceptive or abortion advice or treatment without her prior knowledge and consent until they were 16. The assurance was refused, and after further fruitless correspondence Mrs Gillick went to court in August 1982. She sought declarations (1) against her health authority and the D.H.S.S. to the effect that their advice that children under 16 could be treated without parental consent was unlawful and wrong, and (2) against her health authority to the effect that medical personnel employed by them should not give contraceptive and/or abortion advice and/or treatment to any child of Mrs Gillick's under 16 without her prior knowledge and consent.

Mrs Gillick's concern was with contraceptive and abortion advice and treatment for under-16s. She had no axe to grind in respect of other forms of medical treatment of children. The trouble was that this issue could not that easily be isolated from more general problems. And there was another legal problem to bedevil the debate. Mrs Gillick's counsel pursued a two-pronged attack. They challenged the assumption that the common law had ever permitted medical treatment of children under 16 in the absence of parental consent. And they argued in relation to contraception specifically that as it is a crime for a man to have sexual intercourse with a girl under 16, providing her with contraception amounts to the crime of causing or encouraging sexual intercourse with a girl under 16.

Children under 16 and consent to treatment

The first judge[5] to consider Mrs Gillick's claim rejected emphatically her contention that a doctor may never treat a child under 16 without parental agreement. He saw that issue as a straightforward question of when the consent of a child prevented a contact with the child from constituting a battery. If the doctor examined a girl physically before prescribing the Pill, did he run the risk of committing a civil battery or even a criminal assault on the girl? No, said Woolf J., provided the girl had the maturity and understanding to appreciate the nature of the consent she gave, the doctor could safely go ahead with treatment on the basis of her consent alone. The finding was not limited to contraception but applied to all forms of medical treatment. The nearer the child was to 16, and the more minor the nature of the treatment, the more likely it was that the child would be considered capable of giving the necessary consent. Where treatment with long-term implications was proposed, and the judge gave the example of sterilization, he warned that he doubted whether the consent of the child would ever be sufficient to justify the doctor's action. Woolf J. upheld the assumption as to how the common law approached the issue of consent given by children. Section 8(3) of the Family Law Reform Act, he found, simply preserved the common law position.

Mrs Gillick took her case on to the Court of Appeal and scored a famous victory in that arena.[6] The judgment of Woolf J. and the majority opinion among medical practitioners that the validity of a child's consent depended upon the individual child's maturity and capacity to understand the proposed treatment was rejected by the Court of Appeal as '. . . singularly unattractive and impracticable particularly in the context of medical treatment'.[7]

For the Court of Appeal the issue centred not on whether a child might be sufficiently mature to give consent to any particular contact with another, but on parental rights to control what happened to their children. They held that the common law gave to parents rights of custody and control over their children until either a child reached the age of majority, or common law or statute expressly set a lower age for emancipation from parental control in respect of a specified activity. So the Family Law Reform Act had empowered children to consent to medical treatment at 16. But below 16, at any rate where girls were concerned,[8] the parents' rights were paramount and the consent of a child was irrelevant and of no effect.

Moreover, not only actual treatment was unlawful if given without parental agreement. Any information or advice on contraception or abortion was unlawfully given in the absence of parental knowledge and agreement. After the Court of Appeal judgment a doctor could not safely see a child under 16 in his surgery or clinic without a parent's presence. And the legality of sex education in schools was thrown into doubt.

Arguments that the doctor was entitled to override parental rights to promote the best interests of a child patient were dismissed unequivocally. A doctor could intervene only in an emergency or with the backing of a court order. What amounted to an emergency, whether it referred to general medical treatment to save a child rushed to a casualty ward, or envisaged emergency contraceptive treatment, was not defined by the Appeal Court.

The end of the story?

The D.H.S.S. appealed to the House of Lords. By a majority of 3 to 2 the House of Lords held that the original advice circulated by the D.H.S.S. was not unlawful and that a child under 16 could in certain circumstances give a valid consent to contraception or abortion treatment without parental knowledge or agreement.[9] To consider the implications of their decision for doctors, parents and children, the Law Lords' judgment will be dissected into three parts: (1) the general issue of consent by children to medical treatment, (2) the special problems of contraception and abortion and consent thereto, and (3) the criminal law as it affects contraception.

The general problem of consent

The majority of their Lordships rejected the Court of Appeal's finding that consent given by a child under 16 was of no effect. They accepted the view that the Family Law Reform Act had left the question open. The matter was for the common law to determine. But the common law was not static, fossilized in eighteenth-century notions of the inviolable rights of the paterfamilias. Judge-made law must meet the needs of the times. Parental rights derived from parental duties to protect the person and property of the child. Modern legislation qualified and limited parental rights by placing the welfare of the child as its first priority. Parental rights being dependent on the duty to care for and maintain the child, they endured only so long as necessary to achieve their end. As Lord Scarman put it: '. . . the parental right yields to the child's right to make his own decisions when he reaches a sufficient understanding and intelligence to be capable of making up his own mind on the matter requiring decision'.[10]

Parental rights were thus not absolute. Furthermore, the court found that the common law had never regarded the consent of a child as complete nullity. Were that the case, sexual intercourse with a girl under 16 would inevitably be the crime of rape. That is not so. Provided the girl is old enough to understand what she is agreeing to, intercourse with her with her consent will not be rape. Parliament, to protect girls under 16 from the consequences of their own folly, enacted a separate offence of unlawful sexual intercourse with girls under 16 in the commission of which the girl's consent is irrelevant. And if the girl validly consented, that is the only offence committed, and not the more serious crime of rape. In another context, just a year before the *Gillick* hearing, the House of Lords had considered the crime of kidnapping as it related to children under 16. They held that the central issue was the agreement of the child, not either parent, to being taken away by the accused.[11] In the case of a young child absence of consent could be presumed. With an older child the question was whether he or she had sufficient understanding and intelligence to give consent.

Moving from the general issue of consent by children to the problem of consent to medical treatment, the House of Lords saw no reason to depart from the general rule. Lord Fraser thought it would be ludicrous to say that a boy or girl of 15 could not agree to examination or treatment for a trivial injury. Importantly, Lord Templeman, who dissented on the specific issue of contraceptive treatment, agreed with his colleagues that there were circumstances where a doctor could properly treat a child under 16 without parental agreement. He concurred that the effect of the consent of the child depended on the nature of the treatment and the age and understanding of the child. A doctor, he thought, could safely remove tonsils or a troublesome appendix from a boy or girl of 15 without express parental agreement. With some confidence, then, it may be predicted that in relation to general problems of medical treatment, the *Gillick* case concludes that a child below 16 may lawfully be given medical advice and treatment without parental agreement, provided that child has achieved sufficient maturity to understand fully what is proposed. The doctor treating such a child will not be at risk of either a civil action for battery or criminal prosecution. One would go further and say that on this general issue *Gillick* is the end of the story.

The special problems of contraception and abortion

Lord Templeman, as we have seen, departed from his brethren's views on the specific issue of contraception. The core of his disagreement with them is this. He did not accept that a girl under 16 has sufficient maturity and understanding of the emotional and physical consequences of sexual intercourse to consent to contraceptive treatment. His Lordship put it thus:

> I doubt whether a girl under the age of 16 is capable of a balanced judgment to embark on frequent, regular or casual sexual intercourse fortified by the illusion that medical science can protect her in mind and body and ignoring the danger of leaping from childhood to adulthood without the difficult formative transitional experiences of adolescence. There are many things a girl under 16 needs to practise but sex is not one of them.[12]

The majority of his colleagues disagreed with Lord Templeman. They conceded that a request by a girl under 16 for contraception coupled with an insistence that parents not be told posed a problem for the doctor. Assessing whether she is mature enough to consider the emotional and physical consequences of the course she has embarked on will not be easy. But that question is to be left to the clinical judgment of the doctor. Lord Fraser set out five matters the doctor should satisfy himself on before giving contraceptive treatment to a girl below 16 without parental agreement. They are:

> . . . (1) that the girl . . . will understand his advice; (2) that he cannot persuade her to inform her parents . . . ; (3) that she is very likely to begin or continue having sexual intercourse with or without contraceptive treatment; (4) that unless she receives contraceptive advice or treatment her physical or mental health or both are likely to suffer; (5) that her best interests require him to give her contraceptive advice or treatment or both without the parental consent.[13]

Lord Fraser's carefully devised formula fails to satisfy Mrs Gillick and her many supporters. They regard it as inadequate in two respects. First, in a busy surgery or clinic has any doctor sufficient time to embark on the investigation and counselling of the girl necessary to fulfil the criteria laid down? Second, underlying the judgments of the majority is acceptance of the view that, as significant numbers of young girls under 16 in 1987 are going to continue having sexual intercourse regardless of whether they have lawful access to contraception, it may be in their best interests to protect them from pregnancy by contraceptive treatment. Mrs Gillick disagrees. She contends that if access to contraception without parental agreement were stopped, at least the majority of young girls would (a) be deterred from starting to have intercourse so young by fear of pregnancy and/or parental disapproval, and (b) would have a defence against pressure from their peers to 'grow up' and sleep with someone. Both sides in the debate on 'under-age' contraception agree that early sexual intercourse increases the danger of disease to the child, be it cervical cancer or venereal disease. Most agree as to the emotional damage the child risks. They are no nearer agreement as to how girls under 16 may best be protected than on the day Mrs Gillick first went to court.

The divide between Mrs Gillick and her opponents is too wide and their disagreement too bitter for the Law Lords' judgment to be regarded as definitely marking the conclusion of legal manoeuvres to ban or restrict contraception for children under 16. Two courses of action are open to those who support Mrs Gillick. First, they may be able to persuade an M.P. to promote legislation specifically on contraception for children under 16. The debate could then move to Parliament. Argument would be just as vitriolic, but at least the issue would be clearer for being dealt with independently and apart from the general issue of medical treatment for children. Second, individual parents could pursue legal action against a doctor who had prescribed for their daughter in circumstances which they allege contravene the guidelines put forward by the Law Lords. Such actions would be highly speculative. They would raise the issue of whether Lord Fraser's guidelines are legally enforceable. For if the girl understood what was entailed in the physical examination conducted by the doctor preparatory to prescribing contraception and any physical invasion of her body if mechanical means of contraception were to be fitted, it is difficult to see how a civil suit for battery or a criminal prosecution for assault could lie.[14] The guidelines may represent the pious hopes of their Lordships rather than a statement of law. In the end the Lords' judgment may be seen to have left scope for further bitter litigation. Doctors are not yet free from the threat of legal action by angry parents discovering that their child has been given contraception.

Finally, express mention must be made of abortion. The greater part of the Law Lords' judgment concentrates on contraception. It is clear that the rules for abortions on girls under 16 are the same. If a girl is intelligent and mature enough to understand what is involved in the operation, the doctor, if the girl insists on not telling her parents or if they refuse to agree to an abortion, may go ahead on the basis of the girl's consent alone. The House of Lords endorsed the approach of Butler-Sloss J. in an earlier case.[15] A 15-year-old girl, with one child already, became pregnant again while in the care of the local authority. She wanted an abortion. Doctors considered that the birth of a second child would endanger the mental health of the girl and her existing child. Her father objected. Abortion was contrary to his religion. The local authority applied to have the girl made a ward of court and so seek the court's consent to the operation. The judge authorized the operation. She said the decision must be made in the light of the girl's best interests. She took into account the parents' feelings but held that they could not outweigh the needs of the girl. Her judgment, undermined by the Court of Appeal in *Gillick*, has now been restored to favour by the House of Lords.

The criminal law, sexual intercourse and contraception

So far we have examined only the issues relating to a child's capacity to consent to treatment. The second prong of Mrs Gillick's argument related to the criminal law, which renders it a crime to have sexual intercourse with a girl under 16 regardless of her consent or encouragement. Section 28 of the Sexual Offences Act 1956 provides further that it is an offence '. . . to cause or encourage . . . the commission of unlawful sexual intercourse with . . . a girl for whom [the] accused is responsible'. The majority of the Law Lords found that a doctor who *bona fide* provided a girl with contraception in the interests of her health, to protect her from the further risks of pregnancy and consequently abortion or childbirth, committed no crime. He was not encouraging the continuance of sexual intercourse and implicitly the crime of unlawful sexual intercourse, but offering '. . . a palliative against the consequences of crime'. Doctors should, however, tread carefully. For while in general a doctor commits no crime by giving a young girl contraceptive treatment, the judgment makes it clear that any doctor who fails to assess his patient carefully and make a judgment based on medical indications as to her health may face prosecution. Lord Scarman said:

Clearly a doctor who gives a girl contraceptive advice or treatment not because in his clinical judgment the treatment is medically indicated . . . but with the intention of facilitating her having unlawful sexual intercourse may well be guilty of a criminal offence.[16]

This limb of the judgment, too, failed to satisfy Mrs Gillick. For her, contraception for young girls cannot be medically indicated. Once again the judgment may leave room for further legal disputes. Opponents of 'under-age' contraception will be on the look-out for doctors who appear to prescribe contraceptives too freely to young girls or who express views that intercourse is intrinsically acceptable at such a young age. Such doctors will risk prosecution. Additionally, both Lord Fraser and Lord Scarman stressed the role of the General Medical Council in ensuring that doctors adhered to strict guidelines in providing contraceptive treatment for young girls. Mrs Gillick has already expressed her intention to gather dossiers on doctors who appear over-liberal in their provision of contraception to children under 16. The General Medical Council can expect to be the next forum to which the debate is pursued.

Confidentiality and children under 16

A young girl, embarking on a sexual relationship and considering seeking contraception, probably does not contemplate her capacity to give consent to treatment, but the more immediate issue of 'Will the doctor tell my mum?' The thought that a doctor may be free to give contraceptive advice to a child without the parents even knowing of what is proposed was perhaps at the heart of Mrs Gillick's campaign. The disruption of family life, and the danger that the girl herself might omit to give the doctor information on other drugs she might be taking, horrified many caring parents. The courts paid surprisingly little attention to the issue of confidentiality. This is perhaps because, as we saw in Chapter 3, the legal obligation of confidence owed by the doctor to his patient is still in an embryonic stage. The House of Lords held that in exceptional cases the doctor was free to treat the girl without parental knowledge. The question which remains is whether a doctor *must* preserve confidentiality in his dealings with his young patient. By implication the House of Lords endorsed the view that the doctor owed a duty of confidentiality to his patient under 16. They upheld the D.H.S.S. guidelines, laying down the rule that if the girl was adamant that her parents must not be contacted, confidentiality must be preserved. Will a doctor, faced with a girl of 15 who tells him she has started an affair, be at risk of an action for breach of confidence brought by the girl if he refuses her contraception and telephones her mother?

For a number of reasons an action for breach of confidence is likely to run into difficulties. The major obstacle will be that the doctor may invoke in his defence arguments that disclosure is in the patient's interest and in the public interest. As we saw earlier, the public interest defence to an action for breach of confidence justifies disclosure of iniquity.[17] The doctor may contend that he is acting to disclose to those most closely concerned with the girl's welfare the commission of a crime, unlawful sexual intercourse, upon her. We saw that the extent to which a doctor may lawfully breach his patient's confidence, to disclose crime, is uncertain. Any action by a girl under 16 against a doctor who 'told' her parents, or the police, would open up that issue anew. No certain answer can be given on the outcome.

It is not the courts but the medical profession itself which is most likely to safeguard the child patient's confidences. Breach of confidentiality normally constitutes serious professional misconduct, an offence for which a doctor may be struck off the medical register by the General Medical Council. Before Mrs Gillick first challenged D.H.S.S. guidance on contraception for the under-16s in the courts, the G.M.C. required that, while doctors should always try to persuade girls requesting contraception to involve their parents, if the girl refused to permit her parents to be contacted '. . . the doctor must observe the rule of professional secrecy in his management of the case'.[18] When Mrs Gillick won in the Court of Appeal the G.M.C. had no choice but to amend this rule to comply with the law laid down by the court.[19] To the dismay of many doctors involved in family planning, the G.M.C., after the Lords' ruling, has not returned to its previous stance[20] of *guaranteed* confidentiality for young patients. Whether a doctor informs a girl patient's parents is to depend on *his* judgment of the girl's maturity, welfare and best interests. The ultimate result of the judgment of the House of Lords and the consequent ruling on ethics by the G.M.C. is this. Parents have no 'right to know' if their daughter seeks contraceptive or abortion advice or treatment. Daughters have no 'right' to confidentiality.

Parents and younger children

We must consider now the rights and obligations of parents and doctors in relation to children who have not achieved the degree of intelligence and understanding enabling them to give their consent to treatment. The absence of any arbitrary age limit as to when this stage of development is attained is the doctor's first difficulty. One can perhaps safely say that the child under 12 has virtually never reached sufficient maturity; that the 12 to 14-year-old can rarely be said to be at that stage, and that the grey area revolves largely around the 14+ age group. Nevertheless, in each case it is the maturity of the individual child which the doctor must assess. Once he judges the child to be too immature to decide for himself on treatment, what legal principles determine the doctor's duty to the child and its parents? Do the parents enjoy an unfettered right to approve or reject treatment proposed for the child?

In the straightforward case of a sick child and caring parents, parental consent to treatment required for the benefit of the child authorizes the doctor's actions. The doctor will be safe from an action for battery. Problems surface when either (a) a parent is not available or is simply uninterested, or (b) a parent expressly refuses consent to treatment. The first case is relatively easy to resolve. A casualty officer, faced with a young child injured in a road accident or rushed in from school with an acutely inflamed appendix, may safely go ahead with whatever treatment is immediately required. His legal justification derives either from the defence of necessity or from the reasonable assumption that just as the unconscious adult may be presumed to agree to treatment needed to safeguard his life or health, so may the absent parent be presumed to agree to similar treatment for his child. When a parent is physically present but displays no interest in the care of his child or fails to turn up to meet medical staff, again the doctor must do as he sees fit. It is the parents' duty to obtain adequate medical care for their children. Rights to determine the content of that care are dependent on fulfilling that duty.[21]

It is in the second example, when a caring parent expressly refuses consent to treatment of the child, that an acute legal problem for the doctor is posed. Take the examples of a Christian Scientist refusing to allow any medical treatment of his child, and the Jehovah's Witness refusing to authorize a blood transfusion for his critically injured and haemorrhaging child. What may the doctor lawfully do next? I suggest that where treatment is *immediately* necessary to preserve the child's life or health the doctor may simply proceed with treatment. He does not need first to involve the local authority or make the child a ward of court. The essence of the House of Lords' decision in *Gillick* was that parental rights over children derive from parental duties to children.[22] Parents have a duty to provide adequate medical care for their children. That duty has so far usually been interpreted objectively. What would the average parent do to aid his sick child? A parent who fails to obtain adequate medical care for his child commits the offence of wilful neglect.[23] Should the child die, he may face a charge of manslaughter. The courts have held that it is no defence for a parent who appreciated the gravity of his child's condition that he refrained from seeking conventional medical help out of sincere religious conviction.[24]

Faced by a parent rejecting any medical help, for example a parent seeking to remove his child from Casualty after the child arrives there from school, the doctor's course of action is clear. The parent has no right to refuse *all* treatment for his child. Indeed, he commits a criminal offence if he does so. The case of the Jehovah's Witness parent is rather more problematical. Earlier decisions by courts on when refusal of treatment amounts to the crime of child neglect concern parents refusing any form of medical aid. The Jehovah's Witness, by contrast, accepts any treatment save for the administration of blood. Is his refusal of that form of treatment when the child's life is thereby endangered a sufficient deviation from reasonable standards of parenting to render his conduct criminal? The advent of A.I.D.S. and the fear of contaminated blood engendered by that disease has been called on by Jehovah's Witnesses to support their religious objections to transfusion. In 1987 there must be some doubt as to whether a jury would convict a parent of neglect for refusing to sanction a transfusion.

Nevertheless I believe that the civil law will still protect the doctor who administers a transfusion despite parental opposition. The doctor, too, has a duty to the child, his patient. The criminal law on child neglect serves to illustrate that the content of that duty is to be determined by what is objectively considered medically necessary, and not by sole reference to the parents' individual and idiosyncratic viewpoint. The doctor must act in the best interests of his patient. In 99.9 per cent of cases the best interests of the child are represented by his parents. When doctor and parents disagree, parents' views may not be lightly disregarded. On any form of optional or disputed treatment, such as vaccination for whooping cough, parental views must prevail. When treatment is considered necessary but is not immediately called for, the court must be the arbiter of the dispute between parents and the child's doctors. But if there is no time to seek judicial advice the doctor may go ahead with immediately required treatment such as a blood transfusion. As Lord Templeman put it in *Gillick* v. *West Norfolk and Wisbech A.H.A.*:[25]

Where the patient is an infant, the medical profession accepts that a parent having custody and being responsible for the infant is entitled on behalf of the infant to consent to or reject treatment if the parent considers that the best interests of the infant so require. Where doctor and parent disagree, the court can decide and is not slow to act. I accept that if there is no time to obtain a decision from the court, a doctor may safely carry out treatment in an emergency if the doctor believes the treatment to be vital to the survival or health of the infant and notwithstanding the opposition of a parent or the impossibility of alerting the parent before the treatment is carried out.

The role of the court

The doctor's freedom to act on his judgment alone in defiance of parental views is strictly limited to emergency treatment. An essential transfusion can be performed at once. But take another example of religious objections to treatment: what if a Roman Catholic parent objects to an abortion for an 11-year-old daughter? The doctor must delay and refer the issue to the courts via wardship proceedings. A few days' delay will not usually prejudice the child's health.

What happens then? An application will be made to make the child a ward of court, and judicial approval sought for treatment proposed. The formula then is that the court decides the issue 'in the best interests of the child'. The child's interests include the effect on the family relationship of authorizing the disputed treatment. The family's religious beliefs will be a factor for consideration. There seems little if any doubt that where a normal child's life is at stake, saving that life will prevail over parental religion. In the case of a disputed abortion, if the girl appears to want an abortion or is too immature to form a view on the question, the court will probably authorize the operation.

Religious convictions on abortion and any other form of medical treatment are not the only arena for potential dispute between parents and doctors. We will look at two further examples only. What of the parent who after agonized consideration refuses further 'heroic' surgery on her child? For example, should a parent refuse a heart and lung transplant for a sick infant, would a court order that surgery proceed? No definite answer is possible. The court will be guided, as it was in the 'Baby Alexandra' case,[26] by the prospects of success for the operation, the pain entailed for the child and his future quality of life. The views of the child, if he is old enough to understand anything of his condition, may be sought. The judge takes from the doctor the power of life or death. For the overwhelming majority of Her Majesty's judges the call

235

to exercise this power will never come. Whether a trained lawyer sitting on his own is the appropriate forum to answer these agonizing questions may be open to doubt.

A second example of proposed treatment which might end up before a court concerns mentally handicapped children. Should a severely handicapped child survive babyhood, may his parents allow his life to end later by refusing treatment for a physical condition which develops and threatens his life? Again, so far in England our only source of enlightenment as to the judicial stance is the 'Baby Alexandra' case. The court held that an operation to relieve an intestinal obstruction in a newborn Down's syndrome baby girl should go ahead. Similarly, routine surgery on mentally handicapped children later in life is likely to be authorized. More complex surgery may pose more acute problems. An American court has refused to make a 12-year-old Down's syndrome boy a dependent child, a ward of the court, in order to authorize surgery to repair a congenital heart defect.[27] The court regarded the burden of displacing the parents' loving decision as not met. An English court is unlikely to agree. A distinction, rational or irrational, is made in most minds between never embarking on treatment of a damaged newborn infant, and caring for and treating a child through babyhood and then suddenly, to put it crudely, 'pulling out the plug'. In the balance of deciding whether parental refusal of surgery should be upheld, the presence of mental handicap may be a factor to weigh but should not carry any great weight at all. To decide otherwise is to render children second-class citizens, and to reduce mentally handicapped children to the status of animals who may be 'put to sleep'.

When the child objects to treatment

So far we have considered the scenario where the doctor, and the child, if old enough to have a view, agree to treatment and parents object. What if doctor and parents agree on what is to be done and the child objects? Once the child is sufficiently mature to understand and form a rational view on the treatment proposed, treatment cannot be enforced against his will.[28] A 15-year-old boy refusing to accept further orthodontic treatment cannot be made to comply, however much his mother and dentist may feel he will later regret his crooked teeth. A 15-year-old girl cannot be compelled to undergo abortion if she is of normal intelligence and understands her condition and its implications. However genuine her parents' concern for her 'O' levels and her future, the *Gillick* judgment makes the decision the girl's and not theirs. Roman Catholic parents cannot bar their daughters from having abortions. Pro-abortion parents cannot make their daughters terminate a pregnancy.

At the other end of the age spectrum, the expressed wishes of very young children may safely be ignored. The 5-year-old's vociferous objections to vaccination have no legal effect. The 10-year-old's fear of surgery should be calmed, but if it causes him to denounce the whole procedure that has no legal relevance. Doctor and parents together determine what care is in his best interests. Just as problems in overriding parental objections arise in the grey area between 12 and 16, so do problems in overriding the child's objections. And in this context they are perhaps more acute. At 12 I have suggested that only very, very rarely would a child have attained the capacity to agree to treatment to which its parents object. Yet such a child may still be able to form a view and weigh up the pros and cons of what is to be done. His strong objection, where treatment is optional in nature, as opposed to life-saving, may tip the balance as to whether it is in his best interests to go ahead. Again the issue of abortion highlights the problem. A 12-year-old girl becomes pregnant but expresses adamant opposition to a proposed abortion. If her doctor and her parents genuinely believe that, even taking into account her views, the physical and emotional consequences of childbirth require that the pregnancy be terminated, may they compel her to undergo an abortion? Does the doctor run the risk of the girl taking him to court and suing in battery when she reaches 18? This question raises starkly the issue of the basis of and limits to parental consent to medical treatment of children.

The limits of parental consent

Parental rights to determine medical treatment of their children derive from the parental duty to obtain adequate medical care for them. Their rights over their children are not unfettered. As with all other parental rights, they are to be exercised in the child's best interests. A parent may give '. . . a legally effective consent to a procedure which is likely to be for the benefit of the child, in the sense of being in the child's best interests'.[29] Routine treatment or surgery for an existing physical condition, diagnostic procedures, preventive measures such as vaccination, pose no problem here. The likely benefit is there for all to see. More intricate and even risky procedures cause little difficulty. Not all parents might agree to complex heart surgery on a tiny baby, but if doctors and parents weigh risk and benefit and conclude in favour of going ahead, they have exercised their respective duties properly.

Where problems do surface is in relation to medical or surgical procedures which are not immediately called for to treat or prevent ill-health. Two classic issues are dealt with later – whether a child can donate organs or tissue,[30] and when children can be used for medical research purposes.[31] The issue that has engaged the direct attention of the English courts is the sterilization of children.

In 1976 the case of *Re D*.[32] came before Heilbron J. It concerned a handicapped girl aged 11. She suffered from Soto's syndrome and was afflicted by epilepsy and a number of other physical problems. The girl was also to some extent emotionally and mentally retarded. Her mother was anxious as to her future and considered that she would never be capable of caring for a child, that having a child would damage her, that she might all too easily be seduced and would be incapable of practising any form of contraception. Accordingly she sought to have her sterilized before these risks should materialize. The girl's paediatrician agreed, and a gynaecologist was found who was ready to perform the operation. An educational psychologist involved with the child disagreed and applied to have the child made a ward of court. Heilbron J. ordered that proposals for the operation be abandoned. Her function, she said, was to act as the 'judicial reasonable parent', with the welfare of the child as her paramount consideration. She found that medical opinion was overwhelmingly against sterilization of a child of 11. The irrevocable nature of sterilization, the potential emotional impact on the girl when she discovered what had been done to her, her present inability to understand what was proposed, coupled with evidence that her mental development was such that she would one day be able to make an informed choice for herself on childbearing, all these factors led the judge to conclude that the operation was '. . . neither medically indicated nor necessary, and that it would not be in [the girl's] best interests for it to be performed'.[33]

After *Re D*. it is hard to envisage circumstances in which sterilization may lawfully be performed on a child under 16. I asked at the beginning of this chapter whether a mother discovering her child to be a likely carrier of haemophilia may get her sterilized at 4. The answer must be no. The judgment in *Re D*. offers three important criteria on which non-essential treatment should be judged. (1) When the treatment proposed by doctor and parents is not considered appropriate by the general body of opinion within the medical profession, a heavy burden lies on the parents and the doctors proposing the treatment. (2) Irrevocable treatment with emotional consequences for the child in later life will be regarded with extreme caution. (3) The child's right to decide for herself on the major issues in life, once she reaches an age of understanding, will be protected. The child's best interests embrace her right to self-determination, to make painful choices for herself when she reaches womanhood. She must be left to choose whether to risk pregnancy. Sterilization on eugenic grounds, because a child may be a carrier of any congenital disease, is never likely to be authorized by an English court, especially as many congenital defects can, or will soon, be detectable during pregnancy and the mother offered an abortion.

Debate on various hypothetical cases could be continued endlessly. What is the position *re* cosmetic surgery and children? What of circumcision of male infants, now considered by many doctors as rarely medically indicated? Each issue must be referred back to the criteria we referred to earlier. More important, though, is how effective is the law in safeguarding children from procedures generally regarded as improper and inappropriate? Male circumcision is a matter of medical debate. For Jewish and Muslim parents it is an article of faith. The child suffers momentary pain. Although medical opinion is moving away from regarding circumcision as positively beneficial, it is in no way medically harmful if properly performed. The community as a whole regards it as a decision for the infant's parents. Female circumcision carried out on girls at puberty is regarded by most with revulsion in all its forms. Medical opinion condemns the pain and trauma for the girl and warns of serious risks to her when she comes to bear a child. No English judge would be even remotely likely to regard female circumcision of a girl under 16 as in her best interests. Yet for the practice to be effectively banned here, Parliament had to enact the Prohibition of Female Circumcision Act 1985.

Procedures to protect children

What *Re D*. and the Prohibition of Female Circumcision Act have in common is that they illustrate how random and inadequate the machinery to protect children from inappropriate 'treatment' may be. In the course of the judgment in *Re D.*, it emerged that two similar sterilization operations on mentally subnormal girls had already been performed in Sheffield. D. was lucky. Her psychologist was persistent. Chance took

239

D.'s dilemma to the High Court. And this must always be the case when parents and doctors agree. Only if some interested third party intervenes will the matter reach the light of day in time to prevent the procedure going ahead. Nor is the law much of a deterrent to doctors or parents. Technically if a procedure is not medically indicated and/or in the child's best interests it amounts to a civil battery against the child and may be a criminal assault. In debates on prohibition of female circumcision Lord Hailsham argued that it was already a crime, assault occasioning actual bodily harm. But who will tell the authorities; who will prosecute? Besides which, had the common law been faced with the question of female circumcision, difficult questions would have been set in answering the question of the girl's best interests. What if she agreed, wishing to fall in with the customs of her community? What of arguments that the girl's mental well-being required that she meet the customs of her people? And if ritual male circumcision is permissible, why not female circumcision if carried out by surgeons in aseptic conditions? Litigation, if it started, would have been protracted.

Confidentiality, parents, and children at risk

A further dilemma for doctors caring for young children is this. When, if at all, may they breach confidence with the parents to protect a child whom they believe to be at risk from parental violence, neglect or inadequacy? In Chapter 3 it was suggested that a doctor might lawfully breach confidence with an adult patient when he considered that that patient posed a risk of future physical injury to a third party. Clearly any imminent danger to *his patient*, the child, justifies the doctor in contacting police or social workers as he sees fit to protect the child. Parental rights derive from parental duties and are forfeited if those duties are broken.

Conclusions

All this serves to illustrate not that fundamental legal reform is called for, not that official busybodies should monitor every consultation between doctors, parents and children, but rather to show the limitations of the law. The question of parental rights to refuse to consent to treatment occupied the courts for over three years. *Gillick* produced only a partial answer and posed more questions. The issues of consent, confidentiality and compulsion in relation to children will never go away. There is no simplistic solution. Recognition of the problems of law, ethics and medicine and co-operation in striving to solve them may make them more manageable.

Chapter 15
General Practice

At first sight legal problems concerning general practice appear few and far between. Patients visit their G.P. on average four or five times a year and make one or two hospital visits in a lifetime. Yet malpractice actions against G.P.s are rare and only a handful of reported cases exist. There are several reasons for this state of affairs. First, the N.H.S. arrangements for general practice and the quality of consistent care offered by the vast majority of G.P.s are such that family doctors still occupy a high measure of esteem. Second, patients have traditionally enjoyed a longstanding personal relationship with their G.P. A mistake is more likely to be forgiven and forgotten in the context of a G.P.'s continuing care than in the impersonal hospital atmosphere. The patient is less likely to want to put a man or woman he knows well 'into the dock'. But there are other reasons too. Proving negligence, and that the patient's injury resulted from that negligence, is always difficult. Against a G.P. the problems multiply. How do you prove that the child's sudden deterioration resulted from the G.P. not visiting at once? Would immediate treatment have arrested the condition? Added to these difficulties, the common run of complaints about general practice do not tend to be the sort that make litigation with its expense, pomp and ceremony worthwhile. Patients object to unhelpful receptionists, difficulty in getting home visits, and often simply sense a lack of sympathy. Rarely do these irritations cause injury serious enough to merit litigation. We shall look at what the law, in particular the N.H.S. regulations, has to offer. We shall see how the medical profession seeks to enforce standards. And finally we will examine how far, if at all, recent government moves have undermined the G.P.'s freedom to practise as he or she sees fit.

Terms of service

The National Health Service Act 1977[1] imposes a duty on district health authorities to make arrangements for general practice in their district.

They are required '. . . to provide personal medical services for all persons in the district who wish to take advantage of the arrangements'. The actual administration of such medical services is a matter for the local Family Practitioner Committee (F.P.C.). The F.P.C. is crucial to general practice. It administers arrangements for general practice, maintains the medical list of G.P.s in the area, administers pharmaceutical and other ancillary medical services, and acts as a grievance body for dissatisfied patients. And it is the F.P.C. with whom the general practitioner contracts. The composition of the F.P.C. is designed to ensure a balance of doctors, representatives of other medical professions and lay people.[2]

F.P.C.s are now established by the Health Minister under section 5 of the Health and Social Security Act 1984. He decides which areas a particular F.P.C. will cover, and these do not have to coincide with the administrative areas for district health authorities.

A doctor seeking to enter general practice must apply to have his name entered on the medical list in the area where he wishes to practise. The district health authority will refer his application to a central Medical Practices Committee, who will examine his qualifications and experience.[3] If 'passed' by that Committee,[4] then, save where there is already an excess of doctors in a particular neighbourhood, the doctor's name must be entered on the list. Once on the list the G.P. enters into a contract with the local F.P.C. to provide general medical services. He may additionally apply to be entered on the obstetric list and provide care for his own maternity patients. The terms of his contract with the F.P.C. are laid down in lengthy and detailed Regulations.[5] These Regulations do not of course create a contract with any individual patient. The G.P. and his patient within the N.H.S. have no contractual relationship. But the contract between G.P. and F.P.C. is important to the patient in two respects. First, it provides a detailed framework in which to examine the rights and duties of the doctor towards his N.H.S. patient. Second, the absence of a contract with the G.P. does not leave the patient without a remedy should his G.P. prove incompetent or careless. The G.P. owes him a duty of care just as the hospital doctor does. In any action for negligence the court is likely to look to the obligations undertaken by the doctor as part of his contract with the F.P.C. to determine the scope of the duty owed to the patient.

By contrast with the N.H.S. patient, the private patient paying for his personal physician's services does have a contract with his doctor. The terms of that contract are up to the parties themselves. Two special features of private general practice need noting. First, a G.P. may *not* concurrently provide private services for his N.H.S. patients. He may have an N.H.S. list and a private list but the two must not overlap. Second, the grievance procedures available through the F.P.C. to the N.H.S. patient have no counterpart in private practice. One may wonder whether the growth of private G.P. care may lead to an equal growth in malpractice suits against G.P.s. Without an obvious avenue to channel complaints and having paid directly for the service, will private patients more readily resort to the courts?

G.P.s and negligence

Having as we have seen no contract with his G.P., an aggrieved patient seeking compensation from a G.P. must sue in negligence. I look now at a few of the cases where G.P.s have been taken to court, and I examine too some common complaints about general practice to see how likely it is that a claim would succeed if litigation were started.

Every G.P. must attain that standard of skill and competence to be expected of the reasonably skilled and experienced G.P. It is no defence that he has just entered practice or that he is elderly and infirm.[6] There is no compulsory retirement age for G.P.s. But nor can he be expected to have the skill or qualifications of a consultant specialist. His terms of service with the F.P.C. put the matter in a nutshell: the doctor is not to '. . . be expected to exercise a higher degree of skill, knowledge and care than general practitioners as a class may reasonably be expected to exercise'.[7] Should he offer additional services to his patients, for example, if he is on the obstetric list and is prepared to attend home confinements, then he must show the skill that he holds himself out as possessing. He must attain the standard not of the consultant obstetrician but of the specially qualified and experienced G.P.[8]

In reported cases where negligence has been proved against G.P.s, certain danger areas stand out. The maintenance of proper records and ensuring adequate communication with hospitals and other doctors sharing the care of a patient is one. A failure to record and pass on to a hospital information on patients' allergy to certain drugs is a clear case of negligence.[9] Similarly, a failure to check exactly what treatment has been given by the hospital may result in liability. A G.P. was found liable for a young man's death in this case.[10] The man had gone to a cottage hospital after a lump of coal had fallen on him and crushed his finger. A nurse dressed the wound and instructed him to go to another larger hospital. Either because this was not properly explained to him or because he was in shock he did not go. He went later to his own doctor, who did not inquire as to his earlier treatment and simply put on a new dressing. At no stage did the patient receive an anti-tetanus injection and he died of toxaemia. The cottage hospital and the G.P. were both found to be negligent and responsible for the youth's death. The judge made his views emphatically clear: 'the National Health Service had been developed on the basis that a patient might well be transferred for treatment from one person to another so that the responsibility for the patient shifted . . . Any system which failed to provide for negligent communication was wrong and negligently wrong.'

The careful prescription of drugs is another area where G.P.s must be ultra-cautious, not just out of professional concern for the patient but also in order to safeguard themselves. In 1982 a G.P. prescribed Migril for a Mrs Dwyer. Carelessly he in fact wrote down a prescription for a massive overdose of the drug. A pharmacist dispensed the drug as prescribed. Mrs Dwyer became acutely ill. A partner in the same practice attended her at home. The Migril was on a table in her bedroom but the second doctor did not notice the bottle. Mrs Dwyer suffered gangrene as a result of the overdose. She sued both doctors and the pharmacist. All were originally found liable.[11] Mrs Dwyer received £100,000 in damages. Eventually the second doctor was exculpated on appeal. At the end of the day, the G.P. whose slip caused the over-prescription paid 45 per cent of the damages and the pharmacist 55 per cent. The Pharmaceutical Society were not unnaturally some-what aggrieved. What the case clearly demonstrates is this. Doctors must exercise great care in writing out prescriptions. Pharmacists must exercise even greater care in checking on the doctors.

Other reported cases relating to G.P.s exhibit no consistent pattern. Certain common features with other malpractice suits can be identified. Courts will be unwilling to question the doctor's judgment. In *Hucks* v. *Cole*[12] a G.P. was consulted by a maternity patient with a septic spot on her finger. He put her on a five-day course of antibiotics. At the end of the five days, when he saw her in the maternity home where he had delivered her baby, the lesion was not completely healed but the doctor did not prescribe any further treatment. The patient contracted acute septicaemia. In her claim against the doctor she alleged that (1) a different antibiotic should have been prescribed, and (2) a further course of antibiotics should have been prescribed as the sepsis remained unhealed. The trial judge refused to condemn the doctor's choice of drug but held him negligent for failing to take further measures when he could clearly see that the sepsis persisted. The Court of Appeal upheld his judgment. A clear and definite risk to the woman's health had been proved, and the absence of treatment led directly to her contracting an acute and dangerous disease. Sachs L.J. held that the essence of the doctor's defence was that the patient had been 'just unlucky'. But when grave danger should have been noted by the doctor, however small the risk was of that danger materializing, the doctor must act. Failure to act will lead more swiftly to liability than taking steps which prove with hindsight to be wrong.

One final case may interest those patients who complain that 'the doctor never listens'. In *Langley* v. *Campbell*[13] a patient visited his G.P. with symptoms of fever nine days after his return from East Africa. The G.P. diagnosed 'flu. Six days later the patient died of malaria in hospital. The G.P. was found liable for failing to consider and test for malaria, having been told by the patient of his recent return from the tropics where such disease is rife.

Duty to attend

One frequent complaint about G.P.s is that patients have difficulty getting swift appointments or home visits and that receptionists take it upon themselves to decide when and if someone can see the doctor. What exactly is the G.P.'s duty to attend his patients and who in law are his patients?

The doctor's contract with the F.P.C. provides that his patients are firstly those who are accepted on his list.[14] Provision is made for the F.P.C. to assign various patients to him to ensure that no one is ever without a G.P. And most importantly, the doctor's patients include persons accepted as 'temporary residents' and 'persons to whom he may be requested to give treatment which is immediately required owing to an accident or other emergency at any place in his practice area',[15] providing that *inter alia* the doctor is available and the patient's own doctor is not able to give immediate treatment. The doctor's obligation to the health service then is to provide an umbrella of cover. Wherever an N.H.S. patient goes he should be able to see a doctor. If he falls ill on holiday and can get to a doctor himself, he can go temporarily on to the local doctor's list. In dire emergency he or his friends can call on and count on any G.P. practising in the area to come to his aid. Failure to meet this obligation could lead to the doctor being disciplined by the F.P.C.

But is there any obligation directly to the patient? Could a patient sue if denied treatment so that his condition deteriorated? After all, we saw in Chapter 5 that a doctor on an express train could sit by and watch a fellow passenger die of a coronary. There is no legal duty to be a Good Samaritan. The G.P.'s position is quite different. As far as the patients on his list are concerned, he has a continuing duty to them. A failure to attend such a patient where a competent G.P. would recognize the need for attendance is as much a breach of duty as giving wrong and careless treatment. Patients accepted as 'temporary residents' by a G.P. are in the same position for as long as they are registered with that G.P.

The class of patients whose rights are hotly debated are the 'emergency cases'. The doctor's obligation to the F.P.C. is to treat such cases *in his practice area* when he is available to provide medical care. The G.P. on the Inter-City express is therefore as immune from responsibility for fellow passengers as his consultant colleague. Within his practice area, when he is 'on duty' in surgery or on call at home, does he have a legal responsibility to emergency patients? In 1955 lawyers acting for a doctor being sued by a patient on his N.H.S. list conceded that the creation of the National Health Service had created a legal duty on a doctor to treat any patient in an emergency, whether or not the patient was on his list.[16] A commentator has doubted the correctness of this concession, stating such a state of affairs to reflect '. . . the standards by which the medical profession regards itself as bound and would wish to be judged [but] from the strictly legal point of view too wide'.[17] I cannot see why it is 'too wide'. The doctor has undertaken to provide an emergency service. The area and circumstances in which he must act are closely defined. The obligation on him is not unbearably onerous. Emergency patients within his practice area when he is on duty are a foreseeable class of persons to whom, by accepting the position of G.P. within the health service, he has undertaken a duty, and a duty which should be legal and not merely moral.

Failure to attend and treat

Establishing a duty to treat will rarely be a cause of difficulty, except towards emergency cases. A patient suing a G.P. will find that his problems start when he seeks to prove, as he must, that the G.P.'s failure to treat him was negligent. Some patients make intolerable

247

demands on their doctors. The doctor is not obliged to respond immediately to every call. He may indeed be in breach of duty to his more patient patients if he always responds to the most insistent call on his services. He has to exercise his judgment. In 1953 a G.P. was sued when he failed to visit a child whose mother reported (a) that the child had abdominal pains, and (b) that she had previously been examined by a hospital casualty officer who had sent her home. The child proved to have a burst appendix. The judge found that the casualty doctor was negligent and the G.P. was not. He had acted reasonably on the information available to him.[18]

The information available to the doctor is vital in assessing his obligation to the patient. When a patient changed his address without telling his doctor and then summoned the doctor, the doctor was found not negligent when after an attempt to visit the old address he left to complete other calls. The judge found that he acted reasonably in assuming that if urgent treatment was needed he would be contacted again. The doctor could not be expected to mount a search for his missing patient.[19] Similarly, information as to the patient's condition must be full and accurate. A patient may fail in any action for failure to treat if all he said to the doctor was that he felt sick and had a headache, when in fact he was feverish, vomiting and had severe abdominal pains. We saw earlier that the courts will condemn the doctor who fails to act on information from his patient. The patient must give the doctor the information to act on.

Often, information about requests for visits and appointments is not given directly to the doctor. It is channelled via the receptionist. This makes not a jot of difference to the doctor's legal obligation. His terms of service with the F.P.C. require that he provide treatment during approved hours or, if he operates an appointments scheme, that the patient be offered an appointment within a reasonable time. And if the patient's condition so requires, he must be visited at home. The doctor is obliged to 'take all reasonable steps to ensure that a consultation is not deferred without his knowledge'.[20] He is responsible for his staff and must ensure that their service as well as his is efficient. His liability for them is absolute. Let us imagine a perfect G.P. whose receptionist in a burst of temper totally out of character abuses the mother of a seriously ill toddler and refuses to ask the doctor for a visit. The child has peritonitis and dies for lack of immediate treatment. The reception-ist, not the doctor, was negligent, but as her employer he is legally responsible for her negligence.[21]

248

Deputies and locums

The increasing use of deputizing services at night and at weekends has caused major public concern. Steps have been taken to improve the control exercisable by F.P.C.s over the use of such services, and to limit the hours during which a G.P. may use deputies. From a strictly legal point of view, I have argued earlier that the intervention of a deputy or locum is irrelevant to the patient. His G.P. owes him a duty to provide appropriate medical care. If inadequate or incompetent treatment is given, the G.P. is in breach of that duty, and if that breach of duty results in injury to the patient, he is entitled to compensation.[22]

An intolerable burden of liability?

I have taken a view of the potential liability of the G.P. somewhat wider than may commend itself to the B.M.A. In particular, I maintain that there is a legal obligation to treat emergencies and an absolute responsibility for the negligent actions of deputies. This attitude does not result in any way from a belief that general practice on the whole meets a low standard of health care. Nor do I believe that an increase in malpractice actions against G.P.s is desirable or would promote higher standards. The action for negligence remains in this country the main scheme for providing adequate compensation for personal injury. It requires proof of fault. Fault does not mean moral culpability. Every doctor makes mistakes. They are unlucky when their mistakes cause injury. But so are the patients. The doctor can insure against his mistakes, as does the lawyer, the architect and the lorry driver. G.P.s are not obliged to carry professional insurance. Most do. They all should. Until and unless the law changes to bring about a more adequate system of compensating injury, a patient should be entitled to compensation when he is denied adequate treatment.

Freedom to choose: the patient

Fortunately for the majority of patients, the law relating to responsibility for negligence is relevant only in that it creates a framework within which they enter into a relationship with their G.P. They will never have cause to test it in court. More important to that majority is their ability to select the doctor of their choice. The well-off can always opt for private care. For most people, general practice remains a N.H.S. preserve. The

N.H.S. seeks to embody in the system the principle of choice of doctor. Limitations on freedom of choice are imposed by the need to limit the numbers on doctors' lists[23] and by the number of doctors in practice in the neighbourhood. But the major inhibition on choice of doctor lies in the Regulations governing a change of doctor. Forty years after the inception of the N.H.S., all existing residents of the country who wish to opt for N.H.S. care will be on a doctor's list. Many will be there not by any conscious decision of theirs but because their parents placed them on that particular list in childhood. An opportunity for change will arise if the doctor retires, but how easy is a deliberate change of doctor?

The Regulations provide[24] that a person who moves from the address on his medical card may apply to another doctor for inclusion on his list. He does not have to have moved out of the original doctor's practice area. Should the doctor move his surgery, the patient may opt out of his list. Where the patient simply feels ill at ease with his doctor the solution is less simple. He may change doctor either with the written consent of his original doctor or by making a formal application to the Family Practitioner Committee. He has a right to change. Few doctors would wish to hang on to an unwilling patient. Yet it is extremely awkward to have to go and say to your doctor, 'I would rather see someone else.' Patients fear they will be blacklisted. They are probably unaware that the Regulations make elaborate arrangements to ensure that this cannot happen. No patient can be without access to a health service doctor. The right to change doctor and how it may be done is explained on the back of the medical card. But it needs greater emphasis. One may wonder whether some complaints to the F.P.C. would be made at all if the patient was better aware that he could choose to change his doctor and was not obliged to give reasons.

Two further matters call for note. A woman is entitled to apply to another doctor for maternity services if her own doctor does not provide such services.[25] And a new dimension to choice is emerging. Advertising has been for decades the second most serious 'crime' in the doctors' handbook.[26] A doctor must not tout for clients. Now the government plans to change this. They believe that to exercise a proper choice of doctor, patients need more information. Does the doctor vaccinate his own child patients or refer them to the clinic? Will he readily provide screening and health checks? The cynical say that the reason a Conservative government wants doctors to be free to advertise is so as to promote private general practice. New private health care organizations need to be able to 'sell' themselves. The General Medical Council seeks a middle way. They see the need for information. They may fear perhaps a descent into competitive self-advertisement, and in certain areas a vicious war between private and public medicine which can only damage the profession. Hence it is reported[27] that the G.M.C. will take steps to amend its own regulations on advertising and pre-empt further government action.

Complaints

Litigation is uncertain and expensive. A complainant may not want financial compensation. Money cannot replace a dead relative. And in many cases where a patient is understandably aggrieved there may be no cause of action. The patient's condition might have deteriorated in any case, even if his doctor had treated him promptly and properly. Yet he still has cause to complain if his doctor did not attend him or gave inappropriate treatment. What are the avenues open to complainants unhappy about their treatment by a health service G.P.?

The Family Practitioner Committee

The F.P.C., which administers general practice and with whom the G.P. contracts to offer his services, also investigates any failure by the G.P. to comply with those terms of service. An aggrieved patient makes his complaint to the F.P.C. On receiving a complaint, the F.P.C. may attempt to solve the difficulty by informal means. A 'negotiator' is appointed to mediate between doctor and patient. He will usually be a lay member of the full F.P.C., but may ask that one of the doctors on the medical service committee advise him on the complaint. If informal conciliation is not resorted to or fails, the full complaints procedure comes into play.[28] The F.P.C. is required to set up service committees for the various services they administer, for example a medical service committee for G.P.s, a dental service committee for dentists, and a pharmaceutical service committee for pharmacists.[29] It is the medical service committee with which we are concerned. The service committee is obliged to investigate any complaint made against a doctor. Complaints must normally be made within eight weeks of the event giving rise to the complaint.[30] The D.H.S.S. recently proposed that this period be extended to thirteen weeks.[31] The committee can hear complaints outside this eight-week period if some good cause for the delay is shown, as long as the doctor consents. If the doctor does not agree, the committee can seek approval from the D.H.S.S. to go ahead. The patient must at present act swiftly.

Once the service committee has notice of the complaint, the chairman will make a preliminary decision as to whether it discloses any evidence of failure by the doctor. If after a further opportunity for the complainant to substantiate his complaint nothing further is disclosed, the matter will go forward to the committee without a formal hearing being required. Where a formal hearing takes place, the patient may ask someone else to assist him to present his case. There is no legal aid in such cases. Even where the patient pays for advice from a lawyer, the lawyer is not entitled to act as an advocate or to speak at all at the hearing. The patient himself may speak and put questions to the doctor. The hearing is private and the press are therefore excluded from such hearings.

The procedure before service committees has aroused much disquiet. The patient is dependent to a large extent on his own articulacy in presenting a case. So is the doctor. He too is denied an advocate. The likelihood is, though, that the doctor will be better educated than the patient and will be advised throughout by lawyers and other experts from his defence union.

Once a hearing is complete, the service committee reports to the main F.P.C. The F.P.C. must decide what action to take if breach of the terms of service is shown. They have no power to award compensation as such to the patient. The F.P.C. may (*inter alia*)[32] limit the number of patients for whom the doctor may provide treatment, recommend to the D.H.S.S. withholding of remuneration, or recommend to the D.H.S.S. that the doctor be warned to comply with his terms of service more closely in future. Finally, the ultimate sanction available to the F.P.C. is to recommend to a special tribunal specially established for the purpose that the doctor be removed from the medical list.[33]

From any decision of the F.P.C., either party may appeal if the decision is adverse to him. The appeal lies to the Health Minister.[34] No oral hearing is required to be held. Where an oral hearing is held, proceedings again take place in private. Where a recommendation to exclude a doctor from the medical list is made, that recommendation is only the first step in a lengthy process. The tribunal of three members must be chaired by a lawyer of no less than ten years' standing, appointed by the Lord Chancellor. At least one of the other two members will be a doctor.[35] Proceedings are yet again in private, and the doctor is entitled to legal representation. If the decision goes against the

General Practice

doctor he may appeal to the Secretary of State, or if he challenges a point of law in the tribunal's decision he may go to the High Court.

The system for complaints is not well regarded by a number of commentators. It seems loaded in the doctor's favour. The service committee will have at least three doctor members. Their privacy is guaranteed. The sanction of publicity only operates when a doctor suffers the ultimate penalty of removal from the list. It is alleged that the Family Practitioner Committees take a restrictive view of their powers, refusing to adjudicate on matters of clinical judgment. But striking the correct balance between patient and doctor is far from easy. Publicity in the early stages is not necessarily the answer. Perfectly innocent and conscientious doctors would suffer the 'no smoke without fire' syndrome. Legal aid and representation for patients would assist the less articulate. But where would the money come from? The heart of the problem lies perhaps in the many functions entrusted to the F.P.C. It is essentially an administrative body, a sort of unelected N.H.S. local council. Its utility lies in improving the general working of the service, checking on deputizing services, handling of night calls and so on. Whether such a multi-purpose body is the correct forum to investigate individual complaints needs further consideration by the government, the profession and patients.

The service committees and the F.P.C. itself are both subject to the supervision of the Council on Tribunals. The Council, which surveys the working of all tribunals in England and Wales, made some telling criticisms of F.P.C.s and action by the Council in concert with the Health Ombudsman has led to certain changes in F.P.C. procedure.[36]

General Medical Council

The role of the G.M.C. in regulating the medical profession was discussed fully in Chapter 1 of this book. But the function of the G.M.C. in disciplining doctors deserves mention again. The Professional Conduct Committee of the G.M.C. investigates complaints by patients of serious professional misconduct. Adultery with a patient remains the most notorious example of misconduct, and in 1987 will still often lead to the doctor being struck off the register.[37] Advertising, drug addiction and alcoholism will also bring about the doctor's downfall. Growing public concern has focused on the moral, sober but incompetent doctor. When will the G.M.C. act? An isolated mistake is not the concern of the

G.M.C. Nor is incompetence as such. Failure to attend and treat a patient may be. The case of a doctor in 1982[38] illustrates that the Council can take a tough line. The doctor refused to visit two sick little girls on separate occasions. One died. One suffered brain damage when an appendectomy went wrong. The child who died could not have been saved by the doctor. The brain damage to the other was not his fault. So the parents could not have sued for negligence. Their complaint was of the lack of treatment and the distress caused to them. The Council found against the doctor and he was struck off. This was the first time in fifteen years that a doctor had been struck off for failing to visit a patient rather than being merely suspended for a year. One wonders why it took them so long.

Do the powers of the G.M.C. go far enough? Should they be more able and ready to deal with incompetence? As we have seen, the B.M.A. think so and have given their backing to a Private Member's Bill which would radically expand the powers of the G.M.C.[39]

The N.H.S. Ombudsman

The Health Service Ombudsman, discussed in Chapter 8, has no jurisdiction to investigate general practitioners or the deliberations of medical service committees. He can investigate maladministration by health service employees who administer the F.P.C.s. And he may examine complaints relating to informal procedures.[40] In one case a woman complained to the F.P.C. that her doctor had told her not to waste his time when she asked for a blood test for German measles. She was planning to have a baby and wanted to check that she was immune from that disease. The administrator to whom she handed in her complaint told her to change doctors if she was not satisfied with her treatment. He never passed the complaint on to the F.P.C. The Ombudsman found that to be maladministration.

Doctors: freedom to care

So far we have looked at general practice from a more or less exclusively patient-orientated approach. What of the doctor? The arrangements for general practice, in particular the fact that G.P.s are not salaried employees of the state, were designed to safeguard the doctor's independence to give treatment as he saw fit to the best of his professional ability. Is that freedom still respected?

Just as the patient may choose his doctor, so to some extent may the doctor choose his patients. The health service regulations governing general practice and the doctors' terms of service with the F.P.C. provide that doctors may (a) refuse to accept a patient on to their list, and (b) ask for the removal of patients presently on the list.[41] But the regulations further provide detailed rules that ensure that no patient is ever without a G.P. It is doubtful whether this freedom to choose patients is seen as of central importance by many practitioners. What is important to the competent, conscientious G P is his or her freedom to treat the patients on the list as the doctor sees fit.

Certain restrictions on freedom to practise have existed for some time. Control of dangerous drugs has led to legislation restricting the right of every G.P. to prescribe drugs like heroin or cocaine to addicts. Only certain specially designated doctors may prescribe for addicts. Legislation relating to contagious disease requires a doctor in some cases to breach confidentiality with his patient and notify the disease to community medical officers. These are the sorts of restrictions on clinical freedom that are generally accepted by the profession, the details having been worked out between the profession and the government.

But for some time the government, the Treasury in particular, had been expressing growing concern about the escalating cost of prescribed drugs to the N.H.S. One solution, widely canvassed, which attracted support from many doctors and pharmacists was that prescriptions for drugs should follow a policy of generic prescribing. That is, the doctor should not prescribe any drug by a particular brand name but by its generic description.[42] The pharmacist would then supply the cheapest available drug. The doctor would decide exactly which drug his patient needed. The pharmacist would obtain the drug from the cheapest source. Some doctors objected that different drug companies supplying the same drug provided drugs of different quality. Some patients are particularly enamoured of a particular brand or even colour of pill! But the real outcry came from the drug companies. Had generic prescribing been introduced, there would fairly quickly have been little point in companies competing to prescribe the same drug. Their considerable profits would have suffered. The government accepted these objections, and generic prescribing was rejected for the time being.

The option acted on by the government outraged the B.M.A. and the majority of the medical profession. In 1985 prescription drugs were divided into two categories. There is a 'white list' of drugs a doctor may prescribe on the N.H.S., exercising his clinical judgment. And there is a 'black list' of drugs he may still prescribe but only by a private prescription, so that the patient himself[43] has to meet the full cost of the drug. The 'black list' is at present limited to certain categories of drug including tranquillizers, sedatives, analgesics, laxatives and cough and cold remedies. The government has said that it will not extend it to remedies for serious illness, such as tablets for blood pressure or heart ailments. Even as it stands, it is more than a minimal restriction of the G.P.'s freedom to treat his own patient as he sees best. Two examples will suffice. Among the drugs on the 'black list' are a number of mucolytic drugs. Doctors disagree on their effectiveness, but numbers of G.P.s, consultants, and parents have found that the drugs work to clear 'glue ear' in children, a painful complaint causing a degree of hearing impairment. Now a doctor who wishes to give the drug to a child patient must ask the parents to pay for it. Many will be unable to do so. A second drug to be found on the list is 'Nicorette'. Nicorette is a nicotine chewing-gum used to help smokers kick the habit. In 1984 a Manchester G.P., Dr Steele, persuaded a health service tribunal that Nicorette was a medicine and that he could prescribe it on the N.H.S. for bronchial or asthmatic patients whom he advised to stop smoking. Soon afterwards the 'black list' appeared and Nicorette featured on it. Dr Steele then prescribed Nicorette by its generic name, 'nicotine chewing-gum'. Nicotine chewing-gum did not appear on the 'black list'. Pharmacists had to dispense Nicorette because there is no other brand of nicotine chewing-gum. The D.H.S.S. were not to be outwitted; they made a new additional regulation to ban nicotine chewing-gum from N.H.S. prescription too.[44]

Four legal questions arise from the move to remove certain drugs from the N.H.S. The first relates to the potential liability of the G.P. Let us return to the example of nicotine chewing-gum. Patient X, a heavy smoker with chronic bronchitis, attends his G.P. Treatment is fairly pointless unless he gives up smoking. But the G.P. cannot prescribe on the N.H.S. the substance that he knows will help X. Perhaps the G.P. also knows that the man is unemployed, with several children. Will he be in breach of duty to the patient if he fails to offer him a private prescription and the patient's condition deteriorates? The lawyer will always advise the doctor to play safe. If he believes that a certain drug is the best form of treatment, he should so advise the patient so that the patient can decide whether or not to pay. Then the doctor will have discharged his duty. The inner-city G.P. will be moved to tears or hysterical laughter at the thought of having to give advice he knows his patients will not be able to afford to follow.

The second legal question concerns the relationship between N.H.S. and private practice. General practitioners are prohibited from giving private treatment to patients on their N.H.S. list. Now they are being required to make those same patients pay private rates for certain drugs. Many practitioners resent the anomaly.

The third legal question in this area relates to liability for drugs privately prescribed. Drugs prescribed on the N.H.S. are not supplied under a contract. Consumer protection laws do not apply to N.H.S. prescriptions. Where the patient pays the full cost of the drug, then in law he buys it from the pharmacist just as he might buy any non-prescription cough medicine. Any goods bought must (*inter alia*) be fit for the purpose for which they are bought and be of merchantable, saleable quality.[45] If they are not of such quality, the seller is liable regardless of whether or not he has been careless. An example will clarify this vital point. A bottle of medicine is supplied to a patient. The pharmacist had received it from the manufacturer in the sealed opaque bottle in which he is directed to dispense it. The medicine had been contaminated as a result of negligence by the manufacturer. The pharmacist is in no way to blame. If the medicine is dispensed on the N.H.S. no responsibility attaches to the pharmacist. If he dispenses the same medicine on a private prescription, he *sells* that medicine, and is liable to his customer because contaminated medicine is not goods of the quality demanded by the sale of goods laws. The introduction of the 'black list' has not changed the law here. Private prescriptions have always carried a risk for the pharmacist of strict liability for quality. But now there will be far, far more such prescriptions dispensed. Patients will perhaps be ready to take advantage of the only benefit offered them by the new arrangements!

Finally in 1986 one patient, Belinda Chandler, denied by the 'black list' an N.H.S. prescription for a tranquillizer which her doctors believed to be valuable in controlling her epilepsy, considered suing Norman Fowler, the cabinet minister ultimately responsible. She sought to contend that the introduction of the 'black list' was a misuse of his powers as the minister ultimately responsible for the N.H.S. Mrs Chandler has already won one battle. Her local F.P.C. refused to discipline the G.P. who broke the rules and wrote an N.H.S. prescription for the 'black-listed' drug.[46]

Late in 1985 the D.H.S.S. finally persuaded the professional bodies to agree to participate in monitoring the 'white' and 'black' lists. At least now representatives of the profession will have a say in which drugs the N.H.S. continues to provide free of charge.

The Primary Health Care Review

The government has embarked on a general review of the provision made for general practice within the N.H.S.[47] Specific proposals have been made to effect some small but significant reforms to F.P.C. complaints procedures.[48] Extending the time limits for complaints to thirteen weeks has already been mentioned. Three other important changes are suggested. Regulations would ensure that at service committee hearings equal numbers of lay and professional members of the F.P.C. are represented. Service committees would be given power to summon witnesses and *compel* production of relevant documents. And patients, while paid legal advocates would still be barred, would have a *right* to be represented by a trade union official or community health council representative or some similar person.

Conclusion: the role of the law

It is only too easy to carp at the G.P., only too easy to say that the law ought to do this and that. The limited role the law can play in promoting good general practice needs clear recognition from doctors and patients. The law can provide a scheme for compensating the victims of medical error. The present scheme, based on the law of negligence, will work more effectively if doctors recognize that error does not automatically equal incompetence. The law can and should ensure a better and simpler scheme for the thorough investigation of complaints. It can do little else. The maintenance and raising of standards is for the profession and the government. Proposals by the B.M.A. of greater incentives for the good G.P. ought to arouse the sympathy of this government. Moves by the Royal College of General Practitioners to fix higher entrance standards should be listened to carefully.

Chapter 16
Family Planning

Just over 100 years ago Charles Bradlaugh was convicted of, and imprisoned for, publishing an obscene libel when he issued a pamphlet advocating and explaining methods of birth control. In 1924 Marie Stopes sued for libel after her books and work in slum clinics had been described as a 'monstrous campaign of birth control', with the rider that 'Bradlaugh was condemned to jail for a less serious crime'. In the House of Lords, Viscount Finlay said of the practice of birth control:

> . . . it is impossible to hold that the bounds of fair comment are exceeded by the expression of an opinion that such practices are revolting to the healthy instincts of human nature. There is an old and widespread aversion to such methods on this ground.[1]

And as late as 1954 Lord Denning M.R. said of vasectomy:

> Take a case where a sterilization operation is done so as to enable a man to have the pleasure of sexual intercourse without shouldering the responsibilities attached to it. The operation is plainly injurious to the public interest. It is degrading to the man himself. It is injurious to his wife and any woman whom he may marry, to say nothing of the way it opens to licentiousness, and unlike other contraceptives, it allows no room for a change of mind on either side. It is illegal, even though the man consents to it . . .[2]

Attitudes have certainly changed, but how much? And where does the law stand now?

Can family planning be criminal?

Contraceptives have never been totally banned in England, as they still partially are in Eire, and were in France until 1967. But the criminal law cannot be totally divorced from family planning. The fine line between prevention of pregnancy and early abortion, seen most dramatically in relation to the use of the 'morning-after' pill, has been examined earlier.[3] And prescribing contraceptives to girls under 16 was unsuccessfully argued to be aiding and abetting unlawful sexual intercourse.[4] The

259

campaign has now moved to Parliament to create a specific statutory offence. The diversity of opinion in our society concerning sexual morality, and a range of views, from a position that the use of contraception is always morally wrong, through the view that contraceptives should be solely a means of spacing a family within marriage, to the point where contraception is seen as a right for all regardless of age or status, ensures that the acrimonious debate will continue.

But what of sterilization? Is there any substance in Lord Denning's argument that there are circumstances now in which performing a sterilization could entail criminal liability for the surgeon? That cannot now be the law. His argument was based on the principle that a victim's agreement cannot make lawful an inherently criminal act. So a man who sadistically beat a 17-year-old girl was convicted of a criminal assault upon her despite her consent to be beaten.[5] Inflicting violence on another person for sexual gratification is unacceptable to society. Lord Denning argued that sterilization without medical cause was mutilation of the patient, and unacceptable to society because of its potential for risk-free immorality. Several thousands of Britons every year undergo sterilization. It has become an acceptable option for birth control.[6] It seems most unlikely that any judge would now categorize sterilization as inherently unlawful and put the surgeon on a par with the sadist!

Contraception, sterilization and marriage

Two questions arise in this context. Can the use of contraception by, or the prior sterilization of, one of the spouses affect the initial validity of a marriage? Does a refusal to have children give rise to grounds for divorce?

English law provides that a marriage which remains unconsummated because of the incapacity or wilful refusal of one party to consummate the marriage is voidable and may be set aside as a nullity. The earlier sterilization of one of the spouses, or the use of mechanical or chemical contraception, will not prevent consummation taking place.[7] Consummation means full sexual intercourse regardless of whether or not the act is open to the procreation of children. So a husband who had unwillingly used a contraceptive sheath when engaging in intercourse with his wife failed in his attempt to argue that therefore the marriage had never been consummated. Neither will refusal by one spouse to have intercourse unless contraceptives are used amount to wilful refusal to consummate.[8] This can create a knotty problem. If one party is entirely prepared to engage in normal sexual intercourse only if contraceptives are used and the other, for religious reasons perhaps, only if they are not, the marriage remains unconsummated, but neither spouse is guilty of wilful refusal to consummate and the marriage cannot be set aside.[9] Their remedy lies in divorce. Any hardship in having to await a divorce is alleviated by the Matrimonial and Family Proceedings Act 1984, which now permits divorce in normal circumstances after one year of marriage only.

A divorce will be granted if the petitioner can establish that the marriage has irretrievably broken down. One means of establishing the breakdown is to show that the respondent has behaved in such a way that the petitioner cannot reasonably be expected to live with him or her. This test of 'unreasonable behaviour' has replaced the previous test of cruelty as a ground for divorce and is more liberally interpreted by the courts. Undergoing a vasectomy after the marriage,[10] or insisting on using contraceptives,[11] was held in the past to be cruelty on the part of the husband if the effect was damaging to the wife's health. Today a wife would probably succeed in establishing unreasonable behaviour without having to show evidence of damage to her health. Equally, a husband could prima facie show it to be unreasonable for his wife to refuse, without good reason, to have children. But one difficulty can be outlined. In *Archard* v. *Archard*[12] the parties were both Roman Catholics. The wife was advised on medical grounds not to conceive for a while, and refused to have intercourse without the use of contraceptives. Her devout husband refused to have intercourse if contraceptives were used. She failed to establish that his behaviour was unreasonable, as she was aware of his faith and his views. Equally, he would have failed to establish her behaviour to be unreasonable on the grounds of her medical condition. The reasons for one party's refusal to have children must be examined in determining whether this conduct is such that the petitioner can no longer be expected to go on with the marriage, and today may well not be limited to cases where the wife (or the husband) is medically advised against contraception but may embrace the whole of the parties' lifestyle and aspirations.

Finally, there is one gap in the law. What if one spouse has been sterilized before the marriage and never tells the other? We have seen that that is no ground for nullity. Nor is it evidence of unreasonable behaviour so as to support a petition for divorce. For the conduct, undergoing sterilization, takes place before the marriage. A divorce can only be granted on the basis of conduct *after* the marriage.[13] The unhappy spouse will have to establish the breakdown of the marriage on other grounds. A divorce may be granted after two years' separation where the other party consents. Should the contesting party be obdurate, a divorce can be granted without consent after five years' separation. Five years may be enough to end an older woman's hope of children within a future marriage.

Contraceptives: patients' rights

An infallible contraceptive has yet to be invented. The more sophisticated and convenient contraceptives, such as the Pill and the I.U.D., have carried a price-tag. They all pose some risk to women's health. Contraception has become very much a medical as well as a social issue. And it largely concerns women, for except for the still experimental male 'Pill', all the more sophisticated contraceptives which pose some medical risk are used by women. Women seek two sorts of protection from the law. First, they require definition of the doctor's obligation to assist them to avoid pregnancy at the least possible risk to health. And second, they increasingly demand greater information, and consequently greater control of their own bodies and lives. The law is pretty well equipped for the first task, and almost entirely a futile weapon in the second.

A doctor advising a woman on contraception owes her the same duties as in any other area of medicine. He must offer her competent and careful advice. He must perform any mechanical procedure, for example inserting an I.U.D., skilfully. And he must obtain her consent to any invasive procedure. When a woman consults her G.P. his obligation to her is part and parcel of his ordinary care of her. He will be aware of her medical history, prescribe in the light of that history, and take note of any symptoms of general ill-health that are revealed by any examination he undertakes. But many women prefer to consult specialist Family Planning Clinics. They feel the clinics have greater experience, and some may prefer not to discuss their sexual lives with the family doctor. Clinics must beware. Their obligation is not limited to providing competent advice on how to avoid conception. Contraception cannot be divorced from general health and medical care. The clinic must act on any indication that the woman's general health is at risk, whether it be from the prescription of a particular contraceptive, or independently. In *Sutton* v. *Population Services Family Planning Ltd*,[14] Mrs Sutton visited the defendant's clinic and was examined by a nurse preparatory to being given contraceptive advice. The nurse either failed to note, or failed to act on, evidence of early signs of cancer. The cancer was diagnosed much later, with the result that far more drastic treatment was called for and the disease was likely to recur at least four years earlier than would have been the case had it been promptly treated. Mrs Sutton was awarded damages for her additional suffering. So clinics must act to ensure that women receive treatment when signs of disease are present. This will usually be done by advising the patient to contact her G.P. While the clinic staff may not wish to alarm a patient with what may be a very tentative diagnosis, she must be given sufficient information on which to act, and if she agrees, her G.P. will be directly notified. Of course, the clinic must respect her confidence, and should a woman refuse permission to contact her G.P., say where a sexually transmitted disease is suspected, they must not breach her confidence. In such a case a clinic must take steps to advise the woman on alternative sources of treatment.

Problems with the Pill

Scare stories about the Pill and the risk it poses of cancer, heart disease or thrombosis hit the headlines about once a year. Research into side-effects has had two main medical consequences. A number of brands of Pill once popular have been withdrawn. Women over 35 have been advised to think carefully about its long-term use. Socially, a growing awareness of the potential risks has led many women to demand more information about a substance that so many of them swallow every day. What can the law do for them? First, a doctor prescribing the Pill must be properly informed about the current stage of research and knowledge as to brands of Pill and their risks to particular patients. A G.P. is not required to have the experience of a consultant gynaecologist specializing and himself researching into the control of fertility. But he must be adequately informed if he elects to offer advice personally rather than referring women to a specialist clinic. His terms of service do not oblige him to offer contraceptive services. Second, what degree of information is the woman entitled to? The leaflets accompanying prescriptions of the Pill have lengthened considerably in recent years in their description of side-effects to which women should be alert, and of contra-indications to taking that brand. The test applicable is that the woman should be given sufficient information to enable her to decide whether to continue with that method of contraception. Will what amounts to sufficient information be judged by what current medical practice considers appropriate? A recent High Court judgment suggests not.[15] The judge said that, while medical practice must determine what was adequate advice when a doctor was treating illness, a healthy woman considering sterilization must be as fully informed on the pros and cons of that procedure and other means of permanent contraception as any intelligent woman would wish to be to make an informed choice. That judgment should apply equally to women considering taking the Pill and comparing its risks and benefits with other contraceptives.

What about the drug companies who manufacture the Pill? Doctors as well as patients are heavily reliant on the manufacturer for information about a product's efficacy and potential dangers. Very briefly, a manufacturer's duty is to produce a product which is reasonably safe for eventual use. If it is safe only under certain conditions or for certain users, enough information must be provided to enable the product to be safely used. What is in issue today is again the amount of information made available. In the English courts, a claim that a particular Pill was negligently distributed because it was supported by inadequate information as to risks and side-effects, or that such information was not made available to the eventual user, would first be tested against current pharmaceutical practice at the time that brand was manufactured. The company which failed to change its practice in line with new research and modes of thinking would be brought into line. Certain brands of Pill originate in the U.S.A. They are either originally manufactured there, or formulated there and manufactured under licence in the U.K. Women claiming to have suffered injury resulting from a brand of Pill manufactured here in the U.K. have won compensation from the company which formulated the drug in the U.S.A.[16] This can be done where an aggrieved party can establish that the harm he suffered originated in a state of the U.S.A.; where he can show that the relevant act of negligence occurred in America. American courts not only award far higher levels of compensation but adopt a highly patient-orientated attitude towards the amount of information patients are entitled to. Nor will this be likely to be an isolated claim. Groups complaining of injury from the controversial I.U.D., the Dalkon Shield, are suing in the States.

The Depo-Provera affair

An injectable, long-acting contraceptive sounds ideal. No messy devices, no need to remember to take a pill every day, what more could be desired? Depo-Provera is such a drug and yet has been the source of acute controversy. Depo-Provera is a synthetic form of a natural hormone, which acts like most brands of the Pill to prevent eggs developing and, further, makes the womb hostile to any fertilized embryo which makes it that far. One injection is effective for at least three months. Doctors favour the use of the drug for women for whom the Pill is a health risk, women who are considered too unreliable to be trusted to use other means of contraception and where pregnancy should be completely ruled out, for example when a woman has just been vaccinated against German measles. But Depo-Provera can produce unpredictable and unpleasant side-effects, the most notable of which is severe and irregular bleeding. Long-term fertility may also be affected by the drug. Complaints have been made that (1) some women were injected with the drug without ever being told of its nature, and (2) even where Depo-Provera was expressly prescribed and described as a contraceptive, inadequate explanation of its potential side-effects was given. Fears were voiced that Depo-Provera might be forced on the inarticulate or not particularly intelligent woman.

A woman who is injected with Depo-Provera without being told what is in the syringe or without being asked for her agreement may claim in battery against the doctor. She will get compensation for the unlawful violation of her body, and for any unpleasant side-effects which flow from the injection. She will get some compensation even if the drug does her no harm, for the doctor acted unlawfully in acting without her consent. A Salford woman, Mrs Potts, won £3,000 damages[17] after she was injected with Depo-Provera concurrently with a vaccination against German measles. She later suffered severe bleeding. The injection was given days after the delivery of her third child, and she thought that it was a routine post-natal 'jab'. The aim of her doctor was laudable, to protect her from pregnancy while the vaccine might harm any unborn child, but he had no right to deprive her of her choice of whether or not to accept or decline a controversial drug. Women must be told the nature of the drug offered to them, and if their right to choose is to be effective they must have its advantages and disadvantages explained to them.[18] The judge awarding Mrs Potts's compensation said: 'She should have been given the choice, and she was entitled to know beforehand what the decision entailed.'

The controversy over Depo-Provera and fears that it could be forced on unwilling, uninformed patients led the Minister of Health to take an unusual measure in 1983. The Committee on Safety of Medicines advised the Minister to grant Depo-Provera a full licence for general long-term use. The Minister's concern was such that he established an independent panel to inquire into the use and abuse of the drug[19] and to take evidence from interested parties. As a result of the inquiry's findings, Depo-Provera was granted a licence for long-term use but strict conditions were attached to that licence.

Agreeing to sterilization

When a further pregnancy or the burden of caring for more children may endanger a woman's physical or mental health, therapeutic sterilization may be suggested by doctors. Non-therapeutic sterilization is increasingly sought as a method of permanent birth control, both by older couples who feel that their family is complete and by some younger childless women who are adamant that they never wish to reproduce. Both sorts of prospective patients express some disquiet about present practice. Too many doctors within the N.H.S., it is claimed, regard the decision to sterilize as theirs and not their patients'. They are over-inclined to sterilize women whom they regard as physically or mentally unfit for childbearing or childrearing. They are disinclined to help the fit but unwilling. The latter class will find no legal remedy. A plethora of private clinics has grown up offering female sterilization and vasectomy at a price. To those clinics men and women refused sterilization within the N.H.S. must resort if they can meet the cost. By contrast, any woman alleging that she was hustled into sterilization without her full consent may usefully look to the law for assistance.

A doctor undertaking sterilization of a patient must ensure that the patient understands and agrees to what is to be done. Operating without any consent to the physical invasion of the patient's body would be a battery. Nor can sterilization be automatically performed concurrently with some other gynaecological operation to which the patient has consented. The doctor may correctly adjudge in the course of some other form of surgery that a woman should not risk pregnancy again. He cannot go ahead and act 'in her best interests' without her agreement. In *Devi* v. *West Midlands Area Health Authority*,[20] a married woman of 33 who already had four children entered hospital for a minor gynaecological operation. Her religion outlawed sterilization or contraception.

In the course of the operation the surgeon discovered her womb to be ruptured and sterilized her there and then. She received £4,000 damages for the loss of her ability to conceive again and £2,750 damages for the neurosis caused by the knowledge of what had been done to her. The choice as to whether to accept sterilization is the patient's. It may be more convenient to sterilize the patient on the spot but, again, it is never so *immediately* necessary as to justify acting in an emergency without consent.

A doctor who has obtained the patient's consent to the operation may still be liable for negligence if he fails to discuss properly with the patient the implications of the operation in a manner consistent with good medical practice. The doctor must not only give the patient sufficient information on which to make up her mind, but also do so at a time when she is in a fit state to take a reasoned decision. A Roman Catholic woman of 35 was awarded £3,000 damages in negligence when she was sterilized in the course of a Caesarian operation to deliver her second child. She signed the consent form just as she was about to be wheeled into the operating theatre. The judge said that, although she consented to the additional surgery and understood what would physically be done to her, she had been inadequately counselled as to its implications for her.[21] Sterilizing a woman in the course of an abortion or Caesarian saves time and money for the N.H.S. and cuts down on pain and suffering for the patient. It is a course of action rightly fraught with legal hazard unless the patient has been properly advised as to the physical and emotional consequences of electing to be sterilized. The doctor must assess not just his patient's physical condition but also her religious and moral attitudes to enable him and her to take into account the possible emotional effect of the decision.

The B.M.A. *Handbook on Medical Ethics* states that as a matter of courtesy a surgeon should seek the consent of one spouse for the sterilization of the other. There is no legal obligation to do so. Indeed, if one spouse objected to consultation with the other the surgeon would be obliged to respect his patient's confidence. The surgeon cannot be obliged to operate. And indeed, surgeons have cause to be wary of operating without consultation of the other spouse. Do surgeons have any real grounds to fear litigation if they go ahead and operate without consulting the other spouse? Any sane adult is entirely competent to authorise sterilization without reference to a spouse. The risk is this. The 'secret' operation may end the marriage. Sterilization without the other partner's agreement can form grounds for divorce. Could the divorced patient sue the surgeon? She might argue that he failed to counsel her on the risk to her marriage. A caring doctor will have the happiness of his patient's marriage in mind. But it seems less likely that the courts would hold him liable for any financial loss a later divorce occasioned the patient even if his 'marriage guidance counselling' was inadequate.[22] And if he has advised his patient of the consequences of not discussing the proposed surgery fully at home, he had discharged any duty which might be imposed on him in that respect.

Compulsory sterilization

Unlike a number of American states, there is no Act of Parliament in this country providing for the sterilization of the mentally disabled or of criminals. We have seen that the courts have strongly disapproved of the sterilization of children before they are of an age to understand what is to be done to them.[23] The English courts have in this field placed more emphasis on the patient's right to choose than perhaps in any other field of medicine.

Who pays for the unplanned child?

Contraception is known to be fallible. No doctor guarantees avoidance of conception. He only undertakes to use his skill to maximize a couple's chances of preventing pregnancy. Sterilization is expected and intended to be final. What if it fails? This can happen if the surgeon is negligent. But there is also a minute but real risk inherent in both vasectomy and some forms of female sterilization that tissues will rejoin naturally and conception once again be possible. Who foots the bill for the unexpected infant?

We will look first at the case where the surgeon admits that steriliz-ation failed because he was negligent. The only issue here is the amount of damages he should pay. At first judges limited damages to compen-sation for the mother's pain and discomfort arising from the useless operation and from the subsequent pregnancy. In *Emeh* v. *Kensington, Chelsea and Westminster A.H.A.*,[24] Mrs Emeh discovered that she had become pregnant again when her pregnancy was about 17–20 weeks advanced. She was offered and refused an abortion. Park J. found that the birth of the child resulted from her unreasonable act in refusing to terminate her pregnancy. That decision, he said, eclipsed the doctor's original and admitted negligence. She was responsible for the child's birth. Mrs Udale, who similarly discovered herself pregnant after a negligent sterilization, was refused compensation for her fifth and unexpected infant on the grounds of public policy. Jupp J. held[25] that the birth of a healthy child could not be allowed to create a claim in damages. He argued that the child, when he came to know of the award, might feel unwanted and the family's relationship be disrupted. Doctors might seem to put pressure on women to have abortions. Children were a blessing, and any financial loss was offset by the joy of their birth. One judge did not agree with his brethren. In 1984 Peter Pain J. saw no reason to refuse damages for the birth of a child born after a failed vasectomy.[26] Fortunately Mrs Emeh was persistent and went to the Court of Appeal. That Court unanimously held[27] that (1) her decision not to abort was not such an unreasonable act as to eclipse the defendant's negligence, and (2) there is no reason of public policy to debar a claim for damages in respect of the unplanned child's upbringing.

What are the rules now? The Court of Appeal said forcefully that a court should never declare that a woman in the position of Mrs Emeh ought to have an abortion. Mrs Emeh was over 17 weeks' pregnant. Abortion then would have involved considerable physical pain, emotional trauma and some real risk to her health. What of a woman who discovers her pregnancy early enough to take advantage of the relatively simple procedure for abortion available in the first 12 weeks of pregnancy? She would not be an identical case to Mrs Emeh, and counsel might seek to argue that the Court of Appeal's decision related only to late abortions. So it did. But whenever pregnancy is discovered, refusal of an abortion should not excuse the defendant's original failure. He undertook to exercise care to avoid the necessity for further pregnancies and consequently painful decisions as to whether to continue a pregnancy. Abortion early in pregnancy may be physically risk-free. The emotional impact of the decision to abort takes it totally beyond the realm of routine medical treatment which an injured plaintiff might reasonably be expected to accept to mitigate her loss. The defendant should well foresee that it is an option many women would refuse.

As to public policy, the Court of Appeal warned of the dangers of laying down lines of policy to refuse claims that were on the ordinary principles of negligence clearly sustainable. They were right to do so. Jupp J.'s well-intentioned reasons for refusing Mrs Udale damages do not hold water. Children are a blessing to most parents. They are invariably an expense. A family is far more likely to be disrupted by increased poverty caused by an extra child than by the child discovering it was a 'mistake'. Several thousand 'mistakes' have comfortably survived that experience.

What of the case where conception occurs because tissues heal naturally? The operation has been performed impeccably. An act of God or nature reverses the operation. At first sight it appears that the surgeon is in no way responsible. What could he have done? The practice of most surgeons is to warn patients of the risk when discussing the proposed operation with them. Can a failure to warn give rise to a claim against the surgeon? This happened in *Thake* v. *Maurice*. Mr and Mrs Thake had five children and little money. They wanted no more children. Mr Thake decided to have a vasectomy and paid the defendant £20 for the operation. The judge found that the defendant never warned Mr and Mrs Thake of the small but real risk that nature would reverse the surgery. Mrs Thake became pregnant again. She did not discover her pregnancy until it was nearly five months advanced. The couple sought compensation from the defendant surgeon.

As Mr Thake had paid for his vasectomy, unlike an N.H.S. patient, he had a contract with the surgeon. The trial judge held[28] that Mr Thake had agreed to an operation that he understood would render him irreversibly infertile. That is what he contracted for. The defendant was in breach of contract if he failed to achieve that aim. By failing to warn Mr Thake of the risk of natural reversal of the vasectomy, he guaranteed to make him sterile. He was responsible for the financial loss to the family occasioned by the birth of the unplanned infant.

The Court of Appeal[29] held by a majority that the surgeon never guaranteed to make Mr Thake sterile. Neill L.J. found that no reasonable person would have understood the defendant as giving a binding promise that the operation would achieve its purpose. They nevertheless unanimously found for Mr Thake on grounds which will enable private, and N.H.S., patients to sue if they are not warned of the risk of nature reversing sterilization of either sex. They held that failure to warn of this risk was negligent. That negligence resulted in Mrs Thake being unaware of her pregnancy until abortion was no longer a safe option. The defendant was responsible for that state of affairs and thus for the birth of the child. He was liable in contract to his private patient. He would have been liable in negligence to an N.H.S. patient.

It is now clear that negligence in not warning patients of the potential risk of reversal always inherent in sterilization renders the doctor liable for the birth of a subsequent child if the mother, lulled into a false sense of security, fails to recognize the early signs of pregnancy. His, in law, inadequate advice deprives her of the choice of opting for a medically safe abortion early in the pregnancy. A woman who does detect her pregnancy in the first few weeks and rejects the option of abortion may face some difficulty in establishing any 'loss' resulting from an alleged failure to warn her of the risk that sterilization may fail. She cannot contend that she 'lost' the option to abort. Her claim must be framed differently. In *Gold* v. *Haringey A.H.A.*[30] the plaintiff bore a further child after nature reversed an operation to sterilize her. She had not been warned of this possibility nor counselled on alternatives to the operation she agreed to. The judge found that the risk of natural reversal of vasectomy is lower than that attached to female sterilization. A sensible woman would have regarded that information as crucial to her decision to accept sterilization. The doctor's advice was therefore negligently given. His negligence caused her to lose an opportunity for her and her husband to opt for the more reliable means of sterilization, vasectomy for the husband. The law does not impose liability simply because a child is born after a natural reversal of surgery to sterilize a patient. The patient has to establish (1) that he or she was not adequately counselled as to the likelihood of such an occurrence and (2) that he or she lost an opportunity to avoid the birth of a further child as a result. The problem for doctors is this. They are naturally anxious to stress that sterilization should normally be regarded as *irreversible*. The law now demands that they inform patients of the very slight risk of failure inherent in any form of surgery to sterilize. The advice to be given to the patient now needs as much thought, and maybe time, as the operation itself. That may be one beneficial consequence of medical litigation.

Chapter 17
Organ Transplantation

Rarely has a medical procedure aroused so much emotional and public controversy as transplantation. Controversial debates involving clinical, ethical, scientific, financial and resource considerations have raged on for more than a generation. Public acceptance of, and attitudes towards, what are relatively standard procedures, such as kidney transplants, has been affected from time to time by more controversial matters relating to heart transplantation. Public response to transplantation has been erratic, influenced by the publicity given to dramatic successes and failures. For example, in the early days of heart transplantation the major media publicity given to declarations which described transplant surgeons as 'human vultures', and the headline stories of organs which had been removed from bodies before 'real death' had occurred, all contributed to excite public concern and hostility. On the other hand, the media can be effective in publicizing the benefits of transplantation and creating maximum favourable public awareness on the subject. In 1984 the television programme 'That's Life' campaigned on behalf of Ben Hardwick, a 2-year-old baby who needed a liver transplant: a suitable donor was found and the transplant was carried out. Opinion polls revealed that the programme's publicity had swung public opinion significantly in favour of transplantation procedures generally.

Today, it is not uncommon for surgeons to remove the liver, heart, pancreas, kidneys and eyes from, for example, road accident casualties who have suffered irreversible brain damage. But it will take some time yet before the public accepts as a matter of course such multi-organ harvesting.

The benefits of, and problems associated with, transplantation procedures are best illustrated by looking at kidney disease. Twenty-five years ago, permanent cessation of kidney function was a sentence of death within a few days. But the development of the 'artificial kidney' and kidney transplantation has changed the situation dramatically, and patients now have the opportunity, in theory at least, of lasting relief. Yet the waiting list for kidneys at present in this country is about 2,700;

and several hundred patients still die each year for lack of effective kidney treatment. Indeed, it is alleged that more people are allowed to die of chronic renal failure in the U.K. than in any comparable European country.[1] Renal dialysis is very expensive: the cost of keeping a patient alive on a kidney machine over, say, a five-year period, is far higher than the cost of a kidney transplant and the continuing cost of drugs, even were the supply of kidneys sufficient to meet all demands.

Such a situation obviously poses many social and ethical problems. Should more financial resources be channelled into this specialty to meet the demand for kidney treatment? If the capability of providing treatment is inadequate, then what considerations determine which patients should be treated and which may be left to die? There have been reports of cases where kidney units dealt with the problem by adopting a 'cut-off' point for donees based on age. Patients over a certain age, which has been as low as 45, may be considered too old for treatment.[2] It has been said that the older the patient and the more complications he may have, the less his chance of receiving effective treatment in many N.H.S. regions. What remedy, if any, do patients left in such circumstances have? Can they use the law to obtain treatment? We have already seen how difficult this would be.

Perhaps the major need today with kidney transplantation is to obtain an adequate supply of kidneys to meet the demand. There is a social need to persuade healthy people to think ahead and be prepared to agree to donate their kidneys for use after their death. If it were possible, for example, to have available for use the healthy kidneys of all road traffic accident victims, the problem would be solved.[3] Is the law effective to meet current social needs or should it be changed?

Quite different considerations may apply to other forms of transplantation, especially heart transplantation. Not all surgeons have been persuaded that heart transplantation programmes are justified at present. (The experimental aspects are discussed in a later chapter.) The cost is much higher than that of other forms of transplantation, and some maintain that the use of resources here is an expensive luxury for a limited number of possible beneficiaries: significant progress in healthcare results from wider measures to *prevent* heart disease rather than increasing use of expensive salvage services; and resources might be better pointed in that direction.[4] Apart from resource allocation matters, there are also those who have doubts about the ethical justification for some heart transplantation developments.

What is the law affecting these matters and is it satisfactory? This is a matter to which we now turn.

Live donor transplantation

Is it lawful?

We have examined elsewhere the fact that there is no specific legal ruling which determines what limits, if any, are set to permissible surgical operations. It has always been assumed that surgical operations are lawful, where a patient properly consents, because the intrusive procedures are for the medical benefit of the patient. It also seems clear that the law will not permit a person to consent to any intrusive procedures simply because he is willing, or indeed, anxious, to submit to them. The courts have, on a number of occasions, disregarded the consent of people to mutilating procedures upon themselves in a non-medical context.

Accordingly, an immediate question which must be asked in connection with transplantation from live donors is whether a potential donor can, in law, give his consent to, for example, a kidney being taken from his body; the transplant is of no physical therapeutic benefit to the donor, and in some cases the loss of a kidney could prove to be harmful. Almost certainly, the courts will regard this as a public policy issue. In the very early days of transplantation it is conceivable that the courts might have hesitated to approve of the removal of a healthy organ; and it might have been held that consent to such procedures was not permitted; but we have proceeded too far along the transplantation road for that argument to be of any avail today. Thus, Lord Edmund-Davies has said extra-judicially that he would be surprised if a surgeon were successfully sued for trespass to the person or convicted of causing bodily harm to one of full age and intelligence who freely consented to act as donor. But he then added the proviso that the operation should not present unreasonable risks to the donor's life or health. That proviso was important for 'a man may declare himself ready to die for another, but the surgeon must not take him at his word'.[5]

How voluntary is consent?

Thus a person is permitted to consent to surgeons taking an organ from his body in certain circumstances. There is, of course, the problem of the genuineness of consent. Live donors are usually related closely to the potential donee, and it is often the case that the potential donor is the only person whose compatibility is such that the relative's life can be saved.[6] In such circumstances the psychological pressure which exists on a person can be enormous, and if the consent is not really free the surgeon may well be exposed to moral and legal censure. Full discussion and counselling are essential before a donor is asked to sign an appropriate consent form.

Children as donors

More difficult are those cases where organs are to be taken from young children. Can they be organ donors? If they are under 16 they are often unlikely to have the capacity to give consent themselves for serious medical treatment, or other medical procedures, which are for their benefit. This must be given by a parent or guardian. Can they go further and consent to 'non-therapeutic' procedures upon their charges?

This is a problem which in fact arose in the U.S.A. in the early days of kidney transplantation. The first kidney transplants took place in 1956. Because of the importance of compatibility, the operations were between sets of minor twins aged 19, 14 and 14 respectively. In each case the healthy twin was willing to donate a kidney to his dying brother, but it was not clear whether the law permitted this. Applications were thereupon made to the court for guidance. The court fastened on the psychiatric evidence which was given to show that each donor had been fully informed about the nature of the procedure and also that, if it were not possible to perform the operation and the sick twin were to die, there would be a resulting grave emotional impact on the surviving twin. This enabled the court to be satisfied in each case that the operation was for the benefit not only of the donee but also of the donor, and that accordingly a parent was capable of giving consent to such a 'therapeutic' procedure.[7] This seems to be highly artificial reasoning, although, as a matter of convenience, it solved the immediate issue.

It is less clear whether an English court would be as ready to adopt such reasoning. Our courts have a tendency to be far more paternalistic. In 1977 the Health Minister was questioned in Parliament as to the validity of a transplant from an infant donor; he declined to be drawn as to what the law was in this country and suggested that it may be a question for the courts to decide.[8]

In this connection it is worth noting that the Council of Europe

Resolution on the Harmonization of Transplantation Legislation contemplates the removal of organs from minors or otherwise legally incapacitated persons, provided that the donor and his legal representative are given appropriate information before the removal about the possible consequences, in particular the medical, social and psychological consequences, as well as the importance of the donation for the recipient.[9] It is possible, therefore, that an English court might countenance a transplant from a young donor, but probably only where this is a matter of last resort.

It is far less likely that an English court would go along with an American decision where a 28-year-old married man who was dying of a fatal kidney disease sought the permission of the court for a kidney donation from his 27-year-old brother, who had a mental age of 6 and who was detained in a mental institution. The court emphasized the emotional and psychological dependence of the mentally handicapped person on his brother, and that his well-being would be jeopardized more severely by the loss of his brother than by the removal of a kidney. Accordingly, it applied a doctrine of 'substituted judgment', which curiously was based on some very old English law relating to lunatics, whereby the court was able to act in the same manner as the incompetent would have acted had he possessed all his faculties, and in these circumstances it gave consent on behalf of the donor.[10] In a more recent decision in Texas the court applied the same principles, emphasizing first that nothing should be construed as being applicable to a situation where the proposed donee is not a parent or sibling of the incompetent and, second, that it would be preferable for legislation to provide a proper system of rules in these cases.[11]

In this country the situation would be different. The Mental Health Act 1983, which does not, of course, expressly provide for this kind of case, does provide detailed safeguards before consent can be given for different types of treatment of the mentally ill and, by implication, it would not be possible to remove a kidney from the mentally handicapped brother.

Cadaver transplantation – the Human Tissue Act 1961

Most organs for transplantation today are taken from persons who have died rather than from living donors. Interestingly, a person has no legal right at common law to determine what shall happen to his body after his death. A body, or part of it, cannot ordinarily be the subject matter of ownership, and normally it is the legal duty of the close relatives of a deceased or those who are in 'lawful possession' of the body to arrange for its burial at the earliest opportunity. Thus, it is not legally possible for a person to impose a duty upon others that he be cremated after death. All he can do is indicate that he desires to be cremated, and those concerned with burial are free to comply or ignore such a wish as they see fit. It follows, technically, that a person has no legal power to donate organs from his body after his death under the ordinary law; equally nobody has any right to interfere with a corpse, and any such interference would be a criminal act.[12]

However, the law relating to cadaver transplantation is now governed by statute. In 1952, the Corneal Grafting Act, recently amended by the Corneal Tissue Act 1986, authorized the use of eyes for therapeutic purposes in some circumstances. This statute attracted little publicity at the time; nor was there much more public interest when, in 1961, the Human Tissue Act widened the law to cover any other parts of the body. It is this Act which today governs the use of organs for transplantation purposes and, although at one time it served as a model for similar legislation in many other countries, it is now widely regarded as being unsatisfactory both in connection with its wording and also, in some respects, in its narrowness of approach.

Authority for the removal of parts of the body may be obtained in two ways.

At the express request of the donor

First, there is a 'contracting in' provision whereby any person may in writing at any time, òr by word of mouth in the presence of two or more witnesses during his last illness, express a request that his body be used after his death for therapeutic purposes (or for purposes of medical education or research). If such a request is made, then the person lawfully in possession of his body after his death has the power (though not the duty), unless he has reason to believe that the request was subsequently withdrawn, to authorize the removal from the body of any part or, as the case may be, a specified part, for use in accordance with the request.[13] The problems arising from this provision are mainly practical. The usual way in which a person determines what should happen after his death is by will. Relying upon a will would rarely be of much use in a transplantation situation. It is essential, in order to make use of organs which are taken from a body after death, to remove them within a very short time of death taking place. If the medical authorities had to wait until the will was obtained and read, the body would be too far gone to make the use of any organs from it worthwhile. Hence, there is need for a much better system of communicating a person's wishes in connection with transplantation. This will be discussed shortly.

With the consent of relatives

The second method provided for in the Act, and which does not depend upon the express consent of the deceased, enables a person 'lawfully in possession' of the body of a deceased person to give permission for organs to be removed if, 'having made such reasonable inquiry as may be practicable', he has no reason to believe either that the deceased had expressed an objection to his body being so dealt with after his death, and had not withdrawn it; or that the surviving spouse or surviving relative of the deceased objects to the body being so dealt with.[14]

This particular provision bristles with difficulties and ambiguities. It is also capable of causing serious distress to close relatives unless its exercise is handled with care.

For example, it has not yet been determined authoritatively who is regarded in law as the person 'lawfully in possession of the body'. Take an example, by no means unusual, where a young man has been killed, or fatally injured, in a motorcycle accident, is brought into hospital and there is delay in connection with his identification. In those circumstances, it would appear that it is the hospital which is lawfully in possession of his body until such time as the relatives can be traced and can carry out their normal duties in connection with its disposal.[15] The hospital authorities may wish to use the organs of that person, and the law provides that they may do so if 'having made such reasonable inquiry as may be practicable' they have no reason to believe that the deceased or close relatives object. It is not clear whether the practicability of such inquiry relates to the interests of the relatives or the interest of the hospital. For example, in order to trace relatives and establish their views, it would not be unreasonable to take days or even weeks; the family of the deceased may be on holiday and may not be traceable for some time. If the requirement is concerned primarily with the need to establish their views, then it would be unlawful for the hospital to act before those relatives were contacted; and so the body would be 'wasted' for transplantation purposes. Alternatively, it is possible to interpret the need to make such reasonable inquiry as may be practicable as relating to the particular use for which the parts of the body are required, bearing in mind the very short time in which it is possible to make effective use of a deceased's organs. Thus, it can be argued that if the hospital is unable to trace the relative within a few hours then it has made such reasonable inquiries as it could and is free to act. Those who regard the Human Tissue Act as being far too restrictive in any event would naturally regard the latter interpretation as the better one. One may doubt, though, whether that is the correct interpretation.

But even then, there is a technical problem in connection with which relatives should be consulted to establish whether or not they object. The Act specifies the surviving spouse *or any* surviving relative of the deceased. If there is a surviving spouse, does that mean that it is not necessary to consult any other relatives should that spouse agree to the body being used? If there is no surviving spouse, *any* relative suggests, on a literal reading, that the person lawfully in possession of the body must make inquiries of *all or any* of the relatives, so that even a very distant second cousin would have the power to object. In most cases the hospital authorities would act sensibly and so also would close relatives; and it may be, therefore, that some of the technical difficulties created by the rather wide wording of the section would not raise problems in practice. However, difficulties have arisen from time to time. One woman, who had been separated from her husband for more than six years and who had not been consulted before his kidneys had been removed upon death, afterwards maintained that he had indicated a very strong objection during his life to any organs being transplanted from his body.[16] In other cases, serious distress has been caused to parents upon discovering that children who were crash victims have had organs removed from their bodies and they have not been approached. In all these cases, the hospital authorities maintained that all reasonable inquiries had been made!

The role of the coroner

Where there is reason to believe that an inquest may have to be held on a body, or a post-mortem examination may be required by the coroner, it is necessary to obtain the authority of the coroner to the removal of any part of the body. This, too, could have the effect of delaying for an unacceptably long period the opportunity to remove organs. This may be the case particularly where a coroner regards his duty to act as coroner as being of greater importance than the secondary power which he has to authorize the use of organs before his coroner's duties are complete. In a controversial case in Leicester in 1980, the father of a girl who had died in a road accident had given surgeons permission to use any of her organs, including her heart, which had been removed by surgeons. At a subsequent inquest, the coroner complained that he had not given permission for the heart to be removed since permission had been sought from him only for the removal of a kidney. He therefore directed that in future written permission would have to be obtained from him and countersigned by a pathologist. This incident highlighted the problem that coroners, acting in pursuance of what they regarded as their legal duties, could adversely restrict the use of organs even where parents or other relatives had consented. It was for such reasons that the Home Secretary circularized coroners, stressing that it was not part of a coroner's function to place obstacles in the way of the development of medical science or to take moral or ethical decisions in this matter, and that the coroners should assist rather than hinder the procedure for organ removal. A coroner should refuse his consent only where there might be later criminal proceedings in which the organ might be required as evidence, or if the organ itself might be the cause or partial cause of the death, or where its removal might impede further inquiries.[17]

Life must be extinct

The Human Tissue Act 1961 does not deal at all with live donor transplantation; it is concerned solely with the removal of parts of a body *after death*. What is death? The Act simply states that 'no . . . removal shall be effected except by a fully registered medical practitioner, who must have satisfied himself by a personal examination of the body that life is extinct'. Largely as a result of the need, for transplantation purposes, to act as soon as possible after death has occurred,[18] the traditional medical definition of death has been reformulated, and the implications of this generally will be examined in a later chapter. However, it must be emphasized here that the difficulty of establishing an acceptable criterion of death has operated as the most powerful factor to sustain transplantation issues at the centre of media interest as a matter of high emotional and public concern. Public concern was voiced, for example, at the suggestion that a doctor and his medical team might have conflicting interests in that, on the one hand, their duty would be to act in the best interests of the ill or dying patient to keep him alive and yet, on the other, there might be pressures to certify a potential donor's death at the earliest possible moment to enable organs to be removed for the benefit of other donees. Some suggested that there might be two types of death: one for medical purposes and one for legal! Thus, in one of the early heart transplant cases, a surgeon at the National Heart Hospital was reported as saying that the donor was 'clinically dead but legally alive by some criteria'. Such confusion was more confounded by the need in some cases to maintain a person who was dead, clinically and legally, on what was confusingly described as a 'life-support' machine to ensure that the kidneys to be removed were kept in good condition. The fact that the media and the public may often have been misled and were ill-informed about the correct situation did not affect the major unease about the whole question of certification of death. To this we shall return in a later chapter.

Prospects for reform

It is widely believed that the law is in an unsatisfactory state. The blame, though, lies not at the feet of the draftsmen or the judges but rather with a society which is still unable to make up its mind about changes in the law to meet its demands.

The British Transplantation Society has attributed the shortage of organs for transplantation purposes to several factors. First, and most important, was thought to be apathy in the medical profession. It is taking a very long time to persuade doctors to assist positively in the search for organs and the needs of transplantation. The second factor, which perhaps is now beginning to change, was thought to be ignorance among the public and the medical profession as to how serious the shortage is. Kidney transplantation has been carried out for so long that perhaps many people feel that the state of affairs at present is satisfactory, and that patients who need kidneys can always receive them. But perhaps of greatest importance is the fear among doctors that by being involved in organ donation they may in some way be contravening the law, with its present uncertainty of interpretation, or that they may meet with hostility from relatives by asking permission for kidneys to be removed after death, or that they may be accused of hastening the death of a potential donor.

In 1975 the British Transplantation Society recommended that a Code of Practice for Organ Transplantation Surgery be adopted to provide safeguards (beyond those contained in the Human Tissue Act) for those who needed reassurance about possible abuses of practice by over-zealous transplant teams. Thus, (1) before organs are removed from a body for transplantation purposes, death should be certified by two doctors, one of whom has been qualified for at least five years; and neither of these doctors should be members of a transplantation team. (2) In cases of irreversible and total brain death, where respiration is dependent on mechanical ventilation, the decision to stop ventilation must have no connection with transplantation considerations. Brain death would be established using agreed criteria (as discussed later). Two sets of tests should be carried out, separated by a 24-hour interval. (3) Where it has been decided that death of the brain has occurred and mechanical ventilation is to be stopped, the question of organ removal should be discussed fully and sympathetically with available relatives so that their informed consent is obtained for the removal of organs either before or after mechanical ventilation is finally stopped. (4) If available relatives objected to the use of the deceased's organs for grafting, even if it were established that the deceased himself has not objected, the relatives' wishes would be followed. This Code was agreed in 1979.

Contracting in or out?

But by far the most important consideration from a legal point of view is the question whether or not the present system, which is essentially a 'contracting-in' provision, should be changed to a 'contracting-out' system. This means in effect that the law would allow surgeons to assume that a dead person had not objected to his organs being removed for transplantation purposes unless he had expressly put on record, for example on a public register, that he objected to such use. In most cases this would mean, in law at least, that relatives would lose the right of veto. Such a law, which now exists in Austria, Denmark and France,[19] would, in practice, enable surgeons to acquire all the organs they need, unless there happened to be a dramatic change in public attitude so that large numbers of people went to the trouble of registering their objections. However, attractive as such a change would be to transplant surgeons, it has been felt for some time that such a radical amendment of the Human Tissue Act would be too controversial, bearing in mind the strong objections which members of the public and politicians have expressed over recent years to such ideas. To introduce a contracting-out system, it has been suggested, would be to pay too little respect to minority feelings which may be both strong and inarticulate. Nevertheless, such a change may well come. Thus in 1984 a television poll was commissioned (at a particularly propitious time) which showed that 71 per cent of the public supported an 'opting-out' system.

Until the law is changed the government aims to encourage more public awareness of the need to 'contract in' by campaigning to persuade people to sign and carry transplant donor cards with them. Donor cards, which are the size of credit cards, have been available in their present form since 1981. The holder is able to specify which organs can be removed by deleting any of those listed: kidneys, eyes, heart, liver and pancreas, or can request that 'any part of my body be used for the treatment of others'. The holder's signature and the name and telephone number of a relative are required.[20]

In the longer term the aim is to have a complete list of donor volunteers on computer.

Liability for mishaps

Other, perhaps more peripheral, matters will require consideration in due course. Thus, to give some comfort to the medical profession, the American Uniform Anatomical Gift Act provides an immunity from civil or criminal proceedings to persons who act in good faith in accordance with the relevant anatomical gift laws. The extent of such an immunity is questionable. In a case in France, a recipient of a corneal transplant died shortly afterwards from rabies and it was then discovered that immediately before her death the donor had been in Egypt, where she had been bitten by a dog. The director of the eye bank was charged with manslaughter, presumably because inadequate steps had been taken to check the antecedents of the eyes. Should an immunity from the ordinary processes of law be given in such circumstances? Much may depend upon the meaning of 'in good faith' if the American solution is adopted. Preferable, however, would be the simple recommendation of the Pearson Commission that there should be strict liability imposed on authorities responsible for the supply and distribution of human blood and organs.[21]

It is mentioned in Chapter 18 that the Pearson Commission also recommended that any volunteer for medical research or clinical trials who suffers severe damage as a result should have a cause of action, on the basis of strict liability, against the authority to whom he consented to make himself available. This should be extended on similar reasoning to organ donors.[22]

Trafficking in organs

Patients in need of suitable organs in a scarce 'market' may have problems if they are too far behind in the queue, or not in the queue at all. We have already examined the so-called 'right' of a patient to medical treatment; which will not generally provide much encouragement.

Is it possible, however, for a waiting donee to make use of market forces and set out to buy an organ? There have been such cases; and where the stakes are high enough there will usually be sellers, who may be in desperate need of the money. Nevertheless, most doctors would follow those in the U.S.A. who have condemned the possible practice as 'morally offensive and ethically indefensible'. In one survey of doctors reported by the American Medical Association, the objectors felt that the poor might be sold for spares and the wealthy would have an advantage in a sellers' market; there would also be the potential for such criminal abuse as body-snatching and murder for saleable parts – a return to the days of Burke and Hare! The argument against permitting the sale of organs is even stronger than that relating to blood, which is regenerative: organs should not be treated as a commodity and exposed to the laws and practices of the market place.[23] The law in England, though not clear, is almost certainly unlikely on public policy grounds alone to condone trade in organs, quite apart from the more technical objections about property rights. There have been allegations of illicit trade in human limbs and organs conducted from the mortuaries of London hospitals.[24] It would be preferable to adopt the provision in the Council of Europe's model transplant code that all forms of profit-making from the disposal of human tissue should be illegal.

Chapter 18
Medical Research

In 1981 an elderly widow, Mrs Wigley, died from the effects of an experimental drug she had been given subsequent to an operation for bowel cancer. She died not from bowel cancer but from bone marrow depression induced by the drug. Without her knowledge or consent she had been entered in a clinical trial of the new drug. At the inquest into her death the coroner thought the matter to be one deserving of public notice.[1] In 1984 and 1985 two apparently healthy young medical students died in the course of clinical trials of new drugs. Such incidents arouse great public concern. Yet every time any one of us receives a prescription for antibiotics we benefit from research performed on others in the past. It is becoming a human guinea pig oneself that is at first sight unattractive. But if medicine is to progress to combat cancer and continue the battle against diseases such as diabetes and multiple sclerosis, new drugs and procedures must be subject to trials. The key issue is: how should medical research be controlled and who should enforce controls?

We are concerned in this chapter with the role that the law does and should play in the control of medical research involving human subjects. It must be acknowledged straight away that the law can never be more than a fall-back procedure in the control of medical research. Control lies in the first place in the hands of the medical profession. Bodies such as the Royal Colleges and the B.M.A., and pre-eminently the Medical Research Council, are vigilant in maintaining standards. In England today their control of research is shared with the research ethical committees, established in virtually every N.H.S. hospital where trials are carried out. Projects for research, whether on patients or volunteers, must be submitted to the local ethical committee. Funding for research in the absence of ethical committee approval is virtually unobtainable. The committee's membership embraces doctors, other health professionals, and lay membership drawn from all sections of the local community. The number of lay members differs from committee to committee. Despite many shortcomings, the ethical committees provide a model for co-operation between the medical profession and the public, and a forum for reasoned debate sadly lacking in other areas of medical and ethical controversy. The degree to which the doctors sway the committees and the lack of debate on general principles, however, have been criticized by many observers. The trial in which Mrs Wigley died of a drug she never knew she had been given had been sanctioned by no fewer than eleven ethical committees!

Consent to participation in trials

Outrage over Mrs Wigley's death centred on the revelation that a patient should be the subject of a risky trial without her knowledge or consent. To criticism that this should ever have been allowed to happen, the chairman of one of the ethical committees which had approved the trial responded that consent to the surgery embraced consent to related drugs, albeit the drug was experimental.[2] Furthermore, ethical codes of conduct promulgated by the medical profession accept that in certain limited circumstances consent need not be sought. Let us look first then at the international ethical code on research on humans, the Declaration of Helsinki. Within the Declaration a distinction is made between therapeutic and non-therapeutic research. This distinction, we shall see later, may have vital legal consequences too. Therapeutic research concerns procedures experimental in nature but which it is hoped will benefit the subject of the research, the patient. The medical staff engaged in therapeutic research will be combining care of the patient with the conduct of the experiment. Non-therapeutic research involves generally healthy volunteers to test the efficacy, side-effects, and general operation on the human body of a novel procedure. Patients may become volunteers for non-therapeutic research into conditions unrelated to their illness.[3] The basic principle promulgated by the Helsinki Declaration provides that every subject '. . . must be adequately informed of the aims, methods, anticipated benefits and potential hazards of the study and the discomfort it may entail . . . The doctor should . . . obtain the subject's freely given informed consent, preferably in writing.' In relation to therapeutic research an exception to an absolute requirement for the patient's consent is made. If the doctor considers it essential *not* to obtain informed consent, he must give detailed reasons to an independent scrutiny committee. This was done in Mrs Wigley's case and the ethical committees had approved the trial. No exception to the rule on consent is made in relation to non-therapeutic research.

How far does the ethical code conform with the law? I have dealt earlier with the issue of informed consent in general medical care.[4] The English courts demand that the doctor explain the general nature of the procedure to the patient.[5] In the absence of such explanation any contact with the patient may be a battery. His consent is invalid because he does not know what he consents to. When the patient understands what is to be done to him, but receives no information, or what he sees as inadequate information, on the risks and side-effects of treatment, the *Sidaway*[6] judgment held that he may have an action in negligence if risks or side-effects materialize *and proper medical practice would have required that he be warned of that possibility*.

Let us try and apply these principles to Mrs Wigley and the Helsinki Declaration. To perform a procedure whose nature and purpose are not communicated to the patient at all is to commit a battery. The exception to the need for any consent embodied in the Helsinki Declaration is not recognized as such by the law. Had Mrs Wigley's relatives gone to court, their claim would have turned on whether the experimental procedure could truly have been considered part and parcel of the surgery to which she agreed. Medical opinion appears deeply divided on that issue. On the other hand, the Declaration may go further than English law at present in defining in its basic principles the degree of information on risks, side-effects and discomfort the patient should be given. The question to be resolved is whether the *Sidaway* test of judging what information a doctor must volunteer by reference to current medical practice will be adopted in the context of research. Will doctors engaged in research effectively determine what research subjects are entitled to be told? Probably not. It has already been held that *Sidaway* only applies to therapeutic treatment, not medical interventions for non-therapeutic purposes.[7] Researchers involving healthy volunteers in their projects are likely to be required to give those volunteers all the information relating to the risks and side-effects of the trial which a prudent volunteer would consider necessary to an informed decision on whether to participate. Non-therapeutic research on patients would have to be explained to the *patient's* satisfaction. Drawing a distinct line between therapeutic and non-therapeutic research may be difficult in practice and unsatisfactory in principle. England should follow Canada's lead and require full disclosure of risks to all participants in clinical trials.[8] Should the courts in relation to therapeutic research cling to the test of proper medical practice, then that practice must be assessed in the light of the stringent rules on disclosure in the Helsinki Declaration.

In the case of non-therapeutic research a further problem is whether the volunteers are truly volunteers. Do medical students feel under compulsion to assist in trials mounted by their teachers? Do patients feel obliged to 'help' their doctor if he asks them to participate in non-therapeutic research? Where resort is had to volunteers outside the medical schools and hospital patients, payment is still often made in this country. Amounts paid are trivial but may still constitute an inducement to the growing numbers of the unemployed. The principles of law are clear. Any degree of compulsion renders any written consent given invalid. Proving compulsion would be the difficulty for a medical student. And for an unemployed 'volunteer', economic compulsion arising from his circumstances rather than any action by the research team is as yet unrecognized in English law.

The issue of free and full consent is central to the propriety and legality of clinical trials. Should the public, and patients in particular, come to believe that there is a real likelihood of being involved in a trial unknowingly, or, having agreed to participate, discovering that they have been given inadequate or inaccurate information, the supply of volunteers for research will dry up and patients' confidence in general health care will be seriously undermined. But the issue of what constitutes a proper consent is, as we have seen, far from easy. The line between experimenting on a patient and doing your utmost for him is blurred.[9] For example, if a doctor caring for patient with A.I.D.S. attempts as a last resort a novel treatment, knowing that there is no conventional treatment which will prolong the patient's life, has he crossed that line and made the patient a research-subject? The thorny problem of consent and medical research should not be left for a *cause célèbre* to be fought through the courts. Attempts should be made to work out in advance a statutory code of practice which (a) safeguards the rights of, and protects the interests of patients and research subjects, and (b) ensures that properly regulated research can continue and flourish.

Children in medical research programmes

Very real difficulties beset the question of consent to clinical trials by adults. The problems are even greater where children are concerned. When can a child give his own consent to participation in a trial? If the child is incapable of giving an effective consent, may a parent give consent on his behalf?

The House of Lords' ruling in *Gillick*[10] empowers a minor to consent to medical treatment when he or she has reached an age and individual maturity to judge what the treatment entails and assess its benefits and disadvantages. In the case of therapeutic research where the child may expect benefit from the procedure, the test might be the same. And if the child is over 16, the Family Law Reform Act 1969 statutorily empowering minors over 16 to consent to medical treatment will offer absolute protection to the medical team. Non-therapeutic research poses a more awkward problem. Does the *Gillick* ruling apply to a procedure of no immediate benefit to the minor? There is no reason why it should not. The basis of the judgment is not limited to medical treatment alone but concerns the general capacity of older children to make decisions for themselves. Provided the child or young person truly appreciates what he is agreeing to, provided he is sufficiently mature to make the judgment on whether the benefit to the community justifies any risk to himself, he may give consent as an adult may to participation in a research project. What the medical team must assess is the maturity and understanding of that individual. They must do this with any research subject under 18. The Family Law Reform Act empowers 16 to 18-year-olds to consent to their own medical treatment only. It has no application to non-therapeutic research.

What then of younger children? Therapeutic research poses little difficulty. The agreement of the parents to a procedure, albeit novel, which it is hoped will benefit the child will authorize the doctors' action. Parental consent is legally effective to authorize any treatment of the child aimed at promoting the best interests of that child. Non-therapeutic research on a child offers no immediate benefit to the child. On the present state of authority in England, it is unclear whether parental consent to such research on a child is of any effect.

The arguments on the present law can be put in this way. The test of the legality of procedures performed on children centres on the individual child. What will benefit him? What are the pros and cons as far as he is concerned? So in *Re D.*,[11] sterilization of an 11-year-old girl was prohibited because it was an invasion of her right to choose for herself on reproduction, and because of the emotional damage early sterilization might cause her. Social questions, such as the risk that any baby she had might be a burden on the community or be disabled itself, were barely touched on. By analogy then, is one forced to say that non-therapeutic research on any child must be barred because the risk to the child, however slight, cannot be justified in the absence of some immediate benefit to him?

Paediatricians emphasize the need for some degree of carefully controlled research on children. Children respond differently to drugs, they suffer from illnesses not afflicting adults and, above all, their suffering when afflicted is particularly poignant. The British Paediatric Association considers non-therapeutic research on children to be neither unethical nor illegal. They have laid down guidelines centring on the principles that research should never be done on children which could adequately be done on adults and that the benefit/risk ratio must be carefully assessed.

The Association's belief that experimentation on children is legal can generally only be right if the courts were prepared to accede to the following argument. Parental rights to consent to procedures involving their young children are dependent on the procedure being in the child's best interests. That embraces any procedure, not just strictly medical matters, for example taking blood to ascertain paternity is allowed.[12] The best interests of the child include the interests of the community. The child benefits from serving the community and may in the long term benefit himself. For example, a 3-year-old from whom blood is taken as part of a control group and compared with blood from a group of diabetic children may develop diabetes himself or his child may. Hence may he be said to benefit indirectly from research into the disease? It is by no means certain that in all cases such an argument will succeed. Of crucial importance will be the extent to which the parents genuinely participated in the decision. Did they have the information and understanding to weigh the benefit of the programme against the risk to the child? The slighter the risk to the child, though, the more likely a court will accept parental judgment as the arbiter of their child's interests and welfare. The law does not require that children be mollycoddled from every conceivable physical risk.[13]

This matter is too vital to be left to the unpredictability of the common law. Statutory force should be given to a code of practice which (1) determines when consent may be given, and who may give effective consent, to research on children, and (2) provides for independent expert scrutiny of research proposals involving young children.[14]

Randomized clinical trials[15]

At the heart of much modern medical research lies the randomized clinical trial. Patients suffering from the same illness are divided into two groups and subjected to different treatments. Most commonly, either (a) one group will receive the conventional treatment, and another be given the experimental and hopefully more effective treatment, or (b) one group will be given a new drug, and the other a placebo. For an outsider there are a number of worrying features to R.C.T.s. First, there is again the question of consent. Second, there is concern that the control group is denied a chance of superior treatment. In particular, public anxiety was highlighted by a trial involving 3,000 women at risk of conceiving a spina bifida baby. Studies had shown that similar women appeared to suffer a reduced incidence of carrying a spina bifida baby if treated with special vitamin supplements. The trial involved randomizing the women into four groups. One group received the full treatment under trial, another part only of the supplement, a third the other element of the supplement, and the fourth a placebo. Why should any woman at risk be denied a treatment which *might* help her avoid a spina bifida conception? Further criticism of randomized trials includes this point, that while the control group in a test may be denied a benefit, laymen are also concerned at the risk in some tests to the experimental group. And finally, who controls and monitors R.C.T.s?

The law's involvement in the control of R.C.T.s can only be peripheral unless specific legislation were to be introduced. The role the law plays now is largely restricted to the need to obtain, and the difficulty of obtaining, consent to an R.C.T. There are doctors and researchers who believe that the R.C.T. is most effective if conducted 'blind', i.e. the patient is told nothing at all. The issue then is whether consent to treatment given generally is negated by unwitting participation in the R.C.T. The law will decide the issue on how closely related the R.C.T. is to the condition under treatment and whether consent to treatment impliedly includes consent to what was done in the trial. At best, a patient asked to take part in an R.C.T. will be told just that. The nature of the trial and the purpose of random allocation may be explained. Exactly what will be done to the patient cannot be explained, by virtue of the very nature of an R.C.T. Consent on the strength of a proper explanation of the trial and free acceptance by the patient of its random basis would appear both sufficient and necessary. Entering the patient in a random test with no explanation and no consent places the doctor at risk of an action for battery if the patient finds out. Fears that patients if properly informed will refuse to participate are natural. The erosion of personal freedom resulting from allowing 'blind' trials is not justified by those fears. A patient who will not agree to, or cannot understand the implications of, a trial should not be entered in that trial.[16]

Apart from questions of consent, the other means by which the courts may be invoked to consider the R.C.T. arise when something goes wrong, and a subject suffers injury. Will the law enable him to obtain compensation? I move on to this next, and later consider general procedures to monitor clinical trials.

Compensation for mishap

At present, compensation for personal injury suffered as a subject in a clinical trial is available only either to a subject who can prove negligence on the part of the operator of the trial, or on an *ex gratia* basis. A claim in negligence may arise in two contexts in an R.C.T. A subject from the control group may complain that he was denied an improved prospect of cure. Subjects from the experimental group may allege that unjustifiable risks were taken. Neither is likely to succeed. As long as conventional treatment of the control group remained proper medical practice, the control has no claim in negligence. As long as the novel procedure was a properly conducted piece of research, the subject of that procedure is likely to fail, albeit the court may regard the burden of justifying departure from conventional practice as lying on the doctor.[17] One interesting speculation may be made. In the spina bifida trial, might a court be prepared to consider whether if there was a realistic hope of benefit the trial was really necessary? Could a mother denied the full vitamin supplement allege that her doctor treated her negligently? Or would the issue return full circle to the question of whether she freely consented to take part in the trial?

Next, what about the case where something goes disastrously and unexpectedly wrong? The subject will not know why. It may be an inherent risk in the trial, it may be that the staff conducting the trial were negligent. In principle, carelessness by the research team, be it in selecting subjects on the basis of their previous medical history, or in conduct of the trial or in their monitoring of the effects of the trial, creates a remedy for the patient. His problems lie in proof of negligence, just as any other patient-plaintiff's do.[18] And they are more acute. If proving negligence in the operation of standard procedures is difficult, how much more difficult it is to prove negligence in embarking on novel procedures.

No-fault compensation again!

One issue on which lawyers, doctors and drug companies do agree is that the present law is inadequate as a means to provide compensation for injury suffered as a subject of medical research. The Pearson Commission,[19] which inclined towards retaining the law of negligence for medical accidents generally, nevertheless favoured strict liability in the context of medical research. The person who put himself at risk for the community was entitled to compensation from the community. The Commission recommended that 'Any volunteer for medical research or clinical trials who suffers severe damage as a result should have a cause of action, on the basis of strict liability, against the authority to whom he has consented to make himself available.'[20]

No change in the law has yet been effected. The D.H.S.S. and the pharmaceutical industry operated *ex gratia* compensation schemes. The injured subject's legal rights remain dependent on the vagaries of the law of negligence. In relation to injury suffered in trials of a drug, a limited degree of strict liability will be introduced when the government, as it must, introduces legislation to enact the European Community Directive on Product Liability.[21] The subject injured in a drug trial will then face this dilemma. Does his injury derive from the drug itself? In that case the drug manufacturer is strictly liable. Or was his injury the fault of a member of the medical team? In which case his only remedy is a negligence claim. Either claim will be determined by resort to the courts. The proceedings will be adversarial. The drug company and the medical staff have vested interests in revealing as little as possible as to what went wrong and in blaming each other. The subject is left in limbo. It is the inherent faults in such a state of affairs which led me in Chapter 9 to regard an investigation-based no-fault system of compensation as preferable for all medical accidents. The moral case for no-fault compensation of medical research victims is even stronger.

The case for no-fault compensation of persons injured in the course of research now receives wide support among doctors too.[22] It is patently fairer to doctor and subject than the present law. The Pearson proposal for reform via strict liability against the authority to whom the subject made himself available is seen as causing immense practical difficulties. The problem of insurance is one. The inequity in landing blame on one institution where the risk inherent in a trial happens to materialize is another. And the term 'authority to whom the volunteer made himself available' is hopelessly vague. The burden of compensating those injured in the course of research to benefit us all should have a wide base. A fund could be financed from all bodies promoting research, from the profession, the pharmaceutical industry and the D.H.S.S. The prospects for introduction of a scheme to compensate medical research victims along these lines appear brighter than prospects for a general no-fault scheme for all victims of medical accidents. Practical problems of definition, administration and finance will be faced, but with a will most difficulties could be overcome.

However, a scheme limited to injury suffered as a research subject will confront one very real problem. Exactly who would be entitled to benefit under the scheme? Would eligibility be confined to volunteers for non-therapeutic research? The moral case for automatic compensation for that group is overwhelming. Volunteers put their health on the line with no hope of personal benefit. Yet as patients may be used as subjects in non-therapeutic research into conditions unrelated to their illness, the line between therapeutic and non-therapeutic research may be blurred. If the compensation scheme is to extend to all research subjects, the problem of deciding eligibility moves to determining when a patient suffers injury as a result of a research enterprise, as opposed to in the course of general health care which may include resorting to some novel procedure. Neither of these potential problems is insuperable. They illustrate perhaps that a general scheme of compensation embracing all victims of medical mishaps is to be preferred.

Monitoring research programmes

In the absence of specific legislation, the law's role in the control of medical research is limited to intervention when disaster has struck. At present it is only in relation to new drugs that legislation provides machinery which seeks to prevent disasters.[23] New drugs must be licensed in most cases before being granted a limited clinical trial certificate. The company seeking a licence must disclose results of preliminary research and animal tests. Only if the Committee on Safety of Medicines (C.S.M.), established under the Medicines Act 1968, is satisfied with the information submitted by the company may clinical trials on patients begin. Provision is made for reporting back of adverse reactions to the C.S.M. via the 'yellow card' system. It is this aspect of the process which has been much criticized. The evidence is that the wider the trial, the more doctors and patients involved in the trial, the less reliable is the reporting system. The continuing list of anti-rheumatic drugs withdrawn only after several patients have suffered serious reactions and even death is a poignant instance of the partial failure of the system to monitor drugs. The persistent allegations of high-pressure marketing to persuade doctors to enter their patients for trials of new products cause further disquiet. Review of the Medicines Act is clearly called for. But it does at least seek to regulate experimentation.

What should now be asked is whether central legal control of research programmes concerning new procedures should be imposed. A possible pattern for legislation is provided for by the Medicines Act in its regulation of clinical trials of new drugs. All research procedures could be made subject to approval by a body responsible to the Health Minister. Research would be permitted only under licence from the government. Such a proposal would be anathema to the medical profession. It would be seen as undermining their clinical freedom. And it would. The definition between doing your best to provide optimum care for a patient and experimenting would cause endless dispute. The additional burden in terms of money and time spent obtaining licences would eat into the public purse and valuable professional time. The case is not made out yet. Local ethical committees play a valuable role in representing the public's and the patient's views. Bodies within the medical profession, especially the Medical Research Council, act as central brakes on individual over-enthusiasm. The danger is that a series of incidents in which research victims die or suffer serious injury may lead to litigation. As we have seen, the law, be it on consent or compensation, is unclear and unsatisfactory. Litigation may be bitter. If the reaction of the medical staff involved is to go on the defensive, saying nothing and defending the claim to the bitter end, the probity of medical research in general may be questioned. The call may then be for all-embracing and stringent legislation to control research.

Confidentiality and medical research

To advance the development of medicine and to enable research when completed to benefit other patients, the results of research must be published. Does publication of research findings amount to a breach of confidence to the patient? First, the patient, if he has given full and free consent to his participation in a trial, may at the same time agree to information about him being disclosed once the trial is completed and a report is prepared. This must be the preferable course of action. In setting the ethical standard of confidentiality, the General Medical Council recognizes medical research as an example of an exception to the general rule on confidentiality. Information may be disclosed if necessary for the purpose of a medical research project which has been approved by a recognized ethical committee. The N.H.S. draft code on confidentiality recognizes a similar exception to its general rule. Whether in law disclosure in the course of a research project of confidential information about a patient without his consent amounts to an actionable breach of confidence depends yet again on the nebulous test of whether that disclosure can be justified by the public interest in the advancement of the relevant research.

What is clear, though, is that disclosure should be limited to information strictly necessary to the project and that the anonymity of the patient must be protected. The N.H.S. Ombudsman upheld a complaint from a young man who discovered in a medical textbook a full-face frontal picture of his naked body![24]

The way forward

Three criteria should determine the future of law reform pertaining to medical research. The fundamental principles governing consent to participation in research must be defined and enforced. The option of leaving it hazy until and unless the courts intervene is not good enough. The case for automatic compensation for injury suffered in forwarding the public good must be met. And most vitally, the debate on control of experiments must continue. It cannot be left to the doctors alone. Their interests are too heavily involved in the projects they monitor. Ethical committees in individual hospitals and areas provide for lay involvement in individual projects. Greater lay involvement in central control and debate on principle is necessary if control of experimentation is not to pass entirely from the hands of the doctors and to be replaced by rules and regulations allowing no room for individual initiative and individual brilliance.

Chapter 19
Defining Death

The traditional definition

Biologically, death is a process and not an event. Different organs and systems supporting the continuation of life cease to function successively and at different times.

Traditionally, the key factors in that process which were used to determine whether death had occurred were the cessation of breathing and the cessation of heartbeat, matters which could be verified with simplicity. Thus, the irreversible cessation of heartbeat and respiration implied death of a patient *as a whole*; but that did not necessarily imply the immediate death of every cell in the body.

The need to determine an exact or, at best, approximate time of death may be important for many reasons. The law not infrequently requires such a finding. If a person is to be charged with murder, his victim must have died within a year and a day of the unlawful act; thus he may escape a murder charge if his victim survives beyond that period. Establishing the date of death may be important for property purposes: until death is established, steps cannot be taken to obtain probate or letters of administration to that person's estate; the interest of a beneficiary under a will is usually dependent upon the beneficiary surviving the testator; in some cases, where the testator and the beneficiary die at around the same time, it may be important, certainly for their heirs, to know when each death took place; thus, where parties die in a common accident, there may be a presumption that the elder died before the younger, unless evidence can be established as to the precise time of death of either; and the property consequences of this decision can be significant.[1] There may also be tax factors: if a person gives away property before his death, that property may be free from tax, or be subject to less tax, if he survives the gift for a specified period.[2] There have been many stories written involving relatives of such donors going to great lengths to postpone or conceal the 'true moment' of death so that he 'survives' beyond the relevant statutory period for tax purposes!

Another possibility may be that the spouse of a person who is either dead or dying may wish to remarry and, in the absence of clear evidence as to whether death has occurred, there may be a potential risk of bigamy. Finally, if the victim has a claim for damages for the injuries sustained, the amount of damages may differ substantially between cases where the victim is comatose yet living, or dead.[3]

Until twenty years ago, determining whether a person was dead rarely posed any difficulty in practice. The medical profession accepted and used the traditional methods of establishing death: when a person's heart stopped beating and he stopped breathing, he was dead. Advances in medicine and in medical technology, however, gradually began to reveal that this was not a valid test for all purposes: elective cardiac arrest of open-heart surgery, for example, or cases of spontaneous cardiac arrest followed by successful resuscitation. Machines such as mechanical ventilators or respirators have effected major improvements in techniques of resuscitation and life support for those who are desperately ill or injured. Where these efforts are successful and the patient recovers satisfactorily, one may praise the advances in medical techniques. But sometimes such measures do not provide any satisfactory outcome, for example where the person's heart continues to beat on the machine long after breathing has stopped but his brain is irreversibly damaged.

In such circumstances, keeping a person going on a machine can be as undesirable as it is pointless. It is distressing to relatives. It can have an adverse effect on nursing staff morale; the cost of maintaining the patient in such intensive care can be very high and, indeed, the use of machines in these cases can mean that other patients, better able to benefit from them, may be denied access to them. The major background reason for dissatisfaction, of course, was the rapid development of transplantation programmes, which highlighted the need for speed in diagnosing death and taking organs from the body.

Thus, pressures developed to produce a redefinition of death based upon a new concept of 'irreversible brain damage' or 'brain death'. This concept has been illustrated dramatically by considering a guillotine victim. Nobody would consider the body, after the head has been severed, to represent an individual living being; yet the body could be resuscitated and the organs kept alive for a considerable period.[4] Thus, whereas in most cases brain death follows the cessation of breathing and heartbeat in the dying process, occasionally the order of events is reversed. This occurs in a minority of cases as a direct result of severe damage to the brain itself, from, perhaps, a head injury or a spontaneous intercranial haemorrhage: instead of failure of such vital functions as heartbeat and respiration eventually resulting in brain death, brain death results in the cessation of spontaneous respiration; this is normally followed within minutes by cardiac arrest. If, however, the patient is supported by artificial ventilation, the heartbeat can continue for some days and this will, for a time, enable the function in other organs, such as the liver and kidneys, to be maintained.

This condition of a 'state beyond coma' or 'irreversible coma' or 'brain death' was advanced as a new criterion of death in 1968 in an influential report of an *ad hoc* Committee of the Harvard Medical School.[5] In such cases a doctor could pronounce as dead a comatose individual who had no discernible central nervous system activity; and then the respirator could be turned off. It was emphasized that judgment of the existence of the various criteria of death was solely a medical issue.

But public opinion did not seem willing to surrender control of such matters lightly to the medical profession! Uneasiness was expressed in connection with the relationship between the attempt to redefine death and the needs of transplant surgeons. From the transplant surgeon's point of view, it is desirable and important that organs taken from a deceased person should be taken as soon as possible after death. In 1975 the British Transplantation Society expressed concern at the poor quality of cadaver kidneys being transplanted, mainly because of the delay between the determination of death and the removal of the kidneys from the body; more than 17 per cent of kidneys transplanted in Britain were said never to have functioned at all. It was also important, for the purposes of transplantation, that a machine should not be switched off permanently, but rather that the body be kept on the machine to preserve the quality of the organs until they were required. Two major fears were voiced publicly. First, was the pressure to redefine death being made simply to enable transplant surgeons to obtain better results? Could it be said, for example, that potential transplant donors might be designated 'dead' at a point of time earlier than if they were not potential donors? Second, was it ethically or legally permissible to remove organs from a donor before the respirator had been turned off? Indeed, could a doctor be liable for murder or manslaughter by turning off a machine?

Because of doubts such as these, the British Transplantation Society, as we have seen in an earlier chapter, recommended that the death of a potential organ donor should be certified by two doctors; that neither should be a member of the transplant team and, most important, that the decision to stop a ventilator should be made quite independently of transplant considerations.

In the late 1970s the medical establishment agreed that 'brain death' or, preferably, 'brain stem death' (which is the 'irreversible loss of brain stem function') could be diagnosed with certainty; and, in these circumstances, the patient is dead whether or not the function of some organs, such as a heartbeat, is still maintained by artificial means. A Code of Practice for the recognition and confirmation of brain death was endorsed by the D.H.S.S. for the benefit of all hospital doctors. However, controversy developed over the Code as the result of a 'Panorama' television programme casting doubt on the reliability of the tests. Were patients being diagnosed as brain dead who were not 'really' dead? Or were the few reported examples of such mistakes simply cases where the appropriate criteria for determining brain death had not been properly carried out? Was it possible that organs were being taken for transplantation before a patient had died? In 1986 the continuing anxieties of certain eminent doctors were once again voiced publicly. The validity of procedures to establish 'brain death' had never, they argued, been rigorously tested. Short-cuts in procedures were too often prompted by pressure from the transplant team anxious to 'get at' organs swiftly.[6]

Judicial skirmishes

Surprisingly few cases have occurred in English or American courts requiring any extensive discussion of the legal meaning of death. Those cases which have been reported usually involve a scenario where a person suffering from severe injuries is placed on an artificial ventilator which is switched off, after he has been pronounced dead, and then the body is reconnected to a respirator before organs are removed for transplantation purposes. In one case in the United States, the brother of the victim sued the hospital on the grounds that he was not 'properly dead' when the respirator was first turned off, that the surgeons had hastened his death. The standard and successful defence of the surgeons in such cases has been that the victim was 'brain dead' when the respirator was first turned off; and so the removal of the organs at a subsequent stage was not the cause of death.[7] (In this country, of course, it would also be necessary to show that the surgeons had complied with the Human Tissue Act in connection with the measures taken to attempt to trace relatives.[8])

English courts have, on a number of occasions, been faced with cases where a person who is charged with murder claims that it was not he who killed the victim, but rather the hospital team who disconnected the life-support machine. The courts have not reacted favourably to such arguments, even though they have expressly side-stepped the issue as to what, in law, constitutes death. In *R* v. *Malcherek*[9] the Court of Appeal had to deal with two such cases. In the first, the defendant had stabbed his wife, who was taken to hospital and put on a life-support machine; when, however, it was found she had irreversible brain damage, the ventilator was disconnected and shortly after that all her bodily functions ceased. The second defendant attacked a girl, causing her multiple skull fractures and severe brain damage; she, also, was taken to hospital and put on a life-support machine, which was disconnected when the doctors concluded that her brain had ceased to function. The Court of Appeal upheld the judges' decisions in each case not to leave the issue of causation to the jury, pointing out rather tartly that it was not the doctors but the accused who were on trial. The Court took the crucial fact to be that the original criminal acts by the defendants were continuing, operating and, indeed, substantial causes of the death of their victims. In the ordinary case where treatment is given bona fide by competent and careful medical practitioners, then evidence is not to be admissible to show that the treatment would not have been administered in the same way by other medical practitioners. Thus, without going into any definition of death, the court was not prepared to allow assailants to shelter behind the technical arguments challenging standard medical procedures. But the court did go slightly further than that. Lord Lane C.J. said, '. . . whatever the strict logic of the matter may be, it is perhaps somewhat bizarre to suggest . . . that where a doctor tries his conscientious best to save the life of a patient brought to hospital *in extremis*, skilfully using sophisticated methods, drugs and machinery to do so, but fails in his attempt and therefore discontinues treatment he can be said to have caused the death of the patient'.

Should there be a statutory definition of death?[10]

It seems clear, then, that the courts are not yet unduly concerned about the definition of death. There is no statutory definition, and it is usually accepted as an issue of fact established by medical evidence. The law is content to accept the decisions of medical practitioners.

Had there been a legal definition of death, especially a statutory definition based upon the long-standing medical criteria of irreversible cessation of breathing and heartbeat, then the medical redefinitions of death to take into account irreversible cessation of brain function would have had no legal effect in those cases where there was a difference in time between the two definitions, until the existing definition was changed by statute or high judicial decision. However, so long as the matter is treated as a question of medical fact, changes in medical approach can be accommodated within the law without any requirement for it to be specifically amended.

However, the question must be faced whether there should be a statutory definition of death and of the criteria for its assessment. Those in favour maintain that these should not be matters solely for doctors and medical practice but are matters of legitimate public interest and concern. Why should persons who until recently have always been regarded as alive, albeit dying, now be regarded at the same point of time as dead, simply because there is a national need for the use of such organs for transplantation? If there is a case for this new attempt to define death, then surely it is a matter worthy of public debate and statutory enactment. Another reason sometimes advanced for introducing statutory criteria is that the doctors themselves are affected by the considerable uncertainty which exists in the public mind as to the definition of death, and this, in turn, leaves them exposed to the possibility of civil or criminal proceedings in some circumstances. In addition, it is argued that when the matter is raised in a court of law it is not something which should be left for decision either by a judge and jury (in criminal matters) or by a judge alone (in civil matters). Statutory guidance is preferable.

On the other hand, those who argue against the introduction of a statutory legal formula maintain that legislation would be inappropriate: technical clinical matters are not the proper subject matter for statute; it could prove to be inflexible, unable to keep up with medical advances, and there might be difficulty in revising or repealing a definition which became out of date. This debate does at least provide the opportunity to clarify a number of issues which are of major public importance.

First, in connection with switching off life-support machines, the medical authorities and the public ought to appreciate the sharp difference between the situation where the machine is turned off because it is established, medically, that the patient is dead, and the situation where the machine is turned off because, although the patient is still clinically alive, it is thought that there is no further justification in continuing to support life artificially and that, therefore, the patient ought to be allowed to die. In the latter situation, a decision to discontinue 'extra-ordinary' or 'heroic' treatment involves quite different considerations, including consent, the quality of life of the patient, and the proper use of scarce medical resources. These are discussed elsewhere. None of these issues arise where the machine is turned off because the patient has been declared dead. Second, however, it must be appreciated that without proper safeguards, medical changes in the definition of death could conceal policy decisions to introduce limited forms of euthanasia. At present, comatose patients, whether breathing spontaneously or on a life-support machine, who have no hope whatsoever of regaining con-sciousness – frequently described as 'human vegetables' – are still regarded as living beings because, although irreversible brain damage has occurred, some activity of the brain stem is retained; they are not brain dead in accordance with current medical definitions. It would not be a far cry to modify the definition of death so that some comatose patients in this state are also regarded as dead. Many may believe that this is the most sensible and most compassionate way of dealing with these persons. If the courts are content to recognize flexible and developing definitions of death as valid if they accord with medical practice, this would in effect be a method whereby without full public debate and without Parliamentary approval a limited form of euthanasia could be introduced directly into medical practice.

Alternative tests?

If a statutory definition of death is introduced which would recognize either the cessation of respiration and heartbeat or the cessation of total brain function, would that mean that in some cases it would be possible to establish the point of death at two or more different points of time? This could certainly have strange implications for a variety of reasons, not the least being the uncertainty of knowing when, for property purposes, an estate passes from one person to another. It was primarily for this reason that the first American legislative attempt to define death, made by the state of Kansas in 1970, was criticized. In setting out alternative definitions, the long-established traditional definition and the newer definition, it was said that it would lead the public to believe that there are two separate phenomena of death, one being primarily for transplantation purposes. Notwithstanding the criticisms, many other states adopted similar definitions of death, and the medical profession has also welcomed definitions which are broad enough not to restrict medical discretion and which do not include restrictive medical criteria. More recently, the American Uniform Brain Death Act (1978) has served as a model for a number of states. It provides simply that 'for legal and medical purposes, an individual who has sustained irreversible cessation of all functioning of the brain, including the brain stem, is dead. A determination under this section must be made in accordance with reasonable medical standards.'

It is difficult to see what this would add to English law, were it to be enacted. This lends support to the strong lobby which opposes any statutory definition of death, arguing that it is far more sensible to leave the situation as it is at present, namely that the courts will look at and accept as a matter of fact the criteria which are adopted and used by recognized medical practitioners. In this situation, the introduction of Codes of Practice, which presently obtains, would enable the criteria to be examined from time to time, to be adapted and approved and changed to accord with the developments which may occur in modern medicine. This approach, provided that such changes are introduced after full public discussion, is on balance preferable. However, that does not preclude specific statutory provisions being introduced in any fresh transplant legislation, to ensure that medical practitioners see clearly the distinction between duties towards a dying patient and the power to remove organs from such a person once that person is properly declared dead.

Chapter 20
Death, Dying and the Medical Practitioner

Society has never been comfortable with issues surrounding the process of dying; and as medical personnel are involved with the dying, they inevitably become involved in the ethical as well as the medical dilemmas which are part of that process. The major contrasting dilemmas are, first, whether efforts should always be made to keep a dying person alive in spite of the additional suffering incurred by that person and the cost in terms of human dignity; and, second, when, if ever, attempts may be made to hasten death when there is excessive suffering and when the cause is hopeless.

The practice of 'striving officiously to keep alive' has been facilitated by the vast increase in high-technology rescue equipment which has become available in different areas of medicine, much of it capable of being used to postpone inevitable death for a time. The benefits of such high-technology equipment are considerable; yet there are those who question the cost, both in economic and in human terms. In economic terms it is maintained that the inappropriate use of such equipment in, for example, intensive care procedures, yields marginal, if any, benefits, while preventing the resources involved being put to better use elsewhere. Of course, this argument cannot be carried too far, since there are others who riposte that such fashionable economic theories are but a device to justify unacceptable reductions in the resources available for health care.[1] Whatever the force of economic considerations, few can deny the personal cost to the patient and to those close to the patient in terms of human dignity. The attention which is now being given to the 'rights' of patients includes the right to human dignity and the right to die with dignity. In preserving and sustaining the life of the patient with a helpless prognosis, it is in the true interests of neither the patient, the family, nor the doctor, always to prolong his suffering (unless this is specifically requested). Unlimited access to high technology medicine may sometimes be as cruel as the illness itself. Doctors concerned with terminally ill patients may make professional and human decisions to give up *treatment* which may be merely sustaining the functions of the organs and turn to appropriate *care* at the terminal stage. But matters of this kind, when discussed openly, raise important and emotive ethical and legal issues: the term 'euthanasia' is sometimes used loosely to challenge those who may contemplate unacceptable ways of easing the suffering of patients, and also to inhibit doctors from courses of action which they might otherwise be prepared to take.

The word 'euthanasia' refers to the means of inducing or bringing about a gentle and easy death; death without suffering. One form of euthanasia, characterized as 'mercy killing', is used where somebody, usually a relative, deliberately and specifically performs some act, such as administering a drug, to accelerate death and terminate suffering. Prosecutions for mercy killing, while rare, are sometimes reported, and the courts usually deal with such cases with compassion. Thus, in one case, a man who had for 11 years devotedly nursed his wife, who suffered from disseminated sclerosis, before killing her, was convicted of manslaughter but received a conditional discharge; and, in another case, a mother who shot her 6-year-old son, who suffered from cystic fibrosis, was simply put on probation for three years. But the courts are not prepared to be as lenient in all such cases. In one recent, dramatic case, a woman who was described by a judge as 'caring, sympathetic and compassionate' was sentenced to nine months' imprisonment for attempted murder. She had agreed, reluctantly, to sit with a lonely, elderly woman who was deaf, arthritic and nearly blind, while she committed suicide. Four hours after taking a lethal dose of barbiturates with brandy, she was still breathing; and so the accused placed a plastic bag over the elderly woman's head, and she died soon afterwards. The judge passed sentence in order 'to deter others less altruistic' than her. However, the Court of Appeal did allow for the possibility of alternative approaches to sentencing in these 'shadowy areas' of mercy killing. Sometimes decisions may be taken not to prosecute even where the facts suggest that a case exists. In a much publicized example in 1978, Derek Humphreys, a well-known journalist, assisted his cancer-stricken and dying wife to 'commit suicide'; but in spite of his clear admission of this in his autobiography, no steps were taken against him.

Such cases of mercy killing, where doctors are not usually directly involved, can also be termed active, voluntary or positive euthanasia, in contrast to the term 'passive euthanasia' which might describe, for example, the withholding of life-support treatment so that nature is allowed to take its course.

Official attitudes to euthanasia are fairly consistent. The World

Medical Association has declared that voluntary euthanasia is contrary to the Declaration of Geneva, and this has been endorsed by national medical associations throughout the world. For example, in 1969 in this country a medical resolution affirmed the fundamental object of the medical profession as the relief of suffering and the preservation of life, and condemned euthanasia as such. The churches, too, are against voluntary euthanasia, but a report of the Church of England in 1975, *On Dying Well*, following a similar line to various Papal directives, drew a distinction between voluntary euthanasia and a decision not to preserve life by 'artificial' means when it would be better for the patient to be allowed to die; it would be wrong to prolong life at any cost.

It is widely accepted that some medical practitioners from time to time are involved in forms of euthanasia, although inevitably it is impossible to gauge the real extent of this and, indeed, it is questionable whether 'euthanasia' is not a misleading and inappropriate term to use to describe medical conduct in such cases. When a Dr Mair, in an auto-biography, *Confessions of a Surgeon*, admitted to carrying out a series of mercy killings on incurable patients during his career, politicians and some doctors attempted to institute private prosecutions against him for murder; although letters of support for Dr Mair appeared in *The Times*. When a Scottish nurse, Miss McTavish, was convicted of murdering geriatric patients by administering massive doses of insulin and sen-tenced to life imprisonment, Lord Platt, a distinguished physician, publicly stated that he would wish to be on her ward if he ever became senile, demented and incontinent. The contrary view was put by an M.P. who said that if there had been a verdict of not guilty the case could have become a landmark in establishing the thin end of the wedge to justify the practice of euthanasia.[2]

The uncertainties and doubts which affect public attitudes towards the treatment of the terminally sick and dying are compounded further by widespread misunderstanding about, and lack of clarity of, the relevant law. It becomes appropriate, then, to examine the present state of the law in England and to see how it applies to the various situations in which the medical profession becomes involved. The difficulty with English law is that few of the critical issues have had to be considered by courts, unlike the United States where there has been a great deal of relevant judicial activity. Accordingly, some attention will be paid to American cases, although sometimes English legal analysis proceeds on a slightly different basis.

Murder, suicide and assisting suicide

Deliberately taking the life of another person, whether that person is dying or not, constitutes the crime of murder, and causing the death of another by some reckless or grossly negligent act, without any intention to kill, can constitute the crime of manslaughter. Accordingly, any doctor who, no matter how compassionately, practised voluntary euthanasia or mercy killing would be open to charges of murder, attempted murder or manslaughter, if the facts could be clearly established. An important exception to that simple rule was spelt out by Devlin J. in the case *R*. v. *Adams*[3] in 1957. Dr Adams was charged with the murder of an 81-year-old patient who had suffered a stroke; it was alleged that he had prescribed and administered such large quantities of drugs, especially heroin and morphine, that he must have known that the drugs would kill her. In his summing up to the jury, Devlin J. first restated the law to show that doctors were not in any special category: '. . . it does not matter whether her death was inevitable and her days were numbered. If her life was cut short by weeks or months it was just as much murder as if it was cut short by years. There has been much discussion as to when doctors might be justified in administering drugs which would shorten life. Cases of severe pain were suggested and also cases of helpless misery. The law knows of no special defence in this category . . .'

The judge then went on to suggest that perhaps there was a special category for doctors, for he continued: '. . . but that does not mean that a doctor who was aiding the sick and dying had to calculate in minutes, or even hours, perhaps not in days or weeks, the effect on a patient's life of the medicines which he would administer. If the first purpose of medicine – the restoration of health – could no longer be achieved, there was still much for the doctor to do and he was entitled to do all that was proper and necessary to relieve pain and suffering even if the measures he took might incidentally shorten life by hours or perhaps even longer. The doctor who decided whether or not to administer the drug could not do his job if he were thinking in terms of hours or months of life. Dr Adams's defence was that the treatment was designed to promote comfort, and if it was the right and proper treatment, the fact that it shortened life did not convict him of murder.'

This analysis introduces into the law the 'double effect' principle, much debated in philosophical circles, whereby if one act has two inevitable consequences, one good and one evil, the act may be morally acceptable in certain circumstances. Thus, in the context of abortion, the saving of the life of the mother must entail the 'killing' of the foetus; and here, also, where the giving of morphine to relieve suffering may also accelerate death. Lord Devlin's judgment has been widely accepted as an authoritative statement of the law. However, it will be noticed that the summing up was not precise, since in one passage he referred to the incidental shortening of life by hours and, in another passage, he referred to the shortening of life by hours or months. It may well be a matter of judgment in each case. Clearly he is dealing with terminally ill patients where, in order to alleviate their pain, it is permissible to disregard the fact that the treatment involved may accelerate the patient's death. But, if it could be shown that the administering of the drug was designed to kill, rather than to comfort, that would be a case of murder.

The other area of criminal law which is very important in the euthanasia context is that concerning suicide. Since the Suicide Act 1961 it is no longer a criminal offence to commit, or attempt to commit, suicide. However, the Act does provide that 'a person who aids, abets, counsels or procures the suicide of another or an attempt by another to commit suicide, shall be liable on conviction . . . to a term not exceeding 14 years'. In order to achieve consistency in bringing prosecutions, it is necessary for the consent of the Director of Public Prosecutions to be obtained. It is a crime which may be committed for diverse reasons, ranging from the avaricious to the compassionate. Thus, in *R.* v. *McShane*,[4] a daughter was found guilty of trying to persuade her 89-year-old mother in a nursing home to kill herself so that she could inherit her estate. A secret camera installed by the police showed the daughter handing her mother drugs concealed in a packet of sweets, and pinning a note on her dress saying 'Don't bungle it'! Equally, if a doctor were to be shown to have supplied drugs, with similar intent, whatever his motive may have been, an offence would have been committed. However, in practice, as has been said, it would be very difficult to prove that a doctor who had supplied drugs to a patient was responsible for the patient taking an overdose.

Clear evidence of aiding and abetting a particular act of suicide is, therefore, necessary before a prosecution can be successful. This area of law was examined in *A.G.* v. *Able*,[5] where the court was asked to declare that it was an offence for the Voluntary Euthanasia Society to sell a booklet to its members aged 25 and over, setting out in some detail various ways in which individuals could commit suicide. The Society, which campaigned for the introduction of voluntary euthanasia legislation, claimed that, pending such legislation, they saw no alternative to supplying on request the necessary information to enable its members to bring about 'their own deliverance': the Society neither advocated nor deplored suicide; it had a neutral stance and regarded such decisions as matters of personal belief and judgment. Evidence in the case suggested that over a period of 18 months after the first distribution of the booklet there were 15 cases of suicides linked to the booklet and 19 suicides where documents were found which showed that the deceased was a member of, or had corresponded with, the Society. The court concluded that in most cases the supply of the booklet would not constitute an offence. Normally, a member requesting the booklet would not make clear his intentions, and the booklet would be supplied without any knowledge by the supplier of whether it was required for general information, research, or because suicide was contemplated. To establish an offence it would have to be proved that the Society distributed the booklet to a person who, at the time of the distribution, was known to be contemplating suicide, with the intention of assisting and encouraging that person to commit suicide by means of the booklet's contents, and, further, that that person was in fact assisted and encouraged by the booklet to commit or attempt to commit suicide.

These laws become central to many of the issues now to be discussed. It will be appropriate to consider first the case of the 'competent' patient, that is a person with full legal and mental capacity, who is aware of what is happening and who may wish to make decisions himself about his quality of life: the way he will be treated and how he will continue to live or die. Second, the case of the 'incompetent' patient will be considered: the infant, comatose or mentally handicapped person who does not have the mental or physical capacity to make his own wishes known at the relevant times.[6]

Competent patients: is there a 'right' to die?

The question often posed is whether a person has a legal right to determine that medical treatment be withdrawn so that he be permitted to die. The answer is complex and may turn upon the kind of situation involved. Take first the case where a patient is not terminally ill (a condition which it is often not easy to establish), that is, where the situation is not immediately life-threatening. Here, the legal analysis seems straightforward initially. Patients have a basic right of self-determination: they do not have to seek medical advice and treatment in the first place; and any unconsented interference with them constitutes trespass. Similarly, a patient can discharge himself from medical care; withdrawal of consent would mean that further unconsented treatment would also be trespass. But should this simple analysis apply also where a patient is in, or believes himself to be in, a life-threatening situation? Logically, the wishes of a competent patient, or of a formerly competent patient who had made his wishes known while competent, must similarly be respected. Yet, in such circumstances, patients' wishes often have been overridden and treatment has been given. There are strong medical arguments to suggest that in life-threatening situations patients are not always capable of making rational decisions: they may no longer be 'competent'.

One study of a number of cases in a medical intensive care unit showed the complex factors surrounding the request by different patients for cessation of treatment. One patient, whose request seemed clear, was in fact ambivalent. Another's decision was possibly determined by a depressive condition which, if successfully treated, might have affected his general attitude to treatment. Sometimes patients may use a plea for death with dignity to mask other less 'acceptable' problems or complaints; or the request may be based upon misconceptions, on the part of either the patient or the medical staff. Therefore, it is suggested that superficial and automatic acquiescence to the concepts of patient autonomy and death with dignity threaten sound clinical judgments; and doctors should continue to exercise their professional responsibility for thorough clinical investigation and the exercise of sound professional judgment.[7] The law, however, may be unlikely to consider that the competence of patients is affected in many of these situations. Will it, nevertheless, protect doctors who save or prolong lives of patients against their wishes?

This issue has also been discussed in two related areas: hunger-strikers and Jehovah's Witnesses. In *Leigh* v. *Gladstone*,[8] a suffragette serving a term of imprisonment went on hunger strike and after 3 days was subjected to daily forcible feedings. Later she sued the authorities, unsuccessfully, for trespass, and the judge, in directing the jury, said that 'it was wicked folly for the plaintiff to attempt to starve herself to death' and ruled: 'as a matter of law . . . it was the duty of the prison officials to preserve the health of the prisoners, and . . . to preserve their lives'. This decision, which stands alone in this area of law, might suggest, if applied to hospital situations, that not only would doctors have a defence of 'necessity' to a trespass action following the overriding of a patient's request to have treatment discontinued, but also that it was a doctor's *duty* to act against a patient's wishes, certainly outside the situation where medical treatment is imposed upon prisoners.[9] However, this decision has been criticized, and it is doubted whether, if medical personnel did so act, they would always be able to plead the defence of necessity. Thus, modern prison practice no longer is to forcibly feed hunger-strikers. Similarly, when adult Jehovah's Witnesses refuse life-saving blood transfusions, the advice given to doctors is to abide by that refusal regardless of the consequences if the mental and legal competence of the Jehovah's Witness is clear. Where a patient's decision to refuse further treatment does not involve the medical personnel in committing any further positive acts to hasten the patient's death, it would seem that the medical authorities would be liable neither for manslaughter nor for assisting suicide.

More difficult, however, is the situation where positive acts which have the effect of accelerating death, such as turning off a life-support machine, have to be taken by medical personnel. The play *Whose Life Is It Anyway?* concerned a traffic accident victim paralysed from the neck down; his mental faculties were unimpaired and he wanted to die, but he could not turn the machine off by his own efforts. A similar situation arose in America in *Satz* v. *Perlmutter*.[10] An elderly man lay terminally ill in hospital. His affliction had progressed to the point of virtual incapability of movement, inability to breathe without a mechanical respirator, and he could speak only with extreme difficulty. Even linked to a respirator, he would die within a relatively short time. Yet he remained in full command of his mental faculties. He had attempted to 'kill himself' by removing the respirator from his trachea, but hospital personnel, activated by an alarm, had reconnected it. He sought, with the full approval of his adult family, the court's authority to have the respirator removed. Interestingly, the court saw the law's role as involving a balancing exercise between a citizen's right of self-determination and his constitutional right of privacy against the state's interest, in some cases, of overriding such rights. In the U.S.A. the right of an individual to refuse medical treatment is tempered by several factors. First, there is the state's interest in the preservation of life generally. But there 'is a substantial distinction in the state's insistence that human life be saved where the affliction is curable, as opposed to the state interest where, as here, the issue is not whether, but when, for how long and at what cost to the individual his life may be briefly extended'. In this case the patient's condition was terminal, his situation

wretched, and the continuation of his life temporary and totally artificial; and accordingly there was no compelling state interest on this
ground to interfere with the patient's expressed wishes. The second state
interest which was not really in point here was said to be the need to
protect third parties. The clearest example of this interest would be
where the patient was a parent of young children and, by refusing
treatment, would be abandoning them; and the state, as *parens patriae*,
would be justified in seeking to prevent this. The third factor is the duty
of the state to prevent suicide. But is the patient seeking to commit
suicide? The court reasoned strongly that a request to turn off a
life-support machine in this situation is not necessarily assisting suicide.
Its disconnection, far from causing an unnatural death by means of a
'death-producing agent', in fact would merely result in death, if at all,
from natural causes. The patient had demonstrated that he really
wanted to live but under his own power. This basic wish to live, plus the
fact that he did not self-induce his horrible affliction, precluded his
further refusal of treatment being classed as attempted suicide. The
court found it difficult to distinguish the situation from the case where a
mortally sick patient refuses to undergo a further operation which
constitutes the only hope for temporary prolongation of his life. The
fourth, and last, interest which the state is said to have is the requirement that it should help maintain the ethical integrity of medical
practice. In some cases important *medical* decisions should be left as the
responsibility of physicians, and there should be no attempt to remove
such responsibility from the control of the medical profession and place
it in the hands of the courts. It is a matter of medicine only. That
interesting and controversial proposition was not applicable in this
case. Accordingly, balancing the competing interests, the court, on the
facts of this case, came down in favour of the patient being allowed to
decide to die with dignity; the right to refuse treatment in the first
instance carried with it the concomitant right to discontinue it, even
though the withdrawal of the life-support machine would certainly
hasten death.[11]

On the same facts an English judicial approach would be less flexible
and more direct. The central question would be whether a doctor who,
at a patient's request, facilitated death by switching off a life-support
machine could be liable for aiding and abetting a suicide. The third
argument adopted in *Satz* v. *Perlmutter* would certainly be advanced:
the refusal of medical treatment does not necessarily constitute suicide
since, first, in refusing treatment the patient may not have the specific

intent to die, and, second, even if he did, the decision to switch off the machine is a decision to refuse treatment and not a decision to commit suicide.

The acceptability of such an argument is also linked to the question whether those responsible for turning off a life-support system can be liable for murder or conspiracy to murder. A Californian doctor was recently involved in such a murder trial. In *Barber* v. *Superior Court*[12] a patient, following an operation, lay in a deeply comatose state, suffering severe brain damage, with little prospect of recovery. After full discussion with his family it was decided that he should be taken off all life-sustaining machines; but after a few days he was still breathing. Accordingly the intravenous tubes which provided him with fluids and nourishment were removed, and he received only nursing care which preserved his dignity and provided a clean and hygienic environment until he died. The lower court adopted a simple approach and ruled that intentionally shortening life by a period of time was an intentioned, unlawful killing and so constituted murder. The appeal court struggled to avoid this conclusion, in much the same way as an English court would have to, if it were similarly sympathetic to the doctor. First, it looked at the distinction between acts and omissions and concluded that the cessation of 'heroic' life-support measures is not an affirmative act but rather a withdrawal or omission of further treatment.

Even though these life-support devices are, to a degree, 'self-propelled', each pulsation of the respirator or each drop of fluid introduced into the patient's body by intravenous feeding devices is comparable to a manually administered injection or item of medication. Hence 'disconnection' of the mechanical devices is comparable to withholding the manually administered injection or medication.

An alternative argument which has also been used to reach the same conclusion is that a machine is turned off to enable a doctor *during treatment* to decide whether there is any medical advantage in turning it on again. That decision not to turn the machine on again is the omission which leads to death! Having reached the decision that turning off a machine is an omission to act, there is no criminal liability for omissions unless there is a duty to act. Thus the critical issue then turns on the legal duty owed by a doctor to a patient in this situation, which has already been touched upon. Here, whether the patient is competent and refuses further treatment, or incompetent, a doctor is under no duty to continue treatment once it has proved to be ineffective. Thus the court held that the doctors' omission to continue treatment, though intentional and with knowledge that the patient would die, was not an unlawful failure to perform a legal duty. Further, the court decided that there was no difference between switching off mechanical breathing devices such as respirators and mechanical feeding devices such as intravenous tubes.

Medical nutrition and hydration (fluids) may not always provide net benefits to patients. Medical procedures to provide nutrition and hydration are more similar to other medical procedures than to typical human ways of providing nutrition and hydration. Their benefits and burdens ought to be evaluated in the same manner as any other medical procedure.

There is a strong medical view that in certain circumstances the maintenance of fluid and nutritional intake should be regarded as 'treatment' rather than the provision of food and care, a controversial issue which has yet to be finally resolved.

Another argument which has been advanced to justify a doctor withdrawing a life-support system at the patient's request is that such machines are part of the 'extraordinary' or 'heroic' measures used to save life and that a doctor is under no duty to use, or persevere with, extraordinary measures. While this argument also has some theological support, it is a distinction which bristles with difficulties. What was an 'extraordinary' machine a decade ago may be in everyday use now. Would its use still constitute 'extraordinary' treatment? In *Barber* the court rightly felt that the use of these terms begs the question. A more rational approach might involve the determination of whether the proposed treatment is proportionate or disproportionate in terms of the benefits to be gained versus the burdens caused.

Thus, undesirable as it may be, it seems at present that doctors who switch off life-support machines at the request of mentally and legally competent patients, with knowledge that death will follow, cannot be totally reassured that they will not be exposing themselves to criminal and civil liability. The courts will be faced with fine, and uncomfortable, verbal distinctions. But if the law is to cope with these matters, in the absence of legislation, the courts will be driven into these artificial arguments.

'Incompetent' patients

In cases where a patient does not have the legal or mental capacity to make decisions for himself, the issues under discussion become even more difficult and uncertain. Legal incapacity may exist, for example, where the patient is unconscious and so cannot make a decision, where the patient is a child and does not have the capacity or understanding to decide,[13] and in cases where the patient is suffering from some mental disorder or mental illness which affects his legal capacity to make decisions for himself. Does the medical profession, with or without the concurrence of close relatives or others, have the ethical or legal right to take decisions on behalf of incompetent patients in such cases?

The unconscious, dying patient

The leading decision in the United States is the *Karen Quinlan* case.[14] Karen Quinlan, a young woman suddenly stricken with illness, lay in a coma attached to a life-support machine and presented a terrible dilemma to her family and the hospital authorities. Although she was not dead by the applicable medical criteria for determining brain death, the medical authorities were satisfied that there was no hope that she would ever recover to a cognitive state: she was characterized as being in a 'chronic, persistent, vegetative condition', kept alive only with the assistance of the respirator.

In those circumstances, the parents of Karen Quinlan decided that it would be best for her to be removed from the life-support machine. Accordingly, her father applied to the court to be appointed her guardian and claimed that, as guardian, he would be entitled to authorize the discontinuance of all 'extraordinary' medical procedures sustaining Karen Quinlan's vital processes and hence her life.

The Supreme Court of New Jersey upheld the father's claim in the following way. First, had Karen Quinlan been conscious and lucid, she would have had a right, by virtue of her constitutional right of privacy, to decide to discontinue life-support treatment in circumstances where it was simply prolonging for a short period a terminal condition.[15] But she was not conscious or lucid. Second, because of her condition, her father was appointed guardian and the question then arose whether he could make a decision of that kind on her behalf. He was entitled to go to the court to seek assistance; and the court was prepared to 'don the mental mantle of Karen Quinlan' to make a decision for her which she would have made had she been able to do so. Thus, by applying a 'substituted judgment' test, the court decided that if, upon the concurrence of the guardian and the family of the patient, the attending physicians should conclude that there was no reasonable possibility of her ever emerging from her comatose condition to a cognitive state and that the life-support apparatus should be discontinued, they should consult with the Hospital Ethics Committee and, if that body agreed, the present life-support system might be withdrawn, without any civil or criminal liability on the part of any participant. Following that judgment, a Hospital Ethics Committee was appointed comprising five lay persons and one physician, and the decision was taken to remove the life-support system machine. It is an interesting reflection on the medical evidence given in the case that withdrawal of the life-support system did not lead to a swift death and Karen Quinlan survived for 10 long years after falling into the coma.

This decision in the United States was hailed by many as a humane and sensitive development of the law. But it was not without its critics. Thus, it has been said that:

The *Quinlan* case has gone a long way towards obliterating the distinction between voluntary and involuntary euthanasia. The court imputed to Karen a will to die; it did not discover it. Then the court permitted others also to impute a will to die to an uncomprehending patient and to act on behalf of that patient's privacy so construed. It does not matter who is the designated agent; others now have an extraordinary extra legal power to bring death.

Another critic has observed that this decision 'may have provided the euthanasiasts with something that has eluded them for decades – the bridge between voluntary and involuntary euthanasia, between the "right to die" and the "right to kill"'.

It has already been noticed that much of the reasoning in *Quinlan* is unlikely to be of direct relevance to an English court faced with a similar situation. There is no constitutional right of privacy in England and thus the initial basis of the argument would not be so clear cut. Even so, a fully competent and lucid patient may have the right under English law to authorize discontinuance of extraordinary treatment. But a court would then have difficulty in taking the next steps. The power to appoint a guardian is fairly limited and, even if a comatose patient were to come within the provisions of the Mental Health Act 1983, which authorize a guardian's appointment in respect of patients suffering from mental disorder, it is doubtful whether the guardian could consent to withdrawal of a life-support system on behalf of the comatose patient.

The doctrine of 'substituted judgment', referred to in the *Quinlan* case, and which the American courts are beginning to use, is open to criticism because it is conceptually questionable whether it is appropriate to treat a non-autonomous person as if autonomous, particularly if

317

the desires and preference of incompetents are generally unknowable. It is also a curious development, since the substituted judgment concept in fact originated in early English cases involving the disposition of the estates of mental incompetents. In spite of its English roots, the concept has never been used in English cases in recent times, and it seems unlikely that it would be brought out of cold storage for use in modern English family law. Even if it were, it would take a very policy-orientated court to introduce by judicial fiat the procedure whereby an appropriately appointed Hospital Ethics Committee could make such a decision and be free from legal responsibility for doing so. Whatever the attraction of the reasoning in *Quinlan*, it is likely that an English court would have to proceed on the more traditional, tortuous reasoning already discussed; namely, that turning off a life-support machine is simply an omission; or that it is the cessation of extraordinary treatment.

Mental incompetence

Similar reasoning has been used by American courts in connection with mentally incompetent patients. Thus, in the *Saikewicz* case,[16] a court approved the appointment of a guardian to make medical decisions on behalf of a profoundly retarded 67-year-old man with an I.Q. of 10 and a mental age of under 3 years who was suffering from leukaemia. The medically indicated course of treatment of chemotherapy would cause him significant adverse side-effects and discomfort while possibly prolonging his life for a matter of months, whereas without such treatment he would die within weeks or months without discomfort. In addition to the substituted judgment doctrine the court also added a related doctrine of doing what was 'in the best interests' of the incompetent person. The court accordingly concluded that respect for the patient's right to privacy and self-determination justified the withholding of further treatment.

This decision excited additional controversy in the United States because it raised openly the procedural question whether such life and death decisions should be left primarily to the medical community, as may have been implied by the *Quinlan* case, or whether there should be overall judicial control so that it might be necessary for an application to court to be made in each case as it occurred. That question has yet to be finally decided in the U.S.A.[17] In this country, as we have seen, the law is far less developed, and there is nothing in the mental health legislation which gives any greater powers to medical personnel to withhold treatment than to any other persons; indeed, the whole tenor of such legislation suggests that such patients should be treated no differently from any others so far as basic legal rights are concerned.

To resuscitate or not to resuscitate

Particularly difficult, though not uncommon, problems for doctors and nursing staff arise in connection with the resuscitation of patients, that is, restoring breathing and heartbeat. Is a decision not to resuscitate a patient whose prognosis is poor a purely medical one, or can that also be challenged as passive euthanasia? Where a patient is under medical care and has not vetoed particular forms of treatment, doctors and medical staff remain under a duty to take proper care of a patient, and may be liable civilly, and possibly criminally, for failing to do so. Thus, what say should a patient have in such decisions?

Because resuscitation decisions have to be taken in emergency situations, guidelines for issuing 'do not resuscitate' orders for individual patients have long been commonplace in America.[18] Some of these codes indicate a scaling down of active treatment for patients who are hopelessly ill by defining several levels of care, including, in some cases, a controversial slow-code procedure, which is a deliberately slow response to a patient who has suffered cardiopulmonary arrest. This procedure has been used when a patient's prognosis suggests that resuscitation is medically inappropriate and the family has refused, or is thought likely to refuse, 'do not resuscitate' status.[19] American courts have recognized the appropriateness of codes of guidance: it would be an impossible situation if every decision not to resuscitate a patient had first to be sanctioned by a court, for that would mean that it would be necessary for attempts to be made to resuscitate dying patients in most cases, without exercise of medical judgment, even when that course of action could aptly be characterized as a pointless, even cruel, prolongation of the act of dying.[20]

In England procedural guidelines whether or not to resuscitate are less frequently available. There is less open discussion, although a recent report on cardiopulmonary resuscitation in the elderly in an English hospital listed a series of circumstances in which this should be withheld.[21] As far as English law is concerned, the uncertain principles which have already been discussed would have to be applied to the specific resuscitation cases.

Attempts to introduce legislation

The relevant English law is imprecise and uncertain. Doctors cannot always be given clear advice about the legality of various procedures. Is this fair to the medical profession? Is it right that some doctors, acting with the best of motives, may under a screen of silence do things which they believe may be unlawful? If what is taking place in medical practice is acceptable to society, should not the law be changed to set out clearly the parameters within which they should be acting? If society disapproves of certain procedures, how can they be controlled? Is it right, again, for the law to be left obscure but that when clear evidence of euthanasia occurs the prosecution may elect not to enforce the law? On the other hand there are those who oppose legislation on the grounds that the current fog allows for maximum flexibility for a caring medical profession.

Furthermore, one must be clear about the type of legislation which may be introduced. Should there be laws relating to certain forms of euthanasia, or more limited provisions dealing, for example, with certain types of high-technology treatment? Proposals for legislation which expressly or implicitly involve euthanasia will immediately come up against all the emotional, religious, social and other objections which are advanced passionately by many people. All kinds of arguments can be advanced against voluntary euthanasia legislation. Just how voluntary would such euthanasia be? Would the introduction of such laws result in a change of attitude by society towards the sanctity of life generally, towards the elderly and the infirm and towards the mortally sick? Would the existence of such laws impose pressures upon elderly and terminally ill patients to seek euthanasia rather than remain a burden on relatives or on society? Would the existence of such legislation provide opportunities for fraud and abuse and also undermine the relationship of trust between doctor and patient? How easy would it be to apply such a law? The experience of the Abortion Act shows the danger of imprecise drafting and the variability of interpretation by those who wish to go beyond, or retreat from, the rather uncertain compromise which the legislation was designed to provide.

Further, voluntary euthanasia legislation could well contravene Article 2 of the European Convention on Human Rights, which provides that 'Everyone's right to live shall be protected by law. No one shall be deprived of life intentionally . . .'[22] Neither the European Court nor the European Commission on Human Rights has yet been called upon to decide to what extent the consent of a person to voluntary euthanasia procedures would negate what could well be a prima facie violation of the Convention.

Nevertheless, there are strong voices in favour of some clarification of the law. Thus, in connection with the possibility of withholding or withdrawing treatment, it should be made clear whether or not a person who is legally and mentally competent has the right to refuse further treatment, whether ordinary or extraordinary. When that is determined, it should also be made clear whether a person has the right to specify in advance what he would wish to happen in any future situation, when he may not then be competent to make a rational decision. If these matters were clarified, then it would seem natural to move to the next question, which is whether, in cases where there has been a prior indication (for example by a 'living will'), it is possible to use a substituted judgment procedure to enable a decision to be made on behalf of an incompetent patient. In these situations it would also be important to decide whether such decisions could be made only where a patient was terminally ill or in other situations as well. Also important, and in need of major clarification, is the extent to which the distinction between omissions and positive acts in medical practice should be legally significant. To prohibit doctors from committing positive acts but to allow them to achieve desired objectives by omission may satisfy some who are prepared to accept rather tenuous philosophical distinctions, but in practical terms adherence to such distinctions is capable of working cruelly against a patient and his family. If it is likely that there would be strong objections to empowering doctors to take positive steps to kill upon the request of a patient, then surely it would be far better to decide which positive actions are acceptable and which are not, rather than to draw the line between acts and omissions as such. Procedural matters are also of major importance. Who takes such decisions? Should these be matters of such importance that an objective review by a court of law is required; should there be a quasi-judicial review body such as a Hospital Ethics Committee; or is this a matter which should be left primarily as a matter of medical responsibility alone or in consultation with members of the family or a guardian?

The history of euthanasia reform in this country has not been encouraging for those who are in favour of legislation. The first measure in 1936 was a curious and bizarre Euthanasia Bill, designed to deal with a situation in which the doctor could no longer control a patient's pain. The procedural requirements were that the patient had to be over 21, suffering from an incurable and fatal illness, and he then had to sign a form in the presence of two witnesses asking to be put to death. This form and two medical certificates were then to be submitted to a 'euthanasia referee', whose task it was to interview the patient to ensure that he understood the nature of his request, and the referee might then also question doctors and relatives. Then, if the referee gave his certificate of approval, the matter would go to a special court which had the right to question any parties and consider objections; if the court was then satisfied, it would issue an appropriate certificate which would authorize a practitioner to administer euthanasia, which would have to be effected in the presence of an official witness. This Bill, with its prolonged procedural requirements, was received with no enthusiasm and was quickly rejected. In any event, the primary purpose of such legislation is now less important, since it is possible in most cases to control pain.

Another Voluntary Euthanasia Bill, introduced in 1969, was designed to allow a patient or prospective patient to sign in advance a declaration requesting the administration of euthanasia if he was believed to be suffering from a fatal illness or was incapable of rational existence. Again, the Bill was severely criticized by some as being inadequately thought out, ill-drafted and riddled with loopholes and ambiguities of the most dangerous kind; and above all 'because it failed in what it chiefly sought to do . . . it provided no reliable safeguards for the patient'. Perhaps the *coup de grâce* was applied with the following comment: 'Such a Bill is medically unnecessary, psychologically dangerous and ethically wrong. Unnecessary, because legal rigidity should not be substituted for medical discretion. Dangerous, because this Bill would diminish the respect for life, blurring the line between crime and medicine. Ethically wrong, because it infringes on the absolute value of life.'

Subsequent Bills in the mid 1970s were more modest and attempted to avoid being seen as attempts to legalize euthanasia or 'mercy killing'. They were designated 'Incurable Patients Bills' and were described as being attempts to enlarge and declare the rights of patients to be delivered from incurable suffering. Thus, one Bill set out to state the rights of an incurable patient to receive whatever quantity of drugs may be required to give full relief from pain or physical distress, and to be rendered unconscious if no other treatment was effective to give such relief, and also to approve the right of a patient to specify in advance that he should not receive life-sustaining treatment if by reason of brain damage or degeneration he became incapable of giving such directions. Once again, the Bill was seen by its opponents as being the thin end of the wedge and that even if the Bill was strictly not about euthanasia, it could lead to it.

The reaction in the United States has been quite different. Stimulated by the *Karen Quinlan* case, which focused the attention of the public on the problems involved in dealing with terminally ill patients, many states introduced 'advanced directive' or 'living will' legislation, enabling persons to direct in advance the conditions for their own terminal care. For example, the first statute of this kind, passed in 1976, was the California Natural Death Act. Its preamble recited that 'In recognition of the dignity and privacy which patients have a right to expect' the law recognizes 'the right of an adult person to make a written directive instructing his physician to withhold or withdraw life-sustaining pro- cedures in the event of a terminal condition'. It should be noticed that the Act refers to a 'terminal condition', and there are stringent pro- cedures laid down which means that its provisions operate fairly nar- rowly. Thus, in one case, a patient had signed a directive but did not come within the provisions of the Act. In his application to the court to have a life-support system removed he stated: 'I understand that I am not a "qualified patient" . . . in that I have not had a written diagnosis of "terminal illness" submitted to me. I do not wish to wait to become a "qualified patient" before proceeding with my earnest desire to have the ventilator disconnected.'[23] Another criticism of such legislation is that it did nothing to deal with those rendered incompetent by their injuries or illness and who had not indicated in advance their views as to terminal care. Surveys also have shown that few doctors have changed their previous practices by virtue of the introduction of new laws about which they tended to have only the most hazy knowledge. Nevertheless, similar legislation or, as an alternative, 'durable powers of attorney' statutes by which an agent can make decisions on the patient's behalf, have been enacted in many American states.

The situation in the United Kingdom, however, appears to be static. The cause of reform has not been helped by the adverse publicity received by Exit, the voluntary euthanasia society, when its director and another member were convicted on a number of counts of aiding and abetting suicides in circumstances which cast a major shadow over what had been a highly respected organization.[24] There is little prospect at present of the law being amended.

In view of the criticisms which have been levelled against the

American statutes, there are those who would prefer codes of practice for doctors, leaving appropriate development to the courts. In my view, however, because of the rather limited way in which the law has developed and particularly bearing in mind some of the difficult conceptual distinctions which have been discussed, there is a strong case for legislation on some matters.

In Canada, a Law Reform Commission has produced an important report in which, first, the right of competent patients to refuse treatment, even if the refusal would inevitably lead to death, was recognized; and, second, the question of discontinuance of medical treatment of the incompetent patient was also considered. While it was stressed that medical treatment of the incompetent patient should be discontinued only for very clear reasons, it was also emphasized that they, too, should have the right to die in peace and dignity, assisted by whatever palliative care is needed at the time. The appropriate mechanism for ensuring consent and protection for patients in such situations was thought to be primarily through the medical profession, after discussion, explanation and consultation with those close to the patients, and it was recommended that there be no criminal liability on physicians for decisions in these situations, including decisions not to treat or to discontinue treatment previously instituted as long as the decision was valid medically; that is, made on reasonable medical grounds under the circumstances, in the best interest of the incompetent patient and in conformity with other standards set by criminal law. When consideration, with a view to possible legislation, is given to these matters in Britain, it would be well to consider seriously such recommendations.

Chapter 21
Reviewing and Reforming the Law

A survey of the law regulating medical practice reveals a state of affairs disturbing to doctor and patient alike. The procedures which judge when a patient is entitled to compensation if treatment goes wrong appear on occasion loaded against the patient. Litigation is expensive and usually protracted. The system encourages the doctor, backed by the resources made available to him by his medical protection society, to defend a claim against him to the last gasp. The defensive, embattled attitude engendered by litigation, and the ever-present threat of litigation, colours medical attitudes to complaints procedures. Too often proper investigation of patients' grievances may be hampered by lack of co-operation from medical staff. And complaints procedures within the N.H.S. are complex and not always well publicized. Finally, the law as it affects sensitive health care decisions is frequently ill-defined. The rights of doctors and parents to decide whether to treat or not to treat a severely damaged baby, the legal restraints on medical research programmes, the law as it relates to 'test-tube' babies and consequent advances in reproductive technology are just three examples of areas of medicine where the law can offer the doctor and his patients little clear guidance as to their rights and obligations to each other and to the community.

The reaction of some members of the medical profession to this apparent legal vacuum is to welcome the absence of legal interference in medical affairs. 'Keep the lawyers out of things' is a natural but unwise response to the problems the law can pose.[1] First, the last 20 years have shown a dramatic increase in the number of patients willing, despite the expense and the stress involved, to resort to litigation. And when a patient gets into court, the judges no longer exhibit quite the same deference to their brethren in another related and learned profession, that of medicine, as they did in times gone by. Second, the legal vacuum is only apparent and not real. The legal principles governing when one person may make contact with another's body, when consent is freely and fully given to that contact, the rights of parents to make decisions for

325

their children, the criminal law of murder and manslaughter, apply to doctors as much as to anyone else. Doctors are not above the law. It is the application of the general rules of law to the particular context of the doctor–patient relationship which is unclear. Crucial questions of the doctor's right to take decisions, the patient's rights to autonomy and control over his own body, and even the doctor's power of life and death, are subjects of fascinating debate among law students. They are material for agonized debate within the medical profession and groups representing patients' interests. While the only means of concluding the debate remains litigation started by an aggrieved patient or concerned citizen, the sword of Damocles hangs over every doctor's head. He may be following a practice accepted and applied by many of his colleagues, but he happens to be the unlucky man who receives the writ or, in an extreme case, the prosecution summons.

There is one sense in which this 'threat' against each individual doctor may be seen as beneficial. It emphasizes the personal and individual responsibility of each and every doctor. It forces him to examine his conscience and his ethical stance in every phase of his career. At least it should! The problems are these. First, until the sword falls the threat of litigation is fairly remote. Other doctors get sued, not you. Second, if one considers the huge areas of medical practice where the law is hazy and uncertain, is it fair to the medical profession? Everyone, doctors included, is presumed to know the law. In medico-legal matters the honest answer to a question on the law is very frequently that there is no answer, unless and until a claim has taken several years to work its way through the hierarchy of the courts up to the House of Lords.[2] This state of affairs is equally unfair to the patients. They cannot know with any precision what their rights are without resort to expensive and protracted litigation. Finally, are the courts the right forum to lay down rules to act as the framework for health care decisions? The judge can consider only the particular claim before him. He cannot evaluate the overall implications of a particular practice. He has no power to call for evidence beyond the facts of the case before him on how a disputed practice affects the care of patients other than the plaintiff. He will necessarily be influenced by the facts and merits of that particular claim. In considering what the doctors consider to be proper medical practice, and in ascertaining the ethical standards applied by the profession, the judge relies on expert evidence from either party. The evidence will be prepared in order to support the party the expert appears for.[3] The judge cannot *investigate* the practice in any sense. He merely adjudicates in a battle between opposing views, each with a personal and emotional stake in the litigation in process.

The proper role of the law

The law should have three aims in regulating medical practice. First, sensible and equitable rules and procedures should determine when compensation is payable in respect of medical mishaps. Second, procedures should exist and be easily available to patients to ensure (a) that individual complaints are fully investigated, (b) that appropriate action is taken to remedy any error found in the course of investigating the complaint, and (c) that any doctor found to be at fault should be dealt with in such a way as to prevent that fault recurring and harming other patients. Finally, the law should strive to provide a clearer and more certain framework within which doctors and patients may make difficult and sensitive decisions on health care.

To achieve these aims three steps need to be taken. (1) Either (a) a system of 'no-fault' compensation should be introduced, or (b) radical reform of the procedure in medical litigation should be embarked on. (2) Complaints procedures within and beyond the N.H.S. must be reviewed and rationalized. (3) A Commission on Medicine, Law and Ethics should be established to examine the relationship between law and ethics in health care decisions, and to recommend codes of practice to guide the decision-makers in the future.

I(a) 'No-fault' compensation

At the end of Part II a case for the replacement of the law of negligence by a scheme of 'no-fault' compensation as the primary means of compensating a patient injured in the course of medical treatment was outlined. I recap on just a few of the reasons. For the patient the benefits of a 'no-fault' system are these. Compensation to enable him to take steps to adapt his lifestyle to his disability would be available much more swiftly and easily. The ever-awkward problem of whether his condition resulted from his medical treatment or the natural progression of his original disease or injury would be investigated, and not fought over in a modern version of trial by battle. The patient would be spared the trauma of facing two medical examinations, by his own experts and by the defence experts. Availability of compensation would be more equitable. Resort to law at present depends on whether you are rich enough to pay for legal representation yourself or poor enough to qualify for legal aid. From the doctors' viewpoint, the threat of a judgment in negligence blighting their careers because one mistake is made would be removed. The inhibition about confessing that something has gone wrong to a patient for fear of litigation would go. Frank communication between doctor and patient would be encouraged.

Progress towards introduction of 'no-fault' compensation would take some time and great care. Two major difficulties must be confronted. First, eligibility to claim under the scheme must be defined. Will, or should, 'no-fault' compensation be limited to N.H.S. patients? What must the patient establish to prove that his disease or injury arose from his medical treatment? Second, the funding and administration of the scheme must be worked out. A tribunal to decide disputed cases would have to be established. I made some suggestions on these matters in Chapter 9. The D.H.S.S. should act to create a committee of inquiry, composed of representatives from medicine, the law, patients' associations, the medical insurance societies, and the drug companies, to consider the options for reform. Their first task may be to weigh the benefits of radical change to 'no-fault' liability against the more limited step of simply reforming existing procedures in medical litigation but keeping the action for negligence. Should they opt for a 'no-fault' scheme, the committee should then take evidence and make recommendations on the funding and general outline of feasible schemes. Once general proposals are made and accepted by government, those proposals should be referred to the Law Commission for examination and the preparation of a draft Bill on the necessary legislation. One final issue for the Law Commission to consider would have to be whether the system of 'no-fault' compensation should entirely replace the action for medical negligence, or whether resort to the courts should remain an option open to a patient who feels that his case merits public litigation and that compensation alone on a 'no-fault' basis is an inadequate remedy. In deciding this question it must be remembered that a number of 'medical negligence' claims deal not with allegations that something went wrong with the treatment, but that the doctor failed to give the patient sufficient information to make his own decision on treatment.

1(b) Reform of existing rules

An alternative and less drastic reform would be to leave untouched the general principles of negligence as they apply to medical litigation and to effect reform of the procedures in medical litigation alone. While I prefer the option of 'no-fault' compensation, reform of evidential and procedural rules alone would clearly be simpler, and would recommend itself to those who see the sanction of liability for negligence imposed by a court as an important instrument in controlling medical practice, and ensuring medical accountability.

The Lord Chancellor has initiated a civil justice review to consider the delays in, and costs of, all claims for compensation for personal injuries. Any reduction in the time claims take to come to court, or to be settled, and in the overall costs of taking legal action will clearly benefit victims of medical accidents as much as any other personal injuries claimant. But specific and urgent attention should be given to two questions central to the problems of medical litigation. First, the manner in which judges hear and assess expert evidence must be reformed. The present adversarial procedure has, as we have seen, several drawbacks. Expense, the trauma for patients, and the presentation of expert views for the plaintiff and defendant in what appears to be partisan form, are but a few. At the very least the task of ascertaining whether the injury complained of resulted from something done or omitted in the course of treatment should be assigned to an impartial expert selected by the court. Better still, the whole of the evidence as to the conduct of the practice in question, its conformity with proper medical practice and questions of disputed medical practice would be put before the court by expert witnesses selected from a panel nominated by the Royal Colleges and the Lord Chancellor's Department. The air of trial by champion, with each side advancing its own claims to good medical practice backed by experts with as many letters as possible after their names, would be dispersed. One problem must be noted here if patients and defendants are to lose their right to nominate their own experts. The panel must be seen to be impartial. Patients' groups may fear that doctors chosen essentially by the medical establishment would protect their peers. The Lord Chancellor's Department should, therefore, actively seek a representative panel from a broad spectrum of the profession. In internal audits doctors can be frank and forthright about professional disagreements and each other's failings. They must be prepared to be equally frank in open court when necessary.

The second urgent reform of procedure involves the patient's right to access to the records, and reports into his treatment and any mishap, drawn up by the health authority. At present doctors and health authorities are often at liberty to withhold from the patient material essential to the pursuit of his claim. The Master of the Rolls, Sir John Donaldson, has already criticized[4] this state of affairs. If the action for negligence is to remain the main means of compensating injured patients, this criticism might be acted on swiftly.

Weighing up the choices of radical reform via 'no-fault' compensation against more limited reform of the existing system is primarily a task for the D.H.S.S. in the first instance. If the government is unhappy, but not totally opposed to the more radical option, they might perhaps refer both options to the committee of inquiry which I have suggested should be set up to consider ways and means of effecting a 'no-fault' scheme.

2 Complaints procedures

Acceptance of comprehensive and effective complaints procedures is the price doctors must pay for introduction of 'no-fault' compensation. If in the majority of cases the role of the courts in adjudicating on negligence is to cease, then patients must have the means to ensure that any complaint of lack of care, or inadequate or improper care is fully investigated. Complaints procedures ought to be a much better means of establishing a failure in care than the courts. They will be concerned with finding out exactly what happened. They will be able to distinguish between the understandable error and the blameworthy mistake. The responsibility of the health authority will be properly looked at. Did the medical staff have adequate facilities to provide proper care? What sort of hours had the doctor been working? Procedures will involve the doctors in judging their peers. But they must, if they are to be seen to be fair, involve significant lay representation to assess and evaluate the opinions on medical issues arrived at by the medical investigators.

The Hospital Complaints Procedures Act 1985 requires the D.H.S.S. to review existing procedures within N.H.S. hospitals. That review should be extended to take in procedures available to pursue complaints against G.P.s. And the role of the G.M.C. must not be forgotten. The G.M.C. exercises ultimate authority over doctors. Other procedures exist to discipline and warn doctors within the N.H.S., even to prevent them practising within the N.H.S., but only the G.M.C. can ensure that a truly incompetent or uncaring doctor never sees another patient. Another issue demanding attention is whether some official body should monitor complaints of malpractice in the private sector. That will arouse political controversy. Now that something like 8 per cent of families are covered by private health insurance, the issue of whether standards of care in the private system are adequately monitored must at least be considered. In Scotland the Medical Practitioners Union have backed a review of private hospital practice, after a boy died in the course of a minor operation performed in a private hospital.

Above all, complaints procedures must be rationalized. Whether medical staff should always be obliged to co-operate in an inquiry into a complaint needs consideration. At present compulsion is rare, and, as we have seen, refusal of co-operation can prevent an inquiry achieving any result. Once 'no-fault' compensation is introduced, then the justification that it is unfair to ask a man to incriminate himself will have lessened. Central to review of complaints procedures must be the role of the N.H.S. Ombudsman, the Health Service Commissioner. Should his jurisdiction be extended to embrace questions of clinical judgment? What added resources and support would be needed if this were to be the case?[5]

In view of the crucial importance of the Health Service Commissioner, perhaps the appropriate body to review complaints procedures is the Select Committee of the Commons, which already monitors the Health Service Commissioner's progress. This course of action has the advantage of referring review of procedures to an existing body with substantial experience in the field and the ability to obtain whatever expert assistance is required and to take evidence from all interested parties.

3 Commission on Medicine, Law and Ethics

The first two proposals that I have outlined aim to ensure (1) that an injured patient is offered a fair and simple remedy by way of monetary compensation, and (2) that complaints procedures investigate any alleged failure in medical care. Both are procedures designed to provide a remedy once something has already gone wrong, after the doctor–patient relationship has broken down. My final proposal is intended to improve the framework within which decisions on medical care are taken.

At the heart of many of the problems in medical decision-making discussed throughout this book lies the question of the patient's right to determine what treatment he receives and how to reconcile that right with the doctor's duty to give the patient the best treatment available. This arises in many forms. Did the patient have sufficient information to enable him to decide whether or not to agree to treatment proposed by the doctor? How far may parents consent or refuse consent to treatment of their children? Is a patient asked by his consultant to take part in a research programme genuinely free to refuse?

The debate on consent has concentrated on the concept of informed consent. On one side it is argued that it is the patient's fundamental right to decide for himself on health care. To promote that right, the doctor should be under a duty to disclose any unusual and material risks inherent in the proposed treatment and explain any feasible alternative treatment. Deciding whether a risk is unusual or material should be based on what the prudent patient would want to know. Members of the medical profession respond that informed consent is a myth. No unqualified person can adequately comprehend the necessary information relating to the risks and benefits of many procedures and treatments. And, say many doctors, patients do not want to know. They place themselves without qualification in the hands of their doctors.

'Informed consent' is an issue which has been pronounced on by the House of Lords. Their judgment in *Sidaway*[6] appeared at first sight to be a victory for those who maintain that what patients should be told is a matter for medical judgment alone. Careful study of the individual judgments reveals that if there was such a victory, it was partial in effect. Curious patients must be answered. The extent to which patients in clinical trials or volunteers in non-therapeutic research programmes must be counselled and informed was not touched on. A later judgment sought to restrict the scope of *Sidaway*, making it a 'rule' to which the judges could later develop 'exceptions'. Several years of litigation failed to result in much clarification of legal principles.

Two other medico-legal *causes célèbres* illustrate the fallibility of the present system of leaving the judges and the common law to develop guidelines for medical practice through contested litigation. Mrs Gillick's campaign to prevent girls under 16 being prescribed contraceptives without parental agreement also reached the Lords,[7] and ended in apparent defeat for her. Yet the judgments of their lordships left loopholes for further litigation, and the G.M.C.'s attempt to interpret their rulings as they affected confidentiality met with bitter criticism. Nor does the law manage to evolve principles relating to the potential criminal liability of doctors any more successfully. The trial of Dr Arthur for murder took place in a glare of publicity. The essence of the charge laid against him revolved around the extent to which parents and doctors together may decide to withhold treatment from a damaged newborn infant. The practice followed by Dr Arthur was disputed but mirrored practices current in many other paediatric units. Dr Arthur was acquitted. The law emerged no clearer for his ordeal.[8]

The inadequacy of *ad hoc* case by case litigation is a major reason why many commentators are now pressing for a commission to investigate the law as it relates to medical practice. In the U.S.A. the President's Commission for the Study of Ethical Problems in Medicine reported in 1982. In Canada the Law Reform Commission reported in 1980 on *Consent to Medical Care*. We should follow suit. We can learn from American experience in deciding on the constitution and membership of a Commission. The Canadian report offers valuable insight into the workings of the common law and its application to consent to medical treatment. But a British Commission must start afresh in evaluating law in the context of medical practice in the U.K. Health care here is largely still free of charge. How the existence of the N.H.S. affects the doctor–patient relationship must be carefully evaluated. Many of the factors which influence medical practice and litigation in the U.S.A. are absent here. The patient does not pay the doctor directly. The doctor has no profit motive to influence his decision on appropriate treatment. The contingency fee system, whereby lawyers in personal injury cases will act for no charge unless the patient wins and in that case pocket a third of the damages, is banned in the U.K. Some of the factors which led to an explosion of malpractice claims across the Atlantic exist here. Others do not. Similarly, fears of defensive medicine, of doctors opting for the legally safe rather than the best medical option, may in part have counterparts in England to U.S.A. experience. But any similarity is only partial. Doctors who are paid may have financial reasons to opt for an unnecessary series of tests and check-ups and second opinions. British doctors generally have no such financial incentives. The marked differences in law and medicine between Britain and America mean that a British investigation of law and health care must largely start afresh on its task.

How would any such Commission be constituted? The first question is, who would sit on it? The membership should have a wide base. Clearly the medical profession, doctors and other health professionals, should be represented. The consumers of health care, the patients, should, via representatives of patients' associations, and/or lay members of ethical committees and other existing N.H.S. committees, be given their say. The disciplines of philosophy and theology have a contribution to make, determining proper criteria for decision-making and the formulation of the rights and obligations of those involved in decision-making. And as the legal framework for medical practice and the application of medical ethics would be referred to the Commission, the lawyers cannot be excluded.

In practical terms, even before the selection of members for the Commission comes the issue of its formal establishment and status. Either this could be by means of a statute creating and constituting the Commission, or in the first instance a Committee of Inquiry along the lines of the Warnock Committee could be established by the D.H.S.S. That committee could itself consider the appropriate formal constitution for pursuit of its purpose. My preference, tentatively, is for establishment by statute from the beginning, with Parliament giving its seal of approval to the process of review and having a say in the provision for membership and terms of reference of the Commission.

The Commission's terms of reference will need careful drafting. Certain specific issues should be referred expressly to the Commission. Primarily, the question of consent as it affects so many areas of medical care and medical research must be referred to the Commission at once. The problems of confidentiality, where the law at present is extremely superficial, must be addressed. A decision needs then to be taken as to which other of the issues surveyed in Part III of this book require immediate examination. Perhaps those which put the doctor at risk of criminal liability should be given priority. Thereafter the Health Minister should be empowered to refer specific issues to the Commission for consideration and the Commission should be empowered to propose to the Minister problems which it believes require its attention. What I envisage is not a short-term institution to conduct a limited inquiry, make recommendations and then be wound up. The Commission would remain in existence first to complete its initial review of problems apparent today, then to be there to deal with problems which arise as medicine and technology advance, and finally to keep the law relating to medical practice and medical ethics under constant review.

The Commission's powers should be two-fold, to investigate and to recommend. Investigation is the keynote of its function. It must examine the present constraints the law places on medical practice, the feasibility and application of the principles relating to consent as developed by the courts. It must investigate the claims and counter-claims as to what patients want and need to be told about proposed treatment, and how informed consent will help or hinder good health care. The spectre of defensive medicine must be confronted to see whether it has substance.[9] The Commission must extend its remit beyond the issues already litigated or debated in the context of the common law on consent. The question of payments to research volunteers, the time available for and manner of communications with patients, and the role nursing staff do and can play, must be looked at. From investigation the Commission would move on to reports and recommendations. The Commission would have three options. (1) It may simply issue a report on its findings and outline its views of the appropriate development of the common law. The report should relate general principle to specific practice, distinguishing between and illustrating various spheres of medical practice. Thus a report on consent to medical care would deal with general health care, problems arising out of particular procedures, the question of parents and children, the problems with mentally handicapped adults and the specific difficulties inherent in medical research. (2) The Commission could go further and append to its report recommended Codes of Practice. A Commission created by Act of Parliament could be empowered to make proposals on codes of practice to the D.H.S.S., so that by ministerial regulation the codes could be given statutory force. (3) Finally, on occasion, the Commission might in appropriate cases recommend specific legislation. For example, were the Abortion Act to be referred to the Commission, new legislation would be called for to amend the law embodied in that Act.

It is the second possibility, that the Commission be empowered to propose codes of practice, which needs some further consideration. Codes of practice have the attraction of introducing a greater degree of practical certainty into health care decision-making. They can distinguish between different areas of medical enterprise, providing, for example, for a separate discrete code on research. They create, too, certain problems for the doctor, the patient and lawyer. A code of practice may represent in the end a negotiated compromise. It offers to the doctor greater precision in the legal framework within which he practises. Its provisions are unlikely to command uniform support for each and every clause in the code. Take the example of therapeutic research on patients. While the common law governs what degree of information is required for the patient's consent to be valid and effective, until and unless a case comes to court it is not clear whether such patients fall within the *Sidaway* rules on disclosure, or the higher standard pertaining to non-therapeutic procedures. Patients and doctors are in a legal vacuum. Within a code on medical research a precise rule will be formulated. The compromise arrived at may not please research teams if they feel it would inhibit their clinical freedom. A high standard of disclosure with exceptions to the standard built in to accommodate the needs of doctors combining health care with research may be unsatisfactory to some patients and potential patients.

Two questions about the legal effect of codes of practice formulated by the Commission call for careful consideration. First, what force would the codes have to bind medical staff in their practice of health care? At the lowest they could be advisory only. Breach of the code would be a factor to be taken into account in investigating complaints and deciding on any disciplinary action against health care staff. If litigation were in progress, the codes would clearly be referred to as evidence of what constitutes proper medical practice. To give further emphasis to the codes, the statute empowering the Minister to give statutory force to a code of practice could expressly require that the codes be taken into account when a court considers questions of medical liability. Finally, it would be feasible but unlikely that a criminal sanction could attach to breach of a code of practice.

The most realistic option, then, may be to construe the codes as guidance as to the civil liability of the doctor. The code would set the legal framework for his relationship with a patient. But if 'no-fault' compensation is introduced, the action for negligence used by Mrs Sidaway and others to litigate the issue of informed consent may be barred in medical claims. The Commission would need to consider whether some new form of civil proceedings to test in the courts the application and interpretation of codes of practice is required. I suggested earlier that the relationship between reform making available 'no-fault' compensation and the existing action for medical negligence will need consideration by the Law Commission. Liaison, perhaps even a formal link, between the Law Commission and the Commission on Medicine, Ethics and Law would be of the utmost importance.

So far I have concentrated on the Commission's role in examining and developing the law. The Commission's task should be wider than this. It must also consider ethical standards, and when it is appropriate for the ethical standard to be set higher than the law. The law can never be more than a crude basepoint in deciding what is proper and ethically accepted. Just as the Commission should liaise with the Law Commission in devising a legal framework for decision-making in medical practice, it must also liaise with the General Medical Council in advising on ethics. Nor must the Commission confine itself to formal procedures, whether via legal regulation or the control exercised over professionals by the

G.M.C. and other professional bodies. Health Service procedures must be examined. For example, the role of ethical committees in scrutinizing medical research, and of family practitioner committees in supervising general practice, may be crucial in day-to-day decision-making. The Commission offers a forum for general debate, for co-ordination between groups working in this field, throughout the U.K. This is an opportunity, which should not be missed, for all those involved in and concerned about health care to co-operate rather than to confront each other.

Some Suggestions for Further Reading

Medical ethics and law is a growing field of interest. In the Notes to the text I refer to several books and articles. In this short bibliography I suggest a few works which will be especially helpful to the reader wanting to extend his knowledge of the subject matter of this book.

Dugdale, A., and Stanton, K., *Professional Negligence*, Butterworths, London, 1982.

Faulder, Carolyn, *Whose Body Is It? The Troubling Issue of Informed Consent*, Virago, London, 1985.

Finch, J. D., *Health Services Law*, Sweet & Maxwell, London, 1980.

Glover, Jonathan, *Causing Death and Saving Lives*, Pelican, Harmondsworth, 1977.

Glover, Jonathan, *What Sort of People Should There Be?* Pelican, Harmondsworth, 1984.

Harris, John, *The Value of Life*, Routledge & Kegan Paul, London, 1985.

Hawkins, Clifford, *Mishap or Malpractice*, M.D.U., Blackwells, London, 1985.

Hoggett, Brenda M., *Mental Health Law*, 2nd edn, Sweet & Maxwell, 1980.

Jackson, Rupert M., and Powell, John L., *Professional Negligence*, Sweet & Maxwell, London, 1982.

Kennedy, Ian, *The Unmasking of Medicine*, Allen & Unwin, London, 1981.

Lamb, David, *Death, Brain Death and Ethics*, Croom Helm, London, 1986.

Leahy-Taylor, J. (ed.), *Medical Malpractice*, John Wright & Sons, Bristol, 1980.

Lockwood, M. (ed.), *Moral Dilemmas in Modern Medicine*, O.U.P., Oxford, 1986.

McLean, S. A. M. (ed.), *Legal Issues in Medicine*, Gower, Aldershot, 1981.

McLean, S. A. M., and Maher, G., *Medicine, Morals and the Law*, Gower, Aldershot, 1983

Martin, C. R. A., *The Law Relating to Medical Practice*, Pitmans, London, 1973.

Mason, J. K., and McCall Smith, R. A., *Law and Medical Ethics*, Butterworths, London, 1983.

Nathan, P. C., and Barrowclough, A. R., *Medical Negligence*, Butterworths, London, 1957.

Nicholson, R. H. (ed.), *Medical Research with Children: Ethics, Law, and Practice*, O.U.P., Oxford, 1986.

Some Suggestions for Further Reading

Palmer, G., *Compensation for Incapacity: A Study of Law and Social Change in New Zealand and Australia*, O.U.P., Wellington, 1979.

Phillips, M., and Dawson, J., *Doctors' Dilemmas*, Harvester Press, London, 1984.

Savage, Wendy, *The Savage Inquiry*, Virago, London, 1986.

Skegg, P. D. G., *Law, Ethics and Medicine*, Clarendon Press, Oxford, 1984.

Speller, S. R., *Law of Doctor and Patient*, H. K. Lewis, London.

Speller, S. R., *Law Relating to Hospitals and Kindred Institutions*, 6th edn, H. K. Lewis, London, 1978.

Williams, Glanville, *The Sanctity of Life and the Criminal Law*, Faber & Faber, London, 1958.

Wood, Clive (ed.), *The Influence of Litigation on Medical Practice*, Academic Press, London, 1977.

Notes

Chapter 1: The Practice of Medicine Today

1. Ian Kennedy, *The Unmasking of Medicine*, Allen & Unwin, London, 1981, Ch. 1, p. 9 ff.
2. ibid., p. 8.
3. Medical Act 1983, s. 49; and see *Younghusband* v. *Luftig* [1949] 2 K.B. 354; *Wilson* v. *Inyang* [1951] 2 K.B. 799. Unregistered practitioners are expressly prohibited from certain fields of practice, e.g. venereal disease; Venereal Disease Act 1917. And they are barred from holding certain positions; Medical Act 1983, s. 47.
4. Medical Act 1983, s. 46.
5. Theft Act 1968, s. 15.
6. He was initially sentenced to 6 years imprisonment. His sentence was reduced on appeal to 18 months!
7. *R.* v. *Donovan* [1934] 2 K.B. 498.
8. Medical Act 1983, Sched. I.
9. Medical Act 1983, s. 2 and see ss. 30–34.
10. ibid., s. 35.
11. ibid., s. 37. And see *Crompton* v. *G.M.C.* (*No. 1*) [1981] 1 W.L.R. 1435 and (*No. 2*) [1985] 1 W.L.R. 885.
12. ibid., s. 36.
13. ibid., s. 40.
14. G.M.C. 'Bluebook' *Professional Conduct: Fitness to Practise* (April 1985), p. 10.
15. Earl Halsbury, *Laws of England*, Butterworths, London, Vol. 30, para. 125.
16. *Bhandari* v. *Advocates' Committee* (1956) 1 W.L.R. 1442, P.C.
17. See *Rodgers* v. *G.M.C.*, 19 November 1984, P.C.
18. *Evans* v. *G.M.C.*, 19 November 1984, P.C.
19. Medical Act 1983 (Amendment) Bill.
20. *Rodgers* v. *G.M.C.* (above).
21. *The Times*, 27 June 1985.
22. G.M.C. 'Bluebook' *Professional Conduct: Fitness to Practise* (April 1985), p. 10. And see M. Brazier, 'Doctors and Discipline II' (1985) Vol. I, *Professional Negligence*, p. 179.
23. Medical Act 1983, s. 41.
24. *R.* v. *G.M.C. ex p. Gee*, [1986] 1 W.L.R. 226; *The Times*, 22 May 1986, C.A.

25. See *Rodgers* v. *G.M.C.* (above) and M. Brazier 'Doctors and Discipline I' (1985), Vol. I, *Professional Negligence.*, p. 123.

26. Medical Act 1983, s. 50.

27. See *The Times*, 23 May 1985.

28. See the forceful views expressed to the American Bar Association by Dr Havard, Secretary to the B.M.A., *The Times*, 19 July 1985.

29. See J. D. Finch, *Health Services Law*, Sweet & Maxwell, London, 1980.

30. See Finch, op. cit., Chapter 1; his book preceded the latest turnabouts in the Health and Social Security Act 1984.

31. *R.* v. *Secretary of State for Social Services, ex p. Hincks.* The first instance judgment is reported (1979) 123 Sol. Jo. 436. The appeal judgment remains unreported but is discussed by Finch, op. cit., pp. 38–9.

32. See Finch, op. cit., p. 39.

33. *Thake* v. *Maurice* [1984] 2 All E.R. 513.

34. *Thake* v. *Maurice* [1986] 1 All E.R. 497, C.A.

35. See pp. 99 ff.

36. Chapter 6.

37. Chapter 8.

Chapter 2: Medicine, Moral Dilemmas and the Law

1. See J. K. Mason and R. A. McCall Smith, *Law and Medical Ethics*, Butterworths, London, 1983, Chapter 11; G. H. Mooney, 'Cost-benefit Analysis and Medical Ethics' (1980) 6 J. Med. Ethics 177.

2. See J. Finnis, *Natural Law and Natural Rights*, O.U.P., 1980.

3. See the correspondence in *The Times*, 27 August to 2 September 1985, following an article by Paul Johnson (*The Times*, 26 August) calling for a ban on abortion and embryo research but a return for the death penalty.

4. See M. Phillips and J. Dawson, *Doctors' Dilemmas*, Harvester Press, London, 1984, pp. 22–6; and see that same work generally for its support of the 'middle ground' of the debate.

5. See in particular two persuasive and lively works: Jonathan Glover, *Causing Death and Saving Lives*, Pelican, Harmondsworth, 1977; John Harris, *The Value of Life*, Routledge & Kegan Paul, London, 1985.

6. Glover, op. cit., Chapter 3.

7. Harris, op. cit., Chapter 1.

8. For the Declaration of Geneva, the Hippocratic Oath and other codes of medical ethics, see Mason and McCall Smith, op. cit., Appendices A–F, pp. 251–61.

9. See Phillips and Dawson, op. cit., p. 26.

10. ibid., pp. 47–9, 82–5; Mason and McCall Smith, op. cit., pp. 60–62.

11. See Chapter 19, and also Ian Kennedy, *The Unmasking of Medicine*, Allen & Unwin, London, 1981, Chapter 7. And see the *Guardian*, 6 August 1986, expressing disturbing doubts on brain death.

12. Glover, op. cit., pp. 43–5.

13. See Chapter 20, and also Phillips and Dawson, op. cit., pp. 33–4.
14. ibid., p. 34.
15. See Chapter 20.
16. Contrast the public sympathy attracted by a divorced mother convicted of the manslaughter of her son, who was dying of cystic fibrosis, with the crowds who gathered to hurl insults and hate at Paul Brown, convicted of the murder of his Down's syndrome baby daughter.
17. See I. Kennedy, 'Switching Off Life Support Machines; the Legal Implications' [1977] Crim. L.R. 443.
18. See I. Kennedy, 'The Karen Quinlan case; problems and proposals' [1976] 2 J. Med. Ethics.
19. Glover, op. cit., Chapters 7 and 15; Harris, op. cit., Chapter 4.
20. See Phillips and Dawson, op. cit., p. 34, and B.M.A. *Handbook on Medical Ethics*, 1984, p. 64.
21. See D. Brahams, 'A Doctor's Justification for Withdrawing Treatment' (1985) Vol. 135 N.L.J. 48.
22. See Glanville Williams, *The Sanctity of Life and the Criminal Law*, Faber & Faber, London, 1958; P. D. G. Skegg, *Law, Ethics and Medicine*, Clarendon Press, Oxford, 1984; Mason and McCall Smith, op. cit.
23. J. Havard, 'Legislation is likely to create more difficulty than it resolves' (1983) 9 J. Med. Ethics. See also Chapter 20.
24. [1981] B.M.J. p. 569.

Chapter 3: A Relationship of Trust and Confidence

1. For a lively discussion of the complex ethical dilemmas faced by doctors in relation to confidentiality, see M. Phillips and J. Dawson, *Doctors' Dilemmas*, Harvester Press, London, 1984, Chapter 5, 'Secrets'. And see J. K. Mason and R. A. McCall Smith, *Law and Medical Ethics*, Butterworths, London, 1983, Chapter 8.
2. See J. E. Thompson, 'The Nature of Confidentiality' (1979) 5 J. Med. Ethics 57.
3. See F. Gurry, *Breach of Confidence*, Clarendon Press, Oxford, 1984.
4. See Law Commission Report No. 110, *Breach of Confidence*, para. 3.1 (Cmnd. 8388), and see G. Jones, 'Restitution of Benefits Obtained in Breach of Another's Confidence' (1970) 86 L.Q.R. 463.
5. Gurry, op. cit., Chapters 8 and 9.
6. *Argyll* v. *Argyll* [1967] 1 Ch. 302.
7. *Attorney-General* v. *Jonathan Cape Ltd* [1976] 1 Q.B. 752.
8. *Wyatt* v. *Wilson* (1820), unreported but referred to in *Prince Albert* v. *Strange* (1849) 41 E.R. 1171, 1179.
9. *Hunter* v. *Mann* [1974] 1 Q.B. 767, 772.
10. *Gartside* v. *Outram* (1856) 26 L.J. Ch. 113, 114.
11. *Lion Laboratories Ltd* v. *Evans* [1984] 2 All E.R. 417, 433.
12. Law Commission Report No. 110, paras. 6–106, but see the Scottish

Notes

decisions *A B* v. *C D* (1851) 14 Dunl. (Ct of Sess.) 177; *A B* v. *C D* 1904 7F (Ct of Sess.) 72; discussed in Mason and McCall Smith, op. cit., pp. 108–9.

13. *Gillick* v. *West Norfolk and Wisbech A.H.A.* [1985] 3 All E.R. 402.
14. G.M.C. 'Bluebook' *Professional Conduct: Fitness to Practise* (G.M.C., April 1985); and see B.M.A. *Handbook on Medical Ethics* (B.M.A., 1984) pp. 12–13. And see the (Körner) Report of the Working Party on Confidentiality.
15. The publication of memoirs by Lord Moran, physician to Winston Churchill during the Second World War, provoked a great furore: see Mason and McCall Smith, op. cit., pp. 109–10.
16. Care should be taken, however, even when transmitting information to other medical staff, to ensure that only those who 'need to know' are communicated with, and that they accept the obligation of confidentiality. And the amount of information collected for statistical and similar purposes causes some concern for the future of confidentiality.
17. See Chapter 18.
18. Criminal Law Act 1967, s. 5(5).
19. ibid., s. 5(1).
20. *Kitson* v. *Playfair* (1896), *The Times*, 28 March.
21. Birmingham Assizes (1914) 78 J.P. 604; see Mason and McCall Smith, op. cit., p. 99.
22. *Initial Services Ltd* v. *Putterill* [1968] 1 Q.B. 396, 405.
23. See Pereira Gray, 'Legal Aspects of Violence within the Family' (1981) 282 B.M.J. 2021.
24. See *Hubbard* v. *Vosper* [1972] 2 Q.B. 84; *Church of Scientology* v. *Kaufman* [1973] R.P.C. 635 (disclosure of matter threatening the health of members of the public), see Gurry, op. cit., pp. 334–8.
25. Law Commission Report No. 110, paras. 6-94–6-96.
26. See Paul Sieghart, 'Professional Ethics – for Whose Benefit' (1982) 8 J. Med. Ethics 25.
27. *Carmarthenshire C.C.* v. *Lewis* [1955] A.C. 549.
28. *Tarasoff* v. *Regents of the University of California* (1976) 551 P 2d 334. ↩
29. Law Commission Report No. 110 (Cmnd. 8388).
30. [1977] 1 All E.R. 589.
31. *Hunter* v. *Mann* [1974] 1 Q.B. 767.
32. Police and Criminal Evidence Act 1984, ss. 8–14 and Sched. 1.
33. For a comprehensive list see Phillips and Dawson, op. cit., pp. 204–6.
34. See generally on the implications of record keeping for medical confidentiality, *Report of the Committee on Data Protection (Lindop Report)* (Cmnd. 7341). And see the draft Code on confidentiality of personal health information within the N.H.S. D.A. (84) 25.
35. See Sieghart, op. cit., and Pheby, 'Changing practice on confidentiality; a cause for concern' (1982) 8 J. Med. Ethics 12.
36. Considerations of questions of copyright in records and inter-health service

communications confuse the picture even further. The technical legal arguments have one common feature. They do nothing to help the patient obtain access to information about himself.

37. Supreme Court 1981, ss. 33–5; see Chapter 6.
38. Notably the Inter-Professional Working Group on Access to Personal Health Information and the Working Party on Confidentiality set up by the Steering Group on Health Services Information (Körner).
39. See Körner, p. 17.
40. See ibid., p. 31, Chapter 11 and Annex C; and see D.A. (85) 23.
41. For a view that ethics are more important than law, see J. Jacob, 'Confidentiality: the dangers of anything weaker than the medical ethic' (1982) 8 J. Med. Ethics 18.

Chapter 4: Agreeing to Treatment

1. *Allan* v. *New Mount Sinai Hospital* (1980) 109 D.L.R. (3d) 536. cf. *Wilson* v. *Pringle* (below).
2. *Devi* v. *West Midlands A.H.A.* [1980] 7 C.L. 44.
3. *Cull* v. *Butler* [1932] 1 B.M.J. 1195.
4. *Freeman* v. *Home Office* [1984] 2 W.L.R. 130.
5. See *Wilson* v. *Pringle* [1986] 3 W.L.R. 1, C.A.
6. *O'Brien* v. *Cunard S.S. Co.* (Mass. 1891) 28 N C 266.
7. *Chatterton* v. *Gerson* [1980] 3 W.L.R. 1003.
8. See the *Guardian*, 23 July 1983. This case is further discussed in Chapter 16.
9. *Hills* v. *Potter* (NOTE) [1984] 1 W.L.R. 641, 653.
10. *Sidaway* v. *Board of Governors of the Bethlem Royal and the Maudsley Hospital* [1984] 2 W.L.R. 778, 790; and see *Freeman* v. *Home Office* [1984] 2 W.L.R. 802, 813.
11. *Sidaway* v. *Board of Governors of the Bethlem Royal and the Maudsley Hospital* [1985] 2 W.L.R. 480.
12. *Reibl* v. *Hughes* (1980) 114 D.L.R. (3d) 1.
13. [1957] 2 All E.R. 118.
14. *Hatcher* v. *Black*, *The Times*, 2 July 1954.
15. *O'Malley-Williams* v. *Board of Governors of the National Hospital for Nervous Diseases* [1975] 1 B.M.J. 635.
16. (1972) 464 F. 2d 772, 780.
17. *Reibl* v. *Hughes* (above).
18. *Sidaway* v. *Board of Governors of the Bethlem Royal and the Maudsley Hospital* [1985] 2 W.L.R. 480.
19. ibid., p. 497.
20. ibid., p. 505.
21. ibid., p. 493.
22. ibid., p. 493.
23. *The Times*, 24 May 1985.
24. *Gold* v. *Haringey H. A.*, *The Times*, 17 June 1986.

25. *Beatty* v. *Illingworth* (1896) B.M.J. 21 November, p. 1525.
26. See P. D. G. Skegg, 'Justification for Medical Procedure Performed without Consent' (1974) 90 L.Q.R. 512; 'Consent in Medical Practice' by S. A. M. McLean and A. J. McKay in S. A. M. McLean (ed.), *Legal Issues in Medicine*, Gower, Aldershot, 1981; *Wilson* v *Pringle* above n. 5.
27. *Devi* v. *West Midlands A.H.A.*, see note 2 above.

Chapter 5: Medical Negligence

1. *Barnett* v. *Chelsea and Kensington H.M.C.* [1969] 1 Q.B. 428; but see *Hotson* v. *Fitzgerald* [1985] 3 All E.R. 167, in Chapter 6, p. 101.
2. See J. K. Mason and R. A. McCall Smith, *Law and Medical Ethics*, Butterworths, London, 1983, pp. 126–7.
3. *Barnett* v. *Chelsea and Kensington H.M.C.* (above).
4. *Phillips* v. *William Whiteley Ltd* [1938] 1 All E.R. 566.
5. [1957] 1 W.L.R. 582, 586, 118.
6. *Maynard* v. *West Midlands R.H.A.* [1984] 1 W.L.R. 634, 638.
7. *Nettleship* v. *Weston* [1971] 2 Q.B. 691 C.A.
8. *Wilsher* v. *Essex A.H.A.*, *The Times*, 6 August 1986.
9. See *Jones* v. *Manchester Corporation* [1952] 2 Q.B. 852, 871.
10. *Bolam* v. *Friern H.M.C.* [1957] 1 W.L.R. 582, 587–8.
11. [1980] 1 All E.R. 650, 658, C.A.
12. *Whitehouse* v. *Jordan* [1981] 1 W.L.R. 246, 258, H.L.
13. *Maynard* v. *West Midlands R.H.A.* [1984] 1 W.L.R. 634, 639, H.L.
14. *Sidaway* v. *Board of Governors of the Bethlem Royal and the Maudsley Hospital* [1984] 2 W.L.R. 778, 792, C.A. Lord Bridge endorsed this view in the House of Lords [1985] 2 W.L.R. 480, 505.
15. *Clarke* v. *Adams* (1950) 94 Sol. Jo. 599.
16. *Hunter* v. *Hanley* (1955) S.C. 200.
17. See A. J. Gamble, 'Professional Liability', in S. A. M. McLean (ed.), *Legal Issues in Medicine*, Gower, Aldershot, 1981, p. 89.
18. *Crawford* v. *Board of Governors of Charing Cross Hospital*, *The Times*, 8 December 1953, C.A.
19. *Whiteford* v. *Hunter* (1950) 94 Sol. Jo. 758, H.L.
20. H.M. (72) 37.
21. *Roe* v. *Ministry of Health* [1951] 2 K.B. 66 at p. 84.
22. [1983] 1 All E.R. 416.
23. *Hunter* v. *Hanley* 1955 S.L.T. 213, 217.
24. *Newton* v. *Newton's Model Laundry*, *The Times*, 3 November 1959.
25. *Wood* v. *Thurston*, *The Times*, 25 May 1951.
26. *Langley* v. *Campbell*, *The Times*, 6 November 1975; and see *Tuffil* v. *East Surrey Area Health Authority*, *The Times*, 15 March 1978, p. 4. (Failure to diagnose amoebic dysentery in a patient who had spent many years in the tropics.)
27. Annual Report of the M.D.U. 1982, pp. 22–3.

28. Annual Report of the M.D.U. 1983, p. 24.
29. *Maynard* v. *West Midlands R.H.A.* [1984] 1 W.L.R. 634; see pp. 73–4.
30. Annual Report of the M.D.U. 1982, p. 24.
31. *Chin Keow* v. *Govt. of Malaysia* [1967] 1 W.L.R. 813.
32. *Hucks* v. *Cole* (1968) 12 Sol. Jo. 483.
33. Annual Report of the M.D.U. 1984, p. 18.
34. See J. Finch, 'A Costly Oversight for Pharmacists' (1982) Vol. 132 N.L.J. 176.
35. Annual Report of the M.D.U. 1982, pp. 14–16.
36. Annual Report of the M.D.U. 1984, pp. 34–5.
37. *Collins* v. *Hertfordshire C.C.* [1947] K.B. 598.
38. *Jones* v. *Manchester Corporation* [1952] 2 Q.B. 852.
39. [1964] 2 Q.B. 66 C.A.
40. *Ashcroft* v. *Mersey A.H.A.* [1983] 2 All E.R. 245, 247.
41. *Urry* v. *Biere*, *The Times*, 19 July 1955.
42. *Corder* v. *Banks*, *The Times*, 9 April 1960.
43. [1985] 3 All E.R. 167.
44. *Wilsher* v. *Essex A.H.A.*, *The Times*, 6 August 1986, C.A.
45. See *Cassidy* v. *Ministry of Health* [1939] 2 K.B. 14; see Chapter 6.
46. *Sutton* v. *Population Services*, *The Times*, 7 November 1981.
47. *Smith* v. *Brighton and Lewes H.M.C.*, *The Times*, 21 June 1955.
48. Annual Report of the M.D.U., 1984, pp. 24–5.
49. Unfair Contract Terms Act 1977, s. 2.
50. *Eyre* v. *Measday* [1986] 1 All E.R. 488; *Thake* v. *Maurice* [1986] 1 All E.R. 497, C.A.
51. (1925) 41 T.L.R. 557.
52. Annual Report of the M.D.U. 1982, p. 64.

Chapter 6: Medical Litigation

1. For common-sense, practical advice see C. J. Lewis and N. Staite, 'How to Start a Medical Negligence Action' (1984) 81 L.S. Gaz. 3432; and see Diana M. Kloss (1984) Vol. 289 B.M.J. 66.
2. National Health Service Act 1977, Sched. 5 para. 15, as amended by the Health Services Act 1980.
3. Consider also the problem of agency nurses. Increasingly health service cuts force N.H.S. hospitals to rely on nurses casually engaged from nursing agencies. Inadequate nursing care may be proved, but it may be impossible to determine whether the fault was that of an agency or a full-time N.H.S. nurse. Agency and authority may each try to shift the blame to the other. Nor in many cases is the agency an employer of its nurses. In that case the only remedy lies against the nurse herself.
4. See *Wilsher* v. *Essex A.H.A.* in Chapter 5, p. 82.
5. See *Cassidy* v. *Ministry of Health* [1951] 2 K.B. 343, pp. 359–60; and *Roe* v. *Ministry of Health* [1954] 2 Q.B. 66, p. 82.

Notes

6. *Street on Torts* (7th edn), Butterworths, London, 1983, p. 423; *Winfield and Jolowicz on Tort* (12th edn), Sweet & Maxwell, London, 1984, p. 577.

7. See below, pp. 98–9.

8. Note the Supply of Goods and Services Act 1982, s. 13 (implied term that service will be carried out with care and skill); and Part I of that Act imposing conditions as to goods supplied in the course of a contract for services; see A. P. Bell, 'The doctor and the Supply of Goods and Services Act 1982' (1984) 4 L.S. 175.

9. If the deputizing service actually employs the doctor working for it, the service may be sued. This is unlikely; deputies are usually engaged on a 'casual labour only' basis.

10. Administration of Justice Act 1970, ss. 32–5 (the legislation was based on recommendations of the Winn Committee, Cmnd. 3691 (1968)).

11. *MacIvor* v. *Southern Health and Social Services Board, Northern Ireland* [1978] 2 All E.R. 625.

12. *Dunning* v. *United Liverpool Hospitals' Board of Governors* [1973] 2 All E.R. 454.

13. *Waugh* v. *B.R.B.* [1980] A.C. 521; and see Diana M. Kloss (1984) Vol. 289 B.M.J. 66.

14. *Lee* v. *South West Thames R.H.A.* [1985] 2 All E.R. 385.

15. See *Sidaway* v. *Board of Governors of the Bethlem Royal and the Maudsley Hospital* [1985] 2 W.L.R. 480; see Chapter 4.

16. Supreme Court Act 1981, s. 35.

17. *Hall* v. *Avon A.H.A.* [1980] 1 All E.R. 516 C.A.

18. *Megarity* v. *Ryan (D.J.) & Sons* [1980] 1 W.L.R. 1237 C.A.

19. *Rahman* v. *Kirklees A.H.A.* [1980] 3 All E.R. 610.

20. *Ashcroft* v. *Mersey A.H.A.* [1983] 2 All E.R. 245.

21. [1981] 1 All E.R. 287 H.L.

22. [1980] 1 All E.R. 650, p. 655.

23. See *Hall* v. *Avon A.H.A.* (above).

24. See *Street on Torts*, pp. 124–31.

25. *Mahon* v. *Osborne* [1939] 2 K.B. 14.

26. *Roe* v. *Ministry of Health* [1954] 2 Q.B. 66.

27. *Cassidy* v. *Ministry of Health* [1951] 2 K.B. 343.

28. See pp. 87 ff..

29. *Roe* v. *Ministry of Health* [1954] 2 Q.B. 66, p. 82.

30. [1983] 1 All E.R. 416.

31. This is known as compensation for the 'lost years'; see *Pickett* v. *B.R.B.* [1980] A.C. 136.

32. Fatal Accidents Act 1976 as amended by the Administration of Justice Act 1982.

33. See p. 90.

34. *Hotson* v. *Fitzgerald* [1985] 3 All E.R. 167 in Chapter 5, pp. 80–81.

35. Law Reform (Personal Injuries) Act 1948, s. 2 (4).

36. *The Times*, 21 December 1985, p. 3.
37. *The Times*, 11 March 1985.
38. See Ian Kennedy, 'Patient on the Clapham Omnibus' (1984) 47 M.L.R. 454.
39. See H.M. (54) 32.
40. Civil Liability (Contribution) Act 1978, s. 1.
41. ibid., s. 2.
42. *Jones* v. *Manchester Corporation* [1952] 2 All E.R. 125.

Chapter 7: Drug-induced Injuries

1. But see H. Teff and C. Munro, *Thalidomide: The Legal Aftermath*, Saxon House, London, 1976, pp. 101–4, discussing the doubts expressed about the 'pharmaceutical miracle' and suggesting that eradication of disease had as much to do with improved standards of living and hygiene as with the invention of new drugs.
2. See J. Braithwaite, *Corporate Crime in the Pharmaceutical Industry*, Routledge & Kegan Paul, London, 1984; S. Adams, *Roche versus Adams*, Jonathan Cape, London, 1984.
3. For a full and lively history of the events surrounding the thalidomide tragedy, see Teff and Munro, op. cit.
4. No reported English case of an award of damages for personal injury resulting from drug-induced damage can be discovered; see Teff, 'Regulation under the Medicines Act 1968' (1984) 47 M.L.R. 303, 320–22.
5. In contrast to West Germany, which after the thalidomide disaster enacted a special regime of liability for injury caused by drugs.
6. A particular difficulty here has been establishing which manufacturer made the actual drug taken by the mother. There were several brands of the same drug on the market; see *Sindell* v. *Abbott Laboratories* (1980) 26 Cal. 3d. 588, and on this and other problems of liability for defective drugs see Newdick, 'Liability for Defective Drugs' (1985) 101 L.Q.R. 405.
7. See *Sindell* v. *Abbott Laboratories* (above).
8. See Teff, 'Regulation under the Medicines Act 1968', (1984) 47 M.L.R. 303; Steward and Wibberley, 'Drug Innovation – What is slowing it down?' (1980) 284 *Nature* 118–20.
9. Sale of Goods Act 1979, s. 14(2)(b).
10. ibid., s. 14(3).
11. *Pfizer* v. *Ministry of Health* [1965] A.C. 512; *Appleby* v. *Sleep* [1968] 1 W.L.R. 948.
12. See the Supply of Goods and Services Act 1982; A.P. Bell, 'The Doctor and the Supply of Goods and Services Act', [1984] *Legal Studies* 175.
13. *Donoghue* v. *Stevenson* [1932] A.C. 562, 599.
14. *Watson* v. *Buckley and Osborne, Garrett & Co. Ltd* [1940] 1 All E.R. 174 (duty imposed on distributors of hair dye).
15. Teff and Munro, op. cit., Chapters 1 and 2.
16. *Wright* v. *Dunlop Rubber Co. Ltd* [1972] 13 K.I.R. 255; and see Forte,

'Medical Products Liability', in S.A.M. McLean, (ed.), *Legal Issues in Medicine*, Gower, Aldershot, 1981, p. 67.

17. For details see Teff and Munro, op. cit., pp. 111–18.
18. Medicines Act 1968, s. 6.
19. ss. 7 and 35; for limited exemptions to the requirement for a clinical trial certificate see Medicines (Exemption from Licences) (Clinical Trials) Order 1981 S.I. No. 164.
20. s. 2.
21. s. 4.
22. s. 20(3).
23. s. 19(1).
24. s. 19(2).
25. s. 24.
26. s. 38.
27. s. 21(5).
28. Discussed fully in Teff, 'Regulation under the Medicines Act 1968' (above).
29. H. C. Deb. Vol. 847 Col. 440–41, 29 November 1972.
30. See the *Guardian*, 23 July 1985, p. 4.
31. [1978] A.C. 728.
32. R.S.C. Ord. 11, r.l(f); Civil Jurisdiction and Judgments Act 1982 enacting the European Convention on jurisdiction and judgments; Art. 5(3).
33. *Distillers Co. (Biochemicals) Ltd* v. *Thompson* [1971] A.C. 458 (New Zealand mother allowed to sue the British company Distillers in New Zealand over thalidomide manufactured here; essence of the negligence alleged was failure to warn her, in New Zealand, of the danger to her baby).
34. Notably the Law Commission in their report 'Liability for Defective Products' (1977) Law Com. No. 82, Cmnd. 6831; Royal Commission on Civil Liability and Compensation for Personal Injury (1978) Cmnd. 7054 (the Pearson Report).
35. See Law Commission No. 82 (above), para. 23.
36. Council Directive of 25.7.85.
37. The pharmaceutical industry has repeatedly argued that pharmaceutical products should remain exempt from any regime of strict liability, mainly on the grounds (1) that scientific research and innovation will be severely affected; (2) that the nature of drug disasters means that strict liability could have catastrophic results for the industry; (3) the difficulty of defining defect in a drug is too great: these arguments have been consistently rejected, see Law Commission No. 82 (above), pp. 19–21; Pearson Report, para. 1274.
38. See the thorough and excellent discussion of this problem in C. Newdick, op. cit., pp. 409–20.
39. Council Directive Article 7(e).
40. The Pearson Commission considered and rejected arguments that in the case of drugs the grant of a product licence should be a complete defence; Pearson Report (above), para. 1260.

41. Pearson Report, para. 1259; and see Law Com. No. 82.
42. H.C. Deb. Vol. 1357 Col. 808.
43. See in particular the Pearson Report, Chapter 25.
44. *The Times*, 7 July 1984.
45. See the *Sunday Times*, 10 November 1985.
46. See Newdick, op. cit., p. 429.
47. *Davies* v. *Eli Lilly & Co.*, *The Times*, 2 August 1986.
48. *Guardian*, 11 June 1986.

Chapter 8: Hospital Complaints Procedures

1. *The Times*, 28 June 1985; and see *Kralj* v. *McGrath* [1986] 1 All E.R. 54.
2. See the *Sunday Times*, 21 July 1985, p. 3.
3. H.C. Deb. Vol. 1337 Col. 1377 (1985).
4. National Health Service Act 1977, s. 17.
5. See H.L. Deb. Vol. 1285 Cols. 781–4 (1985).
6. See H.C. Deb. Vol. 1337 Col. 1379 (1985).
7. See the Report of the Davies Committee on Hospital Complaints Procedures, H.M.S.O., 1973.
8. H.C. (81) 5 which adds to but does not replace H.C. (66) 15.
9. There are separate Commissioners for England, Wales and Scotland, see s. 110 of the National Health Service Act 1977.
10. For complaints procedures re G.P.s, see Chapter 15.
11. The relevant bodies within the Commissioner's jurisdiction are set out in National Health Service Act 1977, s. 109.
12. National Health Service Act 1977, s. 114.
13. ibid., s. 111.
14. ibid., s. 113.
15. See ibid., Part I, Sched. 13.
16. Report of the Select Committee on the Parliamentary Commissioner for Administration H.C. 53 (1981–2).
17. Annual Report of the Health Service Commissioner 1984–5 H.C. 445 (1984–5).
18. ibid., pp. 39–45.
19. Annual Report for 1981–2 H.C. 419 (1981–2) p. 36.
20. See the analysis of complaints submitted to and dealt with by the Commissioner in the Annual Report for 1984–5, pp. 46–8.
21. Case W 415 83–4; H.C. 418 (1984–5) p. 39.
22. See Case W 189 84–5; H.C. 418 (1984–5) p. 194.
23. Case W 309 83–4; H.C. 33 (1984–5) p. 94; and see Case W 336 82–3; H.C. 33 p. 59 (*nine*-hour delay in getting a doctor to a geriatric hospital).
24. Case W 24 84–5; H.C. 418 (1984–5) p. 141.
25. Annual Report for 1984–5.
26. Case W 696 83–4; H.C. 418 (1984–5) p. 110.
27. e.g. Case W 309 77–8; H.C. 1 (1979–80) p. 67.

28. e.g. Case W 61 77–8; H.C. 98 (1978–9) p. 224.
29. Case W 236/75–6; H.C. 160 (1976–7) p. 23.
30. Case W 241/79–80; H.C. 51 (1982–3).
31. In 1984–5, 42 complaints were rejected because a legal remedy was open to the complainant. Annual Report, p. 46.
32. Annual Report for 1979–80, H.C. 650 (1979–80).
33. See tables at p. 46, Annual Report for 1984–5. Sched 13, part 2. National Health Service Act 1977.
34. Case W 439/79–80; H.C. 9 p. 105 (1981–2).
35. Case W 342/76–7; H.C. 130 p. 73 (1977–8); and see Annual Report for 1977–8 H.C. 417 p. 13.
36. Report of the Select Committee on the Parliamentary Commissioner for Administration H.C. 45 (1977–8).
37. Annual Report for 1977–8; H.C. 417 (1977–8).
38. Annual Report for 1979–80; H.C. 650 (1979–80).
39. H.M. 81 (5).
40. Report for 1981–2; H.C. 53 (1981–2).
41. For details see H.C. 81 (5).
42. See the *Guardian*, 6 March 1986.
43. H.C. 66 (15).
44. Reported [1979] Vol. B.M.J. 1232.
45. See the *Sunday Times*, 7 March 1982; and see H.C. Debates, Vol. 14 Cols. 965–9 (1981–2).
46. See the address by Dr Havard, Secretary of the B.M.A., to the American Bar Association; *The Times*, 19 July 1985.
47. For Mrs Savage's own account of the 'affair', see *The Savage Inquiry*, Virago, London, 1986.
48. See *The Times*, 9 July 1986.

Chapter 9: Radical Reform: An End to Fault Liability

1. See in particular P. S. Atiyah, *Accidents, Compensation and the Law*, Weidenfeld & Nicolson, London, 3rd edn, 1980; T. C. Ison, *The Forensic Lottery*, Staples Press, London, 1967.
2. The Pearson Report (Report of the Royal Commission on Civil Liability and Compensation for Personal Injury), Cmnd. 7054 Vol. 1 paras. 246–63.
3. In evidence to the Lord Chancellor's review of civil justice, *The Times*, 5 August 1986.
4. [1981] 1 All E.R. 287 H. L.; see pp. 73, 95–7.
5. Pearson Report, Vols. 1–3.
6. ibid., paras. 1304–71.
7. ibid., paras. 1372–1413; and see Chapter 7.
8. ibid., paras. 1340–41 (opinion among the medical profession and the drug industries has moved towards favouring a centrally funded no-fault scheme

for injury sustained by volunteers in clinical trials; see C.I.B.A. Foundation Study Paper (1980) B.M.J. 1172).

9. ibid., paras. 1193–1278. The Commission's proposals related to all defective products and not drugs alone. And see Chapter 7.

10. ibid., paras. 1488–1535.

11. ibid., paras. 1370–71.

12. Richard Smith, 'Problems with a no-fault system of accident compensation' (1982) 284 B.M.J. 1323, at p. 1325. This is the second of three excellent articles on the New Zealand scheme by Richard Smith, assistant editor of the B.M.J. See (1982) 284 B.M.J. 1243–5, 1323–5, 1457–9.

13. For detailed studies of the New Zealand and Swedish schemes in the 1970s see the Pearson Report, Vol. 3.

14. See Richard Smith, op. cit.; and for a detailed survey see G. Palmer, *Compensation for Incapacity: A Study of Law and Social Change in New Zealand and Australia*, O.U.P., Wellington, 1979.

15. [1983] 2 All E.R. 245.

16. [1981] 1 W.L.R. 246 H.L.

17. [1985] 2 W.L.R. 480 H.L.

18. See C. Oldertz, 'The Swedish Patient Insurance Scheme: 8 years of experience' (1984) 52 *Medico-Legal Journal* 43–59; D. Brahams, 'No Fault Compensation: Reform of Present System Overdue' [1985] *The Lancet* 1 1403–4.

19. See Brahams, op. cit.

20. ibid.

21. ibid.

22. Treatment would be defined to include treatment given to the mother and injuring the child. Consideration of the implications of ante-natal treatment would be required, e.g. (1) would treatment necessary for the mother but injuring the child be excluded? (2) what about pre-conception injury to either parent?

23. For detailed discussion of proposals for a no-fault scheme for drugs see A. L. Diamond and D. R. Lawrence, 'Product Liability in respect of drugs' (1985) 290 B.M.J. 365–8.

Chapter 10: Pregnancy and Childbirth

1. For a thorough discussion of the legal implications of the thalidomide tragedy see H. Teff and C. Munro, *Thalidomide: The Legal Aftermath*, Saxon House, London, 1976. And see Chapter 7.

2. Liability at common law was conceded in *Williams* v. *Luft*, *The Times*, 14 February 1978; and see *McKay* v. *Essex A.H.A.* [1982] 2 All E.R. 771.

3. *S.* v. *Distillers Co.* [1970] 1 W.L.R. 114.

4. On the difficulties in proving causation of birth defects see the Report of the Royal Commission on Civil Liability and Personal Injury (Pearson Report) Cmnd. 7054 (1978) paras. 1441–52, and see the essay 'Ante-Natal Injuries'

by S. A. M. McLean in S. A. M. McLean (ed.), *Legal Issues in Medicine*, Gower, Aldershot, 1981.

5. She is liable for injuries caused through negligent driving of a vehicle on the road; s. 2. A claim against the mother was in general seen as (a) not likely to be pursued by the child within a happy family relationship. The child would have to act through a 'next friend'. The mother would not proceed against herself. The father would do so only where the marriage had broken down, and (b) women are subject to such contradictory advice as to the management of pregnancy that establishing negligence would be extremely difficult. Negligence while driving a car, by contrast, is easy to prove, and in reality the claim would be against the mother's insurers.

6. The mother may be able to claim for the pain and suffering of miscarriage or stillbirth.

7. *The Times*, 26 July 1986; the hospital conceded liability.

8. See the defences provided by s. 1 (4) and s. 1 (7) below at pp. 167–8.

9. On drug-related damage generally, see Chapter 7.

10. [1983] 1 All E.R. 416.

11. [1982] 2 All E.R. 771.

12. It has been argued that the Act does not apply to a 'wrongful life' claim. The Act provides a scheme to compensate for disability inflicted by human error, not to a claim for allowing a disabled foetus to be born at all. The argument is of academic interest only. For the Court of Appeal were adamant that at common law no such action lay either.

13. See *Lazenvnick* v. *General Hospital of Munro City Inc. Civ. Act* 78–1259 Cmnd. Pa., 13 August 1980.

14. At p. 787.

15. *The Times*, 3 January 1983.

16. [1984] 3 All E.R. 1044.

17. See p. 1048.

18. At p. 1053.

19. *Emeh* v. *Kensington, Chelsea and Fulham A.H.A.* (above, note 15).

20. *Lion Laboratories Ltd* v. *Evans* [1984] 2 All E.R. 417.

21. Nurses, Midwives and Health Visitors Act 1979, s. 17. An exception is made for emergencies to protect family, policemen and ambulance crew from liability for helping in emergencies. For thorough discussion of the monopoly on childbirth see J. M. Eekelaar and R. W. J. Dingwall, 'Some Legal Issues of Obstetric Practice' [1984] J.S.W.L. p. 258, and J. Finch, 'Paternalism and Professionalism in Childbirth' (1982) 132 N.L.J. pp. 995 and 1011.

22. For further discussion of this case see Finch, op. cit.

23. *R.* v. *Senior* (1832) 1 Mood. C.C. 346; and see *R.* v. *Bateman* (1925) 19 Cr. App. R. 8.

24. See Finch, op. cit., pp. 995–6.

25. Eekelaar and Dingwall, op. cit.

26. See pp. 139–40.

27. *Kralj* v. *McGrath* [1986] 1 All E.R. 54.
28. *Whitehouse* v. *Jordan* [1981] 1 W.L.R. 246 H.L.
29. Eekelaar and Dingwall, op. cit., pp. 264–6.
30. s. 1(2).
31. Eekelaar and Dingwall, op. cit., p. 265.
32. See Eekelaar and Dingwall, op. cit., p. 270.

Chapter 11: Problems of Infertility

1. Report of the Committee of Inquiry into Human Fertilization and Embryology, Cmnd. 9314 (1984): The Warnock Report.
2. A body of distinguished lawyers who keep the current state of the law under review and recommend reform; see the Law Commissions Act 1965. The Law Commission's proposals *re* A.I.D. children are to be found in Law Com. Report *Illegitimacy*, No. 118 (1982); Law Com. Working Paper No. 74, *Family Law, Illegitimacy* (1979).
3. pp. 25–6.
4. On the ethics of extending A.I.D. to unmarried women, see J. K. Mason and R. A. McCall Smith, *Law and Medical Ethics*, Butterworths, London, 1983, pp. 34–6.
5. p. 16.
6. *MacLennan* v. *MacLennan* 1958 SC 105.
7. Children Act 1975, s. 26.
8. p. 15 and pp. 24–5.
9. pp. 24–5.
10. See Chapter 10, pp. 164–5.
11. *L.* v. *L.* [1949] P. 211.
12. At p. 55.
13. At p. 23.
14. *The Times*, 2 April 1984.
15. See Chapter 6, pp. 87 ff.
16. [1984] 3 All E.R. 1044.
17. See Chapter 10 of the Report.
18. At pp. 63–4.
19. At p. 37.
20. At p. 40.
21. At p. 38.
22. Surrogacy Arrangements Act 1985.
23. At p. 46.
24. s. 50.
25. *In re a Baby*, *The Times*, 15 January 1985.
26. *A.* v. *C.* (1978) 8 Fam. Law 170.

Notes

Chapter 12: Abortion

1. *R.* v. *Sockett* (1908) 72 J.P. 428.
2. *R.* v. *Whitchurch* (1890) 24 Q.B.D. 420.
3. *R.* v. *Bourne* [1939] 1 K.B. 687.
4. Report of the Committee on the Working of the Abortion Act (Cmnd. 5579).
5. In *McKay* v. *Essex A.H.A.* [1982] 2 W.L.R. 890 (see above, p. 167), a mother claimed that had tests for German measles been properly conducted, she would have known that she had the disease, and had an abortion. Her claim for negligence resulting in the birth of her handicapped daughter is still proceeding.
6. *R.* v. *Smith (John)* [1974] 1 W.L.R. 1510 C.A.
7. In *R.* v. *Price* [1969] 1 Q.B. 541, a prosecution for criminal abortion was brought against a doctor who inserted an I.U.D. into a woman who was some months pregnant. The prosecution failed because it was not proved that he knew her to be pregnant.
8. H.C. Official Report, 10 May 1983, Col. 238–9.
9. Prosecution of Offences Regulations, 1985.
10. Exchange of letters with Renée Short M.P. See V. Tunkel, 'Abortion: how early, how late, how legal' [1979] 2 Brit. Med. J. 253.
11. Glanville Williams, *Textbook on Criminal Law*, 1st edn, p. 264; but he modifies this view substantially in the 2nd edn, see p. 304.
12. *The Times*, 1 June 1984.
13. *The Times*, 2 June 1984.
14. *R.* v. *West* (1848) 2 Cox C.C. 500.
15. *Royal College of Nursing* v. *D.H.S.S.* [1981] A.C. 800.
16. [1979] Q.B. 276.
17. [1980] 3 E.H.R.R. 408.
18. *Re P. (A Minor)* (1981) 80 L.G.R. 301.
19. [1985] 3 All E.R. 402, H.L.
20. See Chapter 14.
21. See Chapter 14.

Chapter 13: The Handicapped Newborn: Whose Rights? Whose Decision?

1. Medical News (1981) 283 Brit. Med. J. 567.
2. See, in particular, J. K. Mason and R. A. McCall Smith, *Law and Medical Ethics*, Butterworths, London, 1983, Chapter 7.
3. J. Lorber, 'Results of the Treatment of Myelomengole', *Developmental Medicine and Child Neurology*, 1971; and 'Spina Bifida Cystica', *Archives of Disease in Childhood*, 1972.
4. See Jonathan Glover, *Causing Death and Saving Lives*, Pelican, Harmondsworth, 1977, Chapter 12. And see earlier in Chapter 2 of this book.
5. *Re B.* [1981] 1 W.L.R. 1421.
6. *The Times*, 6 October 1981.

7. See 'Dr Leonard Arthur: His Trial and its Implications' (1981) 283 Brit. Med. J. 1340; H. Beynon, 'Doctors as Murderers' [1982] Crim. L.R. 17; M. Gunn and J. C. Smith, 'Arthur's case and the right to life of a Down's Syndrome child' [1985] Crim. L.R. 705.

8. Some dispute exists as to the moment in childbirth when this occurs. The child need not have breathed apparently. See *R.* v. *Poulton* (1832) 5 C. & P. 329, and *R.* v. *Brain* (1834) 6 C. & P. 349; and see J. C. Smith and B. Hogan, *Criminal Law*, 5th edn, p. 274.

9. See (1981) 283 Brit. Med. J. 1340, 1341.

10. *R.* v. *Adams* [1957] Crim. L.R. 365, discussed more fully in Chapter 20. See also Lord Devlin's account of the trial, *Easing the Passing* (1985).

11. Children and Young Persons Act 1933, s. 1(1).

12. *R.* v. *Lowe* [1973] Q.B. 702.

13. *R.* v. *Senior* [1899] 1 Q.B. 823.

14. *R.* v. *Gibbins and Proctor* (1918) 13 Cr. App. Rep. 134.

15. Children and Young Persons Act 1969 s. 1(2).

16. As happened in *Re B.* (the Baby Alexandra case).

17. See Beynon, op. cit., pp. 27–8.

18. See Rachels (1975) 292 New Eng. J. Med. 78.

19. (1981) 78 Law Soc. Gaz. 1342.

20. *Law and Medical Ethics*, 1983, p. 89.

21. (1983) Journal of Medical Ethics 18.

22. See Chapter 20.

Chapter 14: Doctors and Child Patients

1. *Gillick* v. *West Norfolk and Wisbech A.H.A.* [1985] 3 All E.R. 402 H.L.

2. See P. D. Skegg, 'Consent to Medical Procedures on Minors' (1973) 36 M.L.R. 370, pp. 370–75.

3. N.H.S. (General Medical and Pharmaceutical Services) Regulations 1974, S.I. 1974/160 as amended by S.I. 1975/719. As to persons under 16 away from the parental home, see Lord Fraser in *Gillick* (above) at p. 408.

4. Mental Health Act 1983 s. 131(2).

5. [1984] 1 All E.R. 365 (Woolf J.).

6. [1985] 1 All E.R. 533, C.A.

7. At p. 540.

8. The Court of Appeal invoked the ancient common law concept of the age of discretion as relevant to determine parental rights to physical control of their children. This was set at 16 for girls and 14 for boys.

9. [1985] 3 All E.R. 402.

10. At p. 422.

11. *R.* v. *D.* [1984] 2 All E.R. 449.

12. At p. 432.

13. At p. 413.

14. See Glanville Williams, 'The Gillick Saga I and II' (1985) 135 N.L.J. 116 and 1180.

15. *In Re P. (A Minor)* (1982) 80 L.G.R. 301.

16. At p. 425. For trenchant criticism see Glanville Williams, op. cit.

17. See Chapter 3, pp. 38–9.

18. G.M.C. 'Bluebook' *Professional Conduct: Fitness to Practise*, August 1983, p. 20.

19. *Professional Conduct: Fitness to Practise*, April 1985, p. 21.

20. See the *Sunday Times*, 16 February 1986, for G.M.C. ruling and critical comment. But has anything really changed? In 1971 Dr Browne was acquitted of professional misconduct after he informed the parents of a girl of 16 of her request for contraception. The G.M.C. found he acted 'in the girl's best interests'. *G.M.C.* v. *Browne*, *The Times*, 6 and 8 March 1971. See J. K. Mason and R. A. McCall Smith, *Law and Medical Ethics* Butterworths, London, 1983, p. 103; *Handbook on Medical Ethics* B.M.A. (1984), p. 20.

21. 'Emergency, parental neglect, abandonment of the child or inability to find the parent are examples of exceptional situations justifying the doctor proceeding to treat the child without parental knowledge and consent . . .' *per* Lord Scarman in *Gillick* v. *West Norfolk and Wisbech A.H.A.* (above), p. 424.

22. *Per* Lord Fraser at p. 410 in *Gillick*.

23. Children and Young Persons Act 1933, s. 1(1).

24. *R.* v. *Senior* [1899] 1 Q.B. 283.

25. At p. 432.

26. See Chapter 13.

27. *Re Phillip B.* App. 156 Cal Rptr 48 (1979).

28. There is some slight authority pre-*Gillick* that treatment of a minor capable of consenting but who refuses consent may lawfully be continued on the basis of parental consent: see Skegg, op. cit., p. 376. I believe this to be no longer good law after *Gillick*.

29. See Skegg op. cit. p. 377.

30. See Chapter 18, pp. 288–9.

31. See Chapter 17, pp. 275–6.

31. See Chapter 17, pp. 271–2.

32. [1976] 1 All E.R. 326.

33. At p. 335.

Chapter 15: General Practice

1. s. 29(1). And see the Health Services Act 1980, s. 1(7) and Sched. I.

2. See now the Health and Social Security Act 1984, Sched. 3.

3. National Health Service Act 1977, s. 30(1); Health Services Act 1980, s. 1(7) and Sched. I.

4. As to experience and qualifications demanded of G.P.s, they must complete a course of training and apply for a certificate from the Joint Committee on Postgraduate Training for General Practice. Between 1981 and 1985 fewer

than 15 out of 7,000 applications were refused; see N.H.S. Vocational Training Regulations 1979, S. I. 1979 1644; 1980 No. 1900; 1981 No. 1790; 1984 No. 215.

5. See the N.H.S. (General Medical and Pharmaceutical Services) Regulations 1974 S. I. No. 160 Sched. I as amended by amending regulations S. I. 1975 No. 719; 1976 No. 1407; 1980 No. 288; 1982 No. 1283.

6. See, for example, *Nickolls* v. *Ministry of Health*, *The Times*, 4 February 1955 (surgeon working on while fatally ill).

7. S. I. 1974 No. 160 Sched. I. para. 3.

8. See *Hucks* v. *Cole*, *The Times*, 9 May 1968.

9. *Chin Keow* v. *Government of Malaysia* [1967] 1 W.L.R. 813.

10. *Coles* v. *Reading and District H.M.C.*, *The Times*, 30 January 1963.

11. Recounted in 'A Costly Oversight for Pharmacists' (1982) Vol. 132 N.L.J. p. 176.

12. *The Times*, 9 May 1968.

13. *The Times*, 6 November 1985.

14. The patients the doctor undertakes to treat within the N.H.S. are defined in S. I. 1974 No. 160 Sched. I. para. 4.

15. ibid., para. 4 (h).

16. *Barnes* v. *Crabtree*, *The Times*, 1 and 2 November 1955.

17. P. C. Nathan and A. R. Barrowclough, *Medical Negligence*, Butterworths, London, 1957, p. 38.

18. *Edler* v. *Greenwich and Deptford H.M.C.*, *The Times*, 7 March 1953.

19. *Kavanagh* v. *Abrahamson* (1964) 108 Sol. Jo. 320.

20. See S. I. 1974 No. 160 paras. 16, 17, 25 and 26.

21. Because of the doctrine of vicarious liability discussed earlier in Chapter 6.

22. See Chapter 6, pp. 89–90; and see the G.P.'s terms of service S. I. 1974 No. 160 para. 17 as amended by S. I. 1982 No. 1283.

23. S. I. 1974 No. 160 Reg. 17 (3,500 for single doctor; 4,500 for doctor in partnership subject to an average of 3,500 per partner).

24. S. I. 1974 No. 160 Reg. 18; and see S. I. 1982 No. 1283.

25. S. I. 1974 Sched. I. Part I. para. 9.

26. See Chapter 1.

27. The *Sunday Times*, 7 July 1985.

28. For a G.P.'s perspective on the F.P.C. procedure, see J. Oldroyd, 'Any Complaints' (1981) 282 B.M.J. 29, 117, 193.

29. See National Health Service (Service Committees and Tribunals) Regulations 1974 S. I. 1974 No. 455.

30. Reg. 4(1).

31. *Family Practitioner Services: Complaints Investigation Procedures*. Consultation Document, D.H.S.S., August 1986.

32. Reg. 10.

33. See National Health Service Act 1977, s. 46 and Sched. 9.

34. Reg. 11.

Notes

35. National Health Service Act 1977, Sched. 9.
36. See Annual Report of the Council on Tribunals 1981–2, 1982–3, H.C. 64.
37. *Evans* v. *G.M.C.*, reported in (1985) Vol. 1 *Professional Negligence* p. 114.
38. *Rodgers* v. *G.M.C.* reported in (1985) Vol. 1 *Professional Negligence* p. 111.
39. See Chapter I, pp. 12–3.
40. See Annual Report of the Health Service Commissioner 1979–80 H.C. 650 at pp. 65–7.
41. S. I. 1974 No. 160 Sched. I. Part I. para. 10.
42. See the Generic Substitution (National Health Service) Bill, a Private Member's Bill which never got past a first reading in the Commons.
43. N.H.S. (General Medical and Pharmaceutical Services) Amendment Regulations 1985 S. I. No. 290, 1985.
44. S. I. No. 803, 1985.
45. Sale of Goods Act 1979. Supply of Goods and Services Act 1982. See A. P. Bell, 'The Doctor and the Supply of Goods and Services Act' [1984] Legal Studies 175.
46. See the *Guardian*, 11 February 1986.
47. *Primary Health Care: An Agenda for Discussion* (Cmnd 9771), H.M.S.O.
48. See above, note 31.

Chapter 16: Family Planning

1. *Sutherland* v. *Stopes* [1925] A.C. 47 at p. 68.
2. *Bravery* v. *Bravery* [1954] 3 All E.R. 59 at pp. 67–8.
3. See Chapter 12, pp. 202–3.
4. See Chapter 14.
5. *R.* v. *Donovan* [1934] 2 K.B. 498.
6. See the discussion on this matter in the essay on 'Sterilization' by S. A. M. McLean and T. D. Campbell in S.A.M. McLean (ed.), *Legal Issues in Medicine*, Gower, Aldershot, 1981.
7. *Baxter* v. *Baxter* [1948] A.C. 274.
8. ibid.
9. See P. M. Bromley, *Family Law*, 6th edn, Butterworths, London, 1981, p. 87.
10. *Bravery* v. *Bravery* (above), p. 62.
11. *Baxter* v. *Baxter* (above).
12. *The Times*, 19 April 1972; see Bromley, op. cit., p. 206.
13. *Sullivan* v. *Sullivan* [1970] 2 All E.R. 168 C.A.
14. *The Times*, 7 November 1981.
15. *Gold* v. *Haringey A.H.A.*, *The Times*, 17 June 1986.
16. See the *Guardian*, 2 August 1986.
17. See the *Guardian*, 23 July 1983, p. 24.
18. *Blyth* v. *Bloomsbury A.H.A.*, *The Times*, 24 May 1985 (Mrs Blyth won compensation in negligence. She knew the injection was Depo-Provera. She was not warned of its side-effects.) See Chapter 4, p. 65.

19. See the discussion in *The Times* of 13 April 1983, p. 8. And see Chapter 7, p. 114.
20. [1980] 7 Current Law S. 44.
21. *Wells* v. *Surrey Area Health Authority*, *The Times*, 29 July 1978.
22. *Pritchard* v. *J. H. Cobden Ltd*, *The Times*, 27 August 1986.
23. See Chapter 14, p. 238.
24. *The Times*, 3 January 1983.
25. *Udale* v. *Bloomsbury A.H.A.*, [1983] 2 All E.R. 522.
26. *Thake* v. *Maurice* [1984] 2 All E.R. 513.
27. [1985] 3 All E.R. 1044.
28. [1984] 2 All E.R. 513.
29. [1986] 1 All E.R. 497, and see *Eyre* v. *Measday* [1986] 1 All E.R. 488.
30. *The Times*, 17 June 1986.

Chapter 17: Organ Transplantation

1. Dr Antony Wing, Ed. European Dialysis and Transplantation Association. *The Times*, 20 March 1980; also *The Times*, 2 April 1984.
2. *The Times*, 19 May 1977.
3. It is now being suggested, however, that the recent change in the law making the wearing of seat belts compulsory has reduced considerably the number of car accident donors.
4. The government has commissioned a cost-benefit report into the heart transplant programmes at Papworth and Harefield hospitals.
5. (1969) 62 Proc. Roy. Soc. Med. 633, 634.
6. In one American case a court, not surprisingly, refused to *order* the only possible donor to submit to a bone marrow transplant; *McFall* v. *Shimp* (1978).
7. Curran, 'A Problem of Consent: Kidney Transplantation in Minors' (1959) 34 N.Y. Univ. L. Rev. 891.
8. *The Times*, 25 January 1977.
9. Council of Europe Resolution (78) 29. Art 6.
10. *Strunk* v. *Strunk* (1969) 35 A.L.R. (3d) 683.
11. *Little* v. *Little* (1979) 576 S.W. 2d 493.
12. In *R.* v. *Lennox-Wright* (1973) Crim L. Rev. an unqualified person removed eyes from a cadaver for further use in another hospital. He was successfully prosecuted for contravening s. 1(4) Human Tissue Act 1961, which prohibits removal save 'by a fully registered medical practitioner'. But see Kennedy (1976) 16 Med. Sci. Law 49.
13. Human Tissue Act 1961, s. 1(1).
14. ibid., s. 1(2).
15. This is the view of the D.H.S.S., who require the N.H.S. hospital to designate one of their officers to exercise this function. D.H.S.S. 1975 H.S.C. 15 (156).
16. *The Times*, 8 September 1976.

17. H.C. (77) 28 August 1975.
18. A kidney which is removed from the body and 'cooled' may be kept for at least 12 hours and may function satisfactorily for as long as 2 days, but the longer the delay the greater the damage to the kidney.
19. For a description of the system in France, which has not been entirely satisfactory, see Redmond-Cooper, 'Transplants Opting-out or In – the Implications' (1984) 134 N.L.J. 648.
20. What has to be overcome is apathy. A recent survey revealed that 66 per cent of people would be willing to donate kidneys after death, but of those only 20 per cent actually carried a donor card.
21. Royal Commission on Civil Liability and Compensation for Personal Injury (1978) Cmnd. 7054, para. 1276.
22. cf. *Colton* v. *New York Hospital* (1979) 414 N.Y.S. 866.
23. See R. M. Titmuss, *The Gift Relationship: From Human Blood to Social Policy,* Allen & Unwin, London, 1971.
24. *The Times*, 29 September 1976.

Chapter 18: Medical Research

1. On the debate as to the ethics of the case among doctors, see M. Phillips and J. Dawson, *Doctors' Dilemmas*, Harvester Press, London, 1984, pp. 63–74.
2. For vigorous criticism of ethical committees and professional attitudes see Carolyn Faulder, *Whose Body Is It?*, Virago, London, 1985, pp. 95–100; and see the periodical literature cited by her.
3. See again the Declaration of Helsinki, reproduced in full in appendices to Phillips and Dawson, op. cit., and Faulder, op. cit.
4. See Chapter 4.
5. *Chatterton* v. *Gerson* [1981] Q.B. 432.
6. *Sidaway* v. *Board of Governors of the Bethlem Royal and the Maudsley Hospital* [1985] 2 W.L.R. 480, H.L.
7. *Gold* v. *Haringey A.H.A.*, *The Times*, 17 June 1986.
8. *Halushka* v. *University of Saskatchewan* (1965) 52 W.W.R. 608.
9. On the problems of the development of a doctrine of 'informed consent' in the research context see J. K. Mason and R. A. McCall Smith, *Law and Medical Ethics*, Butterworths, London, 1983, pp. 201–3.
10. *Gillick* v. *West Norfolk and Wisbech A.H.A.* [1985] 3 All E.R. 392; see Chapter 14.
11. *Re D.* [1976] 1 All E.R. 326; see Chapter 14, p. 239.
12. See P. D. G. Skegg, 'Consent to Medical Procedures on Minors' (1973) 36 M.L.R. 370, pp. 379–80.
13. See *S.* v. *S.* [1972] A.C. 24; and see R. H. Nicholson (ed.), *Medical Research with Children, Ethics, Law and Practice*, O.U.P., Oxford, 1986.
14. On experimentation and children generally, see P. D. G. Skegg, 'English law relating to experimentation on children' (1977) Vol. 2 *Lancet* pp. 754–5; G. Dworkin, 'Legality of consent to non-therapeutic medical research on

infants and young children' (1978) Vol. 53, *Archives of Disease in Childhood*, pp. 443–6.

15. For trenchant criticism on ethical and legal grounds of randomized clinical trials, see Faulder, op. cit., in particular Chapters 5–7.

16. See the useful discussion in Phillips and Dawson, op. cit., pp. 61–71.

17. *Clark* v. *MacLennan* [1983] 1 All E.R. 416.

18. See Chapter 6 on the problems of litigation.

19. See Chapter 9.

20. Royal Commission on Civil Liability and Compensation for Personal Injury, Cmnd. 7054 H.M.S.O. 1978 paras. 1340–41.

21. See Chapter 7.

22. See the deliberations and recommendations of the C.I.B.A. Foundation Study Group [1980] B.M.J. 1172–5.

23. See Chapter 7, p. 113.

24. See Chapter 8, p. 129.

Chapter 19: Defining Death

1. See Law of Property Act 1925, s. 184.

2. Inheritance Tax Act 1984; Finance Tax Act 1986, s. 101, Sched. 19.

3. e.g. *Lim Poh Choo* v. *Camden A.H.A.* [1980] A.C. 174.

4. British Transplantation Society (1975) 1 B.M.J. 251, 253.

5. 'A Definition of Irreversible Coma' (1968) 205 J.A.M.A. 337.

6. See the *Guardian*, 6 August 1986 at p. 11; in particular, concern was expressed that the 24 hour gap between sets of tests for 'brain death' was not always observed.

7. *Tucker* v. *Lower* (1972).

8. See p. 276.

9. [1982] 2 All E.R. 422.

10. See Skegg, (1976) 2 J. Med. Ethics 190–91; Kennedy, (1977) 3 J. Med. Ethics 5.

Chapter 20: Death, Dying and the Medical Practitioner

1. e.g. Green, 'Health Cutbacks and Death with Dignity: A Right Wing Trend in Medicine Today', *Radical Community Medicine* [1985], No. 21, 20–26.

2. The conviction in that case was eventually quashed because of a misdirection by the trial judge to the jury, and so the issue faded from public notice.

3. *R.* v. *Adams* [1957] Crim. L. Rev. 773.

4. (1977) 66 Cr. App. R. 97.

5. [1984] Q.B. 795.

6. It should be noticed, of course, that it may not always be an easy issue to determine whether a person is clinically or legally competent.

7. See Jackson and Youngner, 'Patient Autonomy and "Death With Dignity"' (1979) 299 New Eng. J. Med. 404.

8. (1909) 26 T.L.R. 139.

9. cf. *Attorney-General of Canada* v. *Notre Dame Hospital* (1984) 8 C.R.R. 382; *Freeman* v. *Home Office* [1984] 2 W.L.R. 130.
10. (1978) 379 So. 2d. 359.
11. See also *Bartling* v. *Superior Court of California* (1985) 209 Calif. Rep. 220.
12. *Barber* v. *Superior Court* [(1983) 195 Calif. Rptr. 484].
13. Particularly in cases of severely handicapped newborn children, which are discussed in Chapter 13.
14. *In re Quinlan* (1976) 355 A. 2d. 647.
15. This paved the way for the decisions such as *Satz* v. *Perlmutter* which have already been discussed.
16. *Superintendent of Belchertown* v. *Saikewicz* (1977) N.E. 2d 417.
17. See also *Storar* (1981) 420 N.E. 2d 64 and *Spring* (1980) 405 N.E. 2d 115.
18. See Jennett, 'Inappropriate Use of Intensive Care' [1985] B.M.J. and authorities cited therein.
19. Bassom, 'The Decision to Resuscitate Slowly; Troubling Problems in Medical Ethics', *Ethics, Humanism and Medicine*, Vol. 111, 116 (1981).
20. See *Dinnerstein* (1978) 380 N.E. 2d 134.
21. Gulati, Bhan, Horan, 'Cardiopulmonary resuscitation of old people' (1983) 2 Lancet 267.
22. Although this must be balanced against Art. 3, which includes the right to be safeguarded against inhuman and degrading treatment.
23. *Bartling* v. *Superior Court of California* (1985) 209 Cal. Rep. 2d 220.
24. *R.* v. *Reed* [1982] Crim. App. 819; see also *Attorney-General* v. *Able* [1983] 3 W.L.R. 845.

Chapter 21: Reviewing and Reforming the Law

1. See Ian Kennedy, *The Unmasking of Medicine*, Allen & Unwin, London, 1981, Chapter 6, 'Let's Kill All the Lawyers'.
2. See the Preface to J. K. Mason and R. A. McCall Smith, *Law and Medical Ethics*, Butterworths, London, 1983.
3. See the judicial criticism advanced as the way expert evidence was 'settled' by counsel in *Whitehouse* v. *Jordan* [1981] 1 All E.R. 287 (in Chapter 6, pp. 95–6).
4. *Lee* v. *South West Thames R.H.A.* [1985] 1 All E.R. 385 (in Chapter 6, pp. 92–3).
5. See full discussion in Chapter 8, pp. 133–4.
6. *Sidaway* v. *Board of Governors of the Bethlem Royal and the Maudsley Hospital* [1985] 2 W.L.R. 480, see Chapter 4.
7. *Gillick* v. *West Norfolk and Wisbech A.H.A.* [1985] 1 All E.R. 533, see Chapter 14.
8. See Chapter 13.
9. See Kennedy (1984) 47 M.L.R., pp. 467–9.

Index

abortion
and the Church, 19, 20–21
criminal, 199–200
and confidentiality, 38, 40
debate on morality, 8
on demand or request, 201
and double effect principle, 20–21, 308–9
and embryos, 190
fathers and, 208–9
and foetal abnormalities, 163, 164, 165, 170–71, 187
from foetus to baby, 204–6
girls under 16, 209, 230, 235, 236–7, 239–41
and the law, 8, 23–4, 29
mother's consideration of, 167–8
notification, 44
nurses and, 207–8
post-coital birth control, 202–3
research on, ix
and Roman Catholics, 20, 21, 210, 235, 237
and sterilization, 267, 268, 269, 271
Abortion Act 1967, 29, 167, 199–204 passim, 207, 208, 209, 212, 221, 320
Accident Compensation Corporation, 148, 149
accidents at work, 44
Ackers, Margaret, 175
Ackner, L. J., 165, 167
Administration of Justice Act 1982, 101, 102
Adoption Act 1958, 196
advertising (by doctors), 250–51, 253
A.I.D.S., 32, 39, 40, 234, 288

alcoholism, 11, 12, 40, 253
American Medical Association, 284
amniocentesis, 163–4, 165, 167, 170, 171, 206, 212
anaesthesia
and Caesarian surgery, 175
in dentistry, 84
negligence in, 79, 137, 138
and pregnancy, 158
ante-natal clinics, attendance at, 174
aortagrams, 60
Arthur, Dr Leonard, 8, 214–17 passim, 219, 332–3
Artificial Insemination by Donor (A.I.D.), 20, 180–83 passim, 185, 193, 194
Artificial Insemination by Husband (A.I.H.), 184–5
aspirin, and pregnancy, 162
assault, 9, 129, 130, 168, 225, 229
Association for the Victims of Medical Accidents (A.V.M.A.), 95
Association of British Pharmaceutical Industries (A.P.B.I.), 120
avascular necrosis, 80
Avory, J., 38

babies, handicapped
see newborn, handicapped
'Baby Alexandra' case, 213, 217, 235, 236
Barnes, Dame Josephine, 96
Barnet Social Services, 195, 196
Barraclough, Anthony, Q.C., 134
battery, 53, 55–6, 58, 59, 66, 166, 177, 225, 228, 229, 237, 287

365

Benedictin, 160
births and deaths, notification of, 44
blood tests
  and foetal disabilities, 167
  and German measles, 254
blood transfusions, and Jehovah's
    Witnesses, 67–8, 222, 233, 234,
    312
brachial palsy, 75
Bradlaugh, Charles, 259
Brahams, Diana, 219, 220, 221
Brahams, Malcolm, 219, 220, 221
brain damage
  during operation, 136–7, 254
  and euthanasia, 322–3
  see also Whitehouse v. Jordan in
    Table of Cases
brain death, 282, 298–304 passim,
    316
brain surgery, side-effects, 151
breach of confidence
  compulsory disclosure, 43–5
  disclosure in patient's interests, 37
  disclosure in the public interest,
    38–41
  and the G.M.C., 35–9 passim, 43,
    47, 48, 49
  the law, 33–6
  law reform, 42–3
  and negligence, 41–2
  N.H.S. procedures, 47–9
  patients' access to records, 45–7
Breach of Confidence (Law
    Commission), 42
Bridge, Lord, 62–3
British Medical Association, 135
  and consent forms, 57
  and drugs lists, 255
  and embryo research, 24
  and G.M.C., 12, 254
  and health records, 46
  and Hospital Complaints
    Procedures Act, 126
  and medical research, 285
  and 'no-fault' scheme, 18, 145, 147
  and potential liability of G.P., 249

proposals of greater incentives for
    G.P.s, 258
British Medical Journal, 30, 212
British Paediatric Association, 205,
    290
British Rail, 138
British Transplantation Society, 281,
    299–300
Butler-Sloss, J., 209, 230

Caesarian surgery, 7–8, 14, 70, 73, 96,
    97, 132, 147, 149, 175, 176, 177,
    267
California Natural Death Act, 323
Campaign for Freedom of
    Information, 47
cardiac arrest, 298, 299
cardiac disease, and pregnancy, 168
casualty department, duty of care,
    70–71
Chartered Society of
    Physiotherapists, 74
Chemie Grunenthal, 105, 111
chemotherapy, 151, 318
child abuse
  and confidentiality, 32, 39, 43
  and defamation, 40
child patients
  confidentiality and children under
    16, 231–2
  consent to treatment, 225–6
  contraception and abortion,
    228–30, 259, 333
  criminal law, sexual intercourse and
    contraception, 230–31
  Family Law Reform Act 1969,
    222–3
  general problem of consent, 226–8
  Gillick case, 224–5
  limits of parental consent, 237–9
  objections to treatment, 236–7
  parents of younger children,
    232–5
  procedures to protect, 239–40
  role of the court, 235–6
childbirth, 173–7

children
  in medical research programmes,
    288–90
  as organ donors, 275–6
Children Act 1975, 197
Church of England, 21, 307
circumcision, 222, 239, 240
clinical judgment
  and the Health Service
    Commissioner, 133–4
  judging, 139–40
  professional review of, 135
clinical trials
  see medical research
cocaine, 255
Code of Practice for Organ
    Transplantation Surgery, 280–81
coma, 25, 27, 137, 298, 299, 303, 314,
    316, 317
Commission on Medicine, Law and
    Ethics (proposed), 327, 331–7
Committee on Safety of Medicines
    (C.S.M.), 106, 112, 113, 114–15,
    119, 266, 294
Confessions of a Surgeon (Mair), 307
Congenital Disabilities (Civil
    Liability) Act 1976, 157–60
    passim, 162–6 passim, 168, 176,
    177, 183, 187–8
Consent to Medical Care (Law
    Reform Commission), 333
consent to surgery
  definition of, 56–8
  emergencies, 66–8
  explaining operation risks, 58–63,
    132
  future of 'informed consent', 64–5
  negligence/battery, 55–6
  question of who operates, 65–6
contagious disease notification, 255
contraception
  see family planning
contraception in children under 16
  see child patients
Corneal Grafting Act 1952, 277
Corneal Tissue Act 1986, 277

corneal transplant, 283
coroner, role in organ
    transplantation, 279–80
Council of Europe Resolution on the
    Harmonization of
    Transplantation Legislation,
    275–6, 284
Council on Tribunals, 253
cystic fibrosis, 306
cystoscopy, 75

Dalkon Shield, 105, 106, 115, 264
Data Protection Act, 46–7, 48, 49
Davies Committee on Hospital
    Complaints Procedures Report
    1973, 126
Davies, J., 126
death
  competent patients: and the 'right'
    to die, 310–15
  definition of, 297–304
  and 'high-tech' equipment, 305
  'incompetent' patients, 315–16
  legislation, 320–24
  murder, suicide and assisting
    suicide, 308–10
  mental incompetence, 318–19
  resuscitation, 319
  unconscious, dying patients, 316–18
Debendox, 105, 160, 161, 162
Declaration of Geneva, 23, 32, 307
defamation, 40–41
Denning, Lord M. R., 38, 60, 73, 75,
    87–90 passim, 96, 99, 104, 259,
    260
dentists, 84, 251
Department of Health and Social
    Security (D.H.S.S.), 15, 44, 57,
    75, 106, 121, 122, 127, 128, 132,
    134, 169, 201, 224, 226, 231, 250,
    251, 256, 257, 293, 300, 328, 329,
    334, 335
Depo-Provera, 59, 65, 114, 265–6
deputizing services, 249
Devlin, Lord J., 215, 308, 309
Dewhurst, Professor Sir John, 96

Index

dialysis, 19, 20, 26, 28, 273
diethylstibestrol, 107
Diplock, Lord, 62, 63, 64
Director of Public Prosecutions
     (D.P.P.), 203, 213–14, 309
disseminated sclerosis, 306
Distillers, 105, 110–11, 112, 119
divorce, and family planning, 261–2
doctors
    adultery, 11, 12, 253
    delay in attendance, 129, 130
    and drink, 11, 12, 84, 253
    drug abuse, 11, 84, 253
    fraudulent, 9
    and *in vitro* fertilization, 186–8
    moral decisions, ix, 7–8, 20
    power of, 6–7, 8, 19
    suing over damaged newborn,
        162–3
    'superman' image, 5–6
Donaldson, Sir John, 74, 93, 330
donor cards, 283
double-effect principle, 20–21, 308–9
Down's syndrome, 163, 212–18
    passim, 236, 333
drug companies
    changing public view of, 105
    claims for special treatment, 107
    and drug-damaged child, 160–62
    liability of, 110, 258
    and no-fault schemes, 153
    and the Pill, 264
drug-induced injuries
    claims against the Minister and the
        C.S.M., 114–15
    claims brought abroad, 115–16
    the present law: contract, 107–9;
        negligence, 109–12; preventing
        injury, 112–14
    product liability and drugs, 106–7
    proposed reform: 'no fault'
        liability, 120; strict liability,
        116–20
    vaccine damage, 120–23, 144, 145
drug trials
    see medical research

drugs
    abuse in doctors, 11, 84, 253
    control of dangerous, 255
    and damage to embryo, 160–62
    dosage, 79, 245
    failure to supply, 245–6
    generic prescribing, 255
    and medical injuries, 152–3
    mucolytic, 256
    notification of abuse, 44
    and other medication, 78
    and Pearson Report, 144, 145
    reactions, 78
    and sperm/ovum, 165
    'white' and 'black' lists, 255–8
Dupuytren's contraction, 98

Edmund-Davis, Lord, 73, 274
egg donation, 19
electro-convulsive therapy, 60, 72
embryos
    freezing, 188–90
    health of, 157, 158
    research on, ix, 24, 29, 31, 190–92
    test-tube, 186, 187
    transplants, 192, 193, 195
'emergency cases', 246, 247
English law, 3–4
epilepsy
    and driving, 39, 40
    and sterilization, 131–2, 133, 238
episiotomy, 174–5
ethical committees, 285–6, 296, 337
European Commission of Human
        Rights, 208, 320–21
European Community Directive on
        Product Liability, 117, 118, 293
European Convention on Human
        Rights, 208, 320, 321
euthanasia
    and the Church, 19
    debate on, 20, 306–7
    and 'defining' death, 303
    involuntary, 23, 27–8, 317
    legislation, 320–24
    research on, ix

and resuscitation, 319
voluntary, 27, 221, 309–10, 317, 320, 321
Euthanasia Bill 1936, 321–2
Exit, 323

facial surgery, 95, 148, 149–50
Family Law Reform Act 1969, 222–3, 225, 226, 289
family planning
  compulsory, 268
  contraception, sterilization and marriage, 260–62
  contraceptives: patients' rights, 262–3
  and criminal law, 259–60
  Depo-Provera affair, 265–6
  paying for unplanned child, 268–70
  problems with the Pill, 263–4
  sterilization, 266–8
  vasectomy, 270–71
Family Planning Clinic, 82, 262
Family Practitioner Committee (F.P.C.), 46, 108, 243, 244, 246–55 passim, 338
Finlay, Viscount, 259
foetus
  aborted, 204, 205, 206
  injury to, 105, 107, 110, 111, 118, 119, 157, 160, 161
  killing, 21, 309
food poisoning, 44, 137
Fowler, Norman, 257
Fraser, Lord, 227, 228, 229, 231

General Dental Council, 84
General Medical Council (G.M.C.)
  and B.M.A., 12, 254
  and confidentiality, 35–9 passim, 43, 47, 48, 49, 296
  and contraception for children under 16, 16, 231, 232
  disciplining doctors, 253–4
  and doctors' advertising, 250–51, 253
  Health Committee, 10
  maintenance of standards, 3, 10, 330–31
  membership, 9–10
  and Privy Council, 10, 13
  Professional Conduct Committee, 10, 13
  and proposed Commission, 337
  and register of practitioners, 10
  and serious professional misconduct, 10–13
general practice
  deputies and locums, 249
  doctors: freedom to care, 254–8
  and drug-induced injuries, 160
  duty to attend, 246–7
  failure to attend and treat, 247–8
  Family Practitioner Committee, 251–2
  General Medical Council, 253–4
  hospital liaison with, 128, 129, 244–5
  and the law, 258
  liability, 249
  litigation, 89–90, 251
  N.H.S. Ombudsman, 254
  and negligence, 244–6
  patient's freedom to choose, 249–51
  terms of service, 242–4
generic prescribing, 255
genetic counselling, 39, 169–72
German measles, 164, 169, 170, 254, 265
Gillick, Victoria, ix, 35, 222–5 passim, 228–31 passim, 332
Griffiths, L. J., 34–5
Guardianship of Minors Act 1973, 197

haemophilia, 163, 169, 222, 238
Hailsham, Lord, 240
Halsbury, Earl of, 11
Handbook on Medical Ethics (B.M.A.), 267
handicapped
  care of, 129
  children and surgery, 236
  disability allowances for, 144

handicapped – *cont.*
    and transplantation, 276
    see also newborn, handicapped
Hardwick, Ben, 272
Harvard Medical School, 299
Havard, Dr, 221
Hawkins, J., 38
Health and Social Security Act 1984,
    15, 243
health authorities
    code of practice, 126–7
    and complaints, 128, 135–6
    in litigation, 87–8, 92, 93, 98, 102,
        103, 104
health circulars, 15
Health Minister
    and Depo-Provera, 266
    and drugs, 112–13, 114–15
    and F.P.C.s, 243, 252
    and hospital complaints procedure,
        125, 126, 137, 140
    and medical research, 295
    and medical records, 48
    and N.H.S., 15–16
    and proposed Commission, 334
    and transplants, 275
Health Service Commissioner (Health
        Ombudsman), 44, 54, 127,
        128–34, 138, 253, 254, 296, 331
Health Services Act 1980, 15
heart patients
    and the Pill, 263
    transplantation, 273, 280, 281
Heilbron, J., 238
Helsinki Declaration, 286, 287
hereditary disease/defects, and
        pregnancy, 169
heroin, 254, 308
'high-tech' medicine, 6, 8, 19, 173,
        305
hip-replacement surgery, 16, 131
Hippocrates, 19
Hippocratic Oath, 19, 32
Hodgkin's disease, 73, 74
hospices, 25
hospital complaints procedures

the Commissioner and clinical
        judgment, 133–4
the Commissioner and the courts,
        131–3
evaluating inquiry procedures,
        137–9
health authority inquiries, 136–7
Health Minister inquiries, 137
Health Service Commissioner, 127,
        129–31
initial complaints, 126–7
investigating a complaint, 128–9
judging clinical judgments, 139–40
professional review of clinical
        judgment, 135
reform, 330–31
Hospital Complaints Procedures Act
        1985, 125–6, 127, 131, 140,
        330–31
Hospital Ethics Committee, 317, 318,
        321
hospitals
    arrangements for discharge, 129,
        130
    initial handling of complaints, 129,
        130
Hugh-Jones, Dr, 73, 74
Human Tissue Act 1961, 277–82
        passim, 300
Humphreys, Derek, 306
hunger-strikers, 311–12
hysterectomy, 56, 57, 193

in vitro fertilization, 186–90 *passim*,
        192, 195, 198
    see also test-tube babies
Infant Life (Preservation) Act 1929,
        204
infectious diseases, 44
    see also contagious disease
        notification
infertility
    A.I.D. (Artificial Insemination by
        Donor), 180–83 *passim*, 185
    A.I.D. and doctors' liability,
        183–4

A.I.H. (Artificial Insemination by Husband), 184–5
  female, 185–6
  freezing embryos, 188–90
  ova donation and embryo transplants, 192–5
  spare embryos and embryo research, 190–92
  surrogate mothers, 195–8
  test-tube babies and doctors' liability, 186–8
intra-uterine devices (I.U.D.), 202, 203, 262, 264

Jehovah's Witnesses, 67–8, 222, 233, 234, 310, 311
Joint Consultants' Committee, 135
Jordan, Mr (senior registrar), 73, 96, 144, 147, 148–9
Joseph, Sir Keith, 114
judges, and views of medical profession, 53
Jupp, J., 269

Kennedy, Ian, 6–7
kidnapping, 227
kidney transplants, 19, 272–6 *passim*, 279, 280, 281, 299

Lancet, 75
Lane, Dame Elizabeth, 200
Lane, Lord C. J., 301
Lane Committee, 200, 203
Latey, J., 197
law, state of, 17–18
Law Commission, 35, 42, 180, 182, 328, 336
Law Reform Commission (Canada), 324, 333
Law Society, 7, 104
Laws of England (Halsbury), 11
lesbians, 20, 182
Life, 29–30, 203
life-support machines, 24–5, 26–7, 281, 298, 299, 301, 302–3, 313–18 *passim*

Limitation Act 1980, 90
'Limitation of Treatment Bill', 219, 220, 221
litigation
  access to records, 91–3
  burden of proof on doctor, 97–100
  compensation, 100–104
  doctor-patient relationship, 326, 328
  and Health Service Commissioner, 131–3
  increase in, 325
  pre-trial medical examination, 93–4
  problems of, 84–5, 142, 325
  procedure, 86–90
  proving negligence, 95–7, 122
locums, 89, 249

Maclaren, Professor, 96
McShane, 309
McTavish, Miss, 307
Mair, Dr, 307
manslaughter
  convictions for, 84, 306
  and handicapped newborn, 216
  and medical authorities, 312
  and transplantation, 283
Mason, Professor, 220
mastectomy, 133
maternity care, and complaints, 129
Matrimonial and Family Proceedings Act 1984, 261
Maynard, Staff Nurse, 73–4, 78
mediastinoscopy, 73, 74
Medical Act 1983, 3, 8, 10, 12, 13
Medical Defence Union, 14, 57, 77, 78, 79, 86
Medical Practices Committees, 243
Medical Practitioners Union, 331
Medical Protection Society, 14, 57, 86
medical records, 107
  and clinical judgment, 133
  in general practice, 244–5
  and Health Service Commissioner, 129
  patients' access, 45–7, 91–3

medical research
  children in, 288–90
  compensation for mishap, 290
  and confidentiality, 295–6
  consent to participation in trials,
    286–8
  control of, 285–6
  injury from clinical trials, 144, 145
  monitoring, 294–5
  no-fault compensation, 293–4
  randomized clinical trials, 291–2
Medical Research Council, 24, 192,
    285, 295
medical students, 66, 131, 180, 285,
    287–8
Medicines Act 1968, 112, 113, 114,
    294, 295
Medicines Commission, 112–13, 114
Mengele, Dr Joseph, 5
menstrual extraction, 201, 202
Mental Health Act 1983, 276, 317
mental incompetence, 315–16,
    318–19
mental patients, ill-treatment of, 137
'mercy killing', 26, 306, 307, 308,
    322
Migril, 245
misadventure, 148–9
Misuse of Drugs Act, 44
mongolism
  see Down's syndrome
'morning-after' pill, 202, 203, 259
morphine, 308, 309
mucolytic drugs, 256
murder
  and confidentiality, 39, 41–2
  killing and letting die, 25–30
    passim, 307, 308–9, 314

National Health Service, 3, 14–16
  and complaints mechanisms, 125
  draft code on confidentiality, 295–6
  G.P.–patient relationship, 243
  maladministration issue, 129
  medical records, 46, 47–9
  and negligence actions, 70

National Health Service Act 1977,
    15–16, 127, 133, 137, 242–3
National Heart Hospital, 281
negligence
  and A.I.D., 183–4
  'accepted practice', 74–6
  ascertaining standard of care, 72–4
  and battery, 55, 56, 59
  and birth of damaged child, 157,
    158, 163, 164, 169, 170, 171
  and childbirth, 175
  criminal liability, 83–4
  diagnosis, 77–8
  doctors' fatigue, 81–2
  and drug-induced injuries, 109–12,
    114–15, 116, 118, 121, 122
  of drug manufacturer, 257
  duty of care, 70–71
  and G.P.s, 244–9 passim
  and hospital complaints
    procedures, 132, 136
  and the law, 53, 69–70, 98, 109–12,
    114–15, 116
  and medical research, 292, 293
  medical standards of care, 71–2
  nursing staff, 82–3
  operation performed by student, 66
  private patients, 83, 99
  proving, 95, 97, 100, 242
  and reform, 142, 143, 144, 149, 150,
    151, 154
  relating the injury to medical
    negligence, 80–81
  and sterilization, 267–81 passim
  test of, 60, 61
  and test-tube babies, 186–7, 188
  treatment, 78–80
Neill, L. J., 270
neonaticide, 212, 219
New Zealand, no-fault schemes in,
    145–50 passim
newborn, handicapped
  and A.I.D., 183–4, 185
  and abortion, 205, 206
  'Baby Alexandra', 213
  code of practice, 29

debate on keeping alive, 24
deliberate killing, 215–16
euthanasia and neonaticide, 211–13
and frozen embryo, 188–9
and *in vitro* fertilization, 186, 187, 188
proposals for legislation, 219–21
research on, ix
surgery, 19, 20, 21, 27
trial of Dr Arthur, 8, 214–15
withholding treatment, 216–19
Nicorette, 256
no-fault schemes, 144–54, 293–4, 327–30
N.S.P.C.C. (National Society for the Prevention of Cruelty to Children), 43
Nupercaine, 75
nursing staff
and abortion, 207–8
and negligence, 82–3

Offences Against the Person Act 1861, 199
On Dying Well (Church of England), 307
Opren, 105, 106, 115, 123
organ transplantation, 6
from cadavers, 276–81
contracting in or out, 282–3
controversy, 272
and defining death, 298, 302, 303
and heart patients, 273
and kidney patients, 19, 272–3
liability for mishaps, 283
live donors, 274–5
prospects for reform, 281–2
trafficking in organs, 284
ova donation, 192–5 *passim*

Pain, Peter, J., 163, 269
Panorama (TV programme), 300
Park, J., 268
Pearson, Lord, 144
Pearson Commission, 119–20, 122, 144–6, 283, 293–4

Peel, Professor Sir John, 96
Perjury Act 1911, 180
Pharmaceutical Society, 245
pharmacists, 245, 250, 255, 257
'Pill, The', 262, 263–4, 265
Platt, Lord, 307
Police and Criminal Evidence Act 1984, 44
Potts, Mrs (Depo-Provera case), 265
Powell, Enoch, 29, 191, 192
pregnancy and childbirth
amniocentesis, 163–4
children damaged by pre-conception events, 165
the child's rights, 176–7
Congenital Disabilities (Civil Liability) Act, 158–9
drugs and damage to the embryo, 160–62
hospital *v.* home delivery, 173–6
mother's consideration of abortion, 167–9
parent aware of risk, 166
parents and the law, 157–8
pre-pregnancy advice and genetic counselling, 169–73
suing a doctor, 162–3
wrongful life claims, 164–5
President's Commission for the Study of Ethical Problems in Medicine, 333
preventative medicine, 6
Prevention of Terrorism (Temporary Provisions) Act 1984, 38, 44
privacy, 129, 131, 312, 316, 318, 323
Primary Health Care Review, 258
private medicine, 16–17
and complaints procedures, 125, 244
contract between doctor and patient, 243–4
and litigation, 88–9, 99
and negligence, 83
and patients' access to records, 45–6
Prohibition of Female Circumcision Act 1985, 239

Index

prosthetics, 133
public *v*. private medicine, 16–17
publicity, fear of, 139

Quinlan case, 316–18, 323

rabies, 283
rape, 39, 227
receptionists, 89, 246, 248
reform
  compensation and blame, 153–4
  drugs and medical injuries,
    152–3
  experience abroad, 147–50
  'no-fault' scheme, 145–7
  Pearson Report, 144–5
  tort, 143–4
  way ahead for U.K., 150–52
  ways and means, 152
relatives, and consent, 67, 278–9
renal dialysis, 19, 20, 26, 28, 273
res ipsa loquitur, 98, 99
respirators, 298, 300, 312, 316
resuscitation, 24, 298, 319
reviewing and reforming the law
  apparent legal vacuum, 325–6
  complaints procedures, 330–31
  Commission on Medicine, Law and
    Ethics, 331–7
  proper role of the law, 327–30
rhesus incompatibility, 165
Roman Catholics
  and abortion, 20, 21, 210, 235, 237
  and contraception, 260
  and sterilization, 267
Royal College of General
    Practitioners, 24, 258
Royal College of Gynaecologists and
    Obstetricians (R.C.G.O.)
  and A.I.D., 181, 182
  and abortion, 205
  and embryo research, 24
  and ova donation/embryo
    transplant, 193, 194
  and test-tube babies, 186
Royal College of Nursing, 24, 86

Royal Commission on Civil Liability
  and Compensation for Personal
  Injury
  see Pearson Commission

Sachs, L. J., 246
Saikewicz case, 318
sanctity of life
  beginning and end of life, 24–5
  Judaeo-Christian tradition, 20–21
  killing and letting die, 25–8
  and the law, 28–31
  and the medical profession, 23–4
  in a secular society, 21–2
Savage, Wendy, 18, 140–41, 175
Scarman, Lord, 63, 71, 74, 227,
  230–31
Scottish law, 4
Secretary of State for Social Services,
  15–16
Select Committee on the Health
    Service Commissioners, 129, 134,
    139, 331
septicaemia, 245
sex education, 226
Sexual Offences Act 1956, 230
Shewin, Elizabeth, 136, 139
Slade, L. J., 168
Smith, Dr McCall, 220
Soto's syndrome, 238
South West Thames R.H.A., 92, 93
Spearing, Nigel, 12
spina bifida, 163, 171, 212, 214, 215,
  217, 218, 291, 292
Stallworthy, Professor Sir John, 96
Stanley Royde Hospital, 137
statutory instruments, 3
Steele, Dr (Manchester G.P.), 256
sterilization
  compulsory, 268
  and confidentiality, 40
  and consent, 56, 57, 266–8
  and divorce, 261–2
  and epilepsy, 132, 133, 258
  failed, 148, 167, 168, 171, 172
  and haemophilia, 222, 238

Lord Denning on, 260
and mentally subnormal, 239
and ova donation, 193
risk of conception after, 268
Stopes, Marie, 259
Strang, Professor L. B., 96
stress incontinence, 76, 100
suicide, 19, 26, 309–10, 312, 313–14, 323
Suicide Act 1961, 309
Supreme Court Act 1981, 91
surgery
child's objection to, 237
facial, 95, 148, 149–50
negligence, 79–80
side-effects, 151
see also consent to surgery
surrogacy, 185, 194, 195–8
Surrogacy Arrangements Act 1985, 31, 195–6
Sweden, no-fault schemes in, 145, 147, 149, 150, 152
Swedish Patients' Insurance Scheme, 147, 149
syphilis, and pregnancy, 166

teaching hospitals, 66
Templeman, Lord, 62–3, 64, 213, 227, 228, 234–5
'temporary residents', 246–7
'test-tube' babies, 6, 18, 185–8, 325
thalidomide, 105, 110, 111, 112, 114, 119, 153, 157, 159
'That's Life' (TV programme), 272
thrombosis, and the Pill, 263
Tizard, Professor J. P. M., 96
tort system, criticism of, 143–4
transplant surgery
see organ transplantation
tribunals, 150, 253, 328

Udale, Mrs (sterilization case), 268–9

ultrasound scan, and foetal disabilities, 167
Uniform Anatomical Gift Act, 283
Uniform Brain Death Act 1978, 304

vaccination, child's objection to, 237
vaccine damage
as drug-induced injury, 120–24
and Pearson Commission, 144, 145
Vaccine Damage Payments Act 1979, 120, 122, 123
vasectomy
and A.I.H., 184
and divorce, 261
Lord Denning on, 259
private, 17, 83, 266, 270–71
risk of conception after, 268
venereal disease
and defamation, 40
notification of, 44
and pregnancy, 166, 170
ventilators, 19, 20, 137, 282, 298–301 *passim*, 323
Voluntary Euthanasia Bill 1969, 322
Voluntary Euthanasia Society, 309–10

Waller L. J., 168
Warnock, Baroness, 179
Warnock Committee, 179–86 *passim*, 189, 191, 192, 193, 195, 196, 198, 334
whooping cough vaccine, 121–3
Whose Life Is It Anyway? (play), 312
Wigan Health Authority, 175
Wigley, Mrs (drug-induced death), 285, 286, 287
Wilson, Michael McNair, 125–6
Woodhouse, David, 136, 137, 138
Woolf, J., 225
Working Party on Confidentiality, 48
World Medical Association, 306–7